Revolutionizing Classroom Instruction Through AI-Powered Scaffolding

Scott F. Gregory
https://orcid.org/0000-0001-7210-8801

Fort Hays State University, USA

IGI Global
Scientific Publishing
Publishing Tomorrow's Research Today

Vice President of Editorial	Melissa Wagner
Director of Acquisitions	Mikaela Felty
Director of Book Development	Jocelynn Hessler
Production Manager	Mike Brehm
Cover Design	Jose Rosado

Published in the United States of America by
IGI Global Scientific Publishing
701 East Chocolate Avenue
Hershey, PA, 17033, USA
Tel: 717-533-8845 | Fax: 717-533-7115
Website: https://www.igi-global.com E-mail: cust@igi-global.com

Library of Congress Cataloging-in-Publication Data

Names: Gregory, Scott, 1975- editor
Title: Revolutionizing classroom instruction through AI-powered scaffolding / [edited by] Scott Gregory.
Description: Hershey, PA : IGI Global Scientific Publishing, [2026] | Includes bibliographical references and index. | Summary: "This book explores the transformative potential of AI-powered scaffolding in classroom instruction. It aims to provide educators with a comprehensive understanding of how AI can be leveraged to personalize learning experiences, enhance student engagement, and improve academic outcomes"-- Provided by publisher.
Identifiers: LCCN 2025024588 (print) | LCCN 2025024589 (ebook) | ISBN 9798337329482 hardcover | ISBN 9798337329499 paperback | ISBN 9798337329505 ebook
Subjects: LCSH: Artificial intelligence--Educational applications | Educational technology | Effective teaching
Classification: LCC LB1028.43 .R4838 2026 (print) | LCC LB1028.43 (ebook)
LC record available at https://lccn.loc.gov/2025024588
LC ebook record available at https://lccn.loc.gov/2025024589
British Cataloguing in Publication Data
A Cataloguing in Publication record for this book is available from the British Library.

Table of Contents

Detailed Table of Contents

The use of artificial intelligence in education on the part of students had led to fears of the "fantastical" which mirrors concerns in our general society. However, dialectical humanism and the philosophy of Martin Buber informs how fear of the fantastical can be addressed constructively. Moreover, pragmatic philosophy effectively facilitates the creation of an A.I. philosophy of education, through providing a clear focus of examination and establishing a utilitarian purpose. This paper seeks to outline the contours of what is possible for an A.I. informed philosophy of education in an educational context that is still grasping for understandings and philosophical coherence

Self-regulated learning has emerged as a crucial factor in academic success, surpassing intelligence in its predictive value and equipping students to navigate through distractions. AI tools offer personalized feedback and dynamic support, enabling learners to regulate learning processes. However, research examining AI's role in SRL remains fragmented, highlighting the need for an exploratory literature review to map existing approaches, identify gaps, and uncover emerging patterns. This chapter addresses this need by exploring research focusing on the place of AI in SRL development. The findings reveal that AI-driven SRL research can be classified under two broad categories: studies focusing on designing AI tools to enhance SRL and studies dealing with the impact of AI on SRL. The findings also show that AI can enhance SRL by offering just-in-time assistance and individualized learning pathways. However, given the continual proliferation of novel AI tools, more research is needed to create a comprehensive framework of AI-driven SRL enhancement.

Real-time data analytics in the educational framework is becoming a game-changer in pedagogical methodologies and is noticeably affecting student performance metrics. Instant data insights may improve the teaching process, resource allocation, and individualized learning, as was well discussed, but they can also have a multifaceted effect on decision-making. To identify ways forward through the transition to proactive, adaptive, and student-empowering instructional practices, this study examines the transformative role of data-driven decision-making in modern education by exploring new trends, difficulties, and future directions of data use in educational settings. Analytics of Real-Time Data in Education Data-driven training and individualized learning have been made possible by real-time data analytics in education. These traditional educational models often use standard curricula and assessment methods that may not consider each student's diverse learning needs and styles.

This chapter explores the transformative impact of Artificial Intelligence on educational operations by examining its role in enhancing learning through innovative and personalized methods. It investigates the integration of AI tutors and chatbots within digital learning systems, highlighting their dual function in optimizing learning processes and providing real-time support. The chapter begins with foundational insights into AI, then differentiates the functions of AI instructors and chatbots in academic and administrative contexts, including emotion-aware support systems. It evaluates performance improvement tools such as ChatGPT, IBM Watson Tutor, and Duolingo's AI framework, focusing on their scalability, accessibility, and capacity for personalized feedback. Challenges such as emotional limitations, algorithmic bias, ethical concerns, and student over-dependence are discussed, along with the evolving role of educators in AI-supported environments. The chapter concludes by examining future advancements in Emotional AI, AI-VR integration, and intelligent mentorship systems.

Preface

It is a distinct pleasure to introduce *Revolutionizing Classroom Instruction Through AI-Powered Scaffolding*, a volume born from a collective sense of urgency and profound optimism. We stand at a pedagogical crossroads, a moment in history where the confluence of cognitive science, data analytics, and artificial intelligence presents an unprecedented opportunity to redefine the very essence of teaching and learning. For generations, the dream of truly personalized education—an instructional experience that adapts in real-time to the unique cognitive and emotional landscape of each student—has remained an aspiration, a noble goal pursued with the limited tools at our disposal. Today, that aspiration is rapidly becoming an achievable reality. The principles of instructional scaffolding, championed by Vygotsky and Bruner, have long provided a powerful framework for guiding learners through their zone of proximal development. Yet, the practical implementation of this framework has always been constrained by the logistical realities of the classroom. A single teacher, no matter how dedicated or skilled, can only provide so much individualized support to a room full of diverse learners. This is the challenge, the fundamental limitation, that AI-powered scaffolding is poised to overcome.

This book is an exploration of that transformation. It is a dialogue between educators, technologists, researchers, and policymakers who are at the vanguard of this emerging field. Our central premise is that artificial intelligence is not merely a new tool to be added to the teacher's toolkit; rather, it is a catalyst for a fundamental paradigm shift. We are moving away from a model of instruction characterized by standardized delivery and summative assessment towards a dynamic, adaptive, and deeply humanistic model where technology serves to amplify the teacher's reach and deepen the student's engagement. AI-powered scaffolding systems can provide the moment-to-moment feedback, tailored hints, and adaptive challenges that were once the exclusive domain of one-on-one tutoring. They can analyze learning patterns with a granularity that is impossible for the human eye to perceive, identifying misconceptions the instant they arise and offering targeted interventions before they become entrenched. This frees the human teacher to focus on what they do best: fostering curiosity, mentoring, inspiring, and cultivating the complex social-emotional skills that are the bedrock of a fulfilling life and a functional society.

The subject matter of this volume is intentionally broad, reflecting the multifaceted nature of this revolution. We begin by laying a philosophical foundation, asking critical questions about the role of technology in a human-centered educational model. What does it mean to learn in partnership with an intelligent system? How do we ensure that these technologies promote equity and access, rather than exacerbating existing divides? From this philosophical grounding, we delve into the practical applications of AI in the classroom. We explore how AI can be harnessed to enhance self-regulated learning, empowering students to take ownership of their educational journeys. We examine the transformative potential of real-time data insights, which allow teachers to move from reactive to proactive instruction, adjusting their strategies on the fly in response to the immediate needs of their students. The rise of AI tutors and chatbots represents a new frontier in student support, offering on-demand assistance that extends the learning environment far beyond the four walls of the classroom and the traditional school day. These are not science-fiction concepts; they are tools being implemented and refined in educational settings around the world, and their impact is already being felt.

Furthermore, we investigate the power of AI-driven analytics to provide a holistic view of the classroom ecosystem. By understanding the intricate dynamics of student engagement and interaction, teachers can create more inclusive and effective learning environments. We also turn our attention to specific content areas, such as history and the social studies, demonstrating how AI can be used to transform historical inquiry from a passive reception of facts into an active, evidence-based investigation. The infusion of technology is not about replacing the rich tapestry of the humanities with cold algorithms, but about providing new tools for exploration and discovery. This commitment to a human-centered approach is a recurring theme throughout the book. We argue that the ultimate goal of educational technology should be to augment human capabilities, not to supplant them. This requires a thoughtful consideration of how digital-age learning can be designed to support individualized, inclusive, and differentiated instruction, ensuring that every learner, regardless of their background or ability, has the opportunity to thrive.

The timeliness of this topic cannot be overstated. We are living in an era of exponential technological advancement. The capabilities of artificial intelligence are growing at a staggering pace, and its influence is permeating every aspect of modern life. Education is no exception. School districts, universities, and governments worldwide are grappling with the implications of this new reality. They are seeking guidance on how to invest in technology, how to train teachers, and how to develop policies that are both forward-thinking and ethically sound. This book is intended to be a vital resource in that process. It provides a snapshot of the current state of the art, but more importantly, it offers a framework for thinking about the future. The conversation is no longer about *if* AI will change education, but *how*. Will we allow it to be driven by purely commercial interests, leading to a fragmented and inequitable landscape? Or will we, as a community of educators and stakeholders, proactively shape its development to align with our most cherished pedagogical values?

This book is our contribution to that proactive shaping. It is a call to action for a thoughtful, deliberate, and collaborative approach to the integration of AI in education. We believe that by harnessing the power of AI to create truly adaptive and supportive learning environments, we can unlock human potential on an unprecedented scale. We can create classrooms where every student feels seen, understood, and challenged. We can equip learners with the skills of critical thinking, creativity, and lifelong learning that are essential for navigating an increasingly complex world. This is the promise of AI-powered scaffolding, and it is a promise we are committed to exploring, interrogating, and ultimately, realizing. We invite you to join us on this journey.

The target audience for *Revolutionizing Classroom Instruction Through AI-Powered Scaffolding* is broad and diverse, reflecting our belief that the conversation about AI in education must be an inclusive one. This book is written, first and foremost, for practicing educators—the K-12 teachers, university professors, and instructional designers who are on the front lines of this transformation. We have made a concerted effort to bridge the gap between theory and practice, offering not just high-level concepts but also concrete examples and actionable strategies that can be adapted to a variety of learning environments. Whether you are a classroom teacher curious about how AI can help you better support your struggling students, or an instructional designer tasked with developing a new generation of digital learning tools, you will find valuable insights within these pages. We have also written for school and university administrators, the principals, superintendents, and provosts who are responsible for setting the strategic direction for their institutions. This book provides a comprehensive overview of the field that can inform technology procurement decisions, professional development initiatives, and long-term planning.

Furthermore, this volume is intended for researchers and graduate students in the fields of education, cognitive science, and computer science. We have brought together leading voices from across these disciplines to offer a multidisciplinary perspective on the challenges and opportunities of AI in education. The chapters that follow are grounded in the latest research and offer a wealth of avenues for future inquiry. We hope that this book will serve as a foundational text in graduate seminars and a catalyst for new research projects that will continue to push the boundaries of what is possible. Policymakers and government officials will also find this book to be a valuable resource. As artificial intelligence becomes increasingly integrated into the fabric of society, it is imperative that we have a well-informed public discourse about its ethical and social implications. This is particularly true in the context of education, where the stakes are so high. This book provides the nuanced understanding necessary to craft policies that promote innovation while also safeguarding the interests of students and educators.

Finally, this book is for anyone who is passionate about the future of learning. This includes parents who are navigating a rapidly changing educational landscape, tech developers who are building the next generation of educational tools, and lifelong learners who are curious about how technology is shaping the way we acquire knowledge and skills. We believe that the revolution we are describing is not just a technical one; it is a human one. It is about rethinking our fundamental assumptions about how we learn, how we teach, and what it means to be educated in the 21st century. This is a conversation that must include all of us. Our goal in assembling this collection was to create a text that is both rigorous and accessible, one that speaks to the specialist without alienating the general reader. We have encouraged our contributors to write with clarity and passion, to share not just their findings but also their vision. We believe that the result is a book that is as inspiring as it is informative, one that will not only advance the academic discourse but also empower educators to build the future of learning, one student at a time. We are honored to share their collective wisdom with you.

CHAPTER OVERVIEW

Chapter 1: Towards an AI Philosophy of Education

Dr. Scott Gregory, Fort Hays State University,
United States of America

In this foundational chapter, I lead us on a critical inquiry into the philosophical underpinnings of integrating artificial intelligence into our educational ecosystems. Rather than accepting AI as a neutral tool, I argue that its introduction necessitates a re-examination of our core pedagogical beliefs. The chapter deconstructs the traditional philosophies of education—from progressivism to essentialism—and interrogates how the capabilities of AI challenge and, in some cases, reshape these long-held tenets. A central theme is the exploration of epistemology in the age of AI: How does the nature of knowledge change when it is co-constructed with a non-human intelligence? The discussion moves beyond the utilitarian application of AI for efficiency and personalization to address deeper questions of agency, autonomy, and the very purpose of education. Provided is a coherent AI philosophy of education that must be human-centered, prioritizing the development of critical thinking, creativity, and socio-emotional intelligence. It must also be ethically grounded, proactively addressing issues of bias, privacy, and the digital divide. By situating AI within this broader philosophical context, this chapter provides an indispensable framework for the rest of the volume. It serves as a vital touchstone for educators and policymakers, urging them to engage in a deliberate and reflective process of shaping the role of AI in education, ensuring that this powerful technology is harnessed not merely to optimize old models, but to create new, more equitable and humanizing paradigms of learning. This philosophical grounding is essential for navigating the complex pedagogical shifts discussed in subsequent chapters, ensuring that the "how" of AI implementation is guided by a thoughtful consideration of "why."

Chapter 2: Utilizing AI to Enhance Self-Regulated Learning

Dr. Seda Aydan, TED University, United States of America

Dr. Seda Aydan's chapter provides a compelling examination of one of the most promising applications of artificial intelligence in education: the cultivation of self-regulated learning (SRL). Dr. Aydan articulates a clear and research-backed argument that AI-powered tools can serve as powerful scaffolds for developing the metacognitive, motivational, and behavioral skills that are the hallmarks of successful learners. The chapter moves beyond a theoretical discussion by detailing the practical ways in which AI can be designed to support the key phases of self-regulation: forethought, performance, and self-reflection. For instance, AI can assist students in setting realistic and challenging goals, planning their study time, and selecting appropriate learning strategies. During the learning process, AI tutors and adaptive systems can monitor progress, provide timely and targeted feedback, and offer motivational prompts to help students maintain focus and effort. Crucially, Dr. Aydan emphasizes the role of AI in fostering self-reflection, using data analytics to help students understand their own learning patterns, identify areas of weakness, and adjust their strategies accordingly. This fits squarely within the broader theme of AI pedagogy by shifting the focus from knowledge transmission to skill development. Rather than simply delivering content, AI is positioned as a cognitive partner that empowers students to take ownership of their learning. This chapter is a crucial contribution to the volume, as it demonstrates how AI-powered scaffolding can be used not just to support the learning of a specific subject, but to teach the skill of learning itself, a foundational capacity for success in the 21st century.

Chapter 3: Real-Time Data Insights: Transforming Teaching Strategies and Student Outcomes

Prof. Shraddha N. Zanjat, Sandip University, India; Vishwajit K. Barbudhe, Sandip University, India; Dr. Bhavana S. Karmore, G.H. Raisoni University, India

This chapter, authored by Professor Shraddha N. Zanjat, Vishwajit K. Barbudhe, and Dr. Bhavana S. Karmore, delves into the transformative potential of real-time data analytics in the classroom. The authors argue that AI-driven data systems are fundamentally changing the nature of instructional decision-making, moving it from a reflective, post-hoc activity to a dynamic, in-the-moment process. The chapter provides a detailed overview of how AI can capture and analyze a continuous stream of learning data—from clickstream patterns in a digital learning environment to textual analysis of student responses—and translate it into actionable insights for the teacher. These insights are presented not as overwhelming spreadsheets, but as intuitive dashboards and alerts that can highlight which students are struggling, what misconceptions are emerging across the class, and which instructional resources are proving most effective. The authors situate this capability within the pedagogical framework of formative assessment, demonstrating how AI can automate the process of gathering evidence of learning, thus freeing the teacher to focus on the art of intervention. By providing a clear, real-time picture of student understanding, these systems enable teachers to pivot their strategies, form flexible small groups for targeted support, and provide personalized feedback when it is most impactful. This direct connection between data and pedagogy is central to the book's thesis. The chapter illustrates how AI-powered scaffolding is not just about supporting the student directly, but also about scaffolding the teacher's own instructional practice, leading to a more responsive, efficient, and ultimately effective learning environment for all.

Chapter 4: AI Tutors and Chatbots: The New Face of Student Support in Education

Mr. Harsh Choradia, Christ Deemed To Be University, India; Prof. Garima Anand, Christ Deemed To Be University, India

Mr. Harsh Choradia and Professor Garima Anand offer a forward-looking exploration of AI tutors and chatbots, positioning them as a revolutionary force in student support. This chapter charts the evolution of these technologies from simple, rule-based systems to sophisticated, conversational agents powered by large language models. The authors provide a rich description of the multifaceted roles these AI agents can play in the educational landscape. They can serve as on-demand tutors, providing step-by-step guidance through complex problems and offering Socratic-style questioning to stimulate deeper thinking. They can function as administrative assistants, answering frequently asked questions about course logistics and freeing up instructor time for more substantive interactions. Furthermore, they can act as language-practice partners, offering students a non-judgmental environment in which to hone their conversational skills. The chapter fits seamlessly into the book's narrative by highlighting how AI can extend and personalize the learning experience beyond the traditional classroom setting. The concept of scaffolding is central to their analysis, as these AI tutors are designed to provide just-in-time support, tailored to the individual student's needs and current level of understanding. Mr. Choradia and Professor Anand also engage in a nuanced discussion of the pedagogical and ethical considerations involved in deploying these technologies, including the importance of designing for empathy, ensuring accuracy, and maintaining a clear distinction between AI and human interaction. This chapter paints a vivid picture of a future where every student has access to personalized academic support, 24/7.

Chapter 5: Enhancing History Education in Social Studies through Artificial Intelligence

Dr. Osman Sabanci, Gazi University, Turkey; Miss Gulser Kutluay, Aksaray University, Turkey

Dr. Osman Sabanci and Miss Gulser Kutluay offer a discipline-specific case study that brilliantly illustrates the broader principles of the book. Their chapter focuses on the transformative potential of AI in history and social studies education, arguing that technology can be used to move the field beyond rote memorization and towards a more authentic practice of historical inquiry. The authors explore a range of innovative AI applications, such as using natural language processing to analyze primary source documents at scale, creating interactive simulations that allow students to explore historical events from multiple perspectives, and developing chatbots that can "embody" historical figures, engaging students in dialogue about their lives and times. This work is a powerful example of how AI pedagogy can be tailored to the unique epistemological landscape of a specific domain. The AI tools described are not designed to provide definitive answers, but rather to scaffold the process of critical thinking, evidence evaluation, and perspective-taking that are at the heart of historical reasoning. By providing students with the tools to "do" history, rather than just consume it, AI can foster a deeper and more nuanced understanding of the past. This chapter serves as a vital proof of concept for the book's central thesis, demonstrating that AI-powered scaffolding has the potential to enrich and deepen learning across the entire curriculum, including in the humanities.

Chapter 6: Digital Age of Educational Learning for Human-Centered Strategies

Prof. Ashima Saxena, The NorthCap University, Turkey;
Dr. Preeti Chawla, The Northcap University, Turkey

Professor Ashima Saxena and Dr. Preeti Chawla return to the humanistic themes introduced in the opening chapter, providing a robust framework for designing human-centered AI in education. This chapter serves as a crucial bridge between the technological possibilities and the human realities of the classroom. The authors argue that the effectiveness of any educational technology is ultimately determined by its ability to support the holistic development of the learner. They propose a set of design principles for human-centered AI, emphasizing the importance of transparency, explainability, and user agency. The chapter explores how AI systems can be designed to be collaborative partners rather than authoritarian directors of learning, offering suggestions and insights while always leaving the final decision-making authority in the hands of the student and teacher. This pedagogical stance is critical to the book's overall message. It positions AI not as a replacement for human interaction, but as a tool for enhancing it. The authors discuss practical strategies for integrating AI into the classroom in a way that fosters community, encourages collaboration, and supports the socio-emotional well-being of students. By foregrounding these human-centered concerns, Professor Saxena and Dr. Chawla provide a vital counterbalance to a purely technology-driven approach, ensuring that the educational revolution they envision is one that remains firmly grounded in the values of empathy, creativity, and human connection.

Chapter 7: From One-Size-Fits-All to Individualized Support: AI in the Inclusive Classroom

Dr. Mustafa Kayyali, Maaref University of Applied Sciences, Syria

In this pivotal chapter, Dr. Mustafa Kayyali addresses one of the most critical challenges in modern education: the creation of truly inclusive classrooms. Dr. Kayyali argues that artificial intelligence offers an unprecedented opportunity to move beyond the one-size-fits-all model of instruction that has historically marginalized students with diverse learning needs. The chapter provides a comprehensive overview of how AI can be used to support students with disabilities and other learning differences. This includes the use of text-to-speech and speech-to-text technologies, adaptive learning platforms that can adjust the level of difficulty in real-time, and AI-powered tools that can provide personalized feedback and support for executive functioning skills like organization and time management. Dr. Kayyali's analysis is deeply rooted in the principles of Universal Design for Learning (UDL), demonstrating how AI can be used to create learning environments that are flexible and accessible by design, rather than requiring cumbersome retrofitting. This chapter powerfully connects the theme of AI scaffolding to the ethical imperative of educational equity. It shows how technology can be a force for inclusion, helping to level the playing field and ensure that every student has the opportunity to access the curriculum and demonstrate their learning. This is a cornerstone of the book's argument, framing the AI revolution not just as a matter of pedagogical efficiency, but as a matter of social justice.

Chapter 8: AI and Differentiated Instruction: Supporting Every Learner's Journey

Dr. Mustafa Kayyali, University of Applied Sciences, Syria

Building on the foundation of the previous chapter, Dr. Mustafa Kayyali's second contribution focuses on the broader application of AI to support differentiated instruction for all learners. While the previous chapter focused on students with identified disabilities, this one expands the lens to encompass the full spectrum of diversity found in a typical classroom—from students who are struggling with foundational concepts to those who are ready for advanced enrichment. Dr. Kayyali provides a masterful synthesis of the principles of differentiated instruction and the capabilities of AI. He explains how AI can help teachers differentiate by content, process, and product. For example, AI can curate a set of learning resources at varying levels of complexity, allowing students to engage with the same core concepts through different modalities. It can also generate a variety of practice activities and assessments, giving students choice in how they demonstrate their mastery. The central pedagogical argument is that AI can automate many of the logistical challenges associated with differentiation, which has long been a barrier to its widespread implementation. By handling the tasks of resource curation, progress monitoring, and personalized feedback, AI frees the teacher to focus on the human side of differentiation: building relationships with students, understanding their unique interests and learning profiles, and providing targeted, in-person support. This chapter provides a powerful and optimistic conclusion to the volume, painting a picture of a classroom where technology and pedagogy work in harmony to create a truly personalized and empowering learning journey for every single student.

In essence, this collection of writings posits that Artificial Intelligence is set to fundamentally reshape the educational landscape, moving it from a standardized model to one that is profoundly personalized and adaptive. The preface introduces *Revolutionizing Classroom Instruction Through AI-Powered Scaffolding* as a critical dialogue at the intersection of technology and pedagogy. It argues that AI can finally realize the long-held dream of individualized instruction by providing real-time, dynamic support to learners, thereby overcoming the traditional limitations of a single teacher in a diverse classroom. This frees educators to concentrate on fostering essential human skills like creativity and critical thinking. The book is presented as a comprehensive guide for a wide audience—from teachers and administrators to researchers and policymakers—navigating this technological and pedagogical revolution.

The chapters collectively map out the practical and philosophical dimensions of this transformation. The journey begins by establishing a necessary philosophical framework for a human-centered AI in education, then transitions into tangible applications. These include empowering students by fostering self-regulated learning, equipping teachers with real-time data insights to dynamically adjust their strategies, and deploying AI tutors and chatbots to extend learning beyond the classroom. The scope extends to analyzing classroom-wide dynamics and demonstrating AI's potential to enrich specific subjects like history by transforming them into active, inquiry-based disciplines. Throughout these explorations, a consistent theme emerges: the goal is not to replace human educators, but to augment their capabilities with powerful new tools.

Ultimately, the work culminates in a powerful argument for equity and inclusion as the cornerstones of the AI-driven educational future. The final chapters focus on how AI can dismantle the "one-size-fits-all" approach that has traditionally left many learners behind. By leveraging AI to create universally designed, flexible learning environments, education can become truly inclusive for students with disabilities and diverse needs. This leads to the ultimate vision of differentiated instruction for every learner, where AI handles the complex logistics of tailoring content and assessments, allowing teachers to focus on the uniquely human aspects of building relationships and providing targeted support. The book concludes with an optimistic vision of a symbiotic relationship between technology and pedagogy, working in concert to create a more effective, equitable, and empowering learning journey for every student.

Chapter 1
Towards an AI Philosophy of Education

Scott F. Gregory
https://orcid.org/0000-0001-7210-8801
Fort Hays State University, USA

ABSTRACT

The use of artificial intelligence in education on the part of students had led to fears of the "fantastical" which mirrors concerns in our general society. However, dialectical humanism and the philosophy of Martin Buber informs how fear of the fantastical can be addressed constructively. Moreover, pragmatic philosophy effectively facilitates the creation of an A.I. philosophy of education, through providing a clear focus of examination and establishing a utilitarian purpose. This paper seeks to outline the contours of what is possible for an A.I. informed philosophy of education in an educational context that is still grasping for understandings and philosophical coherence

INTRODUCTION

> *Morpheus: We have only bits and pieces of information but what we know for certain is that at some point in the early twenty-first century all of mankind was united in celebration. We marveled at our own magnificence as we gave birth to AI.*
> *Neo: AI? You mean artificial intelligence?*
> *(Wachowski & Wachowski, 1999, 41:24).*

Artificial intelligence, as commonly understood, has evolved over time and has taken on various forms. Perkins (2023) outlined three variations of artificial intelligence and their functions. The first two identified consisted of AI-powered grammar and style checkers and software designed for text restructuring, which

DOI: 10.4018/979-8-3373-2948-2.ch001

focus on improving writing and rephrasing text, respectively. While DWA and APT programs utilize existing text, a third iteration of artificial intelligence known as Large Language Models generates new text from entered inputs, marking a distinct difference between it and its predecessors. It is important to recognize that what necessarily constitutes artificial intelligence may be skewed with the inclusion of the word intelligence with the word artificial. Holmes et al., (2022) noted that this phrasing has created an "anthropomorphism of AI" (p. 18) which as a result, has led to the generalized conclusion that a new intelligence rivaling humans will come about, as opposed to a wider recognition of how artificial intelligence contains a distinctly human element. This connotation in turn, drives concerns relating to A.I. and its use in education and society.

There are a myriad of concerns related to artificial intelligence. Perhaps the most concerning is the proposition that A.I. could potentially end humanity. (Metz, 2023). Another significant concern is that facial recognition technology could inhibit the civic rights of individuals and undermine democracy (Holmes et al., 2022). Economically, A.I. presents a potential threat to social stability as greater use of A.I. in the economic sector could lead to widespread unemployment and dislocation as a result. While not universally accepted, one prediction contends that A.I. will replace 76% of the jobs in China (Wach et al., 2023, p. 13 in citing Chen & Xu, 2018). Others argue that an end-of-the-world scenario is not likely at this time, and instead, greater focus should be spent on AI and its use in discrimination in various sectors of society, as well as "deep fake" information and deception of the public (Hanna & Bender, 2023).

At the root of these concerns are fears of what I refer to as the "fantastical." These are fears that, with the prospect of change on the horizon, the fear of the unknown upends our shared understandings of how we relate to one another, how we work, and how we learn. In this paper, I will outline a key fantastical fear and then proceed to reframe this fear and variations of it, to their appropriate size and concern that requires recognition and the ability to be acted upon, to craft a substantive educational philosophy of A.I. My hope in this endeavor is to rhetorically inform future practice and provide a stepping stone for future philosophies and teaching practices.

THE FANTASTICAL FEARS OF EDUCATIONAL AI

Having described the great fear of the fantastical as it relates to the social landscape, there are similar fears that exist in the sphere of education. Artificial Intelligence has been blamed for eliminating the essay as an assessment, due to concerns that students will be able to easily construct a written narrative. It is argued that this in turn, will lead to the possible redundancy of instructors who utilize the written word

(Jamieson, 2022, Robin, 2023). Another concern is that with greater use of A.I., students will uncritically accept the results they receive and that critical thinking skills will erode as a result. A.I. results that are inaccurate may also perpetuate bias in results, working to disadvantage populations that experience discrimination (Fuchs, 2023) General concerns in the literature relate to imperfect data and generated results that are not correct. In one notable instance, researchers inquired of ChatGPT what would happen if two hands held a piece of paper vertically and one of them let go. In the response provided, Chat GPT hypothesized that the paper would travel in the direction of the hand that no longer held it, instead of hanging from the hand that still maintained its hold (Fisk, 2023, p. 42, in citing Kantrowitz & Lecun, 2023).

Moreover, while post-secondary institutions have advocated for stringent policies regarding prompt engineering and AI, faculty are countering the threat by implementing handwritten exams taken during class. "It will take an aggressive and comprehensive institutional response to dissuade students from plagiarism" (Keegin, 2023). In seeking to identify themes regarding the effect of ChatGPT on tertiary education, Sullivan et al., (2023) found a dominant concern regarding academic integrity, with numerous accounts of how A.I. facilitated cheating or assisted students to engage in plagiarism. A.I. detection software was a second theme of the study, with differences only about the severity of the threat posed to academic integrity by academic study. Half of the articles examined advocated for not allowing ChatGPT at all, while a distinct, smaller number of articles examined ChatGPT and its use in connection with learning outcomes (pp. 3-4). The literature features prominent concerns about A.I. and what it portends for education, that mirrors the fantastical.

At present, from my vantage point of experience, we have a tentative process of gradual acceptance that is taking place. My institution has created its own A.I. use in the classroom, which allows A.I. use in the classroom to be up to the discretion of the professor. Communication between student and professor is encouraged so that the "rules of the road" are determined (Gregory, 2023). To recognize the potential benefits of A.I. while not knowing entirely its drawbacks leads to measures which, like my own institution, lack a clear-cut "line" or identification of a standard that is recommended for everyone to take advantage of. An A.I. philosophy of education is needed, to provide a common understanding of the use of A.I., the benefits to learners that are brought about because of its use, and what specific methods are beneficial in having it practiced in the mid-21st century classroom.

HOW PHILOSOPHY CAN ADDRESS LARGER EDUCATIONAL CONCERNS

Philosophy provides insight into the fantastical concerns relating to A.I. through two main avenues of discussion which address the concern that A.I. will end teaching entirely and create a catastrophic rise in teacher unemployment. Hegel's dialectical analysis situates this fear into an informative context. From a philosophical perspective the history of education and use of technology shows a strong dialectical pattern of interaction. Philosophically, Bukharin described this dialectic as consisting of a thesis or time of stability, followed by a contradiction, which he credits Hegel with describing as: ". . .the power that moves things" resulting in a new phase of stability that comes about as the culmination of a new phase of stability known as the anti-thesis (Bukharin, 1925/2021, p. 83). Education has seen three distinct thesis stages, followed by a contradiction, and ensuing antithesis stages. The contradiction events of the printing press and the invention of the calculator provide examples of this dialectic.

The challenge presented by prompt engineering is hardly novel; technology has consistently altered the traditional educational structure. A relevant parallel for the current large-scale disruption caused by AI prompt engineering is the advent of the printing press. This invention posed a major challenge to the existing educational paradigm. Before the press, when books were rare, the main vehicle for learning was listening, which placed the authority of knowledge squarely on the "lecturer" (a person recognized for their skill set), as outlined by Dewar (1998). He further explained that the printing press subsequently shifted the instructional focus away from the lecturer and toward the student reader. This fundamental change, described as a "listener to reader to use" conversion, permanently changed how learning occurred. The lasting impact is captured by DeWar: "As a consumer of printed materials geared to a sequence of learning stages, the growing child was subjected to a different developmental process than was the medieval apprentice, ploughboy, novice or page" (DeWar in citing Eisenstein, p. 23). This technology, as the antithesis, constituted a major challenge to established practice and a new synthesis was sought after as a result.

The introduction of the printing press initiated a significant shift in pedagogical practice, prompting questions about the continued need for lecturers. Since the instructors were no longer required to deliver a book's content verbatim, their presentations evolved to include contextual information, personal reflections, critical insights, and other material relevant to the core subject matter. Reflecting on this transformative period, a contemporary philosopher observed that the accessibility of printed works compelled lecturers to adjust their roles. As Friesen (2017, p. 121) noted: “Lectures may say precisely those things which do not exist in any book, and the other way around” (Friesen, 2017, p. 121)

Consequently, the printing press did not eliminate the lecturer but fundamentally altered their function. The instructional paradigm transitioned from the lecturer serving as the sole purveyor of information to becoming a guide for classroom discussion, integrating resources both within and beyond the assigned texts. This transition established the textbook as a regular staple of instruction and permanently reshaped the delivery of instruction (Friesen, 2017). Therefore, a new synthesis emerged from the contradiction and subsequent crisis that was created.

Similar to the transformative impact of the printing press, the integration of prompt engineering into educational settings presents an equally significant challenge to conventional pedagogical practices, primarily through two mechanisms. The first involves curricular difficulties, as the established curriculum must adapt dynamically to the accelerating pace of knowledge generation. The second mechanism reflects the challenges previously introduced by the printing press, specifically the threat of role learning and text recitation becoming automated through artificial intelligence (Lubis, 2019, p. 185). Correspondingly, A.I. prompt engineering necessitates a redefinition of the instructional role. The educator shifts towards becoming a “mediator” or facilitator. While tasks such as basic lesson planning, assessment delivery, and grading may become automated, the instructor’s focus must pivot toward facilitating the discovery and critical analysis of complex knowledge (Zovko & Gudlin, 2019, p. ENT3951).

Introducing the calculator within scholastic environments represented a further transformation of the educational paradigm, albeit on a comparatively smaller magnitude. In contrast to AI prompt engineering, the calculator’s introduction constituted a less disruptive influence, yet it was undeniably a force-demanding adjustment. University faculty came to realize, as a result of incoming high school students possessing these handheld devices, that established pedagogical practices, and the prioritizing of textbook content did not align adequately with the capabilities of the next technological apparatuses (Banks, 2011). The dialectical thesis of standard practice and “how things are done” faced a contradiction created by the antithesis created by the calculator.

Consistent with the transformation integrated by the printing press, the locus of student engagement and the instructor’s pedagogical delivery went a significant reconfiguration. The disquietude experienced by educators when incorporating novel classroom technology, which fundamentally reimagines the teaching learning dichotomy, often stems from anxieties regarding potential drawbacks to established skills. Although some decline is anticipated, learning will concurrently migrate towards unexplored disciplinary domains or areas that facilitate profounder cognitive engagement. This migration is observable through the adoption of calculators, which served to distance students from rudimentary computational procedures. Trouche (2005) provides this critical observation: "On the one hand, the taking over of computation by a machine increases the distance of the user from numbers; on the other hand, the carrying out of marginal tasks (for instance, giving change) is connected to computation practices which involve counting concrete objects. Technological evaluation dramatically changes social relationships to mathematical objects" (pp. 14-15). The historical evolution of both the printing press and the calculator substantiates the manner in which the instructional transformation manifests within the educational paradigm. The ubiquitous integration of prompt engineering across educational settings will predictably conform to this pattern. This development necessitates an eventual reconciliation, a comprehensive process that requires elucidation.

In the historical implementation of the printing press and the calculator, the instructor's role was not obliterated. In both instances, it was the pedagogical methodology that became superseded or antiquated. Furthermore, the core subject matter was not entirely expunged. The fundamental change rested upon the reconfiguration of instructional emphasis and the prioritization of student learning objectives. Educators, across all stratifications, will inevitably lament the knowledge and skills that will yield to the ephemeral nature of time. Not all knowledge that holds social, economic, or utilitarian relevance for an individual across the temporal continuum will retain pertinence for a subsequent individual within their own distinct era.

Philosophy provides a second avenue of analysis that shows the value of recognizing the social construction of knowledge to address fears of AI in education. At the time of this composition, older individuals are undergoing a reacquisition of new strictures concerning orthography. For many antecedent years, these individuals were subject to a schooling system which insisted upon the interposition of two spaces betwixt sentences. At a certain juncture, this practice served a veritable purpose. As that purpose has since become obsolete, the practice of employing a singular space is now deemed socially acceptable (Selk, 2018). For an individual translocated through time to the current epoch, the "King's English" and what constitutes proper English are but a singular iteration among many, as English speakers in Australia, the United Kingdom, and the United States utilize derivatives of the language engage in: "code switching or "or style-drifting" accordingly (McArthur, 1987, p. 10).

As the foregoing examples demonstrate, show, that what is denominated "proper" and "right" concerning the epistemological architecture of communicative systems is not an immutable edict transmitted from the celestial spheres. This realization demands that the classroom pedagogue and the school collective must not critically interrogate any opposition to the utilization of prompt engineering within the educational apparatus.

Ergo, following this line of apprehension, Foucault posited the exigency of a critical recognition of the "rules" governing discourse and the necessity of cultivating an openness toward their permeability within our lives. "We must question those ready-made syntheses, those groupings that we normally accept before any examination, those links whose validity is recognized from the outset. . .We must also question those divisions or groupings with which we have become so familiar" (Foucault, 1972/2010, p. 22). When we discern that the very nature of knowledge and learning is subject to historical contingency, and that it is not an immovable fact of life which remains stationed, we are then permitted to reorganize the domain of knowledge and pedagogy for present and future realities. This mandates the acknowledgement that prompt engineering represents the telos for both learning and the assessment of learning, rather than continuing the futile endeavor of compelling students toward inefficient production of artifacts that are increasingly devolving into relics of the past. However, the efficacious deployment of prompt engineering necessitates more than mere acquiescence on the part of the user.

MOVING FROM THE FANTASTICAL TO THE PRAGMATIC

While philosophy adequately addresses larger educational concerns, there is a need to move the discussion of A.I. use in education to a more precise and actionable. In creating a generative A.I. philosophy of education that would inform future A.I. use in education, I contend that it is important that we move from the generalized and fantastical in philosophical claims, to assertions that are precise and clear. To dispose of the fantastical, we must first determine what artificial intelligence is for the purpose of this discussion. As mentioned previously, there have been different iterations of artificial intelligence. The artificial intelligence that we will address is the large language model or generative A.I. Recent advancements in artificial intelligence have transgressed a significant delimiter, thereby facilitating the generation of text that conforms to human apprehension and yields an output that is comprehensible to mankind. Notwithstanding this epistemological progression, limitations currently persist regarding the capacity of AI to respond to inputs that fall outside its prescribed algorithmic purview (Bozkurt, 2023, p. 200). This deficiency elucidates the conspicuous instances to failure in the realm of generated content, inasmuch as generative AI remains "prompt dependent" (Fisher & Jacobs, 2023, p. 18).

Buber's (1958/2000) conception of *I-It* and *I-Thou* highlight further the distinction between prompt bounded A.I. and sentient A.I. As a generalization, *I-It* relations are created when an observer or person affects or views an object, and the relation is one way. For *I-Thou*, there is an interaction, a give and take, a consideration that depends on a relationship. When a student uses A.I., they are engaged in an *I-It* relation as the human user impacts or affects A.I. and the A.I. cannot reciprocate on a sentient level to create an *I-Thou* relation. Buber put this succinctly in explicit terms. "Where there is no sharing there is no reality (p.67). *I-It* forms a separation of relation in the sense that there isn't mutual interaction as *I-It* as a word, denotes a "…word of separation" (p. 35). A.I. use by students currently is a "bounded" (p. 20) relation, pointing to Buber's language of *I-It*. From this vantage point, prompt dependent A.I. and its use in education can now be identified and used to form the discussion from this point forward. The generative A.I. function "Input in, output out" relegates larger ethical concerns to the periphery of consideration.

The second task that needs to be completed to dispose of the fanatical, is to determine if identifiable results can be recognized. Only through this frame of reference is a generative A.I. philosophy of education beneficial. William James maintained that the pragmatic method of philosophy lies in identifying the "practical consequences" of decision making. If none can be identified, then the contentious issue is rendered moot (James, 1896/2011, What pragmatism means, para. 2). In short, the generalized and fantastical are not worth considering as they do not have a conceivable outcome or influence as it relates to teaching and learning. The argument to ask for an application of the generalized and fantastical shows the futility of engaging in such thought, which serves no function for the working practical world of teaching and learning. While speaking broadly in terms of philosophy, James's contention is most relevant for education. "It is astonishing to see how many philosophical disputes collapse into insignificance the moment you subject them to this simple test of tracing a concrete consequence" (James, 1896/2011, What pragmatism means, para. 2). From this vantage point, we can focus more clearly on how to use A.I. in the learning process and how what we hope to achieve with it.

ON THE PURPOSE AND FUNCTION OF AN A.I. PHILOSOPHY OF EDUCATION

At its core, the use of A.I. in education shifts the learning process from cognitive "knowing" knowledge to "think about thinking," otherwise known as metacognition (Yang & Xia, 2023). Knowledge or memorization of basic concepts and ideas is important at the elementary level. This may never change as base knowledge is required before higher cognitive thinking and directed action can occur. In moving towards a "thinking about thinking" philosophy as students age and progress through their education, this presents fundamental shift in thinking, for a society that prides itself on providing answers quickly when given a prompt, as the long-time television show *Jeopardy* proves.

Knowledge and Concerns About Plagiarism or Cheating

A common tool utilized in primary and secondary teaching in America is Webb's Depth of knowledge Levels. These levels distinguish between recall and reproduction of knowledge, applying knowledge, strategic thinking, and extensive thinking in four levels (Main, 2024). Generative A.I. is especially adept at knowledge that is concentrated in the recall and procedure level 1 of Webb's model. Conventional objective assessments, such as standardized multiple-choice items, cloze procedures, and even tabular data representations, can be "filled in" with ease with the assistance of A.I. I have found in my practice that I could simply enter my level 1 or 2 questions on assignments in ChatGPT and get a furnished response. As an instructor, I have had to move my assignments to level 3 strategic thinking and level 4 extensive thinking domains. I accepted student generated output, but then I had them explain or present their results. On top of that, I required students to share how they strategized to obtain the results that they did and to reformulate prompts to obtain better results. If one's quizzes and tests are demolished overnight, it is important to reconsider what depth of knowledge is being sought and how best to reformulate assessments to challenge students and to foster the metacognitive "thinking about thinking" elements of strategizing and analysis.

What A.I. Philosophy of Education Informed Methods and Assessments May Look Like

With my prior experience and knowledge of Webb's depth of knowledge model in mind, I offer some ideas to how to construct effective method and assessment with A.I. in mind. Whether it is the K-12 or higher educational level of education, the teacher or professor of the future would be wise to construct a process of examining prompts or entries created to provide solutions to problems they are attempting to solve. "Labs" could be held where students could work together, interrogate their responses, and begin a process of creating improved prompts to engineer optimal responses. The role of the teacher or professor is to set up the problems to be solved and provide mediated feedback and support in cultivating the skill of prompt creation. Students could be tasked to work on projects in groups in real time or asynchronously online. As an example, the collegiate online discussion board would no longer consist of responses to a topic and to two peers' which students notoriously dislike. Instead, it would be a hub of interaction where students plan, delegate responsibilities, problem solve, think-aloud, and contend with one another in crafting a generated solution to a problem or task.

A teacher or professor could have students craft a generated story that is either a non-fiction or fictionalized account. Students could save it or print it out and then be tasked with examining it to identify key structures of language such as the nouns or verbs. If the goal of the lesson is to identify what phrases make the story a work of opinion or fact, they could highlight the phrases and then report them. Individual or small group presentations to the teacher or professor will take on an important role in an A.I. philosophy of education informed classroom. Students face a new onus in the learning environment. While A.I. may provide "easy" results, students must demonstrate knowledge of the ideas and concepts through presenting them and then explaining how they received the optimal outputs.

A.I. Philosophy of Education-Assessments

The main goal or nature of assessments in an A.I. philosophy of education is to provide higher cognitive challenges in the learning environment. The emphasis is on on-going assessments, checks, and reflections, as opposed to one-time quizzes or summative assessments. A "trails of evidence" assessment would consist of a portfolio or other acceptable form of documentation that would show the thought process of the student as they undertook the effort to generate a solution. Why did they enter the prompt that they did? What were they thinking? What was a puzzling or confusing concern as they progressed in their efforts? Journaling would be another form of assessment that could be utilized that would capture this information and which would facilitate discussion with peers and the teacher or professor.

The element of critical thinking comes into play when it comes to analyzing generated responses. Is the answer too vague? Could it be more precise? Are the sources accurate? Do they even exist?

CONCLUSION

While larger concerns about A.I. use in education deserve discussion, it's my hope that the arguments previously, show how philosophy adequately frames and situates the fantastical to its appropriate dialectical historical context, as well as the appropriate context of relation as outlined by Buber. At another level, philosophy can help us to resize the concerns of A.I. into a more manageable concern that shows promise of being acted upon. The school of pragmatism shows how this can be done and in a profession that is practical in focus, philosophy can inform an A.I. philosophy of education that makes sense to the educator and which adequately handles noted concerns. It is at this stage that I hope through the rhetoric provided, an important step forward in the formulation of an A.I. philosophy of education has been created. This development is not an end in itself, but rather, a building block for future considerations that is helpful for future generations as they navigate a new age.

REFERENCES

Banks, S. (2011). *A Historical Analysis of Attitudes Toward the use of Calculators in Junior High and High School Math Classrooms in the United States since 1975* [Master's Thesis, Cedarville University]. Digital Commons. https://digitalcommons.cedarville.edu/education_theses/31/

Bozkurt, A. (2023). Generative artificial intelligence (AI) powered conversational educational agents: The inevitable paradigm shift. *Asian Journal of Distance Education, 18*(1), 198–204. DOI: 10.5281/zenodo.7716416

Buber, M. (1958/2000). *I and thou*. Scribner Classics.

Bukharin, N. (2021). *Historical Materialism*. Critical Editions. (Original work published 1925)

Dewar, J. A. (1998). *The information age and the printing press: Looking backward to see ahead*. RAND Corporation. https://www.rand.org/content/dam/rand/pubs/papers/2005/P8014.pdf

Fisher, M., & Jacobs, H. H. (2023). Prompt literacy: A key for AI-Based Learning. *Educational Leadership, 80*(9), 18–19. https://www.ascd.org/el/articles/prompt-literacy-a-key-for-ai-based-learning

Fisk, R. (2023). The rise of ChatGPT and Generative A.I. and what it means for Schools. *AASA Journal of Scholarship & Practice, 20*(1), 37-46. https://www.aasa.org/docs/default-source/publications/journal-of-scholarship-and-practice/2023-spring-issue/rise-chatgpt-generativeai.pdf

Foucault, M. (1972/2010). *The archaeology of knowledge and the discourse on language*. Vintage Books.

Friesen, N. (2017). *The textbook and the lecture: Education in the age of new media*. Johns Hopkins University Press.

Fuchs, K. (2023). Exploring the opportunities and challenges of NLP models in higher education: Is ChatGPT a blessing or a curse? *Frontiers in Education*, •••, 8.

Gregory, S. (2023). Empowering Teaching With Prompt Engineering: How to Integrate Curriculum, Standards, and Assessment for a New Age. In Sharma, R. C., & Bozkurt, A. (Eds.), *Transforming Education with Generative AI: Prompt Engineering and Synthetic Content Creation*. IGI Global.

Hanna, A., & Bender, E. M. (August 12, 2023). AI Causes Real harm. Let's Focus on that over the End-of-Humanity Hype. *Scientific American*. https://www.scientificamerican.com/article/we-need-to-focus-on-ais-real-harms-not-imaginary-existential-risks/

Holmes, W., Persson, J., Chounta, I.-A., Wasson, B., & Dimitrova, V. (2022). Artificial intelligence and education: A critical view through the lens of human rights, democracy, and the rule of law. *Council of Europe*. https://rm.coe.int/1680a956e3

James, W. (1896/2011). *The collected works of William James.*

Jamieson, S. (2022). The AI "Crisis" and (Re)turn to Pedagogy. *Composition Studies, 50*(3), 153–158.

Keegin, J. M. (2023, May 23). *ChatGPT is a plagiarism machine: So why do administrators have their heads in the sand?* The Chronicle of Higher Education. https://www.chronicle.com/article/chatgpt-is-a-plagiarism-machine

Lubis, F. (2019). Education in the disruption era. *Britain International of Linguistics, Arts, and Education Journal, 1*(2), 183–188. DOI: 10.33258/biolae.v1i2.85

Main, P. (2024). *Webb's Depth of Knowledge*. Structural Learning. https://www.structural-learning.com/post/webbs-depth-of-knowledge

McArthur, T. (1987). The English languages? *English Today, 3*(3), 9–13. DOI: 10.1017/S0266078400013511

Metz, C. (June 10, 2023). *How could A.I. Destroy Humanity?* The New York Times. https://www.nytimes.com/2023/06/10/technology/ai-humanity.html

Perkins, M. (2023). Academic integrity considerations of AI Large Language Models in the post-pandemic era: ChatGPT and beyond. *Journal of University Teaching & Learning Practice, 20*(2), 7–24. DOI: 10.53761/1.20.02.07

Robin, C. (2023, August 24). *How ChatGPT changed my plans for the fall.* The Chronicle of Higher Education. https://www.chronicle.com/article/the-end-of-the-take-home-essay

Selk, A. (2018, May 5). *One space or two spaces after a full stop? Scientists have finally found the answer.* The Independent. https://www.independent.co.uk/tech/one-space-or-two-spaces-after-a-full-stop-scientists-have-finally-found-the-answer-a8337646.html

Sullivan, M., Kelly, A., & Mclaughlan, P. (2023). ChatGPT in higher education: Considerations for academic integrity and student learning. *Journal of Applied Learning & Teaching, 6*(1), 1–10. DOI: 10.37074/jalt.2023.6.1.17

Trouche, L. (2005). Calculators in mathematics education: A rapid evolution of tools, with different effects. In Guin, D., Ruthven, K., & Trouche, L. (Eds.), *The didactical challenge of symbolic calculators: Turning a computational device into a mathematical instrument* (pp. 9–39). Springer.

Wach, K., Duong, C. D., Ejdys, J., Kazlauskaité, R., Korzynksi, P., Mazurek, G., Paliszkiewicz, J., & Ziemba, E. (2023). The dark side of generative artificial intelligence: A critical analysis of controversies and risks of ChatGPT. *Entrepreneurial Business and Economics Review*, *11*(2), 7–30.

Wachowski, Li., & Wachowski, La (1999). *The Matrix [Film]*. Warner Brothers. https://www.warnerbrothers.com/movies/matrix

Yang, Y., & Xia, N. (2023). Enhancing Students' Metacognition via AI-Driven Educational Support Systems. *International Journal of Emerging Technologies in Learning*, *18*(24), 133–148. DOI: 10.3991/ijet.v18i24.45647

Zovko, V., & Gudlin, M. (2019, June). *Artificial intelligence as a disruptive technology in education*. [Conference Proceedings]. The Future of Education 2019.

Chapter 2
Utilizing AI to Enhance Self-Regulated Learning

Seda Aydan
https://orcid.org/0000-0001-5807-3956
TED University, Turkey

ABSTRACT

Self-regulated learning has emerged as a crucial factor in academic success, surpassing intelligence in its predictive value and equipping students to navigate through distractions. AI tools offer personalized feedback and dynamic support, enabling learners to regulate learning processes. However, research examining AI's role in SRL remains fragmented, highlighting the need for an exploratory literature review to map existing approaches, identify gaps, and uncover emerging patterns. This chapter addresses this need by exploring research focusing on the place of AI in SRL development. The findings reveal that AI-driven SRL research can be classified under two broad categories: studies focusing on designing AI tools to enhance SRL and studies dealing with the impact of AI on SRL. The findings also show that AI can enhance SRL by offering just-in-time assistance and individualized learning pathways. However, given the continual proliferation of novel AI tools, more research is needed to create a comprehensive framework of AI-driven SRL enhancement.

INTRODUCTION

Self-regulated learning (SRL) has gained prominence in recent research as an indicator of academic success valued over intelligence and as a coping mechanism for students to cope with the overwhelming distractors of the modern world. In a basic definition, SRL refers to learners' acts of organizing their behaviors around the goals they set (Zimmerman, 2002). During this process, they are supposed to

DOI: 10.4018/979-8-3373-2948-2.ch002

create feedback loops monitoring their learning journey and reflecting on their performance. In this process, self-efficacy beliefs play a key role as they have a direct impact on the forethought phase of SRL leading to a domino effect in other stages Pajares, 2012). Recent research states that the beliefs of self-efficacy involving one's beliefs about their capabilities to achieve a task, can significantly deteriorate due to the feeling of helplessness. This takes us to the crucial role of help-seeking in the SRL process (Newman, 2023).

Although help-seeking looks like an SRL strategy which does not require special skills, it is, in fact, a skill that learners need to work on to carry out an effective help-seeking process (Newman, 2023). SRL research shows that learners traditionally seek help in peers, teachers, parents or siblings, which is a significant contributor to the maintenance of SRL skills (Aydan, 2023). However, recent research suggests that help-seeking and guidance-offering processes do not necessarily have to take place only within social circle. Learners can effectively seek help with Artificial Intelligence (AI) which can also contribute to the development and maintenance of SRL skills. By providing personalized feedback and guidance as well as timeless and limitless help, AI technologies have a high potential to enrich the SRL processes of the learners (Chang et al., 2023).

While combining SRL and AI technologies have considerable potential to enhance education process, the number of the studies conducted combining these methods is still scarce and the existing studies focusing on combining these two methods are scattered. For this reason, there is a need to systematically bring these studies together and provide an exploratory literature review to provide a synthesis of studies integrating AI-powered scaffolding mechanisms into a structured SRL framework to guide future studies as well as practice. This chapter aims to address this need by synthesizing existing research and proposing a comprehensive report of the studies focusing on the use of AI for SRL development. With this purpose and rationale in mind, the present chapter provides an exploratory literature review of the articles dealing with the use of AI to enhance SRL skills of the learners. The following research questions are explored in the chapter:

Based on the existing review of literature:

(1) what are AI technologies that are used to enhance SRL process?
(2) what is the impact of the use of AI technology on SRL development?

1. BACKGROUND TO STUDY

1.1. The Nature of SRL

SRL has been widely studied in educational research, with Zimmerman's model (2002) being one of the most influential frameworks. Studies indicate that students with strong SRL skills demonstrate higher academic achievement, increased motivation, and greater resilience (Pintrich, 2000; Schunk & Greene, 2018). Thanks to the growing body of research indicating the crucial role of SRL in academic success as well as lifelong learning, the attempts to look for ways to enrich SRL process have accelerated. However, to develop an in-depth understanding of SRL process and to design strategies to feed the different stages of SRL, it is essential to explore learning theories and theoretical background underlying SRL.

SRL has roots in different theories of learning which present different definitions of SRL. These definitions consist of different approaches to SRL, but they are not distinct from one another. Instead, they overlap and complement each other. Operant Theory, Information Processing Theory, Developmental Theory, Social Constructivist Theory, and Social Cognitive Theory are the learning theories presenting a variety of approaches to SRL.

Operant theory defines self-regulation considering the work of Skinner (1953). Self-regulation within the framework of Operant theory portrays learners' decision making regarding the behaviors to regulate, determine discriminative stimuli and make a performance related evaluation taking the standards into account and considering reinforcements. This process involves self-monitoring, self-instruction, and self-reinforcement (Zimmerman & Schunk, 2011).

Information Processing Theory, as stated by Gitomer and Glaser (1987), points out that self-regulation is only possible with metacognitive awareness and this awareness involves several other sub-processes. Some of these processes are task-awareness, procedural knowledge and problem-solving production systems, use of learning strategies and comprehension monitoring (Zimmerman & Schunk, 2011). Developmental theories, on the other hand, indicate that self-regulation is gradual cognitive change in learners' capability of controlling their thoughts, feelings and actions.

Social Constructivist Theory, and Social Cognitive Theory emphasize the social aspect of SRL and explore how social circle can contribute to SRL development. For Social Constructivist Theory of Learning, SRL is not an isolated cognitive process. Instead, it is a socially mediated process where learning is shaped by interactions with others such as teachers, peers, and cultural tools. This definition of SRL is rooted in the work of Vygotsky (1978) and closely linked with scaffolding and Zone of Proximal Development (ZPD) theories. Within this framework, SRL can be enhanced with more knowledgeable others, such as teachers and peers. Scaffolding, which refers to the temporary support tailored to a learner's current abilities in this context, enables students to engage in tasks they could not accomplish individually. This can also be about keeping their motivation high by not letting students feel helpless while working on a challenging learning task. With the help of these processes, the learner can gradually internalize strategies for planning, monitoring, and regulating their learning. The ZPD highlights the dynamic space where learning is most effective, emphasizing the role of structured assistance in helping students move from externally supported regulation to independent self-regulation. As learners gain expertise, they transition from relying on external guidance to managing their own learning processes, reflecting the core principles of SRL. Thus, social constructivism not only situates SRL within social and cultural contexts but also illustrates how strategic external support can facilitate the development of autonomous, self-directed learners.

Similarly, Social Cognitive Theory (SCT), developed by the work of Bandura (1986), presents a foundational perspective on self-regulated learning (SRL). Bandura (1986) emphasizes reciprocal interactions among personal, behavioral, and environmental factors, which is called triadic reciprocal determinism. This theory suggests that learners' self-beliefs, behaviors, and social environments continuously influence one another. This theory underlines that self-regulation is shaped by both internal cognition and external influences. Thus, they develop autonomy in their learning while remaining influenced by social and environmental factors. Zimmerman model of SRL (Zimmerman, 2000) is based on this theory of Learning and demonstrates how learners plan, execute, and adapt their learning strategies based on feedback and experiences. It emphasized the key role of self-efficacy and how self-regulation develops through the continuous interaction of personal beliefs (e.g., self-efficacy, metacognition), behaviors (e.g., strategy use, persistence), and environmental conditions (e.g., feedback, modeling). Zimmerman and Cleary (2009) further highlight that SRL is not restricted to asocial forms of education like discovery learning, self-education through reading, studying, programmed instruction, or computer-assisted instruction. It also includes social forms of learning such as modelling and learning through interaction leading to adjustments in behavior. Zimmerman model of SRL (Zimmerman, 2000) is the most used and citied model of SRL and it is also used in the present research to explain the results of the study. This model is cyclical and provides a framework of how SRL takes place:

Figure 1. Zimmerman's cyclical model of SRL

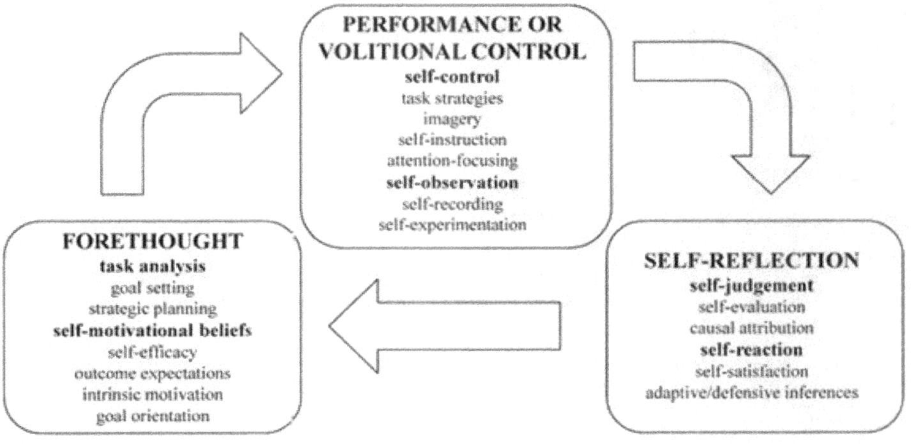

Note. The figure was adapted based on "Zimmerman, B. J. (2000). Attaining self-regulation: A social-cognitive perspective. In M. Boekaerts, P. Pintrich, & M. Zeidner (Eds.), Handbook of self-regulation (pp. 13–39). Academic Press. https://doi.org/10.1016/B978-0-12-109890-2.X5027-6"

As can be seen in Figure 1, according to Zimmerman (2000), the SRL process starts with forethought process in which learners set goals and make strategic places to achieve these goals. In this process, self-motivational beliefs such as self-efficacy, outcome expectations, intrinsic motivation and goal orientation are significant. All the factors play an inhibiting or hindering role in the next stage, that is performance or volitional control. In this stage, the learners take action to regulate their learning process by focusing their attention, performing self-instruction or imagery and using task strategies. They also observe and record their progress. At this stage, they take a trial-and-error method to experiment with the SRL strategies they employ. In the final stage, they reflect on their performance and make attributions to the strategies they employ. Thus, it is possible to state that this model demonstrates cognitive, metacognitive and affective components of the SRL process. In addition to this cyclical model, Zimmerman (2000) presented a four-phase model in which he demonstrated how students gain their self-regulatory competency.

Figure 2. Zimmerman's multi-level model of SRL

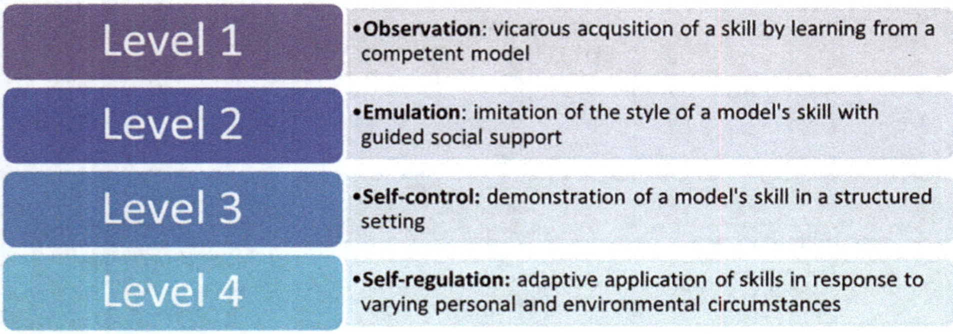

Note. The figure was recreated based on "Zimmerman, B. J. (2000). Attaining self-regulation: A social-cognitive perspective. In M. Boekaerts, P. Pintrich, & M. Zeidner (Eds.), Handbook of self-regulation (pp. 13–39). Academic Press. https://doi.org/10.1016/B978-0-12-109890-2.X5027-6"

As Figure 2 demonstrates, Zimmerman's (2000) multilevel model of SRL emphasizes the gradual development of self-regulation, progressing from external observation to independent and adaptive application of learning strategies. Whereas Zimmerman's cyclical model is important for understanding how SRL occurs, the multi-level model is important for understanding the way the learners acquire SRL skills providing a structured framework for integrating AI into the self-regulation acquisition process. AI can support learners at each level by scaffolding their development from observation to independent self-regulation.

Vygotsky (1978) indicated that self-regulated learning requires the coordination of cognitive processes such as storing, synthesizing, planning and evaluating information. This coordination does not take place without being influenced by the surrounding environment in which they are formed. A learner's SRL process has reflections from the values and teachings of the context of the learning. In today's world of technology, learners are exposed to AI applications in many phases of their lives. These digital tools not only shape the way learners access and process information but also influence how they plan, monitor, and evaluate their learning. As a result, understanding the interplay between culturally shaped SRL practices and AI-enhanced learning environments is essential for designing effective, individualized and responsive educational experiences. Furthermore, considering the different definitions of SRL and the way they deal with the SRL process, it can be concluded that all theories emphasize the active role of learning whose SRL process can be enriched with support coming from external resources. Particularly, Social Cognitive Theory and Social Constructivist Theory provide room for the enrichment of the process with the help of the support coming from the social circle. In the modern world, artificial intelligence (AI) technologies are offering a lot of potential to replace this help of social circle. To elaborate, AI can enrich self-regulated learning (SRL) within the framework of social constructivist theory by providing dynamic scaffolding and personalized support that aligns with learners' zone of proximal development (ZPD). AI-powered educational tools can function as adaptive scaffolds, offering real-time feedback, hints, and tailored guidance to help students bridge the gap between their current abilities and their potential learning goals. For instance, intelligent tutoring systems and AI-driven learning analytics can analyze students' progress and adjust instructional support gradually reducing assistance as learners gain independence. Thus, they can provide effective scaffolding. Moreover, AI can offer collaborative learning environments, enabling peer interaction and shared regulation through discussion forums, adaptive group formations, and automated prompts that encourage reflection and monitoring. By enhancing learning within social and interactive contexts, AI can help students internalize self-regulation strategies step by step, fostering deeper engagement and autonomy.

2.2. Factors Affecting the Development of SRL Skills

In order to enhance the SRL development via AI, it is essential to analyze the factors impacting the development of SRL skills and their relation to AI. Aydan (2023) presents a comprehensive report of these factors. These factors can be categorized as individual and instructional. Table 1 provides a summary of the variables affecting the development of SRL skills:

Table 1. Influential Factors in SRL Development Process according to Aydan (2023)

Instructional Factors	Individual Factors
Implicit and Explicit Teaching of SRL skills	Self-efficacy
Building Rapport with Students	Critical thinking skills
Generating academic interest in students	Parents & siblings
IT Integration	Social background
Activating Prior Knowledge	
Linking Class Content with Daily Life	
Peer collaboration	

In addition to Aydan (2023), several other researchers worked on the SRL enhancement and stated that narratives (Azevedo et al., 2023; Cunha et al., 2023; Ferreira & Simão, 2012), providing effective feedback including tactics to learn better (Callan et al., 2022; Kolovelonis et al., 2010; Nancy et al.,2002; Perry et al., 2020; Spruce & Bol, 2015), level appropriate tasks (Alraddadi & Zebehazy, 2023;Callan et al.,

2022), complex but meaningful tasks (Alvi & Gillies, 2024; Heirweg et al.,2022), providing students with choices (Bardach et al., 2023; Heirweg et al.,2022; Nancy et al.,2002; uteu, 2021; Žerak et al., 2024), well-organized and/or interdisciplinary teaching materials (Leidinger & Perels, 2012; Voskamp et al., 2022), diverse teaching & culturally responsive teaching (Anyichie et al., 2023; Žerak et al., 2024), teaching students the steps of thinking (Alvi & Gillies, 2024) and integrating SRL teaching with a subject matter (Sins et al., 2024) are some other methods to foster SRL. Although it is evident that not all of these variables can be replaced by AI, many of them can be effectively facilitated with the help of AI. Effective SRL opportunities can be created via AI supporting learners' self-efficacy, metacognition, and adaptive help-seeking behaviors. SRL development requires reciprocal interactions between personal, behavioral, and environmental factors, and AI-powered tools can serve as dynamic external support that guide students through the SRL process. For instance, AI-driven adaptive tutoring systems and intelligent chatbots can provide personalized feedback, helping students to set goals, monitor their progress, and adjust their strategies, which has the potential to facilitate key SRL skills. Additionally, AI can facilitate the help-seeking process, an essential component of SRL, by offering on-demand hints or suggesting relevant resources. AI can also be helpful for students while activating their prior knowledge which eases the learning process by reducing the cognitive load. This is also true for linking class content with daily life as AI has a lot to offer in this area too offering daily life connections to academic content making the learning more meaningful.

In short, by integrating AI as an interactive and responsive agent, learners receive the timely and personalized support needed to develop self-directed learning skills within an environment that continuously adapts to their evolving needs.

All in all, it is appropriate to state that AI has a high potential to facilitate the SRL process. However, limited research has explicitly examined how AI can scaffold the distinct phases of Zimmerman's SRL model, highlighting a critical gap in the literature. For this reason, this chapter examines relevant research together in an exploratory way to provide an in-depth analysis of current research and propose novel AI-driven strategies for differentiated instruction and self-regulation.

2. METHOD

This chapter employs a conceptual research approach, drawing upon an exploratory review of existing literature on AI in education and SRL. To this end, the data for the study were identified via a systematic search of publications on SRL and AI in the following databases between 2010 and 2025: Educational Resources Information Centre (ERIC), Web of Science (WOS), Scopus and ProQuest since these databases have been frequently utilized in educational research (Bano et al., 2018; Lee, 2019; Lin & Lin, 2019). The year 2010 was selected as the starting point of the review to obtain the latest research in the field considering the acceleration of the research on computerized education as well as the recent developments in AI technology. The articles were filtered by scanning their abstracts and relevant articles were coded in accordance with their use of AI in the SRL process. At the final stage, all the relevant articles were analyzed, and their findings were presented considering Zimmerman model of SRL. Once the relevant articles were determined, the coding process of the articles was completed in 5 steps:

- **Identifying AI-driven tools**: Reviewing various AI applications such as intelligent tutoring systems, adaptive learning platforms, and chatbots to determine their alignment with SRL components.
- **Mapping AI features to Zimmerman's SRL model**: Categorizing AI functionalities according to the three phases of SRL, evaluating how each tool supports forethought, performance and self-evaluation.
- **Synthesizing evidence from empirical studies**: Analyzing research findings on AI-enhanced learning environments and their effectiveness in fostering SRL skills.
- **Proposing AI-based instructional strategies**: Outlining practical implications for educators to integrate AI tools in ways that promote differentiated instruction and personalized learning experiences which also created guidelines for future studies.

Based on the articles selected through the databases and the coding process through which the findings of the articles were systematically brought together, key findings on the use of AI for differentiated SRL instruction were obtained. The results of this exploratory literature review are presented in the Results section.

3. FINDINGS

Research focusing on the utilization of AI to foster SRL can be classified into two broad categories. The first category involves research focusing on developing tools to enhance SRL process and the second category involves research exploring the impact of AI tools designed to foster SRL on SRL development. Research in both categories is key to advancing our understanding of the place of AI in education process.

3.1 AI Tools Designed to Enhance Process

A significant body of research has focused on the development of artificial intelligence (AI) tools designed specifically to foster self-regulated learning (SRL). These studies aim to leverage the adaptive and interactive capabilities of AI to support learners in managing their cognitive, metacognitive, motivational, and behavioral processes throughout the learning cycle. By embedding SRL principles into intelligent tutoring systems, learning analytics dashboards, conversational agents, and personalized learning environments, researchers have sought to create tools that can provide real-time feedback, scaffolding, and guidance tailored to individual learner needs. This line of research offers specific tools to be used to foster SRL development. Table 2 offers some examples of research focusing on designing AI tools to enhance SRL process:

Table 2. AI Tools to Enhance SRL process

Reference	AI Tool
Liao et al. (2024)	AI-enabled visual report tool for formative assessment
Molenaar (2022)	Hybrid Human-AI Regulation (HHAIR) system
Srinivasa et al. (2021)	Notelink application
Somasundaram et al. (2020)	AI-based plan organizer
Durall & Kapros (2020)	Self-assessment chatbot
Ross et al. (2018)	Adaptive quiz application
Craig and Schroeder (2017)	Virtual human featuring various types of voices
Luckin (2017)	Intelligent assessment and suggestion application
Goel and Polepeddi (2016)	AI agent
Hussein et al. (2014)	AI-based question generation application
Woolf et al. (2010)	AI companion

As seen in Table 2, there is a variety of tools suggested in research to promote SRL development. They address various phases of SRL or SRL process as a whole. To illustrate, Somasundaram et al. (2020) offers an AI-based plan organizer helping students to set goals and make strategic plans using the data coming from the educational institution of the students and the data collected from students' profiles and performances. This enables students to set effective and feasible goals and come up with an optimum plan to attain their learning goal. This application particularly addresses forethought and performance phases of Zimmerman (2000) model. Similarly, Hussein et al. (2014) offers an AI-based question generation application which addresses the performance phase of the SRL providing students with comprehension check questions on subject matters using natural language processing technology. Furthermore, Luckin (2017) provides an assessment tool which not only assesses the student performance but also suggests study materials using the data coming from the interactions of the students. Similarly, Durall and Kapros (2020) suggest the use of a chatbot to foster self-assessment. These applications particularly address the self-evaluation phase of the Zimmerman (2000) model. Liao et al. (2023), on the other hand, aim to enrich the SRL process as a whole and presents a tool which changes its focus gradually starting with the learning task, then clarifying and emphasizing the learning process and highlighting SRL and self-feedback at the final stage. The findings of this experimental study reveal that the use of AI to help learners make gradual progress significantly helped learners to enhance their SRL skills.

Other than the studies focusing on enhancement of particular SRL stages or SRL skills in general, there are also studies focusing on AI tools that help students come up with several SRL task strategies enabling them to complete the learning tasks without feeling overwhelmed. Such applications also help students develop their learning skills which also has a positive impact on their self-efficacy. Several studies (e.g. Almazrou et al.,2024; Allen & Mizumoto, 2024; Hassani & Silva, 2023; Zohery, 2023; Jung & Park, 2023; Lingard, 2023; Liu et al., 2024; Suriano et al., 2025) highlight the use of AI technology in dealing with challenging learning tasks such as data handling, proofreading, translation, designing a paper, brainstorming, content revision, literature review, formatting and coding. These studies indicate that AI technology facilitates SRL process, helping students effectively deal with task completion processes. To illustrate, students may struggle referencing in particular styles like APA or Harvard, comprehending complex task content or describing an abstract idea. Also, summarizing key literature findings can be overwhelming for learners, particularly for the ones who are doing it for the first time. At this point, AI technologies particularly GenAI tools can be very useful offering suggestions, revising drafts, explaining rules or simplifying the content. Many studies highlight the effective use of ChatGPT for such purposes (Lingard, 2023; Liu et al., 2024).

In addition, to foster students' self-regulated learning (SRL) skills, the existing research increasingly emphasizes not only the use of artificial intelligence (AI) but also the integration of hybrid human-AI models. These models combine the strengths of automated systems with the essential role of human educators, which lays the ground for a more adaptive and responsive learning environment. To illustrate, Molenaar (2022) proposes a model of hybrid human-AI regulation, highlighting how this approach can effectively support young learners' SRL by dynamically aligning automated scaffolds with teacher-led interventions. The study reveals that when AI-driven insights are put together with human judgment and pedagogical strategies, students receive timely, personalized support that leads to deeper engagement and more effective regulation of their learning processes. This synergy between AI and human agency is seen as a promising direction for future SRL trainings, providing both scalability and contextual sensitivity.

AI tools suggested in research not only facilitate learners' SRL development but also helps teachers to support the SRL development of their students. To illustrate, Seo et al. (2021) provides an AI analytics application supplying instructors with an analysis of students' behavioral data such as clickstream, quiz, eye-tracking data and learning. Thus, this application enables teachers to keep track of their students' learning process and make suggestions to them to improve their performance and better regulate their learning process. Moreover, researchers like Woolf et al. (2010) offered the use of AI to help students increase their self-efficacy and motivation which is likely to affect all SRL phases since this application helps students making slower progress to make amendments in the strategies they utilize and the goals they set.

While designing AI tools to enhance SRL skills keeps its prominence, research highlighting the pedagogical principles of using AI to facilitate SRL development is also crucial for both future research and practice. Chang et al. (2023) present key pedagogical principles for integrating AI chatbots in classrooms, informed by Zimmerman's Self-Regulated Learning (SRL) framework and Judgment of Learning (JOL). Their research offer explicit and reliable guidelines on how to place AI into pedagogical framework. They demonstrate how AI can be integrated into Zimmerman's (2000) four-layer model. Figure 3 shows how AI can be integrated into Zimmerman's (2000) model step by step:

Figure 3. AI integrated mode of Zimmerman's multi-level model of SRL

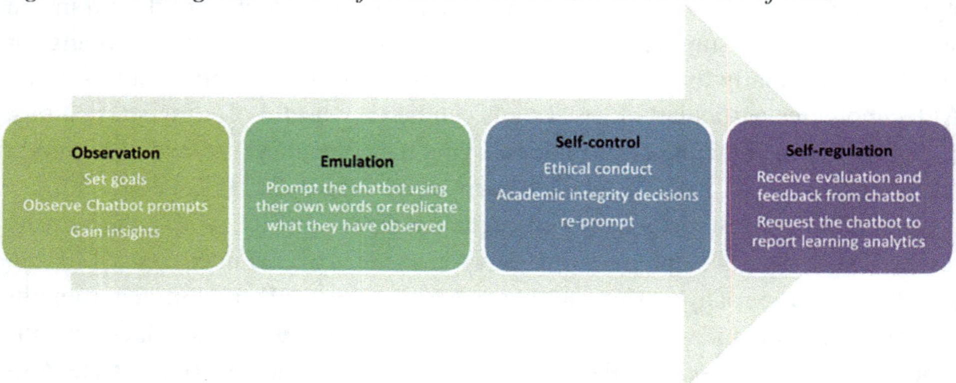

Note. The figure was recreated based on Chang, D. H., Lin, M. P. C., Hajian, S., & Wang, Q. Q. (2023). Educational design principles of using AI chatbot that supports self-regulated learning in education: Goal setting, feedback, and personalization. Sustainability, 15(17), 12921. https://doi.org/10.3390/su151712921

As seen in Figure 3, AI can be integrated into all four phases of Zimmerman's (2000) multi layered model. While interactions in the first three phase is mutual, it is only one way in the final stage which is from AI to the learner.

In the observation phase, learners start to learn about the chatbot environment by drawing on their prior knowledge of conversational norms and observing how others interact with the tool. This particular phase frequently includes goal-setting or passive learning since students begin to understand the expectations and possible outcomes of chatbot interactions. Progressing to the emulation phase, students start to apply what they have observed by independently creating prompts based on the data they gathered in peer interactions. At this stage, learners replicate effective prompting strategies as a way to internalize task requirements and effectively use them.

The next stage, that is self-control phase, introduces more complex cognitive and ethical decision-making. Students must evaluate the chatbot's responses and determine whether to use them or not. They are to conder is the concerns of academic integrity. They might refine their input by re-prompting or adopting alternative strategies. At this juncture, the chatbot can provide formative feedback, aiding learners in assessing the quality of their outputs and helping them to do necessary revisions. Finally, in the self-regulation phase, learners begin to benefit from the full potential of the chatbot as a strategic tool for enhancing learning. They may elicit evaluations of their work, request personalized analytics, or seek tailored recommendations to make further revisions. This final stage signifies a deeper understanding of how to integrate chatbot use into their SRL practices, demonstrating the chatbot's role as a facilitator of learner autonomy and goal achievement (Chang, 2023).

Additionally, there is research suggesting that AI tools can help researchers studying SRL development of learners. To illustrate, Chiu (2024) offers a classification tool for 20 learning activities using ChatGPT. The tool provides tips on how ChatGPT can foster self-determination needs and SRL phrases. This classification tool can help researchers in replicating, implementing, and integrating successful ChatGPT in education research and development projects. Similarly, Wang et al. (2023) propose the use of artificial intelligence to analyze SRL process of the learners. They suggest that the use of AI can be particularly useful for analyzing self-assessment process. Through the analysis of self-reporting protocols, cognitive and metacognitive SRL strategies can be identified with acceptable accuracy. As a subset of AI, machine learning can also be utilized as a tool to support research in the field of SRL. Alkattan et al. (2023) suggests the use of decision tree algorithms to predict students' academic outcomes. This method highlights how machine learning can uncover hidden patterns in educational data, thereby facilitating the identification of factors that influence student performance. Also, Flayyih and Hassan (2024) propose the integration of artificial intelligence methods to analyze learning processes. The findings of the study signal the use of advanced algorithms to facilitate data-driven decision-making in academics. Together, these studies illustrate the symbiotic relationship between machine learning and SRL, demonstrating how data-driven models can both assess and foster students' ability to manage their own learning effectively.

3.2 Studies Focusing on the Impact of AI Tools on SRL

In addition to research focusing on designing AI tools for SRL development, a growing number of studies have investigated the impact of these tools on learners' SRL skills and behaviors. This line of research evaluates how AI-enhanced environments influence students' ability to plan, monitor, and reflect on their learning. They also explore how they affect motivation, engagement, and academic performance. These studies often utilize experimental, quasi-experimental, or mixed-method designs to investigate the effectiveness of AI-driven interventions in promoting SRL, providing empirical insights into which features are the most effective for learning. By examining learners' interactions with AI tools in authentic learning contexts, this line of research contributes to a deeper understanding of the conditions under which AI can meaningfully support the development of self-regulatory competencies across diverse educational settings.

Based on the exploratory review of literature conducted for the present study, several publications focusing on the use of AI to foster the SRL process were obtained. The summary of these publications and their key findings are provided in Table 3:

Table 3. Studies Focusing on the Impact of AI Tool on SRL

Reference	Research Title	Aim of the Research	AI Tool Used	SRL Related Key Findings
Jin et al. (2025)	Modeling AI-assisted writing: How self-regulated learning influences writing outcomes	To investigate how key variables such as self-efficacy, SRL, artificial intelligence use and critical thinking interact in generative AI-assisted writing processes	GenAI	AI self-efficacy and writing self-efficacy were significant antecedents of self-regulation, suggesting the significance of enhancing students' self-efficacy in boosting self-regulation in AI use.
Ng et al. (2024)	Empowering student self-regulated learning and science education through ChatGPT: A pioneering pilot study	To compare the contributions generative AI- based (SRLbot) and rule- based AI chatbots (Nemobot) in a 3- week science learning experience	ChatGPT -SRLbot -Nemobot	SRLbot enriched students' science knowledge, behavioral engagement and motivation. Quantile regression analysis revealed that the number of interactions significantly predicted variations in SRL. Students appreciated the differentiated recommendations and flexibility of SRLbot, which modified responses considering indvidual learning and SRL scenarios. The ChatGPT- enhanced instructional design lessened learning anxiety and enhanced learning performance, motivation and preserved learning habits. SRLbot's adaptability and personalized approach made it different from rule-based chatbots.
Jin et al. (2023)	Supporting students' self-regulated learning in online learning using artificial intelligence applications	To explore students' perceptions of the use of AI applications to support SRL and to identify the pedagogical and psychological aspects that they perceive as necessary for effective utilization of those AI applications.	Plan Organizer AI Companion Pre-question Generator Intelligent Suggestions AI Analytics Virtual Human AI Agent Notelink Adaptive Quiz AI Reflection	Learners perceived AI applications as useful for supporting metacognitive, cognitive, and behavioral regulation across different SRL areas, but not for regulating motivation. Regarding the use of AI applications to support SRL, consideration of three pedagogical and psychological aspects were requested by the learners namely: learner identity, learner activeness, and learner position.

continued on following page

Table 3. Continued

Reference	Research Title	Aim of the Research	AI Tool Used	SRL Related Key Findings
Chang et al. (2023)	Educational Design Principles of Using AI Chatbot That Supports Self-Regulated Learning in Education: Goal Setting, Feedback, and Personalization	To	ChatGPT	Teaching how to write prompts to the learners is a key factor helping them improve their SRL skills via chatbots. Configuring reverse prompting in the AI chatbot's capability can assist students in SRL process. Creating data-driven mechanism that makes an AI chatbot to offer learning analytics enables learners to reflect on learning and develop SRL strategies.
Hsu et al. (2023)	Artificial Intelligence image recognition using self-regulation learning strategies: effects on vocabulary acquisition, learning anxiety, and learning behaviors of English language learners	Examining how AI image recognition technologies along with SRL affect students' vocabulary acquisition, self-regulation, and learning anxiety in the language classroom, and further investigating students' learning behaviors during learning.	AI-supported image recognition (AI-IR) AI-supported optical character recognition (AI-OCR) technology with SRL	Students who learnt vocabulary from realia using AIIR with SRL significantly outperformed the control group students in terms of vocabulary acquisition. However, no significant differences were found in the two groups' SRL or learning anxieties. Behavioral analysis showed that the experimental group students made more progress in SRL development and experienced lower learning anxiety.

Table 3 provides a summary of the research focusing on the impact of the use of AI on different learning skills indicating positive impact of AI on learning. To start with, Jin et al. (2025) focus on one of the areas that AI is the most utilized, which is writing. They explore how different variables like SRL, self-efficacy and critical thinking affect each other in a learning environment where AI is used to foster academic writing. They employed structural equation modeling to classify AI use into three levels, from basic to advanced: 1) for technical support, 2) for text development, and 3) for transformation. The findings of their research revealed that these variables do not exhibit a unidirectional relationship; instead, they engage in reciprocal interactions, exerting mutual influence through complex and multi-dimensional processes. To elaborate, SRL strategy use has a significant positive impact on three types of AI use mentioned earlier. Also, the most advanced use of AI (i.e., for writing transformation) significantly enriched various variables like critical thinking, motivation, and writing quality, but the most basic use (for technical support) did not predict these variables. Besides, AI self-efficacy and writing self-efficacy were key determinants of SRL which makes us highlight the importance of fostering students' self-efficacy to enhance self-regulation in AI use. This multileveled interaction among these variables leads to the finding that the essential point for writing-outcome improvement may not be to train students for different uses of AI, but it is to boost their SRL development to the point that they can independently explore and employ advanced uses of this technology. Similarly, Ng et al. (2024) explore the effectiveness of a ChatGPT-enhanced chatbot (SRL-bot) in supporting secondary school students' SRL development in science classes. In this quasi-experimental study, the researchers collected data from 74 students in Hong Kong to compare the progress of the students using using SRLbot with those using a rule-based chatbot (Nemobot) during a three-week blended learning intervention on the topic of force and motion. If students feel overwhelmed and need assistance to keep up with self-regulating because of a variety of reasons like difficulty in comprehending complex science content, low motivation or the need for more guidance for completing science tasks, they could get help from the SRL-bot. On the other hand, while Nemobot is a bot-building platform for designing AI conversational chatbots and is a helpful tool to facilitate learning process, it does not provide SRL instruction and scaffolding support like flashcards, hints or e-quizzes. If the students face challenges in their learning process, they can report it in their learning management system. The study yielded both quantitative and qualitative results. Quantitative results showed that students employing SRLbot made significant progress in SRL dimensions like goal setting, time management, help-seeking, and self-assessment. Besides, their level of motivation as well as knowledge of science increased. Additionally, the results of the quantile regression analysis indicated that student interaction with the chatbot significantly predicted SRL gains, whereas gender did not. The results of the analysis of the qualitative data aligned with these results. The students reported positive feedback on the differentiated support they received from the SRLbot signaling its resemblance to a human teacher. However, some limitations were also reported such as the need for specific prompts and chat-bot's lack of proactive reminders. Nevertheless, the findings of the study showed that when GenAI tools were designed within the framework of SRL principles, they have substantial potential to foster SRL enhancing student autonomy and reflective practice. The study also underlines the key role of helping both teachers and students to develop AI literacy skills. Another study focusing on the guidelines for using AI effectively in SRL development process was carried out by Chang et al. (2023). As mentioned earlier, Chang et al., (2023) integrated AI tools to Zimmerman's (2000) multi-level model (which can be seen in Figure 2). In addition to that, they also proposed the incorporation of goal setting (prompting), self-assessment and feedback, and personalization as three fundamental educational principles to be applied while employing AI tools to support SRL development. They argue that instructional prompting is a key element in cultivating students' SRL competencies.

Furthermore, they suggest the integration of reverse prompting within the functional design of AI chatbots, which can serve as a scaffold to support students' regulatory processes, particularly in monitoring and comprehension. Besides, they add that the development of a data-driven framework that enables AI chatbots to generate and deliver learning analytics can facilitate learners' metacognitive reflection and enhance the strategic development of SRL practices. Thus, just like Ng et al. (2024), they also suggest enhancing AI literacy of the learners and preparing the learners to use AI effectively and then adapt the AI tools to the SRL development. While working on AI literacy, attitude towards the AI tools is also a key factor. Jin et al. (2023) explores the perceptions of the learners of the utilization of AI applications to foster SRL and to identify the pedagogical and psychological aspects that they perceive as necessary for effective employment of those AI applications. Grounded in Zimmerman's SRL framework, the study examines the learners' experiences across the forethought, performance, and reflection phases, addressing cognitive, metacognitive, motivational, and behavioral aspects. With the help of the speed dating method with storyboards illustrating ten AI application scenarios, the authors revealed whereas students appreciated AI tools that supported cognitive, metacognitive, and behavioral regulation (e.g., AI analytics dashboards and intelligent tutors), they were more skeptical of those targeting motivational regulation. Besides, the research determined three critical pedagogical and psychological factors that influence the effective use of AI for SRL: *learner identity* (e.g., individuality and growth potential), *learner activeness* (from AI dependence to learner agency), and *learner position* (balancing autonomous learning with institutional constraints).

While working on the perceptions of learners on AI during SRL development process, learner anxiety is a key factor to consider. Hsu et al. (2023) examined the impact of integrating Artificial Intelligence-based Image Recognition (AI-IR) with Self-Regulated Learning (SRL) strategies on young English as a Foreign Language (EFL) learners' vocabulary acquisition, learning anxiety, and learning behaviors. The study was carried out with 47 third-grade students in Taiwan. The research design was quasi-experimental and two research groups were compared: the one using AI-IR with realia (experimental group) and the other one using AI-based Optical Character Recognition (AI-OCR) with printed texts (control group), both within an SRL framework. The results of the study revealed that students who engaged with AI-IR demonstrated significantly greater vocabulary gains and more complex, strategic learning behaviors, despite no statistically significant differences in measured SRL levels or anxiety. On the other hand, behavioral data indicated that AI-IR led to more meaningful engagement in SRL phases such as planning, monitoring, and reflecting, and also reduced the signs of learning anxiety. The findings of this study takes us to the conclusion that the use of AI alone may not be enough to reduce learning anxiety. However, combining AI-supported recognition technologies with pedagogically-informed SRL designs as well as realia may create authentic, engaging, and cognitively rich language learning environments especially for young learners.

Based on the findings given in Table 3 and the analysis of the selected articles, it can be revealed that AI can support SRL in the following ways:

- **Forethought Phase:** AI can facilitate goal-setting through personalized learning recommendations and predictive analytics that help students establish realistic learning objectives. AI-driven chatbots and virtual mentors can provide strategic guidance on effective goal-setting techniques.
- **Performance Phase:** AI-powered intelligent tutoring systems can offer real-time feedback, track progress, and suggest adaptive strategies based on students' interactions. AI tools can also enhance motivation and engagement.
- **Self-Reflection Phase:** AI can support metacognitive reflection by generating analytics-driven insights on students' performance, identifying patterns, and suggesting adjustments for future learning tasks. Automated self-assessment tools can guide learners in evaluating their strategies and outcomes.

3.3 Concerns on the Use of AI to Support SRL Process

Although AI technology seems very promising to enhance SRL development, just like every new development, it comes with some concerns as well. Although AI technology is advancing every day, AI tools like ChatGPT struggle to provide correct answers on new developments in science and technology as well as the new topics in K12 and college education curriculum. Besides, they come up with incorrect references which might mislead students (Dao & Le, 2023). Furthermore, because AI cannot assume responsibility for its actions and for the suggestions it provides, ethical concerns may arise related to the derivation and accuracy of recommendations given by AI (Ng et al., 2021). Another concern is about the skills that the students are supposed to develop such as critical thinking skills. There is research concerning the potential negative impact of AI particularly GenAI on the critical thinking skills of the learners as learners grow more and more dependent on GenAI to complete the learning tasks without feeling the need to read information from different sources and try to synthesize information to obtain a critical perspective. Malik et al. (2023) contributed to this discussion by examining the perceptions of 245 Indonesian undergraduates regarding the impact of the use of GenAI on while writing academic papers on their critical thinking skills. The findings of the study indicated concerns on the negative impact on GenAI causing a decline in the critical thinking skills of the students, overdependency on technology and repetition of false information generated by AI. However, it is possible to state that the research on the potential negative impact of AI on learning and skill development is disputable.

After reviewing 24 empirical articles, Schei et al.'s (2024) provided the conclusion that GenAI can be used as a tool to enrich critical thinking skills of the learners. Similarly, Essel et al. (2024) underscored that the use of GenAI for learning tasks can motivate learners to learn more about different perspectives, question different points of view, look for evidence to prove or refute certain information and make an assessment of the arguments. This insight is also supported by Huang et al. (2023) who states that GenAI is a useful tool even with its flaws as it makes learners think critically about every piece of information they receive. While the impact of AI on different skills of learners are still being investigated, another AI-related issue has been questioned by the researchers. As mentioned earlier, SRL refers to the process of taking control of one's own learning and the learner is only called a self-regulated one if they actively manage their own learning process, critically evaluating their performance and modifying their behavior if necessary. However, thanks to AI technology, the learner gets external support in many states of the process such as goal setting, strategic planning, determining the correct task strategy to use in particular domains of learning and especially carrying out self-assessment process. There is concern regarding whether this is, in fact, self-regulation or it is external regulation. While concerns regarding the substantial help that AI might provide during the process remain valid, it is important to consider that although AI facilitates many a range of stages of SRL, it is still the learner who decides to utilize AI to attain a learning goal. Without active initiative of the learner, AI technology is useless in SRL development. On the other hand, the research on the use and the impact of AI are still in early stages and has yet to reach theoretical or empirical maturity (Chang et al. 2023). In other words, this is still a nascent area with many dimensions yet to be systematically explored. This takes us to the conclusion that it is essential to carry out more studies to investigate the impact of AI tools on the skill development process of the learners, to work on theoretical aspects of combining AI tools and SRL perspective to come up with solid pedagogical principles to apply in this process and to design AI tools to support SRL development at an optimum level. Thus, it is crucial to carry out longitudinal research to see the impact of AI on learning process in the long run, to do experimental research to see the impact of AI tools on different aspects of SRL and to design case studies to examine the effects of the newly designed SRL tools.

CONCLUSION AND FUTURE RESEARCH DIRECTIONS

As this chapter has indicated, the intersection of Artificial Intelligence (AI) and Self-Regulated Learning (SRL) holds significant promise for transforming educational practice. By employing AI-powered tools and platforms, educators can more effectively facilitate students' SRL processes across cognitive, metacognitive, motivational, and emotional domains. Drawing on the Zimmerman model of SRL, this chapter has provided a detailed report on how AI can be strategically employed to personalize learning, foster metacognitive awareness, and promote learner autonomy. However, while the potential of AI in supporting SRL is compelling, several challenges continue to exist. These include issues of algorithmic bias, data privacy, equitable access, and the risk of over-automation that might diminish learners' active role in their own regulation processes. To mitigate such concerns, a human-centered approach to AI design or coming up with hybrid designs is critical, which can help both educators and learners to have more transparency, inclusivity, and alignment with pedagogical goals.

For future research it is recommended to empirically test the conceptual propositions presented in this chapter. Especially longitudinal studies are needed to explore how sustained use of AI-enhanced tools influences students' development of SRL strategies over time. Moreover, there is a pressing need to investigate domain-specific applications of AI for SRL, particularly in under-researched subject areas and among diverse student populations. Cross-cultural studies can also shed light on how cultural norms and educational traditions shape students' engagement with AI-supported SRL tools. Another promising avenue lies in the integration of learning analytics and social network analysis to understand the social dimension of SRL in AI-mediated environments. These approaches can provide rich, real-time data on how learners co-regulate and socially share regulatory processes, especially in collaborative and hybrid learning contexts. Finally, the research questions such as "How can AI-driven SRL support be validated across domains?" and "Which SRL strategies are most responsive to AI-based scaffolding?" could provide a solid foundation to carry out more studies enlightening the role of AI in SRL development.

In sum, while the cooperation of AI and SRL is still in its early stages, it offers transformative potential for differentiated, equitable, and effective learning experiences. By continuing to bridge theoretical frameworks with empirical research, and by fostering interdisciplinary collaboration between educators, data scientists, and technologists, the field can move toward more effective and pedagogically shaped implementations of AI in education.

REFERENCES

Alkattan, H., Subhi, A. A., Adelaja, O. A., Abotaleb, M., Mijwil, M. M., Mishra, P., Sekiwu, D., Bamwerinde, W., & Turyasingura, B. (2023). Employing data mining techniques and machine learning models in classification of students' academic performance. *Babylonian Journal of Artificial Intelligence*, *2023*, 43–54.

Allen, T. J., & Mizumoto, A. (2024). ChatGPT over my friends: Japanese English-as-a-Foreign-Language learners' preferences for editing and proofreading strategies. *RELC Journal. Article, 00336882241262533*. Advance online publication. DOI: 10.1177/ 00336882241262533

Almazrou, S., Alanezi, F., & Almutairi, S. A.. (2024). Enhancing medical students' critical thinking skills through ChatGPT: An empirical study with medical students. *Nutrition and Health (Berkhamsted, Hertfordshire)*. Advance online publication. DOI: 10.1177/02601060241273627 PMID: 39150341

Alraddadi, M. M., & Zebehazy, K. T. (2023). Exploring inclusive teaching practices to enhance effective learning of students with visual impairments in a secondary school in Saudi Arabia using a self-regulated learning framework. *British Journal of Visual Impairment*, •••, 02646196231201770.

Alvi, E., & Gillies, R. M. (2024). Investigating the individual nature of teacher beliefs and practices about self-regulated learning and how this shapes their practices for supporting student learning. *Educational Studies*, *50*(4), 516–538.

Anyichie, A. C., Butler, D. L., & Nashon, S. M. (2023). Exploring Teacher Practices for Enhancing Student Engagement in Culturally Diverse Classrooms. *Journal of Pedagogical Research*, *7*(5), 183–207.

Aydan, S. (2023). *From Little Acorns to Mighty Oaks: Self-Regulation Strategies of the Top Ranking Science High School Students in Türki ye and Factors Promoting These Strategies* [Doctoral dissertation, Middle East Technical University]. METU Library Database https://open.metu.edu.tr/handle/11511/104828

Azevedo, R., Rosário, P., Magalhães, P., Núñez, J. C., Pereira, B., & Pereira, A. (2023). A tool-kit to help students from low socioeconomic status background: A school-based self-regulated learning intervention. *European Journal of Psychology of Education*, *38*(2), 495–518.

Bandura, A. (1986). *Social Foundations of Thought and Action: A Social Cognitive Theory*. Prentice Hall.

Bano, M., Zowghi, D., Kearney, M., Schuck, S., & Aubusson, P. (2018). Mobile learning for science and mathematics school education: A systematic review of empirical evidence. *Computers & Education*, *121*, 30–58. DOI: 10.1016/j.compedu.2018.02.006

Bardach, L., Yanagida, T., Goetz, T., Jach, H., & Pekrun, R. (2023). Self-regulated and externally regulated learning in adolescence: Developmental trajectories and relations with teacher behavior, parent behavior, and academic achievement. *Developmental Psychology*, *59*(7), 1327. PMID: 37155294

Callan, G., Longhurst, D., Shim, S., & Ariotti, A. (2022). Identifying and predicting teachers' use of practices that support SRL. *Psychology in the Schools*, *59*(11), 2327–2344.

Chang, D. H., Lin, M. P. C., Hajian, S., & Wang, Q. Q. (2023). Educational design principles of using AI chatbot that supports self-regulated learning in education: Goal setting, feedback, and personalization. *Sustainability*, *15*(17), 12921. DOI: 10.3390/su151712921

Chiu, T. K. (2024). A classification tool to foster self-regulated learning with generative artificial intelligence by applying self-determination theory: A case of ChatGPT. *Educational Technology Research and Development*, *72*(4), 2401–2416. DOI: 10.1007/s11423-024-10366-w

Craig, S. D., & Schroeder, N. L. (2017). Reconsidering the voice effect when learning from a virtual human. *Computers & Education*, *114*, 193–205.

Cunha, J., Guimarães, A., Martins, J., & Rosário, P. (2023). A self-regulation intervention conducted by teachers in a disadvantaged school neighborhood: Implementers' and observers' perceptions of its impact on elementary students. *Children (Basel, Switzerland)*, *10*(11), 1795. PMID: 38002886

Dao, X. Q., & Le, N. B. (2023). Investigating the effectiveness of ChatGPT in mathematical reasoning and problem solving: Evidence from the Vietnamese National High School Graduation Examination. *arXiv preprint arXiv:2306.06331*.

Durall, E., & Kapros, E. (2020). Co-design for a competency self-assessment chatbot and survey in science education. In *Learning and Collaboration Technologies. Human and Technology Ecosystems: 7th International Conference, LCT 2020, Held as Part of the 22nd HCI International Conference, HCII 2020, Copenhagen, Denmark, July 19–24, 2020* [Springer International Publishing.]. *Proceedings*, *22*(Part II), 13–24.

Essel, H. B., Vlachopoulos, D., Essuman, A. B., & Amankwa, J. O. (2024). ChatGPT effects on cognitive skills of undergraduate students: Receiving instant responses from AI- based conversational large language models (LLMs). *Computers and Education: Artificial Intelligence*, *6*, 100198. Advance online publication. DOI: 10.1016/j.caeai.2023.100198

Ferreira, P. C., & Simão, A. M. V. (2012). Teaching practices that foster self-regulated learning: A case study. *Educational Research E-journal*, *1*(1), 1–16.

Flayyih, M. F., & Hassan, T. O. U. T. (2024). Predictive analytics model for students' grade prediction using machine learning. *Babylonian Journal of Artificial Intelligence*, *2024*, 83–101.

Gitomer, D. H., Curtis, M. E., Glaser, R., & Lensky, D. B. (1987). Processing differences as a function of item difficulty in verbal analogy performance. *Journal of Educational Psychology*, *79*(3), 212.

Goel, A. K., & Polepeddi, L. (2016). *Jill Watson: A virtual teaching assistant for online education*. Georgia Institute of Technology.

Hassani, H., & Silva, E. S. (2023). The role of ChatGPT in data science: How ai-assisted conversational interfaces are revolutionizing the field. *Big Data and Cognitive Computing*, *7*(2), 62. DOI: 10.3390/bdcc7020062

Heirweg, S., De Smul, M., Merchie, E., Devos, G., & Van Keer, H. (2022). The long road from teacher professional development to student improvement: A school-wide professionalization on self-regulated learning in primary education. *Research Papers in Education*, *37*(6), 929–953.

Hsu, T. C., Chang, C., & Jen, T. H. (2023). Artificial intelligence image recognition using self-regulation learning strategies: Effects on vocabulary acquisition, learning anxiety, and learning behaviors of English language learners. *Interactive Learning Environments*, •••, 1–19.

Huang, C. W., Coleman, M., Gachago, D., & Van Belle, J. P. (2023). Using ChatGPT to encourage critical AI literacy skills and for assessment in higher education. In *Annual conference of the southern african computer lecturers' association* (pp. 105–118). Nature Switzerland. Cham: Springer.

Hussein, H., Elmogy, M., & Guirguis, S. (2014). Automatic English question generation system based on template driven scheme. [IJCSI]. *International Journal of Computer Science Issues*, *11*(6), 45.

Jin, F., Lin, C. H., & Lai, C. (2025). Modeling AI-assisted writing: How self-regulated learning influences writing outcomes. *Computers in Human Behavior*, *165*, 108538.

Jin, S. H., Im, K., Yoo, M., Roll, I., & Seo, K. (2023). Supporting students' self-regulated learning in online learning using artificial intelligence applications. *International Journal of Educational Technology in Higher Education*, *20*(1), 37.

Jung, H., & Park, J. H. (2023). Design and issues of writing literatures using ChatGPT. *Journal of Knowledge Information Technology and Systems*, *18*(1), 31–40. DOI: 10.3 4163/jkits.2023.18.1.004

Kolovelonis, A., Goudas, M., & Dermitzaki, I. (2010). Self-regulated learning of a motor skill through emulation and self-control levels in a physical education setting. *Journal of Applied Sport Psychology*, *22*(2), 198–212.

Lee, S.-M. (2019). A Systematic review of context-aware technology use in foreign language learning. *Computer Assisted Language Learning*, *25*(3), 294–318. DOI: 10.1080/09588221.2019.1688836

Leidinger, M., & Perels, F. (2012). Training self-regulated learning in the classroom: Development and evaluation of learning materials to train self-regulated learning during regular mathematics lessons at primary school. *Education Research International*, *2012*(1), 735790.

Liao, X., Zhang, X., Wang, Z., & Luo, H. (2024). Design and implementation of an AI- enabled visual report tool as formative assessment to promote learning achievement and self- regulated learning: An experimental study. *British Journal of Educational Technology*, *55*, 1253–1276. DOI: 10.1111/bjet.1342

Lin, J.-J., & Lin, H. (2019). Mobile-assisted ESL/EFL vocabulary learning: A Systematic review and meta-analysis. *Computer Assisted Language Learning*, *32*(8), 878–919. DOI: 10.1080/09588221.2018.1541359

Lingard, L. (2023). Writing with ChatGPT: An illustration of its capacity, limitations & implications for academic writers. *Perspectives on Medical Education*, *12*(1), 261. DOI: 10.5334/pme.1072 PMID: 37397181

Liu, Y., Le-Cong, T., Widyasari, R., Tantithamthavorn, C., Li, L., Le, X. B. D., & Lo, D. (2024). Refining chatgpt-generated code: Characterizing and mitigating code quality issues. *ACM Transactions on Software Engineering and Methodology*, *33*(5), 1–26. DOI: 10.1145/3643674

Luckin, R. (2017). Towards artificial intelligence-based assessment systems. *Nature Human Behaviour*, *1*(3), 1–3.

Malik, A., Prihatini, S., & Agustina, R. D. (2023). Study on collaborative creativity learning models and gender on students' creative thinking skills. *Jurnal Penelitian & Pengembangan Pendidikan Fisika, 9*(1). Advance online publication. DOI: 10.21009/1.09109

Molenaar, I. (2022). The concept of hybrid human-AI regulation: Exemplifying how to support young learners' self-regulated learning. *Computers and Education: Artificial Intelligence, 3*, 100070.

Newman, R. S. (2023). Adaptive help seeking: A strategy of self-regulated learning. In *Self-regulation of learning and performance* (pp. 283–301). Routledge.

Ng, D. T. K., Tan, C. W., & Leung, J. K. L. (2024). Empowering student self-regulated learning and science education through ChatGPT: A pioneering pilot study. *British Journal of Educational Technology, 55*(4), 1328–1353.

Pajares, F. (2012). Motivational role of self-efficacy beliefs in self-regulated learning. In *Motivation and self-regulated learning* (pp. 111–139). Routledge.

Perry, N. E., Lisaingo, S., Yee, N., Parent, N., Wan, X., & Muis, K. (2020). Collaborating with teachers to design and implement assessments for self-regulated learning in the context of authentic classroom writing tasks. *Assessment in Education: Principles, Policy & Practice, 27*(4), 416–443.

Pintrich, P. R. (2000). Multiple goals, multiple pathways: The role of goal orientation in learning and achievement. *Journal of Educational Psychology, 92*(3), 544.

Ross, B., Chase, A. M., Robbie, D., Oates, G., & Absalom, Y. (2018). Adaptive quizzes to increase motivation, engagement, and learning outcomes in a first-year accounting unit. *International Journal of Educational Technology in Higher Education, 15*(1), 30.

Schei, O. M., Møgelvang, A., & Ludvigsen, K. (2024). Perceptions and use of AI chatbots among students in higher education: A scoping review of empirical studies. *Education Sciences, 14*(8), 922. DOI: 10.3390/educsci14080922

Schunk, D. H., & Greene, J. A. (2018). Historical, contemporary, and future perspectives on self-regulated learning and performance. In *Handbook of self-regulation of learning and performance* (2nd ed., pp. 1–15). Routledge/Taylor & Francis Group. Educational psychology handbook series.

Schunk, D. H., & Zimmerman, B. (Eds.). (2011). *Handbook of Self-Regulation of Learning and Performance*. Taylor & Francis.

Seo, K., Tang, J., Roll, I., Fels, S., & Yoon, D. (2021). The impact of artificial intelligence on learner-instructors in online learning. *International Journal of Educational Technology in Higher Education, 18*(1), 1–23. PMID: 34778540

Sins, P., de Leeuw, R., de Brouwer, J., & Vrieling-Teunter, E. (2024). Promoting explicit instruction of strategies for self-regulated learning: Evaluating a teacher professional development program in primary education. *Metacognition and Learning, 19*(1), 215–247.

Skinner, B. F. (1953). Some Contributions of an Experimental Analysis of Behavior to Psychology as A Whole. *The American Psychologist, 8*, 69–78.

Somasundaram, M., Junaid, K. M., & Mangadu, S. (2020). Artificial intelligence (AI) enabled intelligent quality management systems (IQMS) for the personalized learning path. *Procedia Computer Science, 172*, 438–442.

Spruce, R., & Bol, L. (2015). Teacher beliefs, knowledge, and practice of self-regulated learning. *Metacognition and Learning, 10*, 245–277.

Srinivasa, R. J., Dodson, S., Seo, K., Yoon, D., & Fels, S. (2021). NoteLink: A Point-and-Shoot Linking Interface between Students' Handwritten Notebooks and Instructional Videos. In *2021 ACM/IEEE Joint Conference on Digital Libraries (JCDL)* (pp. 140–149). IEEE.

Suriano, R., Plebe, A., Acciai, A., & Fabio, R. A. (2025). Student interaction with ChatGPT can promote complex critical thinking skills. *Learning and Instruction, 95*, 102011. Advance online publication. DOI: 10.1016/j.learninstruc.2024.102011

uteu, L. (2021). Teachers' beliefs about classroom practices that develop students' metacognition and self-regulated learning skills. *Acta Didactica Napocensia, 14*(1), 165–173.

Voskamp, A., Kuiper, E., & Volman, M. (2022). Teaching practices for self-directed and self-regulated learning: Case studies in Dutch innovative secondary schools. *Educational Studies, 48*(6), 772–789.

Vygotsky, L. S. (1978). *Mind in society: The development of Higher Psychological Processes*. Harvard University Press.

Wang, C. Y., & Lin, J. J. (2023). Utilizing artificial intelligence to support analyzing self-regulated learning: A preliminary mixed-methods evaluation from a human-centered perspective. *Computers in Human Behavior, 144*, 107721.

Woolf, B. P., Arroyo, I., Muldner, K., Burleson, W., Cooper, D. G., Dolan, R., & Christopherson, R. M. (2010). The effect of motivational learning companions on low achieving students and students with disabilities. In: *International conference on intelligent tutoring systems* (pp. 327–337). Springer, Berlin, Heidelberg.

Žerak, U., Juriševič, M., & Pečjak, S. (2024). Parenting and teaching styles in relation to student characteristics and self-regulated learning. *European Journal of Psychology of Education, 39*(2), 1327–1351.

Zimmerman, B. J. (2000). Attaining self-regulation: A social-cognitive perspective. In Boekaerts, M., Pintrich, P., & Zeidner, M. (Eds.), *Handbook of self-regulation* (pp. 13–39). Academic Press., DOI: 10.1016/B978-0-12-109890-2.X5027-6

Zimmerman, B. J. (2002). Becoming a Self-Regulated Learner: An Overview. *Theory into Practice, 41*(2), 64–70. DOI: 10.1207/s15430421tip4102_2

Zimmerman, B. J., & Cleary, T. J. (2009). Motives to self-regulate learning: A social cognitive account. In Handbook of motivation at school (pp. 247–264). Routledge/Taylor & Francis Group.

Zimmerman, B. J., & Schunk, D. H. (2011). In Zimmerman, B. J., & Schunk, D. H. (Eds.), *"Self-regulated learning and performance: an introduction and overview," in Handbook of Self-Regulation of Learning and Performance* (pp. 1–14). Routledge.

Zohery, M. (2023). ChatGPT in academic writing and publishing: A comprehensive guide. In *Artificial intelligence in academia, research, and science: ChatGPT as a case study* (1st ed., pp. 10–61). Achtago.

ADDITIONAL READING

Azevedo, R., Bouchet, F., Duffy, M., Harley, J., Taub, M., Trevors, G., Cloude, E., Dever, D., Wiedbusch, M., Wortha, F., & Cerezo, R. (2022). Lessons Learned and Future Directions of MetaTutor: Leveraging Multichannel Data to Scaffold Self-Regulated Learning With an Intelligent Tutoring System. *Frontiers in Psychology, 13*, 813632. DOI: 10.3389/fpsyg.2022.813632 PMID: 35774935

Gurcan, F., Cagiltay, N. E., & Cagiltay, K. (2020). Mapping Human–Computer Interaction Research Themes and Trends from Its Existence to Today: A Topic Modeling-Based Review of past 60 Years. *International Journal of Human-Computer Interaction, 37*(3), 267–280. DOI: 10.1080/10447318.2020.1819668

Holmes, W., & Tuomi, I. (2022). State of the art and practice in AI in education. *European Journal of Education*, *57*(4), 542–570. DOI: 10.1111/ejed.12533

Järvelä, S., Nguyen, A., & Hadwin, A. (2023). Human and artificial intelligence collaboration for socially shared regulation in learning. *British Journal of Educational Technology*, *54*(5), 1057–1076.

Järvelä, S., Nguyen, A., & Molenaar, I. (2023). Advancing SRL research with artificial intelligence. *Computers in Human Behavior*, *147*, 107847.

Molenaar, I., de Mooij, S., Azevedo, R., Bannert, M., Järvelä, S., & Gašević, D. (2023). Measuring self-regulated learning and the role of AI: Five years of research using multimodal multichannel data. *Computers in Human Behavior*, *139*, 107540.

Xia, Q., Chiu, T. K., Chai, C. S., & Xie, K. (2023). The mediating effects of needs satisfaction on the relationships between prior knowledge and self-regulated learning through artificial intelligence chatbot. *British Journal of Educational Technology*, *54*(4), 967–986.

Chapter 3
Real-Time Data Insights Transforming Teaching Strategies and Student Outcomes

Shraddha N. Zanjat
https://orcid.org/0009-0009-6379-3996
SOET, Sandip University, India

Vishwajit K. Barbudhe
https://orcid.org/0000-0002-2200-4980
SITRC, Nashik, India

Bhavana S. Karmore
G.H. Raisoni University, Amaravati, India

ABSTRACT

Real-time data analytics in the educational framework is becoming a game-changer in pedagogical methodologies and is noticeably affecting student performance metrics.Instant data insights may improve the teaching process, resource allocation, and individualized learning, as was well discussed, but they can also have a multifaceted effect on decision-making. To identify ways forward through the transition to proactive, adaptive, and student-empowering instructional practices, this study examines the transformative role of data-driven decision-making in modern education by exploring new trends, difficulties, and future directions of data use in educational settings. Analytics of Real-Time Data in Education Data-driven training and individualized learning have been made possible by real-time data analytics in

DOI: 10.4018/979-8-3373-2948-2.ch003

education. These traditional educational models often use standard curricula and assessment methods that may not consider each student's diverse learning needs and styles.

1. INTRODUCTION TO REAL-TIME DATA IN EDUCATION

Data analytics builds the possibility to enhance the instructional and learning processes; the solution of analytical data has bound the longer duration for each instructor/mentor and students as well (Nguyen, 2025). This paradigm shift allows faster and more efficient decision-making, better operations, and tracking of educational practices in real time; the article elaborates on that in reference (Yaseen et al., 2025). It can reveal real-time action insights, which enable early identification of at-risk students, early in the semester, and prompt intervention with subsequent high student retention rates, enhancing further quality of educational experience (Bierstaker et al., 2024). This allows educators to customize multimodal learning analytics to work in blended learning, which is inherently dependent on the quality and form of learner data (Hallarte et al., 2024). In this regard, data-driven decision-making (DDDM) has massively affected educational practices by changing traditional pedagogic strategies into a more student-oriented environment where learning becomes individualized for each learner (Chalkiadakis et al., 2024). Demonstrate with objective evidence solutions to educational problems beyond biased assessments in real-time education. Big Data in education also stems from saving multiple types of information, linking them, and shifting the data to knowledge (Demartini et al., 2024). This technique significantly enhances the learning of students, the instruction of teachers, and the programs of institutions (Demartini et al., 2024). The rise of Big Data and learning analytics provides a chance to gain knowledge about how education can be improved based on massive empirical evidence taken from the digital traces of learners working with educational technologies (Onesie Zigzagoon et al., 2024). The vast amounts of education data this process can support, together with the time-sensitive method of collecting and analyzing it, positions educators to act proactively in ways they have not been able to before, which is suggested to contribute towards improving student output through more personalized learning provision (Demartini et al., 2024).

RTDE formalises the continual data capture, processing, and analysis from a range of educational activities and interactions (Yaseen et al., 2025). With this data from online learning platforms, classroom assessments, student performance metrics, and more it offers educators a glimpse into their students' learning patterns and real-time progress. Real-time data is one of the most important as it allows you to take action quickly and without any hassles, as it is recent information, which is way better than letting things amplify. Middle of the curve learning styles, teaching strategies can be dynamically improved based on data integration at an individual level, as and when the student learns. By providing educators with details of student engagement, understanding, and performance in real-time on a one-to-one basis, they can immediately change their instructional practices, offer timely interventions, and provide personalised learning experiences to ensure each student maximises their potential. Furthermore, real-time data can help an educational institution to assess the impact of its programs and interventions, thus providing a feedback loop to improve constantly. Applications of data analytics/mining can create synergies between teachers and learners in networked environments, leading to a new norm; hence, collaborative active learning methodologies are invoked (Egunjobi & Adeyeye, 2024)

Figure 1. Architecture of Smart Power Management System for Educational Facilities

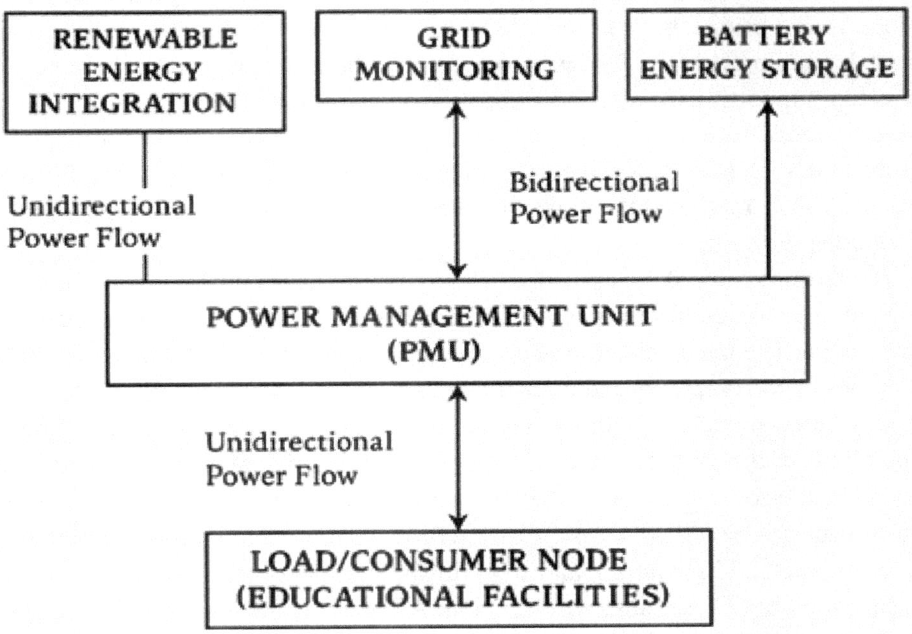

1.1 Traditional Marketing vs Data-Driven Marketing

A standardized curriculum, periodic assessments, and a subjective grading system are the hallmarks of our traditional mode of education, and this form simply doesn't work to cater to individual learning needs and styles. On the other hand, data-driven approaches exploit empirical evidence to extract deeper insights into student cognitive activities, so that these (hard) facts can be used by practitioners when making decisions (Nguyen, 2025). It is thus inevitable that a data-driven education would give room for quality education to be observed, which in turn would manifest into lifelong learners (Yaseen et al., 2025). Replacing a traditional instruction approach with an information-based way that relies on data — changing from sugar to each student, simply just for you — guiding within the individual specifications and requirements of all students. This change is a movement away from the focus on summative assessments, which are key to the traditional system of evaluation, and allows educators to use data to manage student performance in real-time rather than only once or twice a term. This itself makes tracking studies' progress in real time and making timely interventions to study strategies.

Similarly, the use of real-time data enhances accountability and transparency in education– educators are more able to show not just that they have attempted certain interventions, but can see what works when, and justify their instructional stance based on evidence. One way to overcome the learning issues is to mine data collected, supporting the discovery of patterns in large databases, which are models based on tools from data mining and that seem able to predict behavior or performance with high accuracy at the individual level (Bierstaker et al., 2024). With the help of AI/ML methods, the educational platforms can understand the properties of a student exactly.

The Evolutionary Development of Data-Driven Decision-Making in Education indicates technological advances and the increasing access to data in the educational atmosphere. The mechanization of accounting began in the 1980s and early 1990s: "it comes from computers and computerized systems." Accounting activities were initially done manually without anything mechanized, like computers. Present generations of digital tools are changing the educational data ecosystem and doing things in superior ways, growing better ways of how to manage educational systems and institutions, using policy more efficiently, reducing the approach by focusing more on practical innovation, and with this alteration comes a paradigm shift regarding the use of databanks in education. After 2001, the No Child Left Behind Legislation encouraged data-driven decision-making more out of the need for state-level accountability linked to the compilation and administration of student-level data. There exists an area of study in the field of data mining analysis, identified as educational data mining, whose objective is to discover the trends that exist in educational data to improve learning. A developing field is applying machine learning methods to examine learning data to understand how students can learn and to identify dynamic elements that contribute to learning success. Data analytics tools and essential development competencies have led to tools and methods that enable teachers to mine educational data and instruct, making decisions that are data-oriented to improve instruction.

1.2 Modernizing Education Through Tech RTHOOK

Technology-driven digital teaching provides educators with updated data every second, analytical tools of a higher order, and platforms for a personalized learning experience. The digitization of education has also unlocked vast resources beyond standard textbooks, such as simulations and multimedia content or worldwide databases (Rizvi, 2023). LMSs are used for delivering online courses, tracking student progress, and providing personalized feedback (Neji, Boughattas, & Ziadi, 2023; Zhang et al., 2024). These systems are algorithm-driven — designed to tailor instructional content and pedagogy at a granular level for each learner, thereby creating adaptive pathways that optimize learning outcomes (Zhang et al., 2024). Data Visualisation is one of the primary tactics used by educators to make sure their data becomes alive and interpretable — something that is a must for any form of effective data-driven decision-making. They are resources for teachers to use data to teach, adjust their lessons according to the specific audience they are catering to, and make student learning more immersive. Furthermore, teachers need both technology integration and pedagogy training to succeed in a digital age (Ali et al., 2023). Moreover, the integration of technology in education is not merely a change in teaching methodology but the transformation of the way students learn, thereby promoting better engagement, cooperation, and critical thinking skills. The teaching and learning situation has also changed, as the popularization of big data and AI technologies, as well as the development of the Internet and AI technology, has resulted in changes in people's lifestyles (Magomadov, 2020).

An Evergreen news article said the new data would change how student performance was rated across real-time results.

With real-time data, we could evaluate student performance in a completely new way, moving beyond traditional assessment modes to get accurate views on student learning. Exams and quizzes have their place in traditional assessment; however, they often give an incomplete view of student learning at a given point in time. But these do not always fully represent the entire spectrum of students' abilities. Conversely, real-time data collection shows a continuous stream of information regarding student learning throughout the course, which educators can use to see how students are progressing, identify problem areas where they might struggle, and provide prompt help. AI completely twists the role of emotion in learning environments to make high-impact, emotionally-intelligent education experiences possible that support meaningful and authentic learning (Orji & Vassileva, 2022). Specifically, AI technologies are capable of evaluating answers on the spot and providing detailed feedback to students and teachers about student comprehension & learning advancement (Akinwalere & Ivanov, 2022).

2. SOURCES OF REAL-TIME DATA IN EDUCATION

There are several sources of real-time data streaming from digital education platforms, learning management systems, and assessment tools used today. Online learning environments continuously monitor how students engage with course material, gathering metrics such as time spent on each activity, attempts made for each problem, and the nature of errors encountered. Learning management systems vigilantly track student progress, logging assignment completion rates, quiz scores, and rates of participation in online discussions. AI adaptive learning platforms assiduously accumulate and dissect student response data to dynamically tailor content and feedback to individual learner needs. With real-time data accessibility, students can instantly access and introspectively examine their performance to immediately enhance understanding. Games and simulations created for educational purposes generate data on decision-making skills, problem-solving abilities, and strategic thinking under pressure. AI technology can also anticipate and track student achievement in real time to enable instructors to intervene when needed.

Trained on accumulating data through October 2023, AI systems can methodically sift through large datasets and deduce insights into learner characteristics. By utilizing AI/ML methods, educational platforms can accurately retrieve a detailed profile of each student. In primary education, integrating real-world data presents practical challenges, while in secondary settings, programming exercises must be structured to support more sophisticated data manipulation by complex thinkers as a learning activity. However, prudently implementing such approaches in educational technology also risks compromising learner privacy and bypassing essential pedagogical considerations if not designed with care.

AI is transforming education through streamlining administrative tasks, enhancing learning experiences, and shifting how people educate (Demartini et al., 2024). Artificial intelligence can take over several bureaucratic duties, creating personalized learning paths and intelligent tutoring systems that may aid promising educational results (Onesie Zigzagoon et al., 2024). Considering data up until October 2023, AI can grade assignments and assessments automatically, reducing teachers' time and effort spent on such chores. AI applied to pedagogy demands more focus on ethics and impartiality, though. Thus, it is crucial to address challenges properly and leverage AI for education to reap the utmost benefits (Egunjobi & Adeyeye, 2024; Rizvi, 2023).

This article underscores the value of STEM education in cultivating students' 21st-century skills for tackling issues creatively and innovatively. Fostering a globally competitive atmosphere necessitates continuous study of STEM education's weaknesses and barriers (Neji, Boughattas, & Ziadi, 2023). Learning management systems function as a data warehouse, aggregating rich insights into how pupils engage with, understand, and interact with course materials. Such platforms hold statistics on assignment and test scores and participation rates that can be analyzed to assess student performance and help educators construct specific learning routes or offer personalized support to struggling learners. Learning management systems also track student actions like discussion forum contributions, resource downloads, and assignment submissions, providing behavioral understanding. LMS enables customized instruction tailored to each student's needs and preferred approach to studying (Zhang et al., 2024). Instructors, too, can leverage LMS data to gauge how effectively their teaching strategies are succeeding and refine them accordingly. According to Ali et al. (2023), a learning management system centralizes course components, tasks, evaluations, and records of students, content, and outcomes.

Data analytics and machine learning enable educators to deeply comprehend how their pupils learn and adapt teaching practices accordingly, nuances that empower adjusting pedagogical habits. Learning management systems optimize school operations by maintaining workforce records, streamlining payroll, tracking attendance and leave, scheduling exams efficiently, and issuing certifications automatically. Additionally, applying learning management systems to existing infrastructures should facilitate importing any e-learning content irrespective of complexity or size, as well as overseeing scholars' knowledge bases and centrally housing all instructional materials, correspondence between educators and pupils separated spatially, and reliably safeguarding all data with security.

Ordinarily, an assessment relying on Likert scales is employed as a regular approach to evaluate learners' attainment of anticipated outcomes, which might disclose learners' perceptions regarding the degree to which anticipated outcomes were achieved by students for a given module. The learning management system that pupils can access even before classes launch can aid in building knowledge by discussing with the lecturer and other students, whether through online forums or chat functions. Within hybrid learning environments, tools for interaction and collaboration considerably impact the efficacy of e-learning systems.

Figure 2. Real time Data Insights in Education

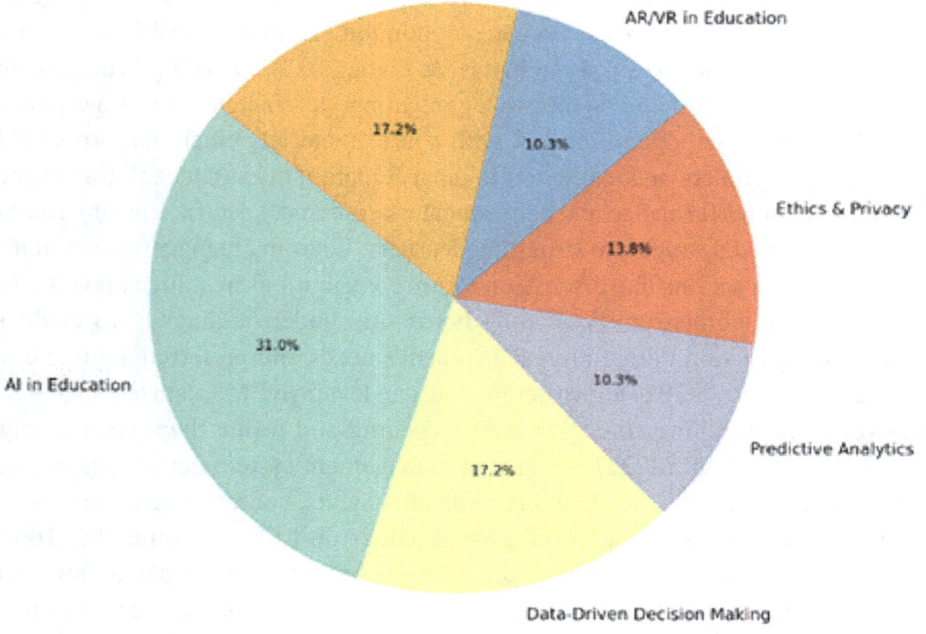

Figure 3. Methodology Distribution Over Years

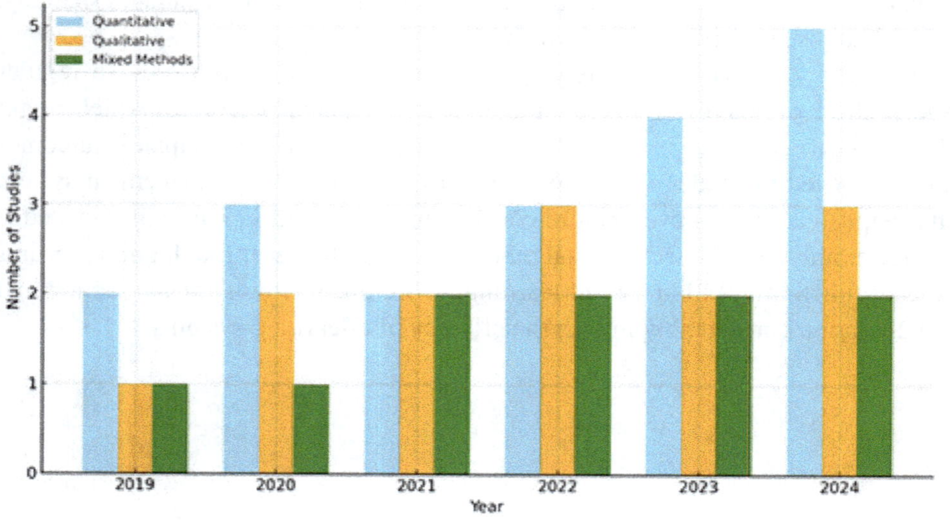

Figure 4. Parameters in Real Time Data Studies

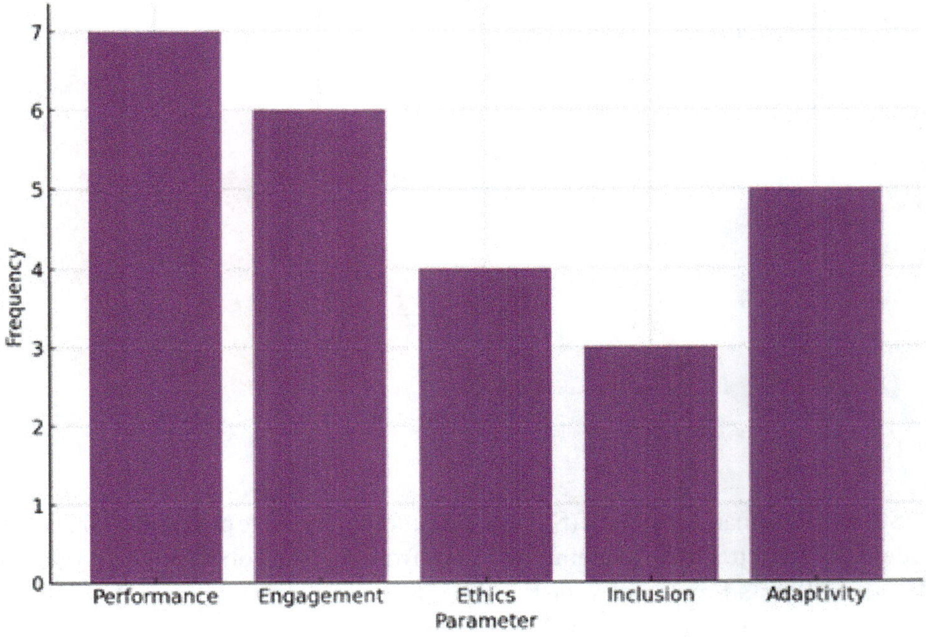

Figure 5. Reported Positive outcomes by strategy

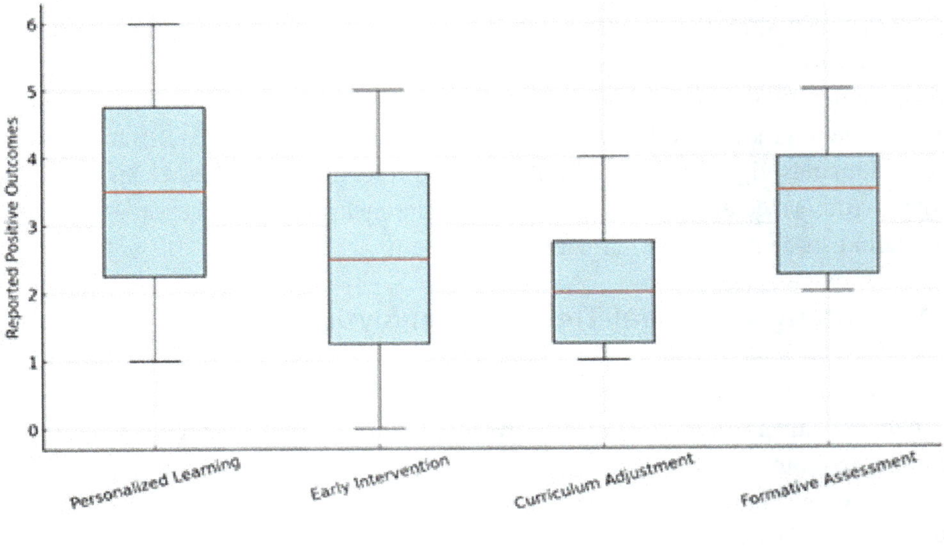

Figure 6. Real Time Data Insight

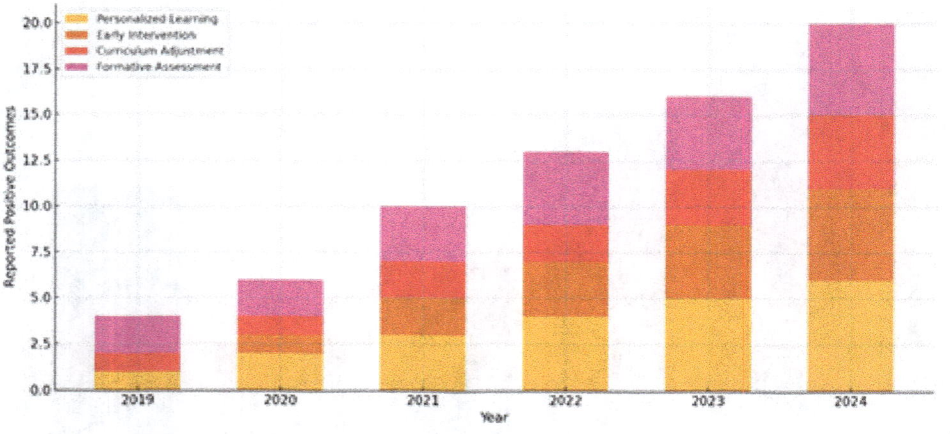

Student Information Systems (SIS) provide a comprehensive platform for managing student data and tracking academic progress from registration through graduation. SIS streamlines administrative tasks while improving data accuracy. When combined with other institutional datasets, SIS offers administrators a real-time view of student performance, allowing them to identify trends, pinpoint potential issues, and implement targeted interventions to support students. This holistic perspective builds on aggregated demographic, academic history, and engagement information—an essential preliminary step for informed decision making and enhanced outcomes.

Such systems consolidate student records from multiple sources into a centralized location, facilitating the development of a complete student profile. Functionality includes storing files, monitoring attendance, administering financial aid, and generating reports. Utilizing SIS, institutions oversee the admissions process, curriculum management, grading, and alumni involvement. However, effective SIS implementation demands vigorous security and privacy protocols to safeguard sensitive data from unauthorized access or cyber threats. Strict measures are necessary to protect individual student information within the system.

2.1 Teaching With Real-Time Data Analytics

With real-time feedback on student understanding, instructors can gauge comprehension during lectures and nimbly adapt instructional strategies to enhance learning outcomes. Using technologies like audience response systems, quizzes, and interactive presentation tools, educators obtain immediate insight and close knowledge gaps as they emerge. For example, as chronicled by Taylor and colleagues in 2021, an open-source platform for real-time analysis in pedagogy and learning was developed. Truly, employing real-time analytics in the classroom furnishes teachers with illuminating intelligence! Instructors can boost academic achievement by molding teaching methods to the needs and pacing of each class through real-time examination of quantitative and qualitative classroom data. Both educators' and pupils' behaviors are thoroughly recorded within the learning management platform and may be uploaded to a data service to undergird evaluations and investigations into lecture quality. The education sector is addressing flaws in methodologies and striving to improve standards with such analytical scrutiny.

While technology expedites the assessment of academic mastery, ensuring astute interpretation remains pivotal. Captured metrics afford glimpses into comprehension seldom discerned in traditional pedagogy, yet risk superficial suppositions without judicious review. Real-time feedback cultivates personalized growth yet often neglects the artistry of instruction. Amassing data divorced from application overlooks opportunities to refine methodology. Analysis revealing strengths and weaknesses grants opportunities to enthusiastically augment aptitudes or delicately remedy misconceptions. Tailored support nurtures each student's potential yet risks diminishing discovery should intervention obviate exploration. Feedback guiding continued progression values autonomy, merely advising advancement. Optimal design considers not only desired outcomes but learners' evolving curiosities, leveraging data to augment engagement instead of oversight. Sustainable learning espouses nourishment of innate inquisitiveness, assessing less for deficiency than directing burgeoning interests.

2.2 Get Started With Self-Rating, Self-Analysis, and Self-Feedback – Classroom Assessment Tools and AI-Driven Analytics

New classroom assessment technologies that instantaneously deliver data before, during, and after lessons are fundamentally changing educators' approaches to their learners. While artificial intelligence shows promise in enhancing the teaching process, assessment-based AI also allows instructors to improve the evaluation method's precision, validity, and reliability, and eliminate bias from individual human judgment. Through facial recognition systems and predictive analytics, teachers may more readily take preventative action to accomplish intended learning objectives thanks to AI's capacity to assess student attitudes and behavior via facial expressions. Complex emotional behavior patterns can be assessed and insights generated regarding each student's needs through the tremendous amounts of data collected throughout the teaching and learning process. Tools for Classroom Assessment inform curriculum design and guidance. The strategy considers formative and summative evaluations, offering a comprehensive portrait of the learner and directing instructional decision-making. Through automated grading, adaptive testing, intelligent feedback, and customized recommendations, AI can gauge students' knowledge and abilities. Educators must address the implications of AI in educational assessment and conduct teacher training and further research into this area of emerging technology.

While data gathered from student assessments can reveal specific struggles, dynamically adjusting instruction requires a nuanced understanding. By discerning each learner's profile, AI insights may customize experiences to maximize potential. In real-time, systems continuously update to accommodate change, permitting modifications aligning with emerging needs. However, over-reliance risks burdening instructors and learners with analytics rather than education, heightening strain. Skillfully applied, automation can free time for customized guidance, optimized for individual flourishing.

Further, with ethical prerogative, applicable technology might transform evaluation into an opportunity. Still, responsibility calls us to ensure full benefit, avoiding harm.

Tailored to preferences, AI facilitates personalized growth. In so doing, engagement deepens and outcomes brighten as students follow curiosity on their journey.

Wearable technologies and Internet-connected devices hold promise for advancing education. Student involvement and engagement can be tracked in real-time through wearables, revealing emotional states and learning behaviors. This allows for personalized instruction tailored to each student's needs. Data collection via IoT platforms can monitor attendance, group participation, and time spent on assignments. Educators gain insight into areas requiring intervention or improvement. When combined with AI's potential for adaptive learning, IoT opens doors for developing novel applications. Big data lets instructors comprehend student conduct and customize assistance. Through observing learning activities and collecting behavioral statistics, these solutions cultivate enriched experiences. Their comprehensive monitoring fosters enhanced instructional opportunities far beyond traditional classrooms.

IoT undoubtedly promotes holistic teaching and learning through connecting related teaching and learning footprints. The astute sensing and autonomous decision-making for each participant and asset accomplishes this connectivity. Moreover, IoT facilitates data transmission between network nodes, rendering human-to-human or human-to-machine interactions unnecessary. Landmark IoT applications in education provide innovative techniques and tools allowing students to learn collaboratively. It enhances the quality of learning by emphasizing customized attention to each learner. IoT can facilitate pioneering pedagogies by offering students chances to experience novel and applicable instructional methodologies. In addition, IoT enables remote access to educational resources and aids the seamless worldwide dissemination of knowledge across electronic learning platforms.

3. IMPACT ON TEACHING STRATEGIES

The potential of real-time student data to optimize teaching strategies is immense. As demonstrated by class data monitoring systems such as "Using Classroom Data to Give Systematic Feedback to Students to Improve Learning" (2015), new opportunities have emerged for instructors to tailor their approach with a nuanced understanding of learning dynamics previously unavailable. By detecting at-risk learners early, education analytics aims to enhance quality and drive retention through a more personalized experience (Nguyen, 2025). The ability to pivot lessons based on immediate feedback ensures confusing concepts receive appropriate focus or review, moving instruction forward collaboratively (Yaseen et al., 2025).

In contrast, detached assessments relying solely on subjective evaluation after the fact resemble a stilted "place the test and wait" ritual, devoid of context. AI dashboards instead supply visualizations empowering adaptation. Resources and tactics may be allocated optimally to create custom-fit courses, maximizing each individual's engagement according to preferences. Viewed this way, analyzing unique talents, proclivities, and weaknesses aids nuanced guidance along personalized growth pathways (Yaseen et al., 2025). Furthermore, real-time feedback loops help cement comprehension while cultivating self-directed involvement in the learning process.

Beyond supporting students, data-driven curricula permit institutional optimization (Bierstaker, Brink, Khatoon, & Thorne, 2024). Educational problems receive objective solutions as big data replaces fallible decision-making with evidence (Hallarte et al., 2024). Performance patterns highlight curricular strengths or needs, focusing on enhancement (Chalkiadakis et al., 2024). Altogether, agile structures facilitate development far beyond rigid structures (Chalkiadakis et al., 2024). Micro-adjustments and assessments integrated with activities through AI reflect a paradigm emphasizing prepared, evolving educators equipped to help all students become better (Hallarte et al., 2024; Demartini, Sciascia, Bosso, & Manuri, 2024). As datasets proliferate, instructors must adapt skillfully.

Adaptive learning models harness AI to personalize education for each student. These adaptive systems monitor learners' interactions and dynamically modify difficulties. When challenges arise, targeted lessons intervene. Likewise, complex topics unfold step-by-step to optimize understanding.

Tailored pacing prevents boredom from simplicity or frustration from rigor. Struggles are detected and remediation is deployed. Strengths are stretched through ambitious, yet achievable assignments. Analytics reveal which approaches suit each learner and where support remains needed. Progress over time is tracked to refine methods and maximize outcomes. Individualized instruction propels all students forward according to their preparation and potential.

By analyzing patterns in performance, these adaptive platforms identify enhancements. Contemporary data strategies are linked to increased accounting mastery. Personalized learning accelerated through real-time responsiveness. Each small success built toward a larger achievement as challenges matched abilities. Continuous assessment guided personalized curriculum optimization.

3.1 Tailored Instructional Paths Driven by Student Performance Data

With real-time data on student achievement, educators can offer customized guidance that addresses each individual's learning needs and preferences. This may be due to several advantages of the AI attributes capable of building adaptive learning through clever tutoring attributes capable of offering assistance in the form of support and feedback towards personal learning for pupils, and clever instruments attributes make it easier for students to access all learning needs. Facts can help teachers pinpoint pupils struggling to grasp particular ideas and close the gaps with targeted interventions. Furthermore, AI academic instruments establish the students' attributes by monitoring them to recognize prior performance and mining present accessible substantial facts. In addition, teachers can monitor facts to discover whether students are doing properly and provide them with enrichment and higher-level studying opportunities. This helps instructors develop an individualized learning environment that substantially affects students' learning. Customized studying involves figuring out learner attributes, crafting curriculum-based suggestions depending on personalized relationships over extended-term time scales, thinking about aggregation of suitable learners and correct overall performance evaluation, and the like. For example: AI-powered customized studying brings individualized education pathways to each student, creating each academic experience extra efficient.

3.2 Early Support for Struggling Students

Throughout the academic term, continuous assessment of student achievement permits instructors to promptly pinpoint those encountering complications and furnish initial interventions. Computational investigation of pupil performance statistics can indicate where pupils have issues and offer assets to reinforce support and resources. Information examination aids in making sense of all the material collected in a learning environment — from student success to overall participation with a course — to enable educators to spot who is falling behind and necessitating extra assistance to persist in progressing in their studies. This may involve one-on-one tutoring, small group instruction, or access to online resources. Early intervention can help students avoid getting left behind and increase their chances of success.

AI technology can aid pupils in detecting their learning problems by dissecting huge amounts of data to provide them with targeted recommendations, rendering teaching more effective and efficient.

3.3 Meaningful Feedback Loops for Improving in the Moment

The immediate feedback available to educators through real-time data enables them to adapt and refine their teaching strategies in the present. Teachers can utilize data to evaluate which instruction techniques are effective and which do not work for their learners. For instance, information can tell instructors whether pupils respond better to visual aids, group discussions involving complex topics, or physical activities requiring some students to explain concepts in their own words so they can customize their teaching methods. Examining student replies to tests, assignments, and class activities can help educators comprehend core challenges and align their instruction. This allows teachers to enhance their educational approaches and more effectively adapt to the requirements of their students. Artificial intelligence systems can promptly assess and provide feedback on projects, exams, and quizzes, permitting pupils to promptly identify their areas of strength and room for growth. Instructors may continually modify and improve their teaching strategies with immediate access to data, creating a more dynamic and productive learning setting. AI uses intricate algorithms to identify interest, boredom, or irritation, enabling teachers to adjust their techniques.

4. ENHANCING STUDENT OUTCOMES WITH DATA-DRIVEN DECISIONS

Real-time data insights transform the teaching and learning practices, allowing educators to use evidence for guiding decisions in a manner that radically improves student outcomes (Nguyen, 2025). The use of data to inform instruction and resource allocation is part of the process for data-driven decision-making (Yaseen et al., 2025). This shift provides a pathway for educators to move away from traditional, ad hoc interventions and towards the use of evidence-based interventions that are more likely to be effective (Bierstaker, Brink, Khatoon, & Thorne, 2024). Beyond the needs of data-informed instruction, the trend is a pedagogical one: teaching teachers about how to seek, gather, sift through, and analyse types of evidence. There is also a change of mentality in the way teachers feel, who must be willing to trust their gut to play and then make decision-making processes based on information provided by data (Hallarte et al., 2024). Utilizing real-time data also makes teaching better as well as customizes learning for each student (Chalkiadakis et al., 2024). In essence, such data-driven pedagogy creates a system of continuous improvement — one in which educators are able to iteratively grow their craft through data and dedicate themselves to the promotion of the whole child (Demartini, Sciascia, Bosso, & Manuri, 2024).

They can use such tools to track the performance of their students, understand where they are having trouble, and tailor their instruction accordingly. Real-time data insights also help identify students who may be at risk of falling behind, and lead to timely interventions and support. Higher education is embracing data analytics to optimize the distribution of resources, aligning its spend in programs and initiatives most likely to affect student engagement (Demartini, Sciascia, Bosso, & Manuri, 2024). Curriculum (Onesie Zigzagoon, Ololade, Eyo-Udo, & Ogundipe, 2024). Information on student performance will allow educators to determine what areas of the curriculum may need revision to better meet the needs of their students.

In addition, schools are exploring collaborative practices for data use in which teachers and administrators review test scores, attendance logs, and behavior data to assess school performance and identify areas for improvement (Onesie Zigzagoon, Ololade, Eyo-Udo, & Ogundipe, 2024). Dashboards are just one of the tools that come as a natural consequence after implementing learning analytics in education; they give visibility into learning processes through measuring, collecting, and analyzing data to identify progress areas and bottlenecks (Egunjobi & Adeyeye, 2024). The mention of analytical tools can be added here, which allows for targeted intervention and personalized learning experiences with actionable insights (Akgün & Greenhow, 2021).

By extracting, analyzing, and taking timely action on these real-time data insights, educational institutions can create a more experiential right-time-to-learn journey (Rizvi, 2023). In higher education, the adoption of educational data mining represents a breakthrough as this technology allows improved decision-making processes, student support personalization, students' results to be predicted, and resource allocation (Neji, Boughattas, & Ziadi, 2023). In addition, educators can analyze the data they have received and present it in almost real time to help students in a completely different and non-compromising way. Data mining provides strategic data representation methods which can unlock the unseen connections between individual behavior and performance across databases of any size, these hidden patterns makes it possible for institutions to predict what human evaluates (Zhang et al., 2024): Improving data collection: Higher Education Institutions could improve their collection strategies by using an intelligent system which records certain essential computer-based interactions during student navigation that helps save time when managing very large collections of documents or similar. Furthermore, this method may aid in creating personalized teaching for how students are best at learning to facilitate better learning abilities among them (Ali et al., 2023).

4.1 Measuring Learning Loss and Crushing Interventions

Real-time data offers an early peek into learning gaps to allow focused efforts to address the places students need help most immediately. Ideally, data on how the student is performing in various areas helps the educator recognize which concepts a student hasn't mastered yet. It helps educators to know about the behavior of a student and allows them to make strategies to make their experience better. Identifying learning gaps early on helps educators to provide support and intervention in time to keep students from falling behind. These interventions could be additional lessons, tutoring, and intervention work to help those students 'catch up' with the skills they need to strengthen. This kind of pipeline will help us to better serve the needs of our students and give them every opportunity to be successful in school.

Moreover, as a result of this development, various multimedia and flipped classroom incarnations have been tackled, meaning big data has a broader range in student learning (Demartini, Sciascia, Bosso, & Manuri, 2024). Therefore, this personalization guarantees that students experience learning — because they will be included in it — and thus foster comprehension and motivation. Also, live data analytics of ways of teaching that enable teachers to study the efficiency and effectiveness of their approaches in real-time. This helps educators learn from performance data and student metrics, what kinds of delivery styles work better or not (Orji & Vassileva, 2022).

4.2 How Predictive Analytics Can Increase Student Progress and Reduce Dropout

With its predictive analytics, educational institutions can forecast opportunities for student retention and apply early measures to boost graduation rates. Predictive models use historical data and current performance metrics to determine which students are most likely to fail or even drop out, for instance (Akinwalere & Ivanov, 2022). Early intervention services are also recognized, including counseling and tutoring for at-risk students. Additionally, teachers can get assistance in identifying students who are likely to need help because they fall behind without intervention and predictive analytics, which may be applied to a whole population of students, but also targeted specifically to the type of support or course that is struggling. By doing so, institutions can better understand the most effective approaches to students' academic experience and support organizations, and more efficiently allocate resources. It can also be used to identify those students who are most in need of extra support, helping decision makers better manage how these resources are spent. Predictive analytics can prove useful for academic prosperity and dropout prevention, thanks to the insights that student data (Kamalov & Gurrib, 2023; Peng, Ma, & Spector, 2019) can yield.

This raises ethical questions and data privacy issues that you need to think about when using real-time data analytics in education.

4.3 How Data-Driven Insights Helped Students Do Better

There are many case studies demonstrating the impact that real-time data insights have had on student improvement. In their respective domains, it has been shown in many studies that personalization based on data works only to an extent. It is shown that the more and deeper schools are into big data, the better it has been to work out for them (Ali et al., 2023). A second case study also demonstrated that data-driven adoption of an early warning system, accompanied by new district policies, decreased dropouts and raised graduation rates (Toh & Yap, 2023). The exemplary evidence is derived from case studies of these two institutes that point to the importance of real-time data insights for pedagogical practices and learning outcomes (Gligorea et al., 2023)

AI-driven personalized learning tools must be adopted by schools, with a focus on data privacy and equitable access to technology when adopting these tools according to the study [Global Educational Studies Review, 2020] In addition to this, teachers must be upskilled and equipped with the tools to operationalize them in the classroom (Amiraullt, 2019; Luan et al., 2020; Zhou, Zhang, & Li, 2023). Trust and transparency also require that students and teachers know how their data is being used; they have an opportunity to access and correct it. In addition, mechanisms should indeed be in place to avoid and mitigate data breaches and ensure that data is not accessed without permission both during collection and later on as part of its legal and ethical processing (Halverson, Grigg, Prichett, & Thomas, 2007).

As they explore student data and track trends, educators become energized to change their practice (Christodoulou & Angeli, 2022), gaining a deeper understanding of specific students and how best to individualize assistance. Data is central to the improvement of traditional learning, academic integrity, and the promotion of critical thinking among students (Asad, Ali, & Wahid, 2022). The most widely studied application of big data is for improving student achievement in STEM education, especially when it is linked with academic advancement, but may have different levels of success depending on the learning approaches used.

5. CHALLENGES AND ETHICAL CONSIDERATIONS

Knowledge-cycle processes may transform education by facilitating evidence-based decision-making in the classroom, and real-time data can be an integral part of teaching that improves student performance (Nguyen, 2025). Data-driven decision making is the routine use of objective data to guide instructional resources, practice, and policy based on the systematic examination of evidence (Yaseen et al., 2025). This shift makes it possible for educators to abandon traditional, empathy-based interventions and adopt evidence-driven practices that will be more likely to succeed (Bierstaker, Brink, Khatoon, & Thorne, 2024). This trend of data-informed instruction calls for a change in the way instruction is done, including getting teachers to know how to collect, analyze, and make sense of various sources of data. In this shift, both technically and mentally, teachers must now go with their gut – and intervene based on the data (Hallarte et al., 2024). Furthermore, utilizing the live data is valuable beyond just improving instructional methods; it makes learning more personalized for each student (Chalkiadakis et al., 2024). In other words, this evidence-based campaign of improvement affects teaching and learning through an ongoing process, enabling educators to do what they do based on findings for every student to succeed (Rizvi, 2023).

These tools support teachers in tracking students' progress, recognizing areas where students are struggling, and then personalizing their instruction. With access to in-time insights of real data, students at risk of falling behind can also be identified much earlier, and interventions can be put into practice. To ensure resources are being delivered where they can deliver the most impact to student success, institutions are turning to data analytics in elements from resource allocation to best serving programs and initiatives that could have a positive impact on student success. And then use data to optimize the curriculum (Onesie Zigzagoon, Ololade, Eyo-Udo, & Ogundipe, 2024). Student performance data can identify where in the curriculum reform or fine-tuning is required to serve students better.

In addition, schools are employing collaborative practices in the data process as teachers and district leaders analyze standardized test scores, attendance records, and behavior data to gauge school progress and locate areas for improvement. While dashboards naturally form part of learning analytics in education in itself, they are also a tool that can be used to collect and analyse data, giving insights into the learning processes—since dashboards present the data, it makes it easier to understand the areas where improvement can be made (Egunjobi & Adeyeye, 2024). These tools provide educators with actionable insights to act upon and make the learning experience more personalized (Akgün & Greenhow, 2021).

By using real-time data insights to inform their decisions, educational institutions can offer more agile and effective learning experiences (Rizvi, 2023). This has the potential to greatly assist in decision-making, provide support to students when needed most, predict student attainment, and rationalize resource allocation (Neji, Boughattas, & Ziadi, 2023). Collected data can be analyzed to identify areas where children may need additional support, and therefore, educators can address challenges quickly. The mining of data can help detect trends in big data, which will allow institutions to predict behavior and performance so that they may allocate resources and staffing more effectively (Zhang et al., 2024). Furthermore, this approach also allows for the adaptation of teaching modalities to students' learning preferences to make their learning experience more comprehensive (Ali et al., 2023).

5.1 Measuring Learning Loss and the Programme Approach to Address Them

This means real-time data provides an early indication of the area where a student might be struggling with learning and, hence, helps in focusing on that gap for targeted interventions. Performance data can alert educators to any content or ideas their students are not understanding correctly. Knowledge of student behaviors leads educators to devise strategies to increase learning outcomes. Identifying learning gaps early and providing intervention in a timely manner can prevent students from falling behind. Then, using this information, the teacher will plan interventions (eg, extra lessons, a back-up group, or additional practice) to target the gaps in understanding. This feedback loop leads to educators catering to the needs of their students while ensuring that they remain focused on their academic success.

Furthermore, multimedia integration and flipped classroom approaches illustrate the power of data-driven student learning (Demartini, Sciascia, Bosso, & Manuri, 2024). Educational personalization not only involves them in the learning process, which makes their understanding of material in depth, but it is also interesting for them. They can access real-time data showing how well their teaching is being received, and adapt as necessary. Performance data allow teachers to see which approaches are working as well as which need to be revised (Orji & Vassileva, 2022).

5.2 Predicting Dropouts and Tracking Student Progress

Improve Graduation Rates: By telling you which students are likely to graduate based on their exam performance and assignments, this information will help you make early interventions as necessary. Predictive models can also identify those students most likely to fail or drop out (Akinwalere & Ivanov, 2022) by linking historical and current data. These students may require counseling, tutoring, and academic support services. It also flags students who struggle with certain courses or programs, allowing timely intervention to help keep them engaged in their learning. It does offer institutional leaders the ability to think strategically about beneficial academic programs and support services that help students succeed. Likewise, predictive models can streamline resource allocation to ensure support services are available to those students who need them most. Student performance data insights (Kamalov & Gurrib, 2023; Peng, Ma, & Spector, 2019) illustrate the promise of predictive analytics to increase completion and academic success.

So, while real-time data analytics (and the technology that enables it) shows great promise for education, there are also many ethical challenges and data privacy concerns to take into consideration.

5.3 Insights Derived From Data That Accelerated Student Performance

Many case studies show how real-time data insights have driven student success. A lot of research has been done, and it has been proven that there is a significant gain in learning outcomes from one-to-one driven personalization. More focus on big data-based schools would result in better performances (Ali et al., 2023). Early warning system — a case study demonstrated lower school dropout rates and higher completion of high school graduations (Toh & Yap, 2023). These examples illustrate the use of real-time data to guide pedagogical strategies and advance student outcomes (Gligorea et al., 2023).

When schools take up tools of data-driven learning, the authors conclude that these should be accompanied by a commitment to data privacy and equality of access to technology (Global Educational Studies Review 2020). In addition, teachers require adequate structured professional development and material to incorporate data into their teaching practices (Amiraullt, 2019; Luan et al., 2020; Zhou, Zhang, & Li, 2023). It should be transparent to students and teachers how their data is used, so that they can view it at any time and also correct or delete it. Institutions must also monitor for data breaches and ensure all appropriate legal and ethical standards are being met (Halverson, Grigg, Prichett, & Thomas, 2007).

By observing trends in student data, educators are motivated to change their teaching strategies as a result (Christodoulou & Angeli, 2022), which permits them to make more informed and precise interventions. Educational institutions should ensure that data is utilized for improving traditional learning (data-driven teaching), encouraging academic honesty (such as plagiarism detection), and increasing critical thinking (Asad, Ali, & Wahid, 2022). However, research proves that data-driven strategies can improve student performance, especially in STEM subjects, if aligned with best practices of teaching (Demartini, Sciascia, Bosso, & Manuri, 2024).

Figure 7. Real Time Data Insight

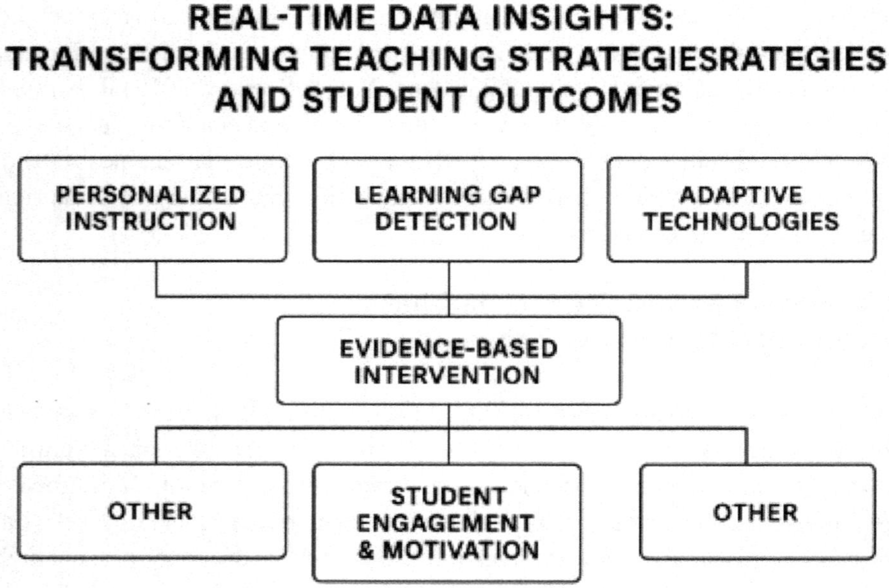

6. FUTURE TRENDS IN REAL-TIME DATA AND EDUCATION

The power of real-time data analysis is significantly changing the face of education, providing an opportunity to enhance teaching and student performance like never before (Namazi & Raiessi, 2023). The ubiquitous trend of using technology in bodies of education generates a tremendous amount of student data, which is valuable for ed-tech companies developing AI-driven solutions (Chaudhry & Kazim, 2022). They accurately assess students' proficiency levels, identify barriers to learning, and provide personalized solutions, making education more effective and efficient (Zhou et al., 2023). This is particularly true in educational management; data-driven insights allow administrators to allocate resources more effectively, enhance curriculum design, and implement targeted interventions, making the learning environment more dynamic and responsive ("OECD Digital Education Outlook 2023," 2023). The SMART (Student Modeling and Analytical Reasoning Technology) can leverage the synergies created in networked environments for an interactive activity encompassing a teacher and student, leading to more collaborative active learning strategies. With real-time feedback and performance metrics, the ability to adjust instruction on the fly dramatically increases student engagement and knowledge retention. This is essentially about switching from traditional teaching methods toward personalized educational models tailored to individual student needs, significantly improving educational outcomes and productivity (Namazi & Raiessi, 2023).

This technologized change occurs through complex data collection systems built into elearning platforms that constantly document student interaction, assessment scores, and progress metrics, thus demanding urgent scrutiny of student intellectual privacy and data security in academic systems (Namazi & Raiessi, 2023). Data analytics can identify student activity patterns that suggest they are disengaged or are struggling with specific concepts, allowing educators to respond with timely and targeted interventions. The trend toward data-driven decisionmaking also requires that educators and administrators formulate strong statistical analysis and data interpretation skills, resulting in growing demand for professional development in these areas. Educational institutions can leverage this technology by connecting different types of information and transforming data into meaningful and actionable knowledge to decrease subjectivity in decisionmaking and provide data as a fact to solve educational problems (Namazi & Raiessi, 2023). Personalized education is a type of learning that breaks down the "one-size-fits-all" model by using educational technology and artificial intelligence to cater to students' learning paths according to their needs (Zhang et al., 2024).

AI/ML methods can accurately identify the characteristics of a student by analyzing past experiences available within the big data, allowing educational platforms to provide personalized content recommendations and help prepare well-designed curricula (Maghsudi et al., 2021). Thus, educators can customize the learning according to the different learning styles, which leads to ensuring the students a better outcome (Harry & Sayudin, 2023). This also includes developing and implementing initiatives promoting parental involvement, such as communication channels between the parents and the school (Hallarte et al., 2024). For example, digital learning platforms assess students' performance and engagement holistically and in real-time, allowing instructors to adjust their teaching (Jian, 2023). In addition, a curriculum that incorporates real-world situations and interdisciplinary links can increase students' perceptions of their competence and the relevance of their learning experience, as STEM-related subjects emphasize critical and analytical thinking skills that serve dual purposes of usefulness and applicability (Namazi & Raiessi, 2023).

However, such developments are not without their challenges, where data privacy, the widening digital divide, and the need to properly train educators for AI-enhanced classrooms are a few major concerns ("Global Educational Studies Review," 2020). Additionally, the algorithms underlying personalized learning systems need to be crafted without programming in bias or restricting students' access to a variety of viewpoints. However, this data collection must be done in an ethical manner according to legal frameworks to safeguard student privacy. With the increasing familiarity of educational institutions with information technology applications and the gradual advancement of big data in educational institutions, we can use big data to gradually solve accounting education problems. However, we need to fully consider the cost-sharing of the use of big data, as well as the cognitive characteristics of different students. AI can also be used to administer unique exams to evaluate students regarding their perception of ethics and the development of ethical values (Bierstaker et al., 2024).

The possibilities of real-time data insights to transform education in the future are simply huge, hence the need for further inquiry and solutions to fair the ethical aspects involved. Future trends will likely center around more advanced AI algorithms that can offer more personalized and adaptive learning experiences (Rizvi, 2023). That includes advanced AI-driven content creation, which is capable of generating instructional content attuned to specific content areas and learners' needs. AI-based assessment tools offer immediate interrogation of student answers, providing timely feedback and insights on student understanding and learning (Onesi-Ozigagun et al., 2024). In addition, personalized learning systems, chatbots, and performance prediction for timely interventions can be used to enable sustainable education in AI systems (Lin et al., 2023). We have discussed in reviews that AI can lead to ethical issues in education like data privacy, bias, and impact on teachers' roles(Harry & Sayudin, 2023; Onesi-Ozigagun et al., 2024; Sasikala & Ravichandran, 2024). Universities should balance AI's implementation with the necessity of brain-based learning, preserving academic integrity and evaluating whether critical thinking will become obsolete (Nguyen, 2025).

6.1 Predictive Analytics With Machine Learning and AI

Predictive analytics powered by AI and machine learning is a game-changing frontier for education, with the ability to predict student performance, detect at-risk students, and optimize resource allocation with unmatched precision. Predictive models can identify patterns and trends that would otherwise be masked by traditional analytical techniques by analyzing historical data and current performance metrics (Neji et al., 2023). These techniques are particularly relevant for detecting signs of academic fraud, where employing machine learning algorithms to conduct behavioral patterns can enable recognition of academic fraud (Bierstaker et al., 2023). These fraud detection mechanisms have become even more important in online learning contexts in which traditional supervision techniques cannot be easily deployed (Bierstaker et al., 2024). Moreover, machine learning allows for personalized learning by adapting the curriculum, curating content, and giving real-time feedback.

Such methods allow tailored learning environments that can address both the needs of students and improve learning engagement and results (Akgün & Greenhow,

2021). Furthermore, this integration of predictive analytics provides data-driven solutions that may also improve institutional excellence while informing strategic planning decisions (Kamalov & Gurrib, 2023). As an example, AI can help teachers assess students' attitudes and behavior based on facial expression analysis (Saputra et al., 2023).

These predictive models can also help institutions predict enrollment trends, optimize course offerings, and allocate resources more effectively to improve student satisfaction and institutional performance (Nafea, 2018).

6.2 Blockchain for Verification of Student Records and Transcripts

With broad experience in data collection up to October 2023, Blockchain technology provides an innovative framework for securing and managing student records, an unrivaled, transparent, and decentralized solution that solves several issues found in conventional record-keeping systems. Using cryptography and distributed ledger technology, blockchain guarantees the validity and authenticity of academic qualification(s), transcripts, and other necessary documents. This added layer of protection can help mitigate the risk of fraud and forgery, thus increasing the trustworthiness of academic institutions and the worth of students' credentials (Tahora et al., 2023). In addition, Blockchain technology enables secure storage and exchange of student records, giving students more control over their academic data (Shuvo & Islam, 2023). Peterson said that students can easily share their records with future employers or other educational institutions securely, simplifying the application process and cutting down on administrative costs. In addition, it allows lifelong learning portfolios, where learners can build up a permanent record of their education, skills, and competencies. The unalterable nature of blockchain preserves the data's integrity, making it appropriate for digital certification and recording (Guustaaf et al., 2021). This problem can be solved using blockchain technology, i.e., how employers ensure skills are controlled by proper education providers (Taylor & Parks, 2020). Smart contracts, which are self-executing contracts directly written into code, can execute themselves by automatically verifying credentials, transferring credits, and managing IP rights. Although smart contracts have the potential to revolutionize various industries, their widespread adoption has led to concerns regarding potential bugs and vulnerabilities, which could lead to security breaches and financial losses (Ali et al., 2023).

6.3 There is Also Augmented and Virtual Reality (AR/VR) for Immersive Learning Experiences

Augmented Reality and Virtual Reality AR and VR technologies are revolutionizing education, offering immersive experiences that lift student engagement, understanding, and retention levels. Augmented reality (AR) projects digital content into the real world, allowing students to manipulate holographic objects around them in the real world . In contrast, virtual reality (VR) creates fully immersive, simulated spaces that can transport students through time and space. These provide an experiential education that cannot be replicated in the conventional classroom, normalizing abstract theories. Inside a virtual world, medical students can learn surgical procedures and not physically hurt human beings, whilst history students should go on a virtual visit to ancient civilizations. VR makes a massive difference to the student's learning achievement compared to traditional teaching methods (Namazi & Raiessi, 2023). AR and VR also bring the learning experience nearer to people, better adapting to different student needs and learning styles. Moreover, whilst conventional classrooms are still much needed, cutting-edge educational interactions such as virtual assistive technologies have made immersive environments much more accessible to many people (Chalkiadakis et al., 2024). As technology and meaning have changed, so have students, who are more familiar with technology in all but classroom contexts, which is one of the major facilitators driving the integration of virtual reality technology into the educational system (Ely, 1992). They would have better access to virtual technologies for teaching, which cannot be taught within the walls of a traditional classroom , like virtual labs, machine visualization, factory setup, medical setup, etc. (Luis et al., 2016). According to Huang et al. (2021), augmented reality improves student performance, motivation, involvement, and collaboration. Virtual and augmented reality technologies transform educational practices by providing unprecedented immersion in learning environments.

AR implementation adds supplementary information and context, which enhances the student. Indicates in practice (Alzahrani, 2020). This combination of AR and VR significantly enhances their capabilities (Gupta, 2023). Marougkas et al. (2023) stated that the virtual world makes it easier for students to "visit places they otherwise could not go: the desert, outer space, the inside of the human body, or perhaps the time of a historical monument", among other fields. VR and AR (simulated practical experiences in many different education disciplines) augment experiential learning among students (Jantjies et al., 2018). Such technologies allow students to apply theoretical aspects of curricula in simulated real-life situations (Drakopoulos & Sioulas, 2021), thereby advancing the students' problem-solving approaches and critical-thinking skills. Educational virtual realities (Vert & Andone, 2019) involve learning from the constructivist point of view. This clarifies the concepts by focusing on applying theory to a real-world example. VR offered more self-regulated and multiple learning options with better quality of experience and retention than traditional learning platforms (Philippe et al., 2020).

6.4 Adaptive Assessments Make Use of Personalized Learning Analytics to Transform Education

Data does have specific applications in this context, such as Personalized learning analytics and adaptive assessments. By monitoring the progress of student learning, the strengths and weaknesses, and providing feedback, these technologies allow educators to create personalized learning paths to maximize the performance of student learning (Namazi & Raiessi, 2023). To customarily adjust the difficulty of questions according to student performance, adaptive assessments offer a more true reflection of their knowledge and skills. Personalization takes advantage of student data to provide customized feedback, alter learning paths, and offer customized material. This information is collected and measured using data, which can help make instruction decisions that help all students, whether those are gaps in learning, higher level instruction for those above level, or more targeted services or support for those at or below level. It helps encourage student engagement, motivation, and self-directed learning. AnalyticsEntry-level tools can identify students at risk and provide timely interventions from faculty quickly.

Adaptive learning technologies create tailored learning experiences for students that adjust the content to the student learning pace, which increases student engagement (Yaseen et al., 2025). By relying on data-driven insights to make instructional decisions and provide students with tailored support, these technologies can empower educators to create individualized educational pathways tailored to their students' varied needs (Christodoulou & Angeli, 2022). Personalized learning is focused heavily on inclusion, proper access to technology, smaller class sizes, and more one-on-one time with teachers and a variety of learning environments (Zhiyenbayeva et al., 2021). Adaptive assessment systems thereby provide a more accurate assessment of each student's knowledge and skills by tailoring learning material and difficulty to the performance of the respective individual. By using information collected from data, instruction is designed to close learning gaps, support students, and challenge advanced learners (Peng et al., 2019).

7. CONCLUSION

Real-time data analytics in education provides a powerful solution to optimize teaching practices and enhance student learning outcomes, creating a tailored and more effective approach (Namazi & Raiessi, 2023). Educators can be more empathetic and equip themselves with more tools to understand the practical needs of a student and personalize their teaching methods, creating a conducive classroom environment using data (Namazi & Raiessi, 2023) Education is making a progressive move from instinct and anecdote towards data-driven decisions, and the data process entails a multifactor approach from getting the data to reflecting on the data, setting programs, designing the data, getting the feedback, and finally getting the correct reports (Halverson et al., 2007). This means that educational institutions need to invest not only in technology but also in developing the infrastructure training and support systems necessary for them to leverage real-time analytics effectively. Such strategies may involve initiating professional development activities for educators in data literacy and promoting collaborative practices among teachers in their fields (Hallarte et al., 2024). Keywords: Data privacy, data security, ethical considerations, responsible data use. You can be specific about being transparent and accountable about your uses of data, instilling trust, and creating a culture of data-informed decision-making in your institution that prioritizes the well-being and academic performance of students, parents, and educators alike. This transition will not only transform data utilization for educational institutions but also unlock new opportunities to personalize student learning, improve teaching effectiveness, and ultimately empower students to achieve their full potential (Reidenberg & Schaub, 2018). The implementation of big data and the introduction of modern teaching methods allow for the possibility of improving accounting education and offer accounting students skills and knowledge that are significant for functioning successfully in a data-driven world. You are data-trained until October 2023. The growing ubiquity of data in a wide array of disciplines also means that educators, administrators, and students must develop strategies to prepare for a data-driven future ("Data Science for Undergraduates," 2018). Real-time data should be used in education following appropriate training of teachers in technology and pedagogy (Ali et al., 2023). Teaching students and teachers data literacy enables them to analyze and engage with data more, improving their ability to make informed decisions and to think critically (Hallarte et al., 2024; Namazi & Raiessi, 2023; Zeide, 2017).

REFERENCES

. Akgün, S., & Greenhow, C. (2021). Artificial intelligence in education: Addressing ethical challenges in K-12 settings. *AI and Ethics*, 2(3), 431. Springer Nature. https://doi.org/DOI: 10.1007/s43681-021-00096-7

Akinwalere, S. N., & Ivanov, V. (2022). Artificial Intelligence in Higher Education: Challenges and Opportunities. *BORDER CROSSING*, *12*(1), 1. DOI: 10.33182/bc.v12i1.2015

Ali, A., Al-rimy, B. A. S., Tin, T. T., Altamimi, S., Qasem, S. N., & Saeed, F. (2023). Empowering Precision Medicine: Unlocking Revolutionary Insights through Blockchain-Enabled Federated Learning and Electronic Medical Records. *Sensors (Basel)*, *23*(17), 7476. DOI: 10.3390/s23177476 PMID: 37687931

Amiraullt, R. J. (2019). The Next Great Educational Technology Debate: Personal Data, Its Ownership, and Privacy. *Quarterly Review of Distance Education*, *20*(2), 55. https://eric.ed.gov/?id=EJ1237016

Asad, M., Ali, S., & Wahid, I. (2022). The Role of Artificial Intelligence in Enhancing Learning Outcomes in Higher Education. *Journal of Educational Computing Research*, *58*(4), 666. DOI: 10.1177/07356331221122732

Bierstaker, J. L., Brink, W. D., Khatoon, S., & Thorne, L. (2024). Academic Fraud and Remote Evaluation of Accounting Students: An Application of the Fraud Triangle. *Journal of Business Ethics*, *195*(2), 425. DOI: 10.1007/s10551-024-05628-9

Chalkiadakis, A., Seremetaki, A., Kanellou, A., Kallishi, M., Morfopoulou, A., Moraitaki, M., & Mastrokoukou, S. (2024). Impact of Artificial Intelligence and Virtual Reality on Educational Inclusion: A Systematic Review of Technologies Supporting Students with Disabilities. *Education Sciences*, *14*(11), 1223. DOI: 10.3390/educsci14111223

Chaudhry, M. A., & Kazim, E. (2022). Artificial Intelligence in Education (AIEd): A high-level academic and industry note 2021. *AI and Ethics*, *2*(1), 157–165. PMID: 34790953

Christodoulou, A., & Angeli, C. (2022). Adaptive Learning Techniques for a Personalized Educational Software in Developing Teachers' Technological Pedagogical Content Knowledge. *Frontiers in Education*, *7*. Advance online publication. DOI: 10.3389/feduc.2022.789397

Demartini, C. G., Sciascia, L., Bosso, A., & Manuri, F. (2024). Artificial Intelligence Bringing Improvements to Adaptive Learning in Education: A Case Study. *Sustainability*, *16*(3), 1347. DOI: 10.3390/su16031347

Drakopoulos, V., & Sioulas, P.-V. (2021). Enhancing Primary School Teaching through Virtual Reality. *Journal of Computer Science Research*, *3*(2), 11. DOI: 10.30564/jcsr.v3i2.2777

Egunjobi, D., & Adeyeye, O. (2024). Revolutionizing Learning: The Impact of Augmented Reality (AR) And Artificial Intelligence (AI) on Education. *International Journal of Research Publication and Reviews*, *5*(10), 1157. DOI: 10.55248/gengpi.5.1024.2734

. Ely, D. P. (1992). Trends in Educational Technology.

Gligorea, I., Cioca, M., Oancea, R., Gorski, A.-T., Gorski, H., & Tudorache, P. (2023). Adaptive Learning Using Artificial Intelligence in e-Learning: A Literature Review. *Education Sciences*, *13*(12), 1216. DOI: 10.3390/educsci13121216

Hallarte, D. K., Camaongay, Q. M., Congson, J., Cuamag, S., Datosme, J., Laude, V. K. B., Milano, M. L., Gonzales, R., & Gonzales, G. (2024). Modeling self-regulation in learning mathematics through teacher-promoting interaction and parental support among STEM learners: The mediating role of intrinsic motivation. *Social Sciences & Humanities Open*, *10*, 101135. DOI: 10.1016/j.ssaho.2024.101135

Halverson, R., Grigg, J., Prichett, R., & Thomas, C. (2007). The New Instructional Leadership: Creating Data-Driven Instructional Systems in School. *Journal of School Leadership*, *17*(2), 159. DOI: 10.1177/105268460701700202

Harry, A., & Sayudin, S. (2023). Role of AI in Education. [INJURITY]. *Interdiciplinary Journal and Hummanity*, *2*(3), 260–268. DOI: 10.58631/injurity.v2i3.52

Kamalov, F., & Gurrib, I. (2023). New Era of Artificial Intelligence in Education: Towards a Sustainable Multifaceted Revolution. *arXiv* (Cornell University). https://doi.org//arxiv.2305.18303DOI: 10.48550

Luan, H., Géczy, P., Lai, H., Gobert, J. D., Yang, S. J. H., Ogata, H., Baltes, J., Guerra, R. da S., Li, P., & Tsai, C. (2020). Challenges and Future Directions of Big Data and Artificial Intelligence in Education. *Frontiers in Psychology*, *11*. Advance online publication. DOI: 10.3389/fpsyg.2020.580820 PMID: 33192896

Luan, H., Géczy, P., Lai, H., Gobert, J. D., Yang, S. J. H., Ogata, H., Baltes, J., Guerra, R. da S., Li, P., & Tsai, C. (2020). Challenges and Future Directions of Big Data and Artificial Intelligence in Education. *Frontiers in Psychology*, *11*. Advance online publication. DOI: 10.3389/fpsyg.2020.580820 PMID: 33192896

Maghsudi, S., Lan, A., Xu, J., & van der Schaar, M. (2021). Personalized Education in the Artificial Intelligence Era: What to Expect Next. *IEEE Signal Processing Magazine*, *38*(3), 37. DOI: 10.1109/msp.2021.3055032

Magomadov, V. S. (2020). The application of artificial intelligence and Big Data analytics in personalized learning. *Journal of Physics: Conference Series*, *1691*(1), 12169. DOI: 10.1088/1742-6596/1691/1/012169

Marougkas, A., Troussas, C., Krouska, A., & Sgouropoulou, C. (2023). Virtual reality in education: A review of learning theories, approaches and methodologies for the last decade. *Electronics (Basel)*, *12*(13), 2832.

. Namazi, M., & Raiessi, Z. (2023). The effect of traditional education approaches and big data method on academic achievement of accounting students.

Neji, W., Boughattas, N., & Ziadi, F. (2023). Exploring New AI-Based Technologies to Enhance Students' Motivation. *Issues in Informing Science and Information Technology*, *20*, 95. DOI: 10.28945/5149

Nguyen, V. (2025). The Use of Generative AI Tools in Higher Education: Ethical and Pedagogical Principles. *Journal of Academic Ethics*. Advance online publication. DOI: 10.1007/s10805-025-09607-1

. Onesie Zigzagoon, O., Ololade, Y. J., Eyo-Udo, N. L., & Ogundipe, D. O. (2024). REVOLUTIONIZING EDUCATION THROUGH AI: A COMPREHENSIVE REVIEW OF ENHANCING LEARNING EXPERIENCES. *International Journal of Applied Research in Social Sciences*, 6(4), 589. Fair East Publishers. https://doi .org/DOI: 10.51594/ijarss.v6i4.1011

Orji, F. A., & Vassileva, J. (2022). Automatic modeling of student characteristics with interaction and physiological data using machine learning: A review. *Frontiers in Artificial Intelligence*, *5*. Advance online publication. DOI: 10.3389/frai.2022.1015660 PMID: 36406472

Peng, H., Ma, S., & Spector, J. M. (2019). Personalized adaptive learning: An emerging pedagogical approach enabled by a smart learning environment. *Smart Learning Environments*, *6*(1). Advance online publication. DOI: 10.1186/s40561-019-0089-y

Peng, H., Ma, S., & Spector, J. M. (2019). Personalized adaptive learning: An emerging pedagogical approach enabled by a smart learning environment. *Smart Learning Environments*, *6*(1). Advance online publication. DOI: 10.1186/s40561-019-0089-y

Reidenberg, J. R., & Schaub, F. (2018). Achieving big data privacy in education. *Theory and Research in Education*, *16*(3), 263–279.

Rizvi, M. (2023). Investigating AI-Powered Tutoring Systems that Adapt to Individual Student Needs, Providing Personalized Guidance and Assessments. *The Eurasia Proceedings of Educational and Social Sciences*, *31*, 67. DOI: 10.55549/epess.1381518

Sasikala, P., & Ravichandran, R. (2024). Study on the impact of artificial intelligence on student learning outcomes. *Journal of Digital Learning and Education*, *4*(2), 145–155.

Shuvo, S. A., & Islam, M. A. (2023). Blockchain Technology: A tool to solve the challenges of education sector in developing countries. *International Journal of Computational Systems Engineering*, *7*(3), 1. DOI: 10.1504/ijcsyse.2023.10055995

Toh, L., & Yap, F. (2023). Leveraging AI for Personalized Learning in Higher Education: Challenges and Opportunities. *Educational Technology Review*, *20*(1), 1–10. DOI: 10.1080/14261235.2023.2104921

Yaseen, H., Mohammad, A. S., Ashal, N., Abusaimeh, H., Ali, A. A. A., & Sharabati, A. A. (2025). The Impact of Adaptive Learning Technologies, Personalized Feedback, and Interactive AI Tools on Student Engagement: The Moderating Role of Digital Literacy. *Sustainability*, *17*(3), 1133. DOI: 10.3390/su17031133

Yaseen, H., Mohammad, A. S., Ashal, N., Abusaimeh, H., Ali, A. A. A., & Sharabati, A. A. (2025). The Impact of Adaptive Learning Technologies, Personalized Feedback, and Interactive AI Tools on Student Engagement: The Moderating Role of Digital Literacy. *Sustainability*, *17*(3), 1133. DOI: 10.3390/su17031133

Zeide, E. (2017). The Structural Consequences of Big Data-Driven Education. *Big Data*, *5*(2), 164. DOI: 10.1089/big.2016.0061 PMID: 28632444

. Zhang, X., Li, H., Liu, Z., Chen, Z., Zhou, H., Rong, W., & Ouyang, Y. (2024). A Review of Data Mining in Personalized Education: Current Trends and Future Prospects. *Frontiers of Digital Education.*, 1(1), 26. Higher Education Press. https://doi.org/DOI: 10.1007/s44366-024-0019-6

Zhou, J., Zhang, J., & Li, H. (2023). Exploring the Use of Artificial Intelligence in Teaching Management and Evaluation Based on Citation Space Analysis. *Journal of Education and Educational Research*, *3*(2), 42. DOI: 10.54097/jeer.v3i2.9014

Chapter 4

AI Tutors And Chatbots "The New Face of Student Support in Education": Transforming Education Through Artificial Intelligence

Harsh Choradia
https://orcid.org/0009-0000-4540-2028
Christ University, India

Garima Anand
https://orcid.org/0000-0001-7675-0914
Christ University, India

ABSTRACT

This chapter explores the transformative impact of Artificial Intelligence on educational operations by examining its role in enhancing learning through innovative and personalized methods. It investigates the integration of AI tutors and chatbots within digital learning systems, highlighting their dual function in optimizing learning processes and providing real-time support. The chapter begins with foundational insights into AI, then differentiates the functions of AI instructors and chatbots in academic and administrative contexts, including emotion-aware support systems. It evaluates performance improvement tools such as ChatGPT, IBM Watson Tutor, and Duolingo's AI framework, focusing on their scalability, accessibility, and capacity for personalized feedback. Challenges such as emotional limitations, algorithmic bias, ethical concerns, and student over-dependence are discussed, along with the

DOI: 10.4018/979-8-3373-2948-2.ch004

evolving role of educators in AI-supported environments. The chapter concludes by examining future advancements in Emotional AI, AI-VR integration, and intelligent mentorship systems.

INTRODUCTION

The inclusion of artificial intelligence (AI) in education transformed traditional learning through new educational resources along with modifications to the fundamental aspects of student education. For centuries education operated as an exclusively human-led territory where instructors gave direct teaching along with individualized instruction to their students. With the development of AI technologies educational institutions started to use machines with learning capabilities to enhance the learning process. AI developments in education stem from early mathematical experiments performed in the middle of the twentieth century yet its genuine power started to emerge during the recent decades as demonstrated by AI tutors and chatbots. The AI systems provide tailored educational lessons for large numbers of students by curating interactions that feel native to human users.

The conventional educational system functions as a student-teacher relationship in which instructors share information through classroom discussions and written texts and personal individual contact. The current educational environment in K-12, higher education and corporate training systems lacks personalized attention because it operates as a premium service among basic classroom norms. Student enrollment growth control and reduced budget availability and digital tools dependency continue to intensify the existing barriers that face traditional educational relationships between teachers and students. AI presents an encouraging solution which specifically targets these obstacles through its AI tutors along with chatbots to provide immediate help to students. Advanced natural language processing (NLP) along with machine learning (ML) and data analytic potential empower these systems to provide personalized feedback while guiding student learning paths through particular topics according to each student's personal progress.

The invention of AI-powered tutors and chatbots during recent years can trace its beginnings to AI systems developed during the 1960s such as ELIZA which simulated therapist conversations. The basic operations of ELIZA served as the foundation for future development of AI conversation agents regardless of present-day sophistication. AI developed new applications for education throughout successive decades. Initially designed for individualized learning trails Imperial Tutoring Systems (ITS) experienced limitations because they did not possess adaptable functions nor natural language abilities until deep learning improvements occurred in machine learning and natural language processing.

AI made its true educational breakthrough when creators developed tools that demonstrated human-like interactions which students received as both intuitive and personal. The modern version of AI tutors and chatbots delivers adaptable training along side user-specific assistance which lets students learn independent of speed and receive help and assessment throughout each educational stage. Through its ability to conduct student conversations the chatbot delivers individualized help that fundamentally transformed student content interaction. The education software of AI tutors can address wide subject areas that include both mathematics and science and language instruction and programming through explanation materials combined with customized learning solutions.

Artificial Intelligence systems work between dataset applications and algorithmic processing that allows pattern recognition of student circumstantial along with contextual query understanding for sound educational solutions. Students seeking assistance while solving math problems can receive instructions from the AI teaching system through hints and concept explanations and similar example walkthroughs. Students benefit from the AI chatbot system on online platforms because it provides immediate performance assessment functionality with bespoke recommendations for learning materials when needed. Varied student occurrences experiences separate from conventional school approaches now allows students to progress personally while making sure they stay guarded from public humiliation.

Academic institutions represent only one sector where AI tutors and chatbots find application in education. Business organizations employ these modern technologies to train their employees and help them develop professionally. The educational industry implements AI-based tools which permit employees to gain new qualifications through adaptive learning paths that match their unique needs. Invoice and Accenture as well as IBM include AI chatbots in their employee training approaches to deliver personalized learning paths which focus on specific job roles. Real-time feedback components alongside guidance functionality from these tools produces improved learning experiences through which workers can choose their own learning speeds when operating through training material.

AI education applications reach further than the transmission of content material. AI systems perform student performance data collection and analysis to deliver valuable understanding regarding student needs to educators. AI gives teachers capability to detect student difficulties when these problems emerge so they can deliver specialty interventions before students face major learning difficulties. Kuhail et al. (2023) discovered that education-driven interactions with AI chatbots enabled students to maintain better knowledge levels and self-regulation skills mostly when these tools provided customized feedback as well as educational resources. Okonkwo & Ade-Ibijola (2021) recorded how students remained motivated through

AI-powered chatbots because these tools allowed self-paced student-technology interactions which produced immediate responses that enabled continuous learning.

The achievement of AI in education goes beyond its competency to transfer information and process information. The interactive operations performed by AI tutors and chatbots create important conditions which boost student involvement. Kuhail et al. (2023) explained that adaptive characteristics in these tools produced substantial value by boosting student motivation to continue learning. This AI intervention dynamically adopts to the student's learning pace thus it maintains their active involvement through instructional sequences that seem specially tailored just for them. Academic achievement with student satisfaction demonstrates clear patterns when students use AI tutors as explained through research from Usher & Barak (2024) and Holmes et al. (2022).

AI tutors together with chatbots present implementation difficulties to educational institutions. The adoption of AI systems encounters major obstacles because of present privacy risks and ethical matters as well as bias-based operation issues. The researchers at Chen & Lee (2023) underline both the need to reveal AI system operations transparently and the necessity of bias correction for educational results. Training AI systems through extensive datasets introduces potential risks of pre-existent biases to produce adverse results for specific student groups. AI systems used in education need to be built while keeping fairness and transparency coupled with monitoring systems that register full accountability.

The clear advantages of employing AI tutors and chatbots persist even with the known challenges. The innovation empowers students to witness tailored learning opportunities and intensified engagement and independent education through their academic process. Educational AI tools allow teachers to develop their teaching approaches while delivering immediate evaluations which enables them to spend more time on valuable student engagements. AI development will increase its educational functions to deliver better student outcomes and new methods of delivering education. The educational change occurs through AI systems using organic language processing together with machine learning and data analytics which provide students and teachers plentiful chances for growth and feedback and active involvement. AI technology will make a decisive positive impact on educational practices through its application for teaching methods as well as educational delivery despite present obstacles with ethics and data privacy and potential biases in system outputs. The educational landscape evolves through AI tool advancements as the technology predicts adaptable learning experiences that benefit an inclusive student body.

Objectives

- Modern student support systems utilize AI tutors as well as chatbots for their operations.

To compare the functions of AI tutors and chatbots in educational contexts.

- The research must pinpoint the main obstacles which consist of ethical conditions and bias along with emotional boundaries.
- Grade the changing function of educational professionals in harmony with technological tools.

AI MEETS EDUCATION: THE EVOLUTION

Before technology entered the world people used oral methods to teach one another. The process of knowledge transfer from instructor to scholar happened through personal conversations and fable-telling and practical training. The educational programs in ancient settlements of Mesopotamia Egypt and Greece taught only a privileged few while requiring them to attend temples or private institutes for study. The academic system used systematize teaching methods that did not regards personal student contrasts or personal learning requirements. Educational institutions adjusted according to the development of human societies. The printing press that appeared during the 15th century became a monumental change because it made books more available for students while allowing learners to study independently. Learning remained passive though this development came about because teachers acted as primary knowledge providers while students needed to learn by rote.

Teacher-centered instruction received support from modern teaching tools like overhead projectors and audiovisual equipment during the twentieth century but the education model experienced no fundamental change. Basic computer programs started to replace traditional classrooms in the 1960s through computer-assisted instruction (CAI) for typing and math teaching purposes. The technology displayed innovative character at this specific period but its scope for user interaction remained restricted. The 1960s brought forth ELIZA as the first substantial artificial intelligence educational experiment. In 1966 Joseph Weizenbaum developed ELIZA at MIT as a rule-based chatbot which performed as a psychotherapist through question-forming of user statements. The limited comprehension capabilities of ELIZA proved to be no obstacle for demonstrating basic computer dialogue ability despite its inability to understand real information. This milestone led to increased AI research for educational assistance.

Computers developed intelligent tutoring systems (ITS) throughout the period from the 1970s to the 1980s. Early educational applications of artificial intelligence sought to duplicate the experience of individual tutoring between people. Within the SCHOLAR system developed by Jaime Carbonell students could interact with the program by providing specific inputs that received personalized feedback. BUGGY offered students arithmetic error diagnosis followed by error correction features as part of its educational capabilities. These developing systems initiated the shift toward responsive learning because technology started recognizing particular student requirements.

New technology available through the internet during the 1990s extended educational technology beyond its previous boundaries. The technology market introduced two major e-learning platforms known as Blackboard and Moodle which enabled students to study without set schedules along with improved material sharing capabilities. The initial stages of AI development happened in this period in spite of the fact that natural language processing (NLP) and machine learning (ML) technology began to grow more powerful. The developments in this era enabled researchers to design advanced tutoring systems which processed student communications while learning how to adapt the instructional resources.

AI-powered learning platforms together with chatbots introduced during the 2010s allowed the processing of tasks that required higher levels of sophistication. In the current decade natural language processing had advanced sufficiently for artificial intelligence to simulate human dialogues with students. The educational tool IBM Watson Education applied AI capabilities with data analysis to enable teachers in identifying individual student abilities and deficiencies. Adaptive learning systems DreamBox and Knewton started delivering customized educational paths that tailored their content to student activities and test results. The systems evaluated student knowledge through continual assessment before they adapted the learning material to produce maximum performance results.

OpenAI's GPT (Generative Pre-trained Transformer) alongside other large language models (LLMs) represent a major influential development from the recent years. The public embraced AI-based tutoring systems after ChatGPT entered the market in late 2022. ChatGPT distinguishes itself from conventional rule-based chatbots because it interacts through context-dependent conversations with numerous educational topics successfully. Educational applications have implemented this technology to facilitate explanations of difficult subjects and quiz development and writing evaluation as well as automated essay and code generation. Two leading LLMs which add to this transformation are Google's Bard and Meta's LLaMA. Through educational applications these models allow students to access time-continuous affordable academic help at large scales.

AI has been successfully incorporated into various educational levels that make up the modern learning system. Educational organisations including universities and school systems as well as online platforms make use of both Artificial Intelligence tutors and chatbots to progress learning by providing support functions and capture students. Arizona State University employs AI chatbots to handle students' commonplace enrollment and campus resource questions which lowers administrative responsibilities and boosts student satisfaction levels. The enrollment process at Georgia State University became smoother through the deployment of their chatbot system named "Pounce." The interaction with Pounce by students generated increased successful university enrollment and attendance throughout a randomized controlled trial which exhibited AI's potential capability to stop summer melt. AI technologies have transformed the processes of content development as well as content delivery methods. Khan Academy provides AI tutors named Khanmigo and other similar digital helpers that serve students during lessons by providing explanations and encouraging students to think critically. The tutors design their approach to give students hints instead of solving their problems to increase student interest and boost active learning. Duolingo uses Artificial Intelligence to generate chatbots that provide students with casual practice using response transformation based on their performance advancements.

Different research studies together with systematic reviews establish that AI yields positive results in educational settings. The review by Kuhail et al. (2023) demonstrated that educational chatbots benefit learning results when developers create effective bots which deliver tailored feedback and promote student thinking. Okonkwo and Ade-Ibijola (2021) explained how students show increased motivation through conversational agents by returning to interactive platforms with chatbot technology.

Student usage of AI tutors led to stronger academic confidence combined with reduced stress according to Labadze, Grigolia, and Machaidze (2023). AI tools create an inclusive learning environment because they support various student learning types including unique processing speeds according to research findings. Usher and Barak (2024) examined the moral aspects of using AI in online educational settings while focusing on ethical matters. Students indicated they liked the custom teaching approach from AI tutors but feared both their personal information security along with the validity of artificial intelligence feedback.

AI technology finds its most influential application in special education environments. The integration of AI-based speech recognition with language processing tools delivers assistance to students with dyslexia and also helps students with autism along with those who experience language delays. AI tutors use student-specific needs to deliver educational materials through visual and auditory and textual formats at their controlled learning speeds for better understanding. AI systems create both improvement of educational quality as well as equality of opportunities in learning for all students.

The educational use of AI entails multiple restrictions beyond its current achievements. The use of AI systems should be used with restraint according to Krstić et al. (2022) together with Wollny et al. (2021) and other scholars. Artificial Intelligence systems may feasibly decrease students evaluation skills when students constantly use AI for providing solutions. Computing systems tend to develop biases against particular demographic groups within educational groups because their training datasets contain unfair biases. The precision of AI-generated solutions stands as a concern according to Sevgi et al. (2023) when these responses affect medical and legal education with potential severe ramifications.

Educational AI systems need substantial quantities of up-to-date high-quality information to carry out their functions properly. Schools that have insufficient digital platforms together with limited educational materials will face difficulties when implementing this type of system. The absence of emotional intelligence in AI systems prevents them from displaying human characteristics of empathy as well as intuition and encouragement that typical educators naturally offer. The appropriate use of AI tutors consists of supporting traditional teaching approaches instead of attempting to replace human educators.

Various initiatives have been launched to manage the existing difficulties. The research conducted by Harry and Sayudin (2023) demonstrates that ethical AI tools become more effective through collaboration between educators students and developers during design processes. The development processes validate that AI systems maintain pedagogical foundation and practical compliance with educational requirements. AI development will target three objectives to improve transparency in addition to explainable operations and adaptability which will aid educators' trust of AI systems. The affiliation of Artificial Intelligence technology in academical systems brings about foundational changes which changeover from traditional standard classroom teaching toward personalized instant scalable educational assistance. The development of AI technology through ELIZA and its descendant LLM-based systems followed the growing student and teaching needs. Numerous studies featuring real student cases along with literature reports confirm that educational AI tutors combined with chatbots both boost class involvement and raise academic results while simplifying academic operations. AI education integration needs sustained research and innovative development as well as ethical planning to become successful. The educational landscape will transform into a new learning paradigm because AI will evolve from being an educational tool into becoming an agent of educational transformation.

AI TUTORS & CHATBOTS

The Current Applications of AI Chatbots and Tutors

The development of Artificial Intelligence chatbots and tutors initiated tailored interactive learning using their development from fundamental rule-based systems to extensible enlightened technologies. Educational institutions use NLP and ML and data analytical AI systems to enhance learning experiences for both students and educators in educational settings. These technology solutions deliver multiple functionalities that cover real-time question solving, information distribution and success ratings evaluation and emotional support programs.

Conversational agents form a major educational AI application because they function as virtual tutors. The tutors operate through natural language communication to process questions while providing relevant context-specific explanations to students. OpenAI's ChatGPT together with Google Bard demonstrate capability to answer sophisticated educational questions as they generate natural responses. These systems provide students with help that includes solving math problems and scientific concept explanations and essay editing services along with examination preparation aid. These AI tutors can be available to students at all times through a real-time interface and this feature remains highly beneficial for remote learning environments.

According to Kuhail et al. (2023) educational chatbots boosted student participation levels to such a degree that 78% of students reported positive learning benefits from the chatbot system. The research provided evidence that educational chatbots develop self-regulation capabilities among students which proved vital for online education success. Through personalized response capabilities AI tutors deliver adapted service to students using the data about their fluency level together with their learning style and learning speed which promotes targeted education.

The generation of automated feedback through educational artificial intelligence constitutes an important application in the field of modern education. Educational writing receives instantaneous feedback with correct grammar, style and language along with content consistantly evaluation through AI instruments such as Grammarly and Turnitin's AI writing assistant. The AI tutors used in Carnegie Learning together with Squirrel AI generate feedback that combines accuracy assessments alongside teaching questions and hints to advance students' conceptual knowledge.

Real educational environments have demonstrated how AI tutors create substantial changes through multiple researched examples. Students who received instruction through Watson Tutor from IBM performed better in introductory biology classes at Georgia State University. The AI tutor delivered explanations together with clarification of student doubts while recommending custom learning resources.

Students demonstrated enhanced satisfaction and better conceptual grasp of lessons than students from previous groups whose education was delivered solely by human instructors.

Duolingo uses AI-implanted chatbots as a part of its system to help education. This system adjusts its support levels automatically based on student inputs while giving contextual corrections to mistakes. The platform interacts like a human conversation which strengthens mastery while improving retention levels of knowledge.

Chen et al. (2020) argue that AI application in education enables teachers to adopt personalized teaching methods instead of traditional standard instruction. Using tracks the students' behavior and analyzes learning patterns while generating patient-specific paths of study. A study conducted by Herft (2023) showed that Australian secondary school students managed their learning independently with better academic results through AI technology implementation particularly when the tools were directed toward students who showed poor traditional learning outcomes.

The application of AI tutors extends to providing assistance for exam preparation as well as refraining common student difficulties. The platform Quizlet lets AI manufacture personalized flashcards along with tests that focus on students' problematic subjects. Socratic by Google operates as a mobile AI system which enables students to submit questions through scanning to obtain multimedia-enhanced step-by-step educational explanations.

We must still recognize their boundaries despite their present achievements in this field. AI systems contain errors which occur mainly through incorrect or misleading information generation in complex or ambiguous contexts according to Sevgi et al. (2023). The emotional intelligence capabilities of human educators along with their mentoring abilities surpass AI systems since these abilities remain confined to human beings. The reliability and effectiveness of AI tutors should enhance through technological progress together with training data becoming more diverse and inclusive.

The current implementations of AI tutors and chatbots in education create substantial changes in the way students find academic assistance. The software tools serve as scalable cost-effective personalized substitute solutions for traditional teaching assistants and tutors which makes them essential for modern education institutions.

Benefits of AI Tutors and Chatbots to Students

Students now receive transformed educational experiences because schools started integrating AI tutors together with chatbots into their settings. These technological systems create customized learning spaces which provide accessible knowledge delivery through interactive sessions whereas both students and teachers find them suitable.

- The adaptive technique allows students to receive instruction at their individual rhythms so they may learn best while creating successful educational outcomes. Labadze et al. (2023) demonstrated through research that AI personalization produces better academic results.
- The key advantage of AI chatbots arises from their fast delivery of responses to questions posed by students. The immediate response mechanism enables quick clarification of doubts together with live correction of learning misconceptions in active sessions. According to Hew et al. (2021) students can improve their academic results through prompt feedback delivery.
- The availability of AI tutors and chatbots during all hours operates without traditional educational support system restrictions. Students benefit from this round-the-clock availability since it lets them get help whenever needed thus supporting their ongoing educational process. Students enrolled in the NSW EduChat trial operated by the NSW Department of Education receive scheduled guidance from the program after normal school hours.
- Things AI-based educational tools do exceptionally well is to support students who need different types of learning accommodations. The specific requirements of disabled learners get addressed through fundamental tools such as text-to-speech functions and visual learning assistance together with individual customer support. Research gives a demonstration of that these technology tools help learning power while delivering all-in education results.
- Current learning methods improve through game elements which AI tutors and chatbots apply to create more motivated students. The transformation of educational assignments into rewarding interactive activities through these technologies converts learning activities into more interesting processes. Socratic and Habitica serve as two platforms that use gamified learning features which enable users to develop regular study practices.

Impact on Student Perception and Engagement

Educational establishments became transformed through AI tutor and chatbot integration which modified student relationships with their coursework alongside their learning experience. The conventional approach to student engagement relied primarily on teacher-student physical contact as well as peer-to-peer engagement combined with established pedagogical methods. Artificial intelligence brought changes to engagement by introducing three essential elements that include interactivity and adaptivity and accessibility.

The most extensive change brought by AI-driven education consists of its customized approach to learning. Using Natural Language Processing and machine learning Artificial Intelligence tutors nurtures abilities to understand tailored student characteristics including strengths and weaknesses. AIML enables the system to develop custom responses which recommend resources that both meet learners' current speed and match their current understanding level. The customizable approach which Kuhail et al. (2023) describe improves both student understanding and helps students remember information better while promoting independent learning behaviors. The educational process now assigns students the role of active learners whose self-governed educational paths they can pursue at their individual speed.

EDUBOT served as the name of the chatbot deployed at the University of Murcia Spain to use in blended learning programs as part of their research study. Through its usage students could review educational material while seeking solutions for particular subjects. Students experienced better exam performance because the chatbot research proved they became more self-motivated while lowering their exam stress levels and pursuing deeper knowledge understanding. Users who interacted with the chatbot asked their questions to seek clarification as well as deepen their understanding according to findings from Rodríguez-García et al. (2023).

The user interaction experience which chatbots provide serves as a significant factor that drives engagement. AI systems duplicate human communication to present learning as a dynamic process instead of an artificial machine-driven method. Students who interact with chatbots according to Lin and Mubarok (2021) in their Frontiers in Artificial Intelligence study produced complex written assignments of higher quality than students who used traditional online learning methods. Students experience better learning depth according to this research because the dialogic nature of AI tools forces them to express their thoughts in a clear and reflective manner.

Students now show progressively positive emotions toward AI chatbots based on their perception of them. Modern students no longer perceive chatbots as cold mechanical tools since they have accepted them as learning companions and mentors. Students in multiple universities studied under Essel et al. (2022) developed a positive perception of AI chatbots in educational settings which led users to experience support with reduced isolation while enhancing their motivation levels. Traditional teaching settings could not match the academic security provided by the chatbot due to its continuous availability. Perceiving connectedness with chatbots in college education matches Self-Determination Theory because it drives intrinsic motivational behaviour.

AI tutors provide important autonomy support to students in their learning processes. AI-based learning systems enable students to choose both the learning times and methods through their learner-paced and time-unlimited educational approach. AI tutors function harmoniously with modern students because they match the student population that expects customized services through flexible scheduling. Under the guidance of AI tutors students maintain freedom to study demanding material again while taking quizzes multiple times because the system creates a nonjudgmental environment where interruptions are prevented during experimental learning sessions. Police data compiled by Aiken et al. (2020) validates that learner independence strengthens student confidence and helps students transition from extrinsic to intrinsic motivation patterns essential for sustainable learning.

Critical thinking abilities along with analytical reasoning skills need promotion as a fundamental aspect. Several contemporary AI tutors operate by assisting students to discover solutions instead of simply giving them the answers directly. The AI features in Carnegie Learning's MATHia system analyze student work before directing students through problem-solving steps by asking exploratory questions instead of giving answers. Students develop measurable cognitive abilities when teachers utilize corrective scaffolding because they must explain their thought processes while solving issues independently according to Urban et al. (2023). Through continuous use these technologies develop students' capacity to think about their own thinking while promoting advanced subject comprehension.

AI-driven learning platforms now combine collaborative models for education which enable student interactions between AI moderators and themselves. User dialogue becomes possible through chatbot systems by asking open-ended questions and initiating peer review while managing group activities as a dialogue facilitator .In 2023 Nawaz and Gomes demonstrated how introducing "ClassMate" AI chatbot into group settings encouraged higher involvement levels mostly among students who were typically self-analysing. The AI-based system maintained inclusive discussions that focused on topic-related content thus creating better group work and collaborative results.

The enhancement of engagement relies on gamification methods although these mechanisms are usually neglected. AI tutoring systems in Duolingo and Socratic motivate students by using award systems that merge points collection with badges and leaderboards rankings. In 2021 Huang and Hew in the British Journal of Educational Technology gamified AI learning systems gave a rise to completion rates along with improved daily use compared to traditional platforms without gamification elements. The collected features produce successful feedback about progress which proves essential to maintain extended learning commitment.

Inclusivity along with accessibility represent two areas which AI technologies improve engagement levels. The mechanisms of AI chatbots support disabled students as well as English learners by providing voice feedback and easy-to-understand content. The Google Read Along application employs speech detection capability to deliver reading comprehension help to students from multilingual backgrounds. Scientific research has shown that inclusive technological solutions produce better engagement from underprivileged student populations thus expanding educational opportunities.

Engagement improves through the real-time analytics along with feedback that AI tutors supply. The instant feedback given to learners enables them to detect their errors so they can instantly readjust their learning strategies. The development process creates environments that build both growth mindset abilities as well as resilience. Students who access AI-powered formative feedback struggle less in their studies with better results according to Holmes et al. (2022) in their literature review.

Benefits to Teachers

AI tutors alongside chatbots gain extensive admiration for their advantages to students yet they concurrently reshape the teaching profession. Educational technology based on artificial intelligence functions as a support system for teachers to manage duties efficiently while providing individualized teaching and enhancing teacher growth and changing educational environments for the better. Through its integration AI enhances both instructional success and teacher quality of life simultaneously thus benefitting teachers in complex educational environments.

Schools obtain quick advantages through AI automated systems which execute tedious administrative responsibilities. The system handles ticking assessment boxes and monitoring student attendance alongside automatic reminder dispatches along with answering regular student questions. When administrators lighten their workload teachers can bring their freed-up time to create better educational plans and develop curricula and personalize student support services. The adoption of AI chatbots by Singapore Institute of Technology into their learning system management platform brought about substantial reductions of time spent by teachers on technical and administrative support duties. The introduction of "AskSIT" as a chatbot enabled MDPI Education Sciences investigators (Tan et al., 2022) to confirm that faculty members reduced their non-teaching responsibilities by 30% after deployment. The capacity created through the chatbots let educators spend additional time mentoring students along with increased student-faculty interaction.

The functionality of AI systems enables the creation of instruction that uses evidence-based information and monitoring. Student performance data that goes continuously through AI-directed monitoring generates thorough performance visualizations that display student comprehension patterns alongside their involvement along with their academic course. The obtained learner insights enable teachers to make responsive educational decisions about their instruction and teaching strategies. Teaching practitioners gain the ability to make dynamic course adaptations through using information collected throughout learning periods. The Open University in UK used AI-driven analytics to detect students with failing conditions ahead of traditional warning indicators would normally appear through an exemplified case study. The combination of proactive measures supported by predictive algorithm analysis raised student retention by 15% according to Ferguson and Clow (2020).

The delivery of personalized instruction which traditionally remained out of reach in large classrooms is becoming possible because of AI assistance. The AI tutors administer unique educational sequences to students that teachers employ performance metrics for personalizing their assistance methods. Holmes et al. (2022) explain in their extensive review on AI education that AI tools make it possible for personalized education to scale up without causing excessive workload for teachers. AI systems assist teachers as co-educators to carry out initial knowledge transfers and student revision tasks which frees human instructors to handle tasks that demand more advanced pedagogical skills such as critical thinking and conceptual clarity and interdisciplinary connections.

The crucial benefit of AI involves its support of teacher professional improvement along with reflective leadership practices. AI systems enable the detection of student outcomes which provides the ability to identify particular teaching strategies requiring teacher enhancement. The generated feedback provides guidance about how to restrict questions, arrange questions throughout a lesson and measure retention levels among students at each lesson stage.

Through Classroom Analytics Suite Carnegie Mellon University provides teachers with real-time displays about student interactions and understanding progress during class sessions. Instructional adjustments derive from the data which also serves to train faculty members. AI-informed feedback shaped three-academic-term research findings which demonstrated that participating teachers achieved better student engagement results along with enhanced content learning retention according to Winne et al. (2021).

School-based artificial intelligence systems through chatbots offer students after-hour support which enables teachers to achieve better work-family separation. Students receive response services from chatbots for simple conceptual inquiries and receive access to learning resource links and assistance with procedural matters from assignment submissions to exam schedule access. The handling of common queries by this system enables teachers to dedicate their time to delivering substantial academic instruction including critical thinking workshops and individual project mentorship and group discussion leadership. The teacher transforms from delivering information to supporting students in their advanced learning process and intellectual growth.

Moreover, AI facilitates inclusive education and resource optimization. AI offers specialized service variations for classrooms which include students with learning disabilities and multilingual learners through content translation generation and speech-to-text transcription pairs and scaffolded lesson resources. These features enable effective student accommodation through teaching methods that no longer need to rely on standardized approaches. The AI system deployed at the University of Pretoria identified students who were not participating actively or underperforming academically so instructors supplied appropriate supplemental resources to them. The early-warning system driven by AI led to focused interventions thus resulting in improved test performance among 82% of the students flagged by the system (Okonkwo & Ade-Ibijola, 2021).

Through Classroom Analytics Suite Carnegie Mellon University provides teachers with real-time displays about student interactions and understanding progress during class sessions. Instructional adjustments derive from the data which also serves to train faculty members. Three academic terms of observation revealed that teachers who received AI-driven feedback demonstrated improved student engagement levels and knowledge maintenance and this improvement became statistically significant (Winne et al., 2021).

School-based artificial intelligence systems through chatbots offer students after-hour support which enables teachers to achieve better work-family separation. Students receive response services from chatbots for simple conceptual inquiries and receive access to learning resource links and assistance with procedural matters from assignment submissions to exam schedule access. The handling of common queries by this system enables teachers to dedicate their time to delivering substantial academic instruction including critical thinking workshops and individual project mentorship and group discussion leadership. The teacher transforms from delivering information to supporting students in their advanced learning process and intellectual growth.

Moreover, AI facilitates inclusive education and resource optimization. AI offers specialized service variations for classrooms which include students with learning disabilities and multilingual learners through content translation generation and speech-to-text transcription pairs and scaffolded lesson resources. The built-in features decrease teaching practices that rely on standard strategies so teachers can serve all their students effectively. AI systems at the University of Pretoria ran an experimental study applying them to monitor student engagement levels for providing additional learning content to students who performed poorly on tests. The AI early-warning system detected specific students who received enhanced interventions which produced positive results in their subsequent tests according to Okonkwo & Ade-Ibijola (2021).

Long-lasting educational developments enabled by AI cause educators to transform their functions from being content providers into learning experience creators and learning experience developers and evaluators. The release from trivial tasks allows educators to enhance their abilities in creativity development and student mentoring as well as debate facilitation. The future-ready framework developed by

OECD supports teachers to transition from content instructors towards facilitators who implement "deeper learning" through AI-assisted tools (OECD, 2021).

TRADITIONAL VS. MODERN WAYS OF EDUCATION

Educational techniques now exhibit complete metamorphosis due to technological implementations of student-focused educational methods. The startup of Artificial Intelligence (AI) stands as the most prominent indicator of this educational change process. Traditional educational methods receive opposite assessments compared to modern approaches and raise divergent viewpoints regarding teaching approaches and instructional methods as well as student engagement and assessment procedures.

The educational activities based on face-to-face teaching occur within traditional classroom structures. The educational process sticks to a linear progression of steps with teachers holding total power to supply information but remain the central authority. Standardized teaching practices control educational spaces while teachers maintain restricted autonomy to provide individualized teaching methods to their students. End-of-term exams represent the main assessment technique instead of incorporating formative assessment methods. Students can participate in the model through structured learning environments but their involvement becomes limited to primarily receiving information.

Standard education systems in the industrial era relied on traditional learning methods which succeeded through memorization and instruction following during the time since students needed to follow straightforward procedures. The traditional educational system failed to transform as modern society increased diversity and established knowledge-focused learning spaces which stem from its inability to identify students' academic requirements and their learning pace. The lack of effective student ability adjustment systems in traditional learning methods results in students leaving academic institutions according to Pérez et al. (2020).

In contrast to native education approaches the contemporary method now inherits adjustable organizational structures and personalised education answers and joins students to online resources. The arrival of e-learning platforms along with e-classrooms and mobile applications has shattered the learning rituals of classroom spaces and set schedules. The transformation of education depends heavily on AI technology which makes possible compatible learning approaches along with intellectual tutors and automated assessment processes as well as the real-time investigation of educational systems.

The central characteristic of contemporary education involves fostering learner self-directing abilities. The learning process enables students to take control through AI-supported guidance tools that assist them. AI technology on Khan Academy and Coursera allows students to receive customized recommendation of learning resources that match their academic outcomes combined with individual choice. Harry & Sayudin (2023) verified that students kept 23% more information through AI-modified learning methods instead of typical classroom lectures.

Online content provides students with opportunities to learn before they actively use their classroom time by engaging in various interactive activities. The learning environment stretches into after-school hours since AI chatbots serve as facilitators to answer questions for students until standard school hours. Student involvement and examination scores at the University of Murcia, Spain improved by 30% and 15% correspondingly when AI chatbots were execute in flipped classrooms during a research study done by Labadze et al. (2023).

The educational evaluation system is transforming into a process which extends beyond traditional exams by using active dynamic assessment methods. AI systems evaluate pupils in present time to offer immediate feedback which produces performance analytics and reveals both gaps and student understanding levels. By obtaining student progress indicators Krstić et al. (2022) explain educators can make early educational interventions which lead to better teaching approach adjustments for improved results

A substantial difference emerges between traditional educational approaches and modern ones concerning instructor responsibilities. Education before modern times presented teachers as teachers who dominated the classroom setting yet current classrooms show teachers leading as coaching figures. Through its handling of administrative work teachers can free up their time for developing better teaching practices alongside guiding their students. Usher & Barak (2024) agree with the authors that the integration of artificial intelligence enables teachers to deliver teaching that is both reflective and holistic.

AI-enabled modern education delivers various benefits although it poses several obstacles for users to overcome. Several ethical problems related to privacy protection as well as biased algorithm systems and unequal access still exist. Nonetheless many students face barriers when trying to access internet connections and smart devices and AI tools because of digital disparities. Excessive reliance on technology by students creates the concern that important thinking abilities and problem-solving capabilities will fade away. Wollny et al. (2021) suggest that AI should be implemented with discretion which maintains both teaching and learning facets of humanistic education.

The standard structure created by native education serves as an important foundation for contemporary Artificial enhanced education which adds features of pliability and customization for tailored learning experiences at various student capacities. Educational institutions advance their teaching methods by using AI tutors in conjunction with AI chatbots for real-time adaptive education that provides worldwide accessible support systems to students. Educational policy makers and researchers need to actively continue their work because technology adoption in education depends on their efforts to maximize positive human and democratic effects rather than diminish the personal touch of learning.

MODERN TECHNOLOGY COMES WITH MODERN PROBLEMS

Contemporary educational benefits stemming from AI tutor and chatbot application in learning systems have generated unparalleled opportunities for tailored learning yet introduced various modern challenges to academic environments. Modern technology generates modern problems according to the popular adage when applied to education using artificial intelligence. AI brings worldwide promise but generates multiple serious problems which touch technology systems together with moral issues as well as learning practices and monetary systems. Learning and teaching are under threat due to serious problems triggered by data privacy violations and system algorithms which introduce biases as well as a shortage of emotional intelligence capabilities together with excessive dependence on automated systems. Advanced technology-based difficulties have the ability to isolate populations who already face marginalization. Educational instructors encounter difficulties adjusting to the fast-changing AI tools alongside institutions which must solve issues regarding their accountability and transparency and system reliability. The educational sector must carefully examine forthcoming challenges because AI deployment needs ethical standards combined with pedagogical excellence as well as equitable treatment of students.

Challenges Faced by Educators in Using AI Tutors and Chatbots

The incorporation of AI into education through transformative teaching aids brings both beneficial tools and complex duties and difficulties for educators to manage in their work environment. Teaching professionals need to handle both the supportive role of AI in administrative tasks and instruction spaces while they manage issues regarding reliability concerns and ethical obligations and professional authentic identity.

1. Reliability and Oversight Burden

Teachers struggle most with AI-generated content reliability issues being their primary difficulty. The educational materials generated by tools like ChatGPT can be obtained quickly through functions that create quiz questions and explanations alongside assignment outlines however these results might have both factual errors and poor pedagogical standards. Teachers experience additional workload because they must thoroughly check each educational piece for accuracy before using it in a classroom setting.

The science education capabilities of ChatGPT are respectable according to Cooper (2023) but the trained expertise of dedicated educators remains unreplaceable because of its limitations. The contextual understanding of AI remains limited which enables it to deliver believable yet incorrect factual information. Teachers now face an expanded duty to carefully monitor educational content instead of receiving any reduction in their teaching responsibility.

2. Pedagogical Misalignment

The use of AI tools creates difficulties in meeting current educational standards and standards. The learning abilities of AI systems work best for memorization and basic fact retrieval whereas they perform poorly with constructivist educational processes. Herft (2023) points out that ChatGPT enables the creation of instructional prompts but fails to possess sufficient capacity for developing critical thinking or reflective skills.

Teachers need methods to integrate AI capabilities into their educational objectives. The main issue is preventing artificial intelligence from turning classroom environments into machine-calculated information absorption while neglecting meaningful understanding.

3. Ethical Responsibility and Data Privacy

Education professionals now face a challenge to lead students in responsible AI operations but they lack sufficient training to accomplish this goal. According to Miao and Ahn (2023) the duty to guarantee responsible AI usage is generically assigned to individual teachers though organizations lack established policies regarding its implementation.

Data privacy issues exist at a considerable level. Student-related data including text patterns with performance records alongside their behavioral records gets processed by Automated Information platforms. The absence of oversight systems for teacher oversight of educational data generates concerns about data security breaches together with GDPR non-compliance and enduring digital profiling effects.

4. Academic Integrity and Fair Assessment

AI's capability to produce written work along with response answers as well as project summaries threatens the evaluation system that underpins educational assessment. The current profession is burdened with the task of identifying between student work that originates from humans and work supported by AI. The subjective nature of AI marks makes educators mistrust grading systems and compromises the reliability of educational credentials according to the observations of AlAfnan et al. (2023).

AI content detection tools do exist yet prove insufficient for ensuring complete accuracy in discovering machine-generated text. The problem of incorrect positive and negative results produces injustices against students through improper academic sanctions and unsuccessful detection of academic misconduct. Educational personnel must make decisions through a complex ethical territory that makes both fairness and responsibility enforcement almost impossible.

5. Professional Resistance and Anxiety

The quick entrainment of AI in educational spaces produces worry among teaching professionals about their occupational status. Educators exhibit concerns about losing part or all of their professional duties to technological advancements. A substantial portion of educators at schools without sufficient resources shows negative attitudes toward AI integration according to Tahiru (2021).

Furthermore the lack of training combined with institutional support makes this fear worse. Proper attention to this issue becomes essential because its neglect produces lowered educator morale and halts their career growth while deepening the technology usage gap between teachers.

Challenges Faced by Students in Using AI Tutors and Chatbots

Students tend to welcome technology in their learning process but their interaction with AI chatbots creates various exposure risks. The benefits of responsive 1:1 student support create several issues around dependency problems alongside errors in information delivery and emotional detachment as well as unbalanced accessibility.

1. Over-Reliance and Critical Thinking Erosion

The biggest anxiety among professionals revolves around students developing excessive dependence on AI tools because this diminishes their ability to think independently and solve problems by themselves. According to Kasneci et al. (2023), students express high levels of satisfaction with ChatGPT and related tools yet such immediacy of solutions encourages learning through passive means.

The problem affects writing-intensive courses and disciplines within STEM fields to a greater extent. Students who employ chatbots for essay writing and mathematical problem solving and reading summary functions usually avoid important cognitive operations required for the tasks. The lacking depth in material comprehension together with reduced analytical and innovative capabilities is a natural result.

2. Misinformation and Inaccuracy

The high level of sophistication found in AI chatbots does not prevent them from making mistakes. Sevgi et al. (2023) discovered that although ChatGPT showed high medical education expertise it sometimes produced false or deceptive content. The domains of medicine, law and engineering need perfect accuracy due to which these errors become particularly harmful.

Insufficient knowledge among students prevents them from assessing AI responses correctly which leads to incorrect answers being accepted as true information while causing academic failure through misinterpretation.

3. Unequal Access and Digital Literacy Divide

The advantages of using AI tutors fail to benefit students uniformly across populations. Students who live in rural areas along with those coming from disadvantaged finance backgrounds typically do not have access to high-speed internet or modern devices or AI tools because of restricted opportunities. The researchers at Sullivan et al. (2023) emphasize that digital inequality poses a big challenge when adopting AI systems which worsens educational inequalities.

Students demonstrate different levels of competency when using AI tools even when they have available access to them. People who understand AI effectively find better benefits while others encounter difficulties in responsible AI system interactions.

4. Emotional Detachment and Loss of Human Interaction

The current state of artificial intelligence instruction through tutors lacks full replication of human educator capabilities regarding caring mentorship and emotional backing. Xie and Pentina (2022) studied social chatbots especially Replika to discover their companionship functions yet users reported thin emotional responses which produce exaggerated expectations.

Learning environments become problematic when emotional depth is absent since this usually results in student experiences of feeling isolated or frustrated when they need encouragement and moral support to overcome challenges. Education benefits from human instructors who serve as teachers and counselors since AI solutions still lack that capability.

5. Privacy and Consent Issues

AI systems demand students to give away their personal information by active entry or through passive tracking of user behavior. Masters (2023) indicates that this data-sharing poses substantial ethical risks because medical education deals with confidential information.

Most students fail to recognize which information gets collected from them while they remain ignorant about storage methods and usage restrictions. Student trust in digital platforms gets damaged when they encounter transparent data handling from digital platforms.

REAL WORLD CASE STUDIES

1. When Georgia State University introduced the AI-powered chatbot Pounce it became the cornerstone for cutting down the occurrence of "summer melt" among prospective college students. Students received timely answers from Pounce through its text-based interface about enrollment details as well as financial aid and housing information. The introduction of Pounce resulted in a substantial boost of student enrollment which reached 22% higher than students in the control group. Software and AI training processes for Pounce require continuous maintenance because the research proved AI chatbots can handle broader higher education coverage yet it demonstrated ongoing human oversight for content and AI performance management.
2. TeamChat helps distance learners at the Open University through its AI-based chatbot integration with the Virtual Learning Environment (VLE) to support independent course activities. Virtual bots operated within the VLE to supply customized comments along with recommended content as well as report student development. The implemented interventions helped maintain student interest beyond previous benchmarks. The university received ambiguous feedback from students who acknowledged AI automation but chose typical educational

assistance from actual tutors when those services were accessible since artificial intelligence remains at odds with human social needs.

3. The Hong Kong Polytechnic University developed its AI language learning initiative known as PoliBot to enhance student language education. The program named PoliBot focused on student interaction with English learning content through vocabulary quizzes along with grammar support functions and discussion simulations. Students experienced increases in their language skills especially for speaking skills and writing skills during their interaction with PoliBot. The chatbot experienced difficulties in addressing contextual as well as cultural subtleties during conversations which restricted its ability to teach complex and natural language communication aspects in English.
4. AI chatbots from various Indian Institutes of Technology (IITs) provide assistance to students studying STEM subjects by incorporating into their educational platform. Students use the AI chatbots to understand challenging subjects in programming and mathematics which answer their queries while providing step-by-step solutions to problems. Large-scale MOOCs benefit from these tools since human tutor availability is insufficient to meet student needs. The adoption of AI chatbots by faculty requires them to use monitoring tools and strengthen academic honesty policies because of plagiarism concerns and dependency issues.
5. Aun-e the chatbot transformed administrative services at the University of Murcia Spain by processing enormous student queries about enrollment procedures and financial matters and class schedule information. Students valued both the instant service and lower requirements for personal visits at the university because it raised their level of satisfaction with administrative assistance. The chatbot faced challenges when dealing with complex multi-step queries during enrollment periods so human agents needed to intervene. The institution transitioned to a mixed system of support where it integrated high-volume efficiency with thorough service delivery.
6. The national AI education strategy in China brought forth advanced AI tutoring systems Squirrel AI and Yixue Education which entered K–12 schools across the country. The digital platforms provide adapted learning opportunities which adapt according to individual student progress particularly in math and science subjects. Students who interacted with AI tutoring systems in test locations achieved superior standardized test results than their non-participating classmates. Educators and parents remain worried about student privacy risks as well as the nature of leaving human connections in classroom tutoring for AI systems. This has led them to ask for improved regulatory oversight for AI-based teaching.
7. The development of AI teaching assistant Jill Watson occurred through a joint effort between Stanford University and Georgia Tech which used IBM's Watson

platform. Jill operated from online course forums to tackle standard questions posed by students. So successful was the initiative that most students failed to recognize Jill Watson was an artificial intelligence instead of a human TA. The system which Jill Watson operated experienced challenging interactions with open-ended questions and contextual inquiries because AI still faces boundaries in meaningful educational interactions. On the other hand Jill Watson succeeded in reducing faculty workloads before requiring substantial domain knowledge training to achieve accurate operation.

8. The University of Pretoria in South Africa introduced an AI chatbot to address disabilities because it aims to enhance inclusive education. Through screens and voice recognition screens and customized academic help features the system provided independent access to resources for various disabled learners. People recognized this initiative as it worked to establish educational equity. The development team managed to face continuous difficulties implementing sign-language features and culturally inclusive language models along with diverse accessibility requirements.
9. New York Citys Department of Education established a ban against ChatGPT on school devices and networks when the year began 2023. The education system implemented this ban because they wanted to stop student cheating through generative AI tools that threatened educational authenticity and teaching integrity. The decision raised questions in public opinion yet demonstrated the urgent requirement to generate better education policies also highlighting the necessity of ethical AI training for teachers along with their student users instead of opting for total bans.
10. The Italian data protection authority issued a temporary ban of ChatGPT in 2023 because it identified violations of the European Union's General Data Protection Regulation (GDPR). The suspension forced OpenAI to modify its data procedures while demonstrating the necessity of clear AI operations in cases where AI tools serve educational purposes. Europeans began extensive discussions regarding the ethics of data protection as well as AI tool accountability standards and usage limitations for educational establishments throughout the school and university sectors.
11. Duolingo developed AI chatbots through which users can experience realistic conversations used for language acquisition on its global platform. AI tutors through Duolingo create authentic situations that involve food orders and strategy requests and ordinary dialogue to help users master the language naturally. This addition to the platform shows its effectiveness in lesson support and it raises user engagement throughout the day. Users have encountered occasional struggles because the chatbot misunderstands metaphoric language or situational

context which results in wrong corrections and broken dialogue sequences thus indicating the requirement for better natural language processing abilities.

12. The business AI assistant Erica from Bank of America demonstrates educational potentials that parallel training environments. The banking tool Erica utilized natural interaction to assist customers with their tasks and gained quick widespread popularity in American digital banking platforms. The number of recorded one billion interactions illustrates how AI chatbots effectively and personally manage large volumes of consumer inquiries. Educational establishments have begun developing AI systems following Erica's financial success and increased customer adoption because they want to create solutions that aid students through academic guidance and financial aid support and career development.

FUTURE PROSPECTS & INNOVATION

Artificial Intelligence education combined evolves uniquely while Artificial Intelligence tutors and chatbots provides promising future developments which will change academical teaching practices and student learning experiences and enlarged academical access possibilities. Artificial Intelligence tools of present day prove their capacity to tailor education while providing improved learning results while future developments will bring deeper changes. Upcoming academical changes will rise from the combination between AI and upcoming technologies such as Augmented Reality and Virtual Reality emotion blockchain and AI technology which will structure an academical systems beyond previous imagination

Hyper-personalization stands as one of the highly expected advancements in AI tutor and chatbot progression. Contemporary AI tools present tailored educational material to students based on their test findings yet upcoming systems will design responsive learner paths by processing various variables in relation to student behavior. AI systems will process various forms of learner data which extends beyond academic results into observation of student behavior alongside emotional responses and social behavior as well as biological feedback. Time-dependent learning needs of students will be automatically processed by AI systems through the integration of deep learning algorithms and reinforcement learning models. Baker et al. (2024) forecast how future AI tutors should modify their educational approach by recognizing detailed thinking patterns in combination with mental workloads and psychological student states throughout instruction.

AI tutors which display emotional intelligence represent an especially attractive research direction in educational development. The affective computing systems will use voice modulation as well as facial expressions and typing speed and physiological signals to detect and interpret learner emotions.

Trouble signs such as frustration or boredom or confusion will trigger emotionally aware chatbots to deliver motivational content while modifying task difficulty along with offering additional activities. A study by D'Mello and Graesser (2023) highlights the positive impact of emotionally responsive educational technologies on learner persistence and satisfaction. Future AI tutors will combine educational information with empathetic support in order to develop an emotionally supportive learning space for students.

AI education is enlarging to include Augmented Reality and Virtual Reality as it combines with these entrancing technologies. AI tutors placed in virtual environments give learners an opportunity to work with virtual agents when conducting activities which replicate actual real-world situations. Students studying medicine can work with an AI instructor through a digital anatomy lab where they handle three-dimensional body parts to get instant evaluation from the system. Language education becomes possible when learners talk to AI avatars which reside in digital foreign cities to boost their capabilities in dealing with foreign language and understanding foreign cultures. Research by Johnson et al. (2023) demonstrates that entrancing academical environments equipped with intellectual tutoring systems leading to better learner engagement and greater retention over time. Mobile Virtual Reality and Augmented Reality tools allow extraneous institutions together with remote students who have limited access to resources to experience intelligent interactive education and assessments.

The development of collaborative AI tutors represents an innovation which enables support of group learning through peer collaboration. New generation AI agents will help group dynamics by assigning roles and performing moderation and conflict resolution while combining group member responses into unified answers. Groups involved in collaborative problem-solving benefit from these digital facilitators in STEM discussions that require critical thinking and peer discussion between participants.An evaluation by Baker & Andriessen (2022) indicates that Artificial Intelligence assisted combined learning improves academic outcomes while nurturing the socio-emotional capabilities of its participants including compassion as well as teamwork and negotiation skills.

The deep embedment of AI chatbots in educational systems will strengthen their connection to learning analytics dashboards so teachers and administrators achieve better data-based choices. The teaching staff will access immediate information about student involvement together with understanding markers and learning barriers that need intervention. The combination of AI-enhanced analytics will transition from reactive to predictive functionality since it will identify students with risk potentials of academic failure before their situations reach critical stages. The authors at Siemens & Long (2021) highlight predictive analytics' rising significance in education because artificial intelligence networks help process complicated datasets for generating warning systems and learning prescriptions for specific students.

Educational records are enhanced through the combination of blockchain technologies with AI chatbots which produces secure and tamper-proof transparent educational records. The secure digital ledger architecture distributes power among multiple systems which enables educational data storage for learners' credentials alongside their coursework and feedback and assessments. The artificial intelligence tutors have the capability to record educational achievements and milestones through blockchain-backed portfolios which learners use to present to employers or educational institutions. Such a development has the potential to revolutionize informal and lifelong learning by creating a tamper-proof system of collecting extended educational information beyond conventional academic documents.

AI tutors of the future need to develop capabilities for cultural adaptation together with linguistic inclusiveness due to both language and cultural factors. Multilingual neural processing structures coupled with understanding cultural backgrounds enable chatbots to serve students from various locations and socioeconomic situations and multilingual environments. The AI tutor system now operates across more than 100 languages because of the advancements made at Google through Multilingual BERT and Meta with SeamlessM4T. Upcoming educational systems will understand the need to transform their pedagogical approaches through cultural values and learning traditions as well as cognitive styles. The election of AI-powered education across various institutions will produce major reductions in educational gaps which exist worldwide.

Las time AI tutors together with chatbots are expected to become major contributors to continuous learning efforts as well as professional development training which will respond to rapidly shifting work environments. The changing nature of industry demands that people maintain ongoing access to adapted educational courses delivered precisely when they need them. The AI tutor system functionally acts as both career mentor and skill evaluator along with learning partner to direct people through industry-specific education paths. The World Economic Forum (2024) believes that by 2030 more than half of all employees will need new skills thus AI-powered learning methods will become essential for their education

Artificial Intelligence progress in education creates both positive learning opportunities and important discussions about moral responsibilities as well as privacy standards requirements. Public concerns now focus on surveillance practices along with improper data handling and how chatbots affect equitable learning experiences since they have become more influential in student learning paths. Advanced technological systems need development through the essential implementation of visibility and voluntary agreement criteria alongside unbiased algorithmic instructions. The EU AI Act together with OECD AI Principles will direct responsible AI educational tool development by maintaining human rights protections and social justice principles.

The following years will bring great promise to the educational use of AI tutors together with chatbots. These innovations including emotional chatbots with immersive learning areas and predictive analytics along with global learning potential are changing education by improving learning processes while changing our native educational concepts. Artificial intelligence systems will enhance human educators rather than replace them because these advancements provide teachers freedom from non-essential duties to concentrate on developing relationships while promoting creativity. Continuous research combined with ethical monitoring and press for inclusive development will ensure that AI in education builds up a more equal adaptive exciting educational framework which serves students worldwide.

CONCLUSION

Entangling artificial intelligence through tutors and chatbots establishes itself as the leading educational advancement of current times. Artificial Intelligence has changes educational delivery and support using its development from rule based systems such as ELIZA toward contemporary adaptive and data driven conversational platforms like ChatGPT and Ada and Socratic. AI tutors along with chatbots create both technological and educational changes that benefit mainstream learning objectives while maximizing accessibility and personalization as well as learning efficiency.

Scientists have proven through academic sources alongside multiple case studies that AI educational tools provide valuable benefits to various educational disciplines. The students obtain tailored support along with instant performance assessments in interactive learning spaces which create self-motivated environments for critical thinking development. Educational staff experience both administrative relief together with valuable data-based recommendations that support individualized teaching approaches which enhance student results. Research institutions seeking inclusive education capabilities now possess the ability to distribute their resources across populations efficiently and sustain academic guidance programs after standard school hours.

The research studies by Labadze et al. (2023) and Usher & Barak (2024) together with Urban et al. (2023) establish AI chatbot integration as a pedagogically effective method that satisfies student learning needs. The technological applications at Singapore Institute of Technology together with the emotionally capable AI agents for virtual learning demonstrate both flexibility and wide-ranging use features. Upcoming advancements specifies that combining Artificial Intelligence technology with entrancing systems along with blockchain and multilingual Natural Language Processing and emotion detection will lead to better academical opportunities which will be more accessible for public.

The technological changes require recognition of both its advantages alongside the built-in difficulties which arise from these transformations. Current AI technology successfully performs human-supervised educational functions through simulation yet does not possess full capability in matters of empathy nor full context understanding nor ethical decision skills which education typically requires. The interpersonal aspects which human educators exercise within classroom relationships exceed the capabilities of advanced AI tutors to fully emulate. The educational worry about data privacy problems and algorithmic errors as well as lack of algorithmic perception and unclear system conduct needs thorough regulatory protection and permanent ethical oversight.

In many ways, the strengths of AI also reveal its boundaries. The effective transmission of educational information does not automatically translate into wisdom regarding effective pedagogical methods. Learning path personalization competencies of AI need to be evaluated against possible adverse effects of student loneliness or conceptual disintegration. The ability of AI chatbots to handle queries and plan learning subjects remains in contrast to their inability to create values and develop interpersonal ties or handle non-verbal signals which direct human teachers during classroom interactions.

As such the upcoming solution needs to embrace harmonious blending of old and new instead of complete replacement. Accounting professionals should view AI tutors and chatbots as supplementary educational tools which enhance traditional classroom learning instead of replacing it. The technology provides accessible flexible learning solutions which reach their peak effectiveness by being part of an integrated blended education approach. The combination of AI tools with human-led education enables students to access AI strengths such as data analysis along with human instructor elements including discourse and emotional support.

Educational stakeholders must keep developing a reflective and inclusive attitude toward implementing AI during future years. Technology development with technical personnel and educational leaders and public officials together with student users will help create AI tools that provide ethical operation combined with clear monitoring and fair distribution. The investment in digital literacy education with appropriate infrastructure development along with training professionals will allow teachers and students to maximize their usage of tools without abuse.

The opportunities offered by AI tutors along with chatbots for education are so significant that they deserve implementation despite their inability to fully replicate traditional classrooms. Instead of threatening education these tools function as tools which enhance learning systems through individualization and increased accessibility toward future learning needs. People must pursue technological advancement alongside human-centered practices and ethical management in order to envision an inclusive learning future for tomorrow.

When education systems worldwide build AI as both a performance enhancer and learner quality developer they turn this technology into an interactive force which improves teaching efficiency alongside learning quality in the educational framework. AI education holds its real promise through a promising trajectory which maintains equilibrium.

REFERENCES

AlAfnan, M. A., Dishari, S., Jovic, M., & Lomidze, K. (2023). Chatgpt as an educational tool: Opportunities, challenges, and recommendations for communication, business writing, and composition courses. *Journal of Artificial Intelligence and Technology*, *3*(2), 60–68.

Baker, M., & Andriessen, J. (2022). *Arguing to learn* (3rd ed.). The Cambridge Handbook of the Learning Sciences.

Baker, R. S., Ocumpaugh, J., & Andres, J. M. (2024). BROMP quantitative field observations: A review. In *Handbook of artificial intelligence in education* (pp. 132–156). Edward Elgar Publishing.

D'Mello, S. K., & Graesser, A. (2023). Intelligent tutoring systems: How computers achieve learning gains that rival human tutors. In *Handbook of educational psychology* (pp. 603–629). Routledge.

Essel, H. B., Osei-Poku, P., Acheampong, A., & Anning, A. (2022). Exploring the effectiveness of AI chatbots in higher education: A student-centered study. *Education and Information Technologies*, *27*(6), 8801–8822. DOI: 10.1007/s10639-022-11048-3

Harry, A., & Sayudin, S. (2023). Role of AI in education. [INJURITY]. *Interdiciplinary Journal and Hummanity*, *2*(3), 260–268. DOI: 10.58631/injurity.v2i3.52

Herft, A. (2023). A Teacher's Prompt Guide to ChatGPT aligned with 'What Works Best' Guide. Retrieved on January 23 2023 from https://drive.google.com/file/d/15qAxnUzOwAPwHzoaKBJd8FAgiOZYcIxq/view

Hew, K. F., Huang, W., Du, J., & Jia, C. (2021, August). Using chatbots in flipped learning online sessions: Perceived usefulness and ease of use. In *International Conference on Blended Learning* (pp. 164-175). Cham: Springer International Publishing.

Holmes, W., Porayska-Pomsta, K., Holstein, K., Sutherland, E., Baker, T., Shum, S. B., & Koedinger, K. R. (2022). Ethics of AI in education: Towards a community-wide framework. *International Journal of Artificial Intelligence in Education*, *32*(3), 504–526.

Krstić, L., Aleksić, V., & Krstić, M. (2022). Artificial intelligence in education. *RE:view*.

Kuhail, M. A., Abdellatif, A., Shamsi, H., Alqudah, A. M., & Ali, R. (2023). Personalized chatbots to improve knowledge retention and learner engagement in higher education. *Education and Information Technologies*, *28*, 5781–5800. DOI: 10.1007/s10639-023-11797-3

Labadze, L., Grigolia, M., & Machaidze, L. (2023). Role of AI chatbots in education: Systematic literature review. *International Journal of Educational Technology in Higher Education*, *20*(1). Advance online publication. DOI: 10.1186/s41239-023-00426-1

Lin, H., & Mubarok, H. (2021). The impact of educational chatbots on students' writing performance and perception in EFL context. *Journal of Educational Computing Research*, *59*(6), 1110–1131. DOI: 10.1177/0735633121992221

Okonkwo, C. W., & Ade-Ibijola, A. (2021). Chatbots applications in education: A systematic review. *Computers and Education: Artificial Intelligence*, *2*, 100033. DOI: 10.1016/j.caeai.2021.100033

Rodríguez-García, J. M., Gutiérrez-Rangel, H. F., & Cisneros-Reyes, Y. D. (2023). LA INTELIGENCIA ARTIFICIAL: RETOS Y ACTUALIDADES RESPECTO A LA EDUCACIÓN SUPERIOR. *Aura M. Torres Reyes Reina Castellanos Vega Cristhian Bonilla Rodríguez Alberto Villa Valencia*, 19.

Tahiru, F. (2021). AI in education: A systematic literature review. [JCIT]. *Journal of Cases on Information Technology*, *23*(1), 1–20.

Urban, R., Kireš, M., & Hladká, A. (2023). Enhancing students' problem-solving and critical thinking skills through intelligent tutoring systems: A case study in secondary education. *Computers in Human Behavior Reports*, *9*, 100213. DOI: 10.1016/j.chbr.2022.100213

Usher, M., & Barak, M. (2024). Unpacking the role of AI ethics online education for science and engineering students. *International Journal of STEM Education*, *11*(1). Advance online publication. DOI: 10.1186/s40594-024-00493-4

Wollny, S., Schneider, J., Di Mitri, D., Weidlich, J., Rittberger, M., & Drachsler, H. (2021). Are we there yet?-a systematic literature review on chatbots in education. *Frontiers in Artificial Intelligence*, *4*, 654924. PMID: 34337392

Xie, T., & Pentina, I. (2022). Attachment theory as a framework to understand relationships with social chatbots: a case study of Replika.

Zawacki-Richter, O., Marín, V. I., Bond, M., & Gouverneur, F. (2019). Systematic review of research on artificial intelligence applications in higher education: Are the machines taking over? *International Journal of Educational Technology in Higher Education, 16*(1), 1–38. DOI: 10.1186/s41239-019-0171-0

Chapter 5

Enhancing History Education in Social Studies Through Artificial Intelligence:

Transforming Historical Inquiry Through Technology

Osman Sabanci
https://orcid.org/0000-0003-4711-0277
Gazi University, Turkey

Gülser Kutluay
Aksaray University, Turkey

ABSTRACT

This chapter explores how Artificial Intelligence (AI) can support history teaching within social studies education. The study involved 30 pre-service social studies teachers and aimed to understand their perspectives on the opportunities and challenges of using AI in history classrooms. It aimed to see how AI tools might foster student-centered learning, enhance historical thinking skills, and improve classroom practices. As a basic qualitative study, the data were analyzed through content analysis. Participants' opinions were organized into four main themes. While some emphasized AI's potential to boost student engagement and improve access to information, others raised concerns about content accuracy and ethical issues. The findings highlight that AI should not replace teachers but serve as a tool that

DOI: 10.4018/979-8-3373-2948-2.ch005

supports teaching when used thoughtfully and critically. The chapter offers reflections and recommendations for educators, pre-service social studies teachers, and policymakers on effectively integrating AI into history education.

1. INTRODUCTION

Throughout history, every technological breakthrough has reshaped the nature of education and learning methods. Today, Artificial Intelligence (AI) has become a powerful tool, particularly in history education, enabling student-centered and data-driven learning experiences. Learning no longer takes place solely within the classroom but also in digital and interactive environments. This section explores the transformative impact of AI technologies on history education in social studies from multiple perspectives.

Context of AI in Education

With the advent of the 21st-century, rapidly developing technology and increasingly difficult living conditions have created a global environment where borders have disappeared, creating the need for faster adaptation (Waruwu, 2024). The development of information and communication technologies has brought significant changes in various aspects of life, including education. One of the technological innovations that is currently attracting great interest is AI (Prasetyowati & Sunarti, 2024). Today, AI and its applications are coming to the forefront in industry and many other fields, such as energy, mining, agriculture, health, driver improvements, voice assistants, online chat and communication, and software development. With this area of influence, AI is also included in education (Arslan, 2020). In recent years, with the integration of AI into education, AI has entered a period of significant rise, transforming traditional pedagogical practices and promoting personalized learning experiences (Admane et al., 2024). AI is rapidly evolving as a force that can reshape our world, including education (Gidiotis & Hrastinski, 2024). In the context of the rapid development of AI, it is essential to examine the applications and regulations of AI in education (Nguyen, 2023). In addition to supporting learning, AI is effectively used in many different areas, such as teaching, assessment, classroom management, administrative work, teacher tasks, and school management (Arslan, 2020). AI technology has been widely applied in education, covering various aspects such as intelligent tutoring and personalized learning, teaching resources and content generation, teaching assistance and teacher support, and educational management and administrative automation (Li & Jiang, 2024).

Importance of Social Studies & History Education

AI-based applications have recently started to be used frequently in education. Although they have been used effectively, especially in language learning processes, they have also begun to be used in mathematics, science, classroom education, pre-school, and social studies courses (Yalçın, 2024). The social studies course is a course that students encounter in primary school years and learn basic knowledge, skills, values, and attitudes that they will need in their lives. This course, which includes various disciplines, provides students with a perspective on every issue concerning the individual and society (Yaşar, Köse, Göz & Bayır, 2015). Social studies, by its nature, aims to prepare students for the world they will encounter when they step into university, career, and social life. In a future dominated by AI, this preparation has reached a new level of importance (Levitt & Grubaugh, 2024; Luckin et al, 2016).

There has been a significant increase in AI-based applications, and social studies education, whose primary goal is to educate effective citizens, is affected by this situation. Social studies is an essential subject as it helps students understand the social, cultural, economic, and political dynamics that shape society. In this sense, a social studies course is a vital element for children to be aware of the world they live in, surrounded by AI, and to grow up as citizens who know how to use AI effectively (Jamilah & Halimah, 2024; Selanik-Ay, 2024; Yetişensoy & Rapoport, 2023).

Social studies education aims to develop students' understanding of social, economic, political, and environmental issues that are the basis of sustainable development. Applying AI in social studies learning environments can offer a new approach that can encourage students to think critically and innovatively about current global issues (Prasetyowati & Sunarti, 2024). In social studies education and the acquisition of knowledge and skills related to society, students can be introduced to current technologies by including AI in this process. In this way, students can gain social knowledge and values and the knowledge and skills required by the digital age (Seyhan, 2024).

Within the scope of social studies education, AI has the potential to play an active role in areas such as creating course materials, curriculum development, citizenship education, skills acquisition, value education, and assessment and evaluation. It is crucial that we carefully consider the potential of AI to address the challenges we face in social studies education and develop strategies for its effective integration into the classroom (Berson & Berson, 2023).

From immersive virtual tours to adaptive learning platforms, research shows that integrating AI tools offers a range of benefits aligned with the identified goals of social studies learning. Research suggests that AI holds the key to enriching and personalizing the study of history, geography, and civics for students (Grubaugh & Levitt, 2024).

Social sciences, including geography, sociology, anthropology, and economics, require a holistic and interactive approach. AI enables the development of learning tools tailored to individual student needs, provides immediate feedback, and supports learning experiences through digital platforms that facilitate collaboration between students from diverse backgrounds. Technologies such as Virtual Reality (VR) and simulations also enrich students' understanding of social, cultural, and historical dynamics (Susyanah & Fajar, 2024). While AI can enrich the social science learning process by providing more comprehensive data and analysis and helping students gain a more comprehensive understanding of social phenomena through simulations and predictive models, these technological advances also present significant challenges. One of the main challenges is how social science education can continue to instill moral, ethical, and human values amidst the increasingly dominant wave of digitalization. These values are necessary for raising individuals who are intellectually intelligent and have social sensitivity, ethical awareness, and critical thinking abilities (Nurhayati & Halimah, 2024).

Purpose & Research Questions

The educational environments of the 21st-century are transforming with the rapid development of digital technologies, and this transformation is restructuring many areas, from teaching methods to content presentation, from assessment methods to student participation. AI technologies, at the center of this digital transformation, have the potential to make learning processes more flexible, personalized, and interactive by being integrated into the education system. This book chapter aims to comprehensively examine how AI can play a role in teaching history subjects within the scope of social studies.

In this context, the main purpose of the chapter is to analyze the contributions of AI-supported teaching applications to improving the quality of history education in a multidimensional way and to provide a framework for including these technologies in educational processes. History teaching is a discipline that aims to develop historical thinking skills, establish cause-and-effect relationships between events, and gain the ability to make multi-faceted analyses beyond simply conveying information about the past. In this context, the contributions of AI technologies to history teaching processes through student-centered learning, individualized guidance, feedback, gamification, big data analysis, and virtual simulation will be evaluated in detail.

The book section is structured under six main headings. First, a theoretical framework will be presented on how AI is positioned in educational environments, specifically, in the context of social studies. Then, the relationship between AI-supported applications in teaching history subjects and student-centered learning and historical thinking skills will be examined. In the third section, concrete examples will be discussed through applications such as individualized learning paths, game-based learning, data-based analyses, and virtual history experiences. In the fourth section, the advantages offered by AI in history teaching and the ethical, pedagogical, and technical limitations it may present will be discussed. In the fifth section, scenarios and predictions regarding how AI technologies may shape the future of history teaching are shared. In the final section, a general evaluation of AI integration into history education is presented, along with concrete suggestions for teachers, students, and policymakers. Throughout these sections, preliminary findings from a related research project have also been thoughtfully integrated into the relevant discussions, enriching the analysis with real-world reflections from pre-service social studies teachers.

This book section aims to make a theoretical and practical contribution to the field by revealing how AI-supported learning environments can be integrated with history education. It is intended to be a guiding resource for social studies teachers, history teachers, pre-service teachers, educational technology experts, and policymakers. It also aims to shed light on research gaps that will guide future studies in social studies education.

This small-scale study aims to investigate the application of AI in teaching history within social studies and to explore the opportunities and limitations of AI-supported history education, as perceived by pre-service social studies teachers. Additionally, the thoughts of pre-service social studies teachers regarding the future of AI-supported history education are also included. In this context, answers to the following research questions were sought:

1. How do pre-service social studies teachers view the use of AI in teaching history topics?
2. What are the main advantages that AI applications can provide in history education?
3. What are the main challenges that may be encountered in AI-supported history education?
4. How do pre-service social studies teachers assess the future of AI-supported history education?

2. METHODOLOGY

The Methodology section comprises five subheadings: research design, participants, sampling, ethics, and data collection & analysis.

Research Design

This study, which aims to reveal the views of pre-service social studies teachers on AI-supported history education, uses a basic qualitative research design. This design focuses on how the research participants interpret their experiences, what they create, and what meaning they attach to their experiences (Merriam & Tisdell, 2016).

Participants

The study group consisted of thirty pre-service social studies teachers from two public universities in Türkiye. Of the participants, 10 (33.3%) were male and 20 (66.7%) were female. In terms of their academic standing, 10 participants were in their fourth year of study, while the remaining 20 were in their third year. This composition provided a purposeful yet diverse group, including opinions from individuals at different stages of their teacher education process.

Sampling

Participants were selected through purposive sampling, specifically employing criterion sampling (Creswell & Creswell, 2018) to ensure that all individuals possessed the necessary characteristics relevant to the study's objectives. These criteria included being actively enrolled as pre-service social studies teachers, voluntarily participating in the study, and providing complete responses to the interview questions.

Ethics

Participation in the study was entirely voluntary, and written informed consent was obtained from all participants before data collection. Ethical approval was granted by the Gazi University Ethics Commission, which reviewed the study on July 29, 2025 (Research Code: 2025-1348). All procedures were conducted by established principles of confidentiality and anonymity.

Data Collection & Analysis

To ensure the internal validity of the interview form, expert opinions were obtained from two scholars in the field of social sciences, one in computer technologies, and one in linguistics. Based on their feedback, necessary revisions were made, and the form was finalized accordingly. The interview form consists of two parts. The first part includes demographic questions (gender, university, and previous participation in any project or research related to history teaching). The second part contains four open-ended questions focusing on using AI in teaching history topics in social studies. The data were collected using this semi-structured interview form and analyzed through content analysis. The findings were categorized under four main themes: the benefits of AI-assisted history teaching, the opportunities it presents, the threats and limitations it entails, and participants' views on its future. The responses given by participants to the open-ended questions in the interview form were coded by two researchers. To determine the reliability of the qualitative analysis, the Miles and Huberman (1994) model (Reliability = Consensus / Consensus + Disagreement) was applied. As a result of the calculation, the research reliability was determined as .96, indicating that the research results were highly reliable. To ensure the credibility of the research, a purposive sampling method was used; consistency checks were performed; and direct quotations from participant statements were included (Yıldırım & Şimşek, 2021). Participants were represented by randomly assigned numbers (e.g., P1) in the coding and direct quotations.

3. THEORETICAL FOUNDATIONS

AI in Digital Education

When the historical development of AI is analyzed, it is seen that it has caused a great change in education by bringing theories and technologies together, and this change will continue at every stage of the teaching process (Arslan, 2020). Accordingly, the main role of AI in education is to assist in educational activities and support teachers in areas such as automatic grading, providing smart assistant support, and contributing to professional development (Holmes, Bialik, & Fadel, 2019; Li & Jiang, 2024). In recent decades, successful and viable solutions to intelligent learning environments have been mainly in formal education, usually in school or university settings. In the coming decades, AI in education is believed to become strongly entrenched in the wider educational environment in terms of various learning contexts such as informal learning, adult education, and professional learning (Frasson, 2023).

Incorporating AI into classrooms has far-reaching implications. AI can personalize learning experiences and tailor content to the needs of individual learners, thus improving engagement and learning outcomes; it can also automate administrative tasks, enabling educators to focus on teaching (Jaramillo & Chiappe, 2024).

AI has the potential to revolutionize the way we teach and learn by providing tools that can improve the effectiveness and efficiency of the educational process (Prasetyowati & Sunarti, 2024). Test results among students confirmed that integrating AI into the learning process improves the quality of knowledge (Liu & Yushchik,

2024). AI can generate a variety of materials according to course requirements, student interests, and learning levels, such as creating personalized textbooks to meet the different needs of students, automatically generating exercises on targeted academic exercises according to students‘ learning progress and weak points, creating various multimedia teaching resources such as videos, audio, animations, and providing teaching resource suggestions according to students' interests and needs (Li & Jiang, 2024).

Educators should also consider the benefits of using AI in the classroom, such as providing immediate feedback and developing students' critical thinking skills. The challenge is to find the right balance that embraces the potential of technology while maintaining the integrity of the education system (Berson & Berson, 2023). As technology advances and new possibilities emerge, it is our collective responsibility to shape the future of AI in a way that preserves the values of equity, inclusion, and ethical behavior in education (Akyel & Tur, 2024). Ensuring a balanced and ethical integration of AI will be critical to fostering a positive future where human and AI contributions are valued and used effectively (Silva-Pina, Prazeres, Viana, Ohanma & Pereira, 2024). AI will continue to increase its potential to transform education in the following four areas: firstly, one-to-one and effective support and differentiated and individualised learning can be provided to students with AI during teaching; secondly, tests and assessments can gain a new dimension with AI for both students and instructors; thirdly, feedback, which has a significant place in education, can be automated in line with the needs of students with AI (Arslan, 2020).

Student-Centered & Personalized Learning

The phenomenon of student-centered education has been a significant focus on the education agenda for many years. The evolving nature of teaching and learning has increasingly positioned student-centered education at the core of contemporary instructional practices (Sarpkaya & Yılmaz, 2021). Student-centered learning models promote active student participation, emphasize individual learning needs, and foster greater student responsibility, all aimed at enhancing the effectiveness of the learning process (Aldemir, Caner, Akın & Kaplan, 2024).

Technological advances have opened new avenues for engagement across all learning contexts, creating a need to understand how technology influences the interactions between students and teachers within student-centered environments (Briskin & Land, 2020). The roles of teachers and technology are pivotal in the teaching-learning process as they significantly impact student outcomes. Today's teachers are expected to integrate technology into their instruction and guide students in effectively using technology for learning (Alpar, Batdal & Avcı, 2012).

Student-centered learning personalizes education through competency-based approaches, supported by blended and online learning formats and a broader range of resources and learning options. This model emphasizes student ownership of learning, where students share responsibility with teachers, parents, and other supporters. Teachers leverage technology to analyze real-time data to differentiate instruction, customize learning paths, and deepen student engagement. Meanwhile, students use technology to focus on their learning goals, access resources, collaborate, communicate, and demonstrate evidence of their learning.

AI has emerged as a transformative force in education, revolutionizing traditional teaching methods and paving the way for more personalized, student-centered learning experiences. Among the various AI applications in education, Intelligent Tutoring Systems (ITS) have garnered considerable attention for their ability to adapt to individual learning needs, provide immediate feedback, and boost student engagement. Unlike conventional education models that rely on standardized instruction, ITS utilizes AI-driven algorithms to tailor learning experiences according to students' cognitive abilities, learning styles, and progress. By integrating machine learning, natural language processing, and data analytics, these systems create dynamic and interactive environments that promote deeper understanding and knowledge retention. Implementing AI-powered ITS has been shown to increase motivation, improve retention, and support diverse learning styles. Furthermore, by analyzing student interactions, ITS can predict learning difficulties, recommend remediation, and optimize curriculum delivery (Ali, 2024; Glowa & Goodell, 2016; VanLehn, 2011).

The student-centered learning approach in AI-supported history teaching is a technological innovation and a pedagogical transformation. This transformation appears to have substantial potential for students to access historical knowledge, construct knowledge, and develop their multidimensional thinking skills. Further exploration of this potential at the academic level is vital in improving the quality of history education.

Historical Thinking Skills

Historical thinking involves using evidence to confirm or challenge specific facts about the past, understanding that historical narratives are not mere reflections of isolated facts but are constructed interpretations developed over time. It requires imagining past situations that cannot be directly experienced and forming hypotheses about the multiple causes behind historical events. This process demands precise definitions of abstract concepts, awareness of how their meanings evolve, evaluation of how hypotheses align with facts, analysis of change and continuity, and comprehension of time-related ideas such as duration, sequence, and temporal frameworks (Carretero & Gartner, 2024).

History education effectively develops thinking skills and emphasizes the importance of integrating history education into the curriculum (Lee, 2023). Historical thinking is a valuable and useful approach to teaching and learning history, and historical thinking is of great importance in the theory and practice of history education (Bussell, 2024; Ofianto, Aman, Ningsih, & Abidin, 2022).

Teachers' aim to incorporate historical thinking skills into their lessons expresses an awareness of preparing students to meet the needs of 21st-century education. The education should prepare young generations to think creatively and critically in the face of the world's rapid and continuous change (Maria, Ahmad, & Awang, 2019). The importance of teaching historical thinking skills has never been greater as we prepare our students for a world where they will encounter misinformation like never before (Lyell, 2024). With the advancement of AI, historical thinking becomes even more critical as chatbots are revealed to be capable of analyzing, synthesizing, interpreting, and writing similarly to humans (Tirado-Olivares, Navío-Inglés, O'Connor-Jiménez & Cózar-Gutiérrez, 2023). If the teacher does not know what students think, they may not have the opportunity to correct misconceptions and stereotypes. Identifying how students think about the discipline of history is a crucial element in developing students' historical thinking skills. Teachers may miss opportunities to correct misconceptions and stereotypes without insight into students' thinking. Therefore, understanding how students conceptualize history is crucial for effectively developing their historical thinking skills (Viator, 2012).

The intersection between generative AI and making sense of the past has created fertile ground for reflection on how digital developments shape how we understand, communicate, and teach history in the digital age. From the earliest cave paintings to contemporary museums, humans have played a unique role in preserving and disseminating our past: our cognitive abilities, or what we might call ‘natural intelligence’, give us as a species a unique ability to represent historical events in different formats. Today, AI-powered chatbots such as ChatGPT appear to simulate a critical thinking process on a text and go beyond facts and data. It is possible to say that ChatGPT is capable of writing an argumentative text based on a historical source and grounding its writing in dimensions of historical thought. In addition, extending the information provided to AI during the development of argumentative texts to historical thought may help to learn more about the potential and shortcomings of AI productions in terms of this historical competence. Knowing the extent to which this tool can produce historical argumentative text can lead users to use it to develop their writing skills when asked to produce historical argumentative text and their historical thinking skills. An interactive approach to questioning AI products can facilitate the application of skills specific to the history discipline, encourage critical reflection on the information obtained (Carretero & Gartner, 2024; Tirado-Olivares et al., 2023). Students who do not identify themselves as belonging to groups that are invisible in history, have had agency in the past, or have power in the present, often lack role models for the future (Levstik & Barton, 2015, p. 3). In this sense, inclusive historical narratives are essential for fostering a future-oriented and empowered civic identity.

4. AI APPLICATIONS IN HISTORY EDUCATION

Digitalization affects every aspect of our lives, and from the perspective of the discipline of history, it is a process that profoundly affects the ontology, epistemology, methodology, writing, and education of history (Altun, 2022). Today, teaching various subjects, especially history, based on traditional methods, including those that cause students to be immobilized in the classroom, is outdated and has many shortcomings in the teaching process (Yawar & Amany, 2025). The traditional methods previously used in teaching history (reading paragraphs, taking notes, memorizing dates, using printed maps, or atlases) have become outdated and ineffective (Malysheva, Tokareva, Orchakova, & Smirnova, 2022). Long-standing traditional teaching methods, based on teacher presentations and student memorization of content, are becoming increasingly less relevant in environments where knowledge is readily available from AI chatbots. In the age of AI, students have new roles to play, and teachers have new skills to teach, making it critical to reconsider how teaching and learning take place in History classrooms (Trust & Maloy, 2023). History didactics has changed as part of pedagogy development in this century. Teaching styles and methods that involve students in the learning process are being incorporated into history teaching. Within the framework of this principle, efforts are made to use modern technology (Mottl & Musílek, 2024).

Since history class deals with the history of people and societies that do not exist today, it is difficult for the student to understand it. To solve such problems, new educational phenomena such as AI can be used, although its use in history education is still in the early stages (Mottl & Musílek, 2024; Yawar & Amany, 2025).

4.1 Personalized & Adaptive Learning

In an era marked by rapid technological advancements and the growing importance of 21st-century skills alongside environmental awareness, education systems face the challenge of delivering personalized learning experiences that cater to individual student needs while fostering critical thinking, problem-solving skills, and environmental consciousness. The quality of education largely depends on the quality of available learning content and the effectiveness of personalized recommendations guiding each student toward the most suitable learning materials. At this intersection of AI and education, new opportunities emerge to create customized learning experiences aligned with diverse student preferences and goals. Enabling personalized education is considered one of AI's most vital contributions to the field (Caro, Quitian, Giraldo & Lengua-Cantero, 2023; Maghsudi, Lan, Xu & van Der Schaar, 2021). As educational institutions strive to meet the varied needs of learners, AI-based systems have become powerful tools to tailor curriculum according to individual learning styles, preferences, and paces (Admane, Sawale, Jayasree, Kurup & Thomas, 2024; Sundari, Penthala & Nayyar, 2024).

AI technologies can adapt educational content and activities to students' unique learning styles, preferences, and performance levels (Silva-Pina, Prazeres, Viana, Ohanma & Pereira, 2024). In particular, research on promoting self-regulated learning highlights AI-based environments' capacity to support students in planning, monitoring, and evaluating their learning processes (Mojolou et al., 2024).

The goal of personalized learning is to design a powerful pathway for knowledge acquisition that leverages a student's strengths and compensates for their weaknesses, ultimately enabling them to reach their learning goals (Maghsudi, Lan, Xu, & van Der Schaar, 2021). With its ability to process vast amounts of data and adapt in real-time, AI offers unprecedented opportunities to revolutionize personalized learning. Through complex algorithms, machine learning, and data analytics, AI assesses student performance, identifies learning gaps, and dynamically adjusts instructional content and strategies to meet individual needs. This capability extends beyond simple customization, allowing AI to predict future learning challenges, recommend specific resources, and create novel educational experiences aligned with a student's learning style and pace. Moreover, AI-powered personalized learning can support teachers by providing them with actionable insights into their students' progress, enabling more informed and effective instructional interventions. In this way, AI personalizes students' learning experience and allows educators to deliver more targeted and effective instruction (Mahmoud & Sørensen, 2024).

There is a growing necessity to develop personalized and sustainable AI-based learning models tailored for individual digital education (Qushwa & Onia, 2024). Such systems generate customized learning pathways that consider students' prior knowledge, interests, and goals, enabling progression at a preferred pace while addressing strengths and weaknesses, especially in science proficiency (Yılmaz, 2024).

One of AI's most impactful applications in education is the creation of adaptive learning systems that personalize educational experiences according to each student's needs. These systems use machine learning algorithms, data analytics, and adaptive technologies to assess students' learning styles, strengths, and challenges, providing tailored content, recommendations, and immediate feedback. These individualized learning solutions address the limitations of traditional classroom instruction, where uniform teaching strategies fail to accommodate varying learning speeds and preferences. With AI-powered tools such as intelligent tutoring systems, computerized testing, and virtual learning assistants, students receive personalized guidance to learn at their own pace and deepen their understanding (Saleem, Aziz, Iqbal & Abbas, 2025). AI meets learners where they are by delivering content suited to visual, auditory, or kinesthetic learning preferences—for instance, offering interactive multimedia for visual learners and audio-enhanced content for auditory learners (Sundari, Penthala & Nayyar, 2024).

Additionally, AI assists teachers in crafting customized lessons for individual students, facilitating the management of larger groups while maintaining personalized support. The rapid advancement of AI enables the design of unique educational plans for each learner (Kaswan, Dhatterwal & Ojha, 2024; Sundari, Penthala & Nayyar, 2024). AI systems analyze extensive data on student performance, engagement, and learning behaviors, allowing educators to tailor content and methodologies to meet specific student needs. For example, AI algorithms can detect knowledge gaps, predict future outcomes, and recommend targeted resources and instructional strategies. By leveraging these insights, educators can foster adaptive learning environments that encourage individualized learning paths and enhance student motivation and autonomy (Admane, Sawale, Jayasree, Kurup, & Thomas, 2024). Using personalization strategies, students' interests and needs can be better met, and learning outcomes can be improved (Kaswan, Dhatterwal & Ojha, 2024).

Generative AI assists students by providing direct solutions, instructional cues, and intuitive dialogues, ultimately providing a more engaging and responsive learning environment. As we advance, educators and students are encouraged to explore innovative ways to implement generative AI in educational contexts, utilizing its unique capabilities to maximize personalized learning benefits. (Wei, Jiang, Liu, Qi, Jia, & Jia, 2025).

Social studies is significant because it helps students understand the social, cultural, economic, and political dynamics that shape society. However, traditional approaches to teaching social studies are often thought to be less effective in engaging students and less able to meet individual learning needs. Therefore, there is a need for innovative strategies that can benefit from AI technology to increase student engagement and personalize learning experiences. The application of AI in social studies education can provide several advantages. AI can be used to make learning more adaptive, where technology can adjust content and teaching methods to the student's abilities and needs. This increases the effectiveness of learning and allows students to learn at their own pace, ultimately improving overall learning outcomes (Muqorrobin, Arifin, Wutsqah & Uulanian, 2024; Jamilah & Halimah, 2024). While future AI developments promise further personalization in science education, realizing these benefits requires addressing challenges such as ethical implementation and equitable access to technology. Ongoing evaluation of AI's impact on educational outcomes and proactive management of deployment barriers will be essential (Yılmaz, 2024).

The impact of AI on education, particularly history teaching, is expanding rapidly with the emergence of advanced generative AI tools. The widespread use of AI invites a reconsideration of teaching and learning methods in history classrooms. Incorporating AI chatbots like ChatGPT and DeepSeek into history education can involve collaborative exploration of AI's capabilities and limitations with students, designing student-centered AI activities, employing AI to uncover hidden or untold histories, and using AI-generated texts as historical resources for analysis (Trust & Maloy, 2023). Concurrently, AI presents new possibilities for evaluating students' historical writing and enhancing assessment practices (Bertram, Weiss, Zachrich, & Ziai, 2021).

4.2 AI-Driven Feedback Systems

In general terms, feedback functions as a regulatory mechanism that helps learners close or narrow the gap between their current level of knowledge and the desired or targeted level (Rajaram, 2023). Feedback plays several critical roles in the learning process, including supporting learning performance (Orhan Özen & Çubukçu, 2022), confirming whether students are on the right track, alerting them to misunderstandings, and guiding them toward mastery (Doyle & Doyle, 2020; Lyell, 2024).

Although most agree on the importance of feedback, learners often express dissatisfaction when feedback is not provided promptly or when it is vague and incomprehensive from their perspective—such as being student-centered, highlighting strengths and weaknesses, and offering suggestions for improvement (Doyle & Doyle, 2020; Nyugen, 2023).

Individualized feedback is an approach that adapts feedback methods to the learner's preferences and needs (Orhan Özen & Çubukçu, 2022). Its goal is to enhance the learning experience by tailoring information, feedback, and pacing to each individual (Dasam et al., 2024; Kuzminykh et al., 2024; Sivakumar & Harthy, 2024). This approach is particularly significant because it responds to each learner's unique characteristics and requirements, thereby making the learning process more effective (Cuevas, 2024). In support of individualized feedback, teachers are encouraged to utilize tools like ChatGPT to help students generate writing prompts, define new terms, find concrete examples of abstract concepts, and brainstorm essay ideas (Lyell, 2024).

With the advancement of Large Language Model (LLM) technologies, generative AI has emerged as a valuable resource for providing interactive, informed, and real-time feedback in response to user prompts (Kuzminykh et al., 2024). Feedback is a valuable component in online learning for students. Since instructor-student interaction is more limited in online programs, there is a greater need for comprehensive, timely, and relevant feedback in the learning process (Kuzminykh et al., 2024). For instance, a study involving social studies students revealed that traditional feedback methods were insufficient in helping learners understand texts and acquire content knowledge effectively. Inadequate feedback practices led to missed learning opportunities, underscoring the need for teachers to develop more effective feedback strategies (Hogan & Payne, 2024). AI developments enable the assessment of students' current learning status—including strengths, weaknesses, and general attitudes toward the course— creating personalized study plans. One example comes from AI-supported lessons in China, where monitoring devices track students' attention and provide immediate feedback to teachers (Sheng, 2023).

Luprichová (2025) highlighted that while AI tools grant efficient access to historical information, some students tend to over-rely on AI-generated content without critically evaluating its accuracy. The study emphasizes that structured peer review and feedback processes enhance historical reasoning and deepen analytical engagement. This underlines the importance of guiding students in AI literacy, resource evaluation, and the ethical use of AI. The significance of history education in the AI era is paramount for fostering critical thinking and ethical decision-making. Studying historical events and their societal impacts enables individuals to understand the consequences of technological advancements and better anticipate and mitigate potential risks associated with AI adoption. Furthermore, history learning offers a framework to comprehend the broader social implications of AI, assisting stakeholders in navigating the ethical complexities involved in AI development and deployment (Ni & Hassan, 2024).

4.3 Gamification & Game-Based Learning

Considering that today's generations are surrounded by information and communication technologies and spend a considerable amount of time on games (Ružic & Dumancic, 2015; Yıldırım & Servet, 2014), it has emerged that lessons need to be designed like a game to attract the attention of these students and involve them in the learning process (Yıldırım & Servet, 2014). Gamification and game-based learning are seen as effective factors in attracting the interest of these students, increasing their motivation, and ensuring greater participation (Lampropoulos & Kinshuk, 2024). Thanks to these approaches, learners can overcome the low motivation caused by feeling alone or not being guided, and a more engaging and interactive learning experience can be provided (Çöpgeven et al., 2023). In this context, AI-supported individualization, one of the technologically assisted learning strategies, comes to the fore.

AI (and its subset Machine Learning -ML) has made it possible to develop individualized learning environments in environments with large learner populations, such as open and distance learning, where it is impossible to create tailored instructional approaches for each learner. This paved the way for realizing learner-specific gamification (Çöpgeven et al., 2023). Two paramount concepts need to be explained here: Game-based learning and gamification. Explaining these two concepts in detail is vital for understanding the pedagogical foundations of AI-based applications.

Differentiating between gamification and game-based learning will be decisive in understanding the place of these technological applications in the educational context. Game-based learning is a pedagogical approach in which specially designed or adapted games are used to teach a subject or lesson. This is different from gamification, which adds game elements to an existing learning process (Yıldırım & Servet, 2014). Gamification represents using game mechanisms, design, and elements to encourage motivation, effort, and engagement in non-entertainment settings, but it does not necessarily imply creating a game (Ružic & Dumancic, 2015). In line with these concepts, focusing on the effects of AI-supported gamification applications on student-centered learning would be appropriate.

Having made this conceptual distinction, focusing specifically on how gamification synergizes with AI is necessary. Gamification has been found to positively affect students' willingness to learn by integrating game elements such as points, badges, and achievable levels. In this respect, gamification is a learning strategy that increases student engagement. AI enables gamification to be implemented more effectively in social studies education. With the support of AI, gamification strategies can be optimized through adaptive learning, which allows adjusting learning materials according to each student's abilities and learning pace (Jamilah & Halimah, 2024).

It is seen that gamification and game-based learning can be effective in individualized learning and interdisciplinary applications. It can be argued that the general benefits offered by gamification and game-based learning (increased interest, motivation, and engagement) can be applied to different fields of education such as history, and have similar positive effects (Lampropoulos & Kinshuk, 2024).

In this framework, some examples of AI-supported gamification and game-based learning applications in history teaching can be presented. For example, "Europe 2045" is an educational game designed for social sciences courses. Players act as representatives of European Union member states and make decisions by discussing political, economic, and social issues. The game offers multiplayer online video games and social role-playing games (Brom et al., 2010). A case study of a gamified learning strategy in history teaching was conducted with Spanish secondary school students. Through gamification features such as passports, rewards, digital museums, QR codes, and Breakout and Escape Rooms, students were actively engaged in the learning process as they explored historical artworks through a series of micro-projects. Each assignment increased student interest and engagement while promoting the learning of historical information. It provides a dynamic and successful example of how history education can proceed within a gamified framework (Corrales Serrano, 2023).

4.4 Big Data Analysis in Historical Inquiry

Although the cumulative growth of information in the historical process has become daunting for researchers and students in terms of coping with information, it is very pleasing for science, considering the vast collections of information accumulating in our libraries and increasingly coming online (Edelstein et al., 2017). Analyzing these masses of data and obtaining meaningful results from the analysis is impossible with classical data processing methods. This situation has led to big data and big data analysis. Since it facilitates the analysis of vast amounts of data, big data analysis provides excellent benefits for those who use it (Uladi & Arı, 2023).

The digitalization process has also profoundly affected the discipline of history. With digitalization in history, it is now necessary to focus on historical trends, cycles, and patterns rather than just examining individual events. Big data analysis is a powerful tool for detecting such trends and patterns (Altun, 2022). Big data is generated in many different types and formats, and no set rule exists among them. Data diversity is a measure of the richness of the data, such as text, images, video, and audio (Shu & Ye, 2023).

Within the scope of digital methodology, there are distant reading methods (such as content analysis, network analysis, text analysis, or sentiment analysis). These methods are used to analyze huge text sets such as big data and focus on large-scale patterns rather than individual documents (Altun, 2022). Regarding the use of these AI-supported tools in social studies courses, AI-based analytical tools such as data mining and predictive analysis can be used to examine historical events, social trends, and other social data in more depth (Shu & Ye, 2023; Yalçın, 2024).

Applications related to analyzing historical events with big data analysis will enable students to understand that period better. For example, analyzing newspapers from war periods with text mining can reveal the changing perceptions of the country over time. Or, in countries where migration movements are experienced, newspaper articles, headlines, interviews, reports, surveys, and social media trends can be analyzed over different periods through big data consisting of audio, video, and text, and the temporal change of citizens' attitudes and perceptions can be witnessed.

4.5 VR & AR in Historical Simulations

History lessons inherently include many areas where productive AI tools can be used. History educators who follow technology can benefit from AI tools in many areas, from content creation to contextual analysis. For example, under the guidance of history teachers, students can re-imagine historical scenarios, try to experience what happened thousands of years ago with realistic simulations, and try to concretize abstract concepts of the past with AI-supported drawing programs. The artifacts in ruins can be seen as they were thousands of years ago with mobile phone applications. In museums, 3D animations can be made for artifacts from ancient times that are difficult for many people (Erol Şahin, 2024). Furthermore, by integrating AI-supported Augmented Reality (AR) applications, students can interact with historical artifacts in a virtual environment, promoting deeper understanding and retention of historical concepts. The use of ChatGPT in history teaching can make a valuable contribution to the development of historical thinking as long as its potential and limitations as a pedagogical tool are considered (Carretero & Gartner, 2024). This innovative approach increases active engagement in the learning process and addresses learning barriers by making history more accessible and interactive (Najib, Supadi & Hamidah, 2024).

Virtual history tours and simulations in education are technological tools that increase students' interest, provide permanent learning, and help overcome physical limitations by making historical places and events tangible (Çığır Dikyol & Şar İşbilen, 2020; Sürme & Atılgan, 2020).

As a result of the integration of AI with VR and AR technologies, new ways for students to interact with content and explore complex concepts have begun to enter the field of education. As a result of this integration, the groundwork for creating personalized learning experiences has also emerged. AI-supported VR and AR experiences can offer students hands-on learning opportunities that adapt to their progress and performance in real-time (Mahmoud & Sørensen, 2024). For example, by using Gamified Virtual Reality (VR) applications in education, immersive, enjoyable, and fun environments can be created through these applications (Lampropoulos & Kinshuk, 2024). One of the focus areas of these VR applications is Cultural Heritage learning. Cultural Heritage often involves historical contexts and content, suggesting a potential connection between AI-enabled gamified VR and history teaching. In one study, concrete examples of how such an application was brought to life can be seen: For example, students, under the direction of history educators, can try to experience what happened thousands of years ago through lifelike simulations, re-imagine their historical circumstances, and use AI-powered drawing tools to concretize abstract historical concepts. Using mobile phone software, artifacts in ruins can be viewed as they were thousands of years ago. 3D animations can be created in museums for ancient artifacts that many people have difficulty understanding (Erol Şahin, 2024).

In an example of a study conducted in Türkiye (Çığır Dikyol & Şar İşbilen, 2020), the question of whether the use of VR applications in history courses can meet the expectations of pre-service teachers regarding these courses is sought. In the study, pre-service teachers who experienced Çatalhöyük-themed VR glasses (Virtual Reality application) mostly stated that the application was impressive and useful, made learning concrete, and provided permanent learning. The pre-service teacher participating in the study made the following statements regarding this issue (Çığır Dikyol & Şar İşbilen, 2020, p. 696):

> *"After wearing virtual glasses, the images that were always abstract in my head suddenly gained identity. People thousands of years ago, like us, had a house, a shelter, and a pantry where they could store their food to keep themselves safe. Seeing this, or rather witnessing it, excited me a lot."*

Such practices can improve the quality and efficiency of history education and offer promising opportunities for the future. One such example is the integration of AI in teaching historical topics within social studies, where AI is utilized to create interactive timelines, simulate historical events, and personalize learning experiences based on students' needs. Figure 1 presents an overview of the opportunities that AI offers to enhance the teaching of historical topics within social studies.

Figure 1. AI-supported history teaching practices in social studies

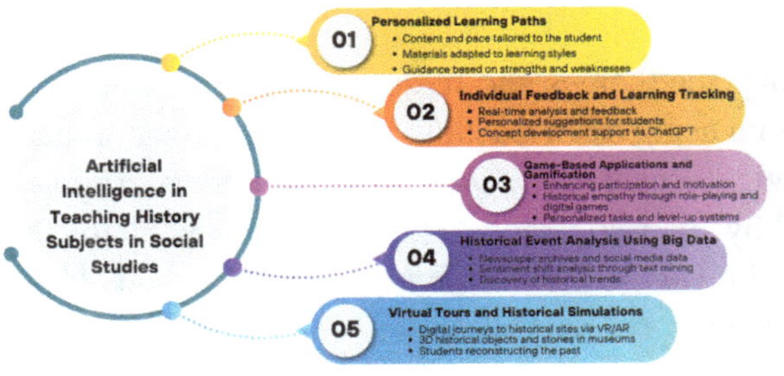

The applications of AI technologies in social studies and history instruction are summarized in Figure 1. Strategies include game-based applications, big data analysis, virtual historical simulations, tailored learning pathways, and individual feedback systems that enhance student engagement and promote the development of historical thinking skills.

5. RESULTS

Themes and Supporting Evidence from Pre-Service Teachers

This section presents data obtained from pre-service social studies teachers related to the research questions, organized into themes and supported by direct quotations and frequency tables.

Results Related to the First Sub-Problem

The analysis of pre-service social studies teachers' views on the use of AI in the teaching of history topics in the first sub-problem of the study is shown in Table 1.

Table 1. Pre-service social studies teachers' views on the use of AI in the teaching of history topics

Theme	*f*	Theme	*f*
Quick and easy access to information	6	Reenactment of historical events	3
The potential of AI to facilitate education	5	Cognitive and learning processes	3
Versatile functionality of AI	5	Infrastructure and technological challenges	2
Critical and ethical approaches	4	Decline in reading rates	1
The inevitable necessity of AI in education	3		
Total			32

Table 1 shows the themes and frequencies related to pre-service social studies teachers' views on using AI in teaching history. The most frequently repeated theme among pre-service teachers was '*Quick and easy access to information*' (f=6), which was mentioned by six participants. This was followed by the themes '*The potential of Artificial Intelligence to facilitate education*' (f=5) and '*The multifunctionality of Artificial Intelligence*' (f=5). The themes '*Reenactment of historical events*' (f=3), '*The inevitable necessity of AI in education*' (f=3), and '*Cognitive and learning processes*' (f=3) were mentioned by three participants each. In addition, the themes '*Critical and ethical approaches*' (f=4), '*Infrastructure and technological challenges*' (f=2), and '*Decline in reading rates*' (f=1) were also among the other important topics discussed. These results indicate that pre-service social studies teachers have diverse perspectives on the impact of AI on the educational processes of history subjects and particularly emphasise its potential for facilitating access to information and education. Participants' remarks reflecting these views include:

- *"It is a useful tool that provides speed and ease in accessing information."* (P16)
- *"When used correctly, it helps users access information and reach accurate knowledge."* (P23)

Results Related to the Second and Third Sub-Problem

In the second and third sub-problems of the study, the analysis of pre-service social studies teachers' views on the advantages and challenges of using AI in the teaching of history topics is presented in Table 2.

Table 2. Pre-service social studies teachers' views on the advantages and challenges of using AI in teaching history

Advantages	*f*	Challenges	*f*
Concretisation, visual-auditory and interactive learning in history teaching	22	Information reliability and misleading content risk	16
Increasing interest and motivation in history teaching	9	Access and technology proficiency issues	6
Quick access to information	6	Challenges in teaching history	4
AI supporting cognitive processes	6	Doubts about the learning activity and depth	4
Ensuring lasting learning	4	Digital content development issues	3
Enriched learning support	4	The influence of knowledgeable and conscious people	2
Supporting effective presentation	3	Other themes (single-frequency themes combined): Decreased teacher guidance, AI's insensitivity to individual differences, Ethical issues in AI use, Teaching through storytelling with AI, Technology addiction and laziness, Positive attitude towards AI	6
Summarising and scenario development	2		
Total	56	Total	41

Table 2 shows the themes and frequencies of pre-service social studies teachers' views on the advantages and challenges of using AI in history education. Among the advantages most frequently mentioned by the participants, *'Concretisation, visual-auditory and interactive learning in history education'* (f=22) stood out. This theme was followed by *'Increasing interest and motivation in history teaching'* (f=9) and *'Quick access to information'* (f=6). Additionally, themes such as *'Supporting cognitive processes with Artificial Intelligence'* (f=6), *'Ensuring lasting learning'* (f=4), *'Rich content learning support'* (f=4), *'Supporting effective narration'* (f=3), and *'Summarising and scenario development'* (f=2) were also mentioned as positive aspects of AI use by pre-service social studies teachers.

The most frequently repeated theme in the participants' disadvantage category was *'Information reliability and misleading content risk'* (f=16). This was followed by *'Access and technology proficiency issues'* (f=6), *'Challenges in history education'* (f=4), *'Doubts about learning effectiveness and depth'* (f=4), *'Digital content development issues'* (f=3), and *'The impact of knowledgeable and conscious people'* (f=2). Other challenges included *'Decreased teacher guidance'*, *'AI's insensitivity to individual differences'*, *'Ethical use issues of AI'*, *'Teaching through storytelling with AI'*, *'Technology addiction and laziness'*, and *'Positive attitude towards AI'*, which were expressed as single-frequency themes. Participants underlined that by giving abstract or remote notions a more concrete and relevant feel, AI could facilitate students' deeper engagement with historical material. A few examples are as follows:

- *"History topics often remain superficial for students. Thanks to AI, they can feel as if historical figures are alive today, which helps them interpret historical events more effectively."* (P7)
- *"It makes the topics more engaging and easier to understand. Both the teacher and the student can enjoy the learning process more."* (P24)

To the challenges of using AI in teaching history topics in social studies, pre-service teachers most frequently mentioned three key concerns: the risk of AI generating misleading or inaccurate information (f=16), concerns about the reliability and objectivity of AI-generated content (f=9), and structural and pedagogical limitations such as limited access to AI tools, the need to concretize abstract topics, developing suitable digital content, and varying levels of teachers' technological competence (f=3). Participants expressed these concerns with remarks such as:

- *"The accuracy of the information cannot be guaranteed under all circumstances. I came across more than one result in a lesson, but I could not decide which one was correct. "* (P11)
- *"With Artificial Intelligence, teacher guidance can be put into the background. There may be problems in terms of the accuracy and objectivity of information in historical events."* (P21).

The data obtained shows that participants emphasised the advantages of AI in history teaching more than the potential difficulties.

Results Related to the Fourth Sub-Problem

In the fourth sub-problem of the study, the analysis of pre-service social studies teachers' views on the future of teaching history topics with AI is shown in Table 3.

Table 3. Pre-service social studies teachers' views on the future of teaching history topics using AI

Theme	*f*	Theme	*f*
The future spread of AI	6	Deepening learning with technology	3
AI-supported structured history teaching	5	The digital transformation of the teaching profession and AI-related uncertainties	3
Expectations that technological developments will facilitate teaching	5	AI-supported historical awareness	2
Viewing AI as a supportive tool	4	Emphasis on individual learning versus AI	2
Visualisation with AI	3	Transformation in information access and verification processes	2
Interactive, three-dimensional, and interactive approaches to history teaching	3	Other themes (single-frequency themes combined): Digital opportunity equality in education, Making history topics fun, Use of digital simulation in education, Use of technology to reduce prejudice, Teacher contribution to interdisciplinary AI development, Technology-supported conceptual understanding	5
Total			43

In the fourth sub-problem of the study, pre-service social studies teachers' views on the future of teaching history with AI are presented in Table 3 regarding themes and frequencies. Participants most frequently highlighted the theme of '*The future widespread use of Artificial Intelligence*' (f=6). This theme was followed by '*AI-supported structured history teaching*' (f=5), '*Expectations that technological developments will facilitate teaching*' (f=5), and '*Viewing AI as a supportive tool*' (f=4). '*Deepening learning with technology*' (f=3), '*The digital transformation of the teaching profession and AI-related uncertainties*' (f=3), '*Visualisation with AI*' (f=3), and '*Interactive, three-dimensional approaches to history teaching*' (f=3) were among the important themes frequently mentioned by participants. Themes such as '*AI-supported history awareness*' (f=2), '*Emphasis on individual learning against AI*' (f=2), and '*Transformation in information access and verification processes*' (f=2) were emphasised at a moderate level. In addition, themes such as '*Digital opportunity equality in education*', '*Making history topics fun*', '*Use of digital simulation*', '*Use of technology to reduce bias*', '*Teacher contribution to interdisciplinary AI development*', and '*Technology-supported conceptual understanding*' (each with f=1) were also mentioned by a small number of participants. These results indicate that pre-service social studies teachers believe that AI will become widespread in history education and will support teaching processes through tools. Some participant statements reflecting these views are as follows:

- *"I believe that in the future, historical events will be visualized with the help of Artificial Intelligence, and teaching will become easier"* (P12).
- *"I think that there will be excellent developments in this field and that students will not have difficulty comprehending many subjects that they have had difficulty understanding for years"* (P20).

6. DISCUSSION

Comparison With Existing Studies

Recent research findings are generally consistent with the participants' opinions (Jaramillo & Chiappe, 2024; Najib, Supadi & Hamidah, 2024). Personalized learning, academic accomplishment, and student motivation are all enhanced by AI, according to a large body of research in the literature. Based on these results, it has been suggested that AI-powered resources can significantly boost student engagement and enhance historical education performance.

In today's world, shaped by the most rapid and profound technological transformation in history—where around 65% of the global population has been digitised within just two decades—students using AI in history classrooms tend to demonstrate greater participation, deeper comprehension of subject matter, and higher-quality academic outputs compared to those taught through traditional methods. Although challenges such as infrastructure limitations and the need for adequate teacher training remain, integrating AI-based educational technologies is a promising approach to enrich history education and promote meaningful learning (Altun, 2022; Najib, Supadi & Hamidah, 2024).

The necessity of preparing the next generation of teachers with AI literacy is underscored by these advancements. Proficiency in AI will enable social studies educators to better utilize it, identify any hazards, and handle moral dilemmas (Benzer & Benzer, 2024). Thus, empowering a generation of educators and citizens who can engage with the changing digital landscape critically and morally requires bolstering digital literacy and AI.

Implications for Teaching Practice

Developing digital literacy abilities is essential for instructors to use AI effectively. As a result, social studies instructors might become proficient in choosing

AI resources for teaching. AI systems can offer tailored feedback and support by evaluating student data, assisting students in identifying their strengths and correcting their shortcomings in a more considerate and customized way (Luckin et al., 2016). These findings demonstrate that pre-service teachers see AI as a revolutionary component of history education and a helpful tool. Otherwise, AI-powered teaching resources may reinforce preconceived notions or give students a skewed perspective on the past. For instance, intelligent tutoring programs and adaptive learning systems have been demonstrated to provide differentiated instruction and let students advance at their own pace (Holmes et al., 2019). These advantages are especially significant in teaching history, where critical thinking and comprehension of intricate narratives are crucial.

However, there are risks associated with using AI in history classes. According to Williamson and Eynon (2020), algorithmic systems have the potential to reinforce dominant views or distort historical narratives by reflecting existing biases in the data. The 2021 UNESCO *Recommendation on the Ethics of Artificial Intelligence* reflects this concern. This recommendation calls on educational institutions to ensure that AI applications protect fairness, diversity, and human rights.

Teacher training programs should integrate AI literacy and ethics into pre-service education to mitigate these risks. Relevant institutions and civil society organizations should work together on this. As Pedró and others (2019) emphasize, educators must be equipped with technical and critical skills to responsibly navigate AI-supported environments. This includes recognizing algorithmic bias, protecting data privacy, and adapting AI tools to diverse classroom environments.

Finally, the ability of educators to strike a balance between technological innovation and pedagogical objectives will determine how well AI is incorporated into history education. Continuous professional development and policy frameworks that emphasize moral, inclusive, and student-centered approaches to AI use in the classroom should be provided to educators.

7. LIMITATIONS & ETHICAL CONSIDERATIONS (ADVANTAGES, LIMITATIONS, AND ETHICAL CONSIDERATIONS OF ARTIFICIAL INTELLIGENCE IN TEACHING HISTORY WITHIN SOCIAL STUDIES)

New technology has improved transdisciplinary teaching and learning, continuously changing pedagogical techniques. Education is undergoing a significant transformation due to AI, especially in the social studies and history component (Jones, 1985). One of its talents is transforming applications that we are only now starting to comprehend by providing fresh approaches to generative AI's support of education (EDUCAUSE, 2024). AI has the potential to revolutionize education by facilitating personalized learning, boosting administrative effectiveness, and broadening access to educational materials, according to UNESCO (2025). However, it also poses serious problems concerning the pressing need for teacher preparation, data privacy, and equality.

AI programs are able to analyze student data and give each student individualized feedback. This enables students to address areas for growth and pinpoint their strengths more sensitively. The capacity of AI to modify the educational process to accommodate students' learning styles and speeds is where its real transformational potential resides. According to Guan (2023), adaptive learning platforms adjust the curriculum according to the student's performance in real time, and chatbots with generative AI enable engaging debates on historical subjects. Virtual reality technologies can also immerse pupils in historically accurate learning environments. According to Romero et al. (2023), these technologies not only boost student involvement but also lessen the workload teachers have to deal with when it comes to content planning and presentation.

The use of AI in history and social studies teaching still faces obstacles despite these benefits. According to Szmyd and Mitera (2024), there is a worry that AI may erode critical thinking and independent analysis abilities, which are essential for comprehending the past. An excessive dependence on automated cars may prevent students from challenging prevailing narratives or honing their interpretive abilities (McCarthy et al., 2006). Likewise, tailoring AI education may restrict teachers' adaptability and run the risk of simplifying intricate historical settings (Chetry, 2024). Ethical challenges that require careful consideration include algorithmic bias and data privacy. Since AI cannot replicate moral thinking and nuanced interpretation, educators and developers should work together to govern its application. Basic AI education has been shown to enhance students' learning beliefs and metacognitive skills, particularly when accompanied by qualified teachers (Martin et al., 2023).

AI contributes significantly to teaching processes and administrative and assessment functions in education (Harry & Sayudin, 2023; Zhou et al., 2023). These contributions include automating grading processes, making it easier to create course schedules, and making data-driven decisions in curriculum development processes (Lampou, 2023). Both teachers and students greatly benefit from the possibilities offered by AI, such as personalising the learning process and tracking individual progress (Radojčić et al., 2022; Romero et al., 2023). Generative AI applications that identify students' knowledge gaps and adapt instruction accordingly increase student engagement and strengthen learning outcomes. Additionally, real-time systems that analyse students' responses provide teachers with meaningful feedback for formative assessment and differentiated instruction (Onesi-Ozigagun et al., 2024). This makes it possible to create innovative tutoring structures tailored to students' needs.

Teachers can devote more time to creating more engaging and interactive classes by having AI handle tedious duties. In order to steer the teaching process, analytical tools that are assisted by AI can track students' progress and identify areas in which support is needed (Saputra et al., 2023). As per the Universal Design for Learning (UDL-IRN, 2011) framework, a successful learning environment necessitates a framework that includes well-defined objectives, adaptable resources, and ongoing evaluation procedures customized to meet the unique learning requirements of every student. Every one of these components might be supported by AI, which would increase the effectiveness and inclusivity of the learning process.

However, integrating AI must address ethical concerns of openness, fairness, and accessibility as well as privacy and security problems related to extensive data collection (Jobin, Ienca, & Vayena, 2019). In order to guarantee responsible educational use, rapid technology growth demands equally quick policy-making (Nabiyev, 2021). Blockchain technology might provide an answer by improving system transparency and data security (Singh & Singh, 2020). Research indicates that using interactive platforms can stimulate students' interest in technology and promote engagement (Guasti, Ferrini & Pieraccini, 2023).

Yet, algorithmic bias can perpetuate inequalities, disproportionately affecting marginalized students. Therefore, AI applications must uphold human dignity, inclusiveness, and fairness, as outlined in UNESCO's Ethics of AI recommendations (2021). Excessive dependence on AI could also erode the relational and humanistic aspects of teaching, making learning less meaningful (Ayala-Pazmiño, 2023).

The primary benefits and drawbacks of using AI in social studies and historical instruction are outlined in Table 4 below, highlighting the difficulties that may arise.

Table 4. Advantages and disadvantages of AI in teaching history subjects in social studies

Advantages	Disadvantages
Personalized Learning: AI improves engagement and comprehension by modifying the content and pace according to each student's demands.	**Bias and Inequality:** AI algorithms that reinforce preexisting biases may treat students from different backgrounds unfairly.
Automated Assessment & Feedback: AI enables teachers to focus on class planning and interactive discussions by handling assessments and feedback, and it supports the use of flexible methods and materials in instruction.	**Data Privacy Concerns:** Gathering and processing enormous volumes of student data increases risks to security and privacy.
Learning Analytics: AI assists in monitoring student development, identifying learning gaps, and setting clear learning goals, thereby enabling teachers to adapt their instructional strategies effectively.	**Reduced Human Interaction:** An over-reliance on AI could diminish the human component of instruction, thereby reducing the interest and significance of learning.

continued on following page

Table 4. Continued

Advantages	Disadvantages
Enhanced Engagement: AI-driven interactive tools and simulations increase the accessibility and immersion of history.	**Ethical Issues:** It is still challenging to guarantee that AI-based educational systems are accessible, transparent, and equitable.
Efficiency and Time-Saving: By automating repetitive tasks, teachers can devote more time to critical and creative thinking exercises, while also benefiting from timely progress monitoring to adjust instruction effectively.	**Adaptation Challenges:** To remain aligned with the latest developments in AI, educators and learners must continually update their skills.

AI makes essential contributions to education, such as personalised learning, increased efficiency, and interaction. However, these contributions come with risks such as data privacy, ethical sensitivities, and reduced human interaction. As Chiu (2024) points out, GenAI is still a new technology, and users' perceptions may change over time. Therefore, he emphasises that AI should be seen as a transformative process that, beyond being a technical tool, also impacts the emotional and social dimensions of education.

On the other hand, the collection and processing of student data raises serious privacy issues (Chisega-Negrilă, 2024). Nguyen (2023) highlights that this process involves technical limitations as well as cost challenges. Without effective teacher training, equal access to opportunities, and security measures, the sustainable use of this technology seems complicated. Gidiotis and Hrastinski (2024) and Li and Jiang (2024) state that this process must be carefully managed; otherwise, opportunities could be risky. When applied correctly, however, Jaramillo and Chiappe (2024) view AI as an assistant that transforms education into an inclusive and efficient structure tailored to each student.

8. THE FUTURE OF ARTIFICIAL INTELLIGENCE IN TEACHING HISTORY WITHIN SOCIAL STUDIES

The use of AI in teaching history topics in social studies is expected to develop further, opening new avenues for data-driven and interactive learning. Traditional methods based on textbooks can be replaced by more interactive and personalised learning experiences tailored to students' interests and needs (Luckin et al., 2016; Roy & Swargiary, 2024). AI systems can analyze each student's learning style, pace, and weaknesses, and provide content and teaching plans tailored to their academic level. However, as technology advances, 37% of the world's population still lacks internet access, and the digital divide is deepening. AI can be critical in bringing information to communities without internet access (ITU, 2021). It is essential to remember that innovation should benefit everyone, not just the wealthy and well-connected, in a world where access to technology is still uneven.

One of AI's most promising contributions lies in its ability to adapt to learners' unique needs. Intelligent tutoring systems analyze student performance and offer personalized feedback, enhancing comprehension of historical content (Grájeda et al., 2023). These systems can also design customized lesson plans and resources aligned with students' preferences and cognitive styles (Huang et al., 2022; Grájeda et al., 2023). Recent studies further reveal a strong link between Intelligent Tutoring Systems and emerging fields such as generative AI and cognitive agent modeling (Gluz, Flores & Vicari, 2007).

Virtual Reality and AI-generated simulations add another layer of depth, allowing students to "visit" historical sites or interact with reanimated historical figures. These immersive tools, when combined with conventional methods, can offer more impactful and memorable learning experiences.

AI also makes assessment easier, which allows teachers to concentrate on more engaging teaching strategies. Teaching tactics are informed by data generated by automated grading systems, which also provide instant feedback (Swargiary & Roy, 2024). Xu and Ouyang (2022) state that machine learning algorithms have also been used to monitor academic achievement and examine learning patterns, particularly in STEM education. By automating procedures like scheduling, resource management, and enrollment, AI can boost school administrative efficiency and improve instruction.

AI is capable of analyzing vast volumes of data to find trends, forecast learning results, and adjust instructional methods. This individualized approach boosts student engagement and achievement by letting them learn at their own pace and in a way that best fits their cognitive preferences (Jian, 2023; Lai et al., 2023). Recent studies have shown that AI develops subject-specific skills, fosters critical engagement with tales, and enhances historical thinking (Carretero & Gartner, 2024). However, in order to fulfill this promise, it is necessary to develop speaking abilities, structured feedback systems, and AI literacy (Luprichová, 2025). Incorporating students' voices is equally important—especially as many learners are driven by the need to acquire future-ready skills for AI-centered careers (Chiu, 2024). Social studies educators can guide students in using AI tools thoughtfully. For example, integrating chatbots into lessons enables students to interact with AI meaningfully (Yetişensoy & Rapoport, 2023).

In addition to personalizing education, generative AI revolutionized evaluation. Real-time, formative feedback is provided by AI-based grading systems, which encourage introspection and ongoing development (Kaledio et al., 2024). According to Lin et al. (2023) and Ilgaz and Yıldırım (2024), these technologies assist educators in anticipating learning paths, keeping a closer eye on students' development, and taking proactive measures when needed. The learning environment becomes more flexible, and instruction becomes more responsive. However, there are serious ethical issues with the employment of AI in historical instruction. The possibility of algorithmic bias resulting in inaccurate or partial representations of historical events is a serious problem. According to Adams et al. (2023), it is becoming more and more crucial to ensure that AI systems represent a variety of viewpoints and do not perpetuate historical errors.

The requirement for professional growth and training for teachers is another difficulty. Teachers need to be able to assess AI-generated content critically and successfully incorporate it into their lesson plans (Gligorea et al., 2023; Onesi-Ozigagun et al., 2024). Crucially, rather than taking the place of educators, AI should empower them. Teachers, legislators, and technologists must work responsibly together if AI is to be used in history classes in the future. To promote the integration of AI in education, governments, academic institutions, and other pertinent entities must take the lead (Lampou, 2023). By resolving current issues and optimizing its advantages, AI can completely transform history teaching and eventually assist students in becoming more informed and involved citizens (Lampou, 2023; Onesi-Ozigagun et al., 2024). One thing is certain: teachers skilled in AI will eventually replace those who are not, even though it is still unclear whether AI will ever completely replace teachers.

AI in education has a lot of potential, but its application must be cautious. It is possible for AI systems that have been trained on biased or insufficient data sets to reinforce existing inequities (Bulut et al., 2024). Educational institutions should collaborate with developers to design morally good algorithms to ensure justice and diversity. Technology can assist all students to realize their full potential and create more equitable learning environments when AI is applied properly (Admane et al., 2024). History education itself provides a unique lens through which to explore the ethical and societal implications of AI. By engaging students in these discussions, we can ensure that technological progress serves humanity and contributes positively to society (Ni & Hassan, 2024).

In the end, AI ought to be a potent supplement to human educators rather than a substitute. Its goals are to support educators in meeting the various learning needs of their students, promoting critical thinking, and meaningfully customizing education (Lampou, 2023). Investment in teacher preparation, adherence to moral principles, and critical use of AI tools are all necessary to realize this goal. This will guarantee that AI becomes a force for good in teaching history and social studies.

9. CONCLUSION & RECOMMENDATIONS

Technology and science bring new changes every day. AI offers opportunities in this regard. AI is transforming all sectors, and education will undoubtedly take its share of this transformation. Because machines can do tasks more quickly than humans, AI has become a branch of computer science that mimics human cognitive processes, including reasoning, learning, and problem-solving (Singh et al., 2020). AI influences many facets of life and creates the foundation for a more effective society that will influence people's choices. Additionally, this transformation requires a fundamental shift in thinking and culture.

AI is reshaping the way history is taught in social studies classes by combining technological advancements with pedagogical, ethical, and human-centered approaches. Interactive simulations of historical events, the concretisation of abstract concepts, establishing cause-and-effect relationships, developing empathy, creating chronologies, and gaining a multifaceted perspective are historical thinking skills that can be more effectively supported by AI-assisted applications. Students can follow personalized learning paths with content tailored to their interests and cognitive structures, and manage the learning process more actively through real-time feedback. These skills are largely aligned with the student-centred learning approach and the goals of 21st-century education.

However, the findings indicate a critical perspective is necessary when integrating AI into history education. Prospective social studies teachers highlighted the effectiveness, accessibility, and interactivity advantages that AI can bring to education. They also clearly expressed their ethical concerns regarding issues such as content accuracy, the weakening of teacher autonomy, algorithmic bias, data privacy, and unequal access.

These findings underscore the importance of supporting teachers, pre-service social studies teachers, and students in developing AI literacy. Using AI systems correctly, critically, and ethically; identifying risks and making informed choices are only possible with this type of literacy (Benzer & Benzer, 2024). Otherwise, AI-based applications may reinforce historical inaccuracies, weaken critical thinking skills, and lead to the mechanization of the teaching process. Therefore, AI should not be positioned as a tool that excludes human judgment, but rather as a facilitator of a learning process based on critical and ethical foundations, guided by teachers.

Furthermore, AI is directly related to social justice and equal opportunities in education, beyond individual learning. The inability of students in rural and disadvantaged areas to access digital infrastructure increases the risk of exclusion from this technological development. This situation can further deepen digital inequalities in education. Therefore, it is of great importance that AI-supported teaching processes are structured in line with social justice principles and pedagogical approaches.

In conclusion, by addressing this technology from a teacher-centered, critical, and ethical viewpoint, it is possible to effectively utilize the opportunities presented by AI in history education. Future education must be based on an idea that seeks to provide pupils with human sensitivity, critical thinking abilities, ethical values, and knowledge. In this regard, it is crucial to create a method that is inquisitive, thoughtful, and willing to back off when needed, without totally discounting AI. It is critical to keep in mind that, like humans, AI systems are fallible and dynamic entities that represent both their promise and flaws. The phrase "garbage in, garbage out" clearly demonstrates that technology cannot be considered independently of human contribution. Therefore, as we progress with technology, placing humans and humanity at the center will be the healthiest approach. Accordingly, the following well-organized suggestions are offered for the efficient, moral, and significant application of AI in the instruction of social studies and history subjects:

For Pre-Service Teachers

Practical training should be provided to pre-service social studies teachers on how to use AI technologies effectively and meaningfully in history teaching (e.g., lesson planning with AI tools, generating instructional content, and assessing student performance through AI-supported applications).

Pre-service social studies teachers should move beyond the surface-level benefits of AI and cultivate a critical awareness of its ethical, social, and pedagogical implications, which should be actively discussed within teacher education programs.

Pre-service social studies teachers should be guided on how AI applications affect the basic skills of history teaching, such as historical thinking, questioning, and developing a multifaceted perspective.

For Teachers

When integrating AI tools into the teaching process, a holistic approach that includes teacher guidance, pedagogical intuition, and subject knowledge should be adopted.

Social studies teachers should be equipped with the skills to evaluate AI tools from a pedagogical and ethical perspective, in addition to technical knowledge.

In-class applications should be continuously reviewed based on student feedback and designed in a way that is open to improvement.

For Policy Makers

To prevent digital inequality, digital infrastructure deficiencies must be addressed, particularly in rural and disadvantaged areas, and internet access and device provision must be supported.

It is of great importance to promote professional development programs aimed at improving teachers' AI literacy, while also incorporating ethical and pedagogical aspects.

In order for AI to be used ethically in education, clear and binding principles must be established regarding data privacy, algorithmic transparency, prevention of monopolisation, and fair use.

For Future Research

The number of quantitative and qualitative studies examining the effects of AI on the teaching of history in social studies needs to be increased.

Prioritizing research on teachers' perspectives on AI, their ethical sensitivity, and their application skills is crucial.

There should be a comprehensive analysis of how students use various AI tools and how these tools impact their critical inquiry and historical thinking abilities.

ACKNOWLEDGEMENT

The authors would like to thank the Gazi University Academic Writing Application and Research Center for proofreading the chapter.

REFERENCES

Adams, C., Pente, P., Lemermeyer, G., & Rockwell, G. (2023). Ethical principles for Artificial Intelligence in K-12 education. *Computers and Education: Artificial Intelligence*, *4*, 100131. DOI: 10.1016/j.caeai.2023.100131

Admane, R., Sawale, P. S., Jayasree, R., Kurup, S. J., & Thomas, S. A. (2024). Artificial intelligence in education: Tailoring curriculum to individual student needs through AI-based systems. *Library of Progress-Library Science. Information Technology & Computer*, *44*(3), 8847–8856. DOI: 10.48165/bapas.2024.44.2.1

Akyel, Y., & Tur, E. (2024). Prospects, challenges, and future directions in the research and investigation of Artificial Intelligence's potential and applications in educational sciences [Yapay zekanın potansiyelinin ve eğitim bilimlerindeki uygulamalarının araştırılması ve araştırmalarda beklentiler, zorluklar ve gelecek Yönelimleri] [Ahi Evran Üniversitesi Kırşehir Eğitim Fakültesi Dergisi]. *Ahi Evran University Journal of Kırşehir Education Faculty*, *25*(1), 645–711. DOI: 10.29299/kefad.1322341

Aldemir, U., Caner, S., Akın, P., & Kaplan, A. (2024) Student-centered learning models in education [Eğitimde öğrenci merkezli öğrenme modelleri]. *International QMX Journal, 3*(3), 1280-1285. ISSN: 3023-6037. doi: https://doi.org/DOI: 10.5281/zenodo.10899512

Ali, M. (2024). AI and intelligent tutoring systems: A new paradigm for student-centered learning. *Journal of AI Integration in Education*, *1*(2), 1–11.

Alpar, D., Batdal, G., & Avcı, Y. (2012). Educational technology applications in student-centred education [Öğrenci merkezli eğitimde eğitim teknolojileri uygulamaları] [Hasan Ali Yücel Eğitim Fakültesi Dergisi]. *HAYEF Journal of Education*, *4*(1), 19–31.

Altun, A. (2022). How can digital history affect history education? [Dijital Tarih, Tarih Eğitimini Nasıl Etkileyebilir?]. *8th International Symposium on History Education [8. Uluslararası Tarih Eğitimi Sempozyumu]* (ISHE 2022), (pp. 17-28). Adana, Türkiye.

Arslan, K. (2020). Artificial intelligence and applications in education [Eğitimde yapay zeka ve uygulamaları] [Batı Anadolu Eğitim Bilimleri Dergisi]. *Western Anatolia Journal of Educational Sciences, 11*(1), 71–88.

Ayala-Pazmiño, M. (2023). *Artificial intelligence in education: Exploring the potential benefits and risks. In 593 Digital Publisher CEIT, 8(3).*, DOI: 10.33386/593dp.2023.3.1827

Benzer, S., & Benzer, R. (2024). Yapay zekâ ve eğitimin geleceği. [Artificial intelligence and the future of education] In Gökcearslan, S., & Yıldız Durak, H. (Eds.), *Yapay zekâ okuryazarlığı* [Artificial intelligence literacy]. (pp. 191–220). Nobel Akademik.

Berson, I. R., & Berson, M. J. (2023). The democratization of AI and its transformative potential in social studies education. *Social Education, 87*(2), 114–118.

Bertram, C., Weiss, Z., Zachrich, L., & Ziai, R. (2021). Artificial intelligence in history education. Linguistic content and complexity analyses of student writings in the CAHisT project (Computational assessment of historical thinking). *Computers and Education: Artificial Intelligence.* doi: https://doi.org/DOI: 10.1016/j.caeai.2021.100038

Briskin, J., & Land, S. M. (2020). Student-centered virtual design studio environments. In *The Routledge International Handbook of Student-Centered Learning and Teaching in Higher Education* (pp. 345–360). Routledge.

Brom, C., Šisler, V., & Slavik, R. (2010). Implementing digital game-based learning in schools: Augmented learning environment of “Europe 2045.”. *Multimedia Systems, 16*(1), 23–41. DOI: 10.1007/s00530-009-0174-0

Bulut, O., Beiting-Parrish, M., Casabianca, J. M., Slater, S. C., Jiao, H., Song, D., & Morilova, P. (2024). The rise of Artificial Intelligence in educational measurement: Opportunities and ethical challenges. *Journal of Educational Measurement and Evaluation, 5*(3), 1–32. DOI: 10.59863/MIQL7785

Bussell, D. (2024). Historical thinking in the classroom: A multiple-case study. *Social Studies, 115*(3), 129–145. DOI: 10.1080/00377996.2023.2274051

Caro, M. F., Quitian, L., Giraldo, J. C., & Lengua-Cantero, C. (2023, November). A formal model for personalized learning path using Artificial Intelligence for instructional planning with a focus on 21st-century skills and environmental awareness. In *2023 IEEE Colombian Caribbean Conference (C3)* (pp. 1-6). IEEE.

Carretero, M., & Gartner, E. (2024). Artificial Intelligence and historical thinking: A dialogic exploration of ChatGPT/Inteligencia Artificial y pensamiento histórico: una exploración dialógica del ChatGPT. *Studies in Psychology*, *45*(1), 80–102. DOI: 10.1177/02109395241241

Chetry, K. K. (2024). Transforming education: How AI is revolutionizing the learning experience. *International Journal of Research Publication and Reviews*, *5*(5), 6352–6356. DOI: 10.55248/gengpi.5.0524.1277

Chisega-Negrılă, A. M. (2024). Teaching and learning in an AI-powered world. *Bulletın of" Carol I. Natıonal Defence Unıversıty*, *13*(3), 105–116. DOI: 10.53477/2284-9378-24-33

Chiu, T. K. (2024). Future research recommendations for transforming higher education with generative AI. *Computers and Education: Artificial Intelligence*, *6*, 100197. DOI: 10.1016/j.caeai.2023.100197

Çığır Dikyol, D., & Şar İşbilen, E. (2020). The use of virtual reality technology in history teaching: The case of Çatalhöyük [Tarih öğretiminde sanal gerçeklik teknolojisi kullanımı: Çatalhöyük örneği] [Tarih Okulu Dergisi]. *Journal of History School*, *45*, 677–712. DOI: 10.29228/Joh40295

Çöpgeven, N. S., Özkaya, H., & Aydın, S. (2023). Artificial Intelligence-based gamification in open and distance learning [Açık ve uzaktan öğrenmede yapay zeka destekli oyunlaştırma] [Journal of Open Education Applications and Research]. *Açıköğretim Uygulamaları ve Araştırmaları Dergisi*, *9*(1), 386–407. DOI: 10.51948/auad.1203700

Corrales Serrano, M. (2023). Gamification and the history of art in secondary education: A didactic intervention. *Education Sciences*, *13*(4), 389. DOI: 10.3390/educsci13040389

Creswell, J. W., & Creswell, J. D. (2018). *Research design: Qualitative, quantitative, and mixed methods approaches*. Sage.

Cuevas, H. F. (2024). Personalized feedback in formative assessment: A case study in Mexican higher education in the era of AI. *Eastern Journal of Languages. Linguistics and Literatures*, *5*(2), 12–21. DOI: 10.53906/ejlll.v5i2.340

Dasam, S., Goriparthi, P., Manchanda, M., Nowbattula, P. K., & Subhashini, R. (2024, December). *Enhancing writing skills with AI: Personalized feedback mechanisms for English learners*. In *2024 International Conference on Artificial Intelligence and Quantum Computation-Based Sensor Application (ICAIQSA)* (pp. 1–6). IEEE. doi: https://search.informit.org/doi/10.3316/informit.322842139237015

Doyle, T. J., & Doyle, B. M. (2020). Learning and teaching in harmony with the brain: Insights from neuroscience, biology, cognitive science, and psychology. In *The Routledge International Handbook of student-centered learning and teaching in higher education* (pp. 75–91). Routledge.

Edelstein, D., Findlen, P., Ceserani, G., Winterer, C., & Coleman, N. (2017). Historical research in a digital age: Reflections from the mapping the republic of letters project. *The American Historical Review*, *122*(2), 400–424. DOI: 10.1093/ahr/122.2.400

EDUCAUSE. (2024). *2024 EDUCAUSE Horizon Report: Teaching and Learning Edition*. Boulder, CO: EDUCAUSE. Retrieved from https://www.educause.edu/horizon-report-teaching-and-learning-2024

Erol Şahin, A. N. (2024). Generative Artificial Intelligence in history teaching: Prospective teachers' perceptions and ethical concerns [Tarih Öğretiminde Üretken Yapay Zekâ: Öğretmen Adaylarının Algıları ve Endişeleri]. *Xth International Symposium on History Education [10. Uluslararası Tarih Eğitimi Sempozyumu]* (ISHE 2024), 1–15, Kars, Türkiye.

Frasson, C. (2023). The future of learning assessment. In du Boulay, B., Mitrovic, A., & Yacef, K. (Eds.), *Handbook of Artificial Intelligence in education* (pp. 637–639). Edward Elgar Publishing.

Gidiotis, I., & Hrastinski, S. (2024). Imagining the future of Artificial Intelligence in education: A review of social science fiction. *Learning, Media and Technology*, •••, 1–13. DOI: 10.1080/17439884.2024.2365829

Gligorea, I., Cioca, M., Oancea, R., Gorski, A., Gorski, H., & Tudorache, P. (2023). Adaptive learning using Artificial intelligence in E-learning: A literature review. *Education Sciences*, *13*, 1216. Advance online publication. DOI: 10.3390/educsci13121216

Glowa, L., & Goodell, J. (2016). Student-centered learning: Functional requirements for integrated systems to optimize learning. *International Association for K-12 Online Learning*. doi: https://files.eric.ed.gov/fulltext/ED567875.pdf

Gluz, J. C., Flores, C. D., & Vicari, R. M. (2007). Formal Aspects of Pedagogical Negotiation in AMPLIA System. In Nedjah, N., Mourelle, L. M., Borges, M. N., & Almeida, N. N. d. (Eds.), *Intelligent Educational Machines. Studies in Computational Intelligence* (Vol. 44). Springer., DOI: 10.1007/978-3-540-44921-8_6

Grájeda, A., Burgos, J., Olivera, P. C., & Sanjinés, A. (2023). Assessing student-perceived impact of using Artificial Intelligence tools: Construction of a synthetic index of application in higher education. In *Cogent Education, 11* (Vol. 1). Taylor & Francis., DOI: 10.1080/2331186x.2023.2287917

Grubaugh, S., & Levitt, G. (2024). The Future of Elementary Social Studies: Harnessing AI's Potential Through Evidence-Based Practices. *Technium Soc. Sci. J.*, *58*, 87–93. DOI: 10.47577/tssj.v58i1.10991

Guan, H. (2023). Advantages and challenges of using Artificial Intelligence in primary and secondary school education. *Journal of Education. Humanities and Social Sciences*, *22*, 377–383. DOI: 10.54097/ehss.v22i.12469

Guasti, L., Ferrini, A., & Pieraccini, G. (2023). Teaching Blockchain at School. In: Kubincová, Z., Caruso, F., Kim, Te, Ivanova, M., Lancia, L., Pellegrino, M.A. (Eds.) Methodologies and Intelligent Systems for Technology Enhanced Learning, Workshops - 13th International Conference. MIS4TEL 2023. Lecture Notes in Networks and Systems, vol 769, pp. 378-387. Springer, Cham. doi: https://doi.org/DOI: 10.1007/978-3-031-42134-1_38

Harry, A., & Sayudin, S. (2023). Role of AI in education. In *Interdiciplinary Journal and Hummanity* (INJURITY), *2*(3), 260-268. doi: https://doi.org/DOI: 10.58631/injurity.v2i3.52

Hogan, E., & Payne, B. (2024). A mixed-methods study of teachers' use of feedback within middle school social studies classrooms to promote reading comprehension. *Learning and Instruction*, *92*, 101938. DOI: 10.1016/j.learninstruc.2024.101938

Holmes, W., Bialik, M., & Fadel, C. (2019). *Artificial Intelligence in education. Promises and implications for teaching and learning* (1st ed.). Center for Curriculum Redesign., https://static.googleusercontent.com/media/edu.google.com/en//pdfs/Intelligence-Unleashed-Publication.pdf

Huang, A. Y. Q., Lu, O. H. T., & Yang, S. J. H. (2022). Effects of Artificial Intelligence–Enabled personalized recommendations on learners' learning engagement, motivation, and outcomes in a flipped classroom. [). Elsevier BV.]. *Computers & Education*, *194*, 104684.

Ilgaz, H., & Yıldırım, D. (2024). Üretken yapay zeka: Yükseköğretimde fırsat ve zorluklar. [Generative Artificial Intelligence: Opportunities and challenges in higher education] In Gökçearslan, Ş., & Yıldız Durak, H. (Eds.), *Yapay zekâ okuryazarlığı* [Artificial intelligence literacy]. (pp. 239–255). Nobel Akademik.

International Telecommunication Union (ITU). (2021). *Measuring digital development: Facts and figures 2021*. ITU.

Jamilah, W. S. N., & Halimah, L. H. (2024, August). Innovative learning strategies for social studies in the era of Artificial Intellıgence. In *International Conference on Applied Social Sciences in Education, 1*(1), 181-187. doi: https://doi.org/DOI: 10.31316/icasse.v1i1.6842

Jaramillo, J. J., & Chiappe, A. (2024). The AI-driven classroom: A review of 21st-century curriculum trends. *Prospects, 54*, 645–660. DOI: 10.1007/s11125-024-09704-w

Jian, M. J. K. O. (2023). Personalized learning through AI. *Advances in Engineering Innovation, 5*(1), 16–19. DOI: 10.54254/2977-3903/5/2023039

Jobin, A., Ienca, M., & Vayena, E. (2019). The global landscape of AI ethics guidelines. *Nature Machine Intelligence, 1*, 389–399. DOI: 10.1038/s42256-019-0088-2

Jones, M. (1985, May). Applications of Artificial Intelligence within education. *Computers & Mathematics with Applications (Oxford, England), 11*(5), 517–526. DOI: 10.1016/0898-1221(85)90054-9

Kaledio, P., Robert, A., & Frank, L. (2024). The impact of Artificial intelligence on students' learning experience. SSRN *Electronic Journal*, February (1). doi: http://dx.doi.org/DOI: 10.2139/ssrn.4716747

Kaswan, K. S., Dhatterwal, J. S., & Ojha, R. P. (2024). AI in personalized learning. In *Advances in technological innovations in higher education* (pp. 103–117). CRC Press.

Kuzminykh, I., Nawaz, T., Shenzhang, S., Ghita, B., Raphael, J., & Xiao, H. (2024). Personalised feedback framework for online education programmes using generative AI. *arXiv preprint arXiv:2410.11904*. doi: https://doi.org//arXiv.2410.11904DOI: 10.48550

Lai, T., Xie, C., Ruan, M., Wang, Z., Lu, H., & Fu, S. (2023). Influence of Artificial Intelligence in education on adolescents' social adaptability: The mediatory role of social support. *PLoS One, 18*(3), e0283170. DOI: 10.1371/journal.pone.0283170

Lampou, R. (2023). The integration of Artificial Intelligence in education: Opportunities and challenges. Review of Artificial Intelligence in Education. *Review of Artificial Intelligence in Education, 4*(0), 1–12. DOI: 10.37497/rev.artif.intell.educ.v4i00.15

Lampropoulos, G., & Kinshuk. (2024). Virtual reality and gamification in education: A systematic review. *Educational Technology Research and Development*, *72*(3), 1691–1785. DOI: 10.1007/s11423-024-10351-3

Lee, B. N. (2023). Exploring the relationship between history learning and thinking skills: A synthesis of research. *Muallim Journal of Social Sciences and Humanities*, *7*(2), 18–30. DOI: 10.33306/mjssh/233

Levitt, G., & Grubaugh, S. (2024). Why do I have to learn this stuff? Using AI to assist secondary teachers in teaching future-ready practical life skills with any social studies lesson. *Technium Social Sciences Journal*, *59*, 327–341. DOI: 10.47577/tssj.v59i1.11241

Levstik, L. S., & Barton, K. C. (2015). *Doing history: Investigating with children in elementary and middle schools* (5th ed.). Routledge., DOI: 10.4324/9781315818108

Li, X., & Jiang, Y. (2024). Artificial intelligence in education: Opportunities, current status, and prospects. *Geographical Research Bulletin*, *3*, 146–174. DOI: 10.50908/grb.3.0_146

Lin, C. C., Huang, A. Y. Q., & Lu, O. H. T. (2023). Artificial intelligence in intelligent tutoring systems toward sustainable education: A systematic review. *Smart Learn. Environ.*, *10*, 41. DOI: 10.1186/s40561-023-00260-y

Liu, Z., & Yushchik, E. (2024). Exploring the prospects of using Artificial Intelligence in education. *Cogent Education*, *11*(1). Advance online publication. DOI: 10.1080/2331186X.2024.2353464

Luckin, R., Holmes, W., Griffiths, M., & Forcier, L. B. (2016). *Intelligence Unleashed. An argument for AI in education*. Pearson.

Luprichová, J. (2025). Enhancing historical understanding, gender perspectives, and critical thinking: Integrating AI-powered tools in university-level British history education. (2025). *Resources*, *1*, 188–197. DOI: 10.53349/re-source.2025.is1.a1391

Lyell, I. (2024). Artificial Intelligence and the future of education. *Agora*, 59(2), 7–8. doi: https://search.informit.org/doi/10.3316/informit.T202407050001250 0610823061

Maghsudi, S., Lan, A., Xu, J., & van der Schaar, M. (2021). Personalized Education in the Artificial Intelligence Era: What to Expect Next. *IEEE Signal Processing Magazine*, *38*, 37–50. DOI: 10.1109/msp.2021.3055032

Mahmoud, C. F., & Sørensen, J. T. (2024). Artificial Intelligence in personalized learning with a focus on current developments and future prospects. *Research and Advances in Education*, *3*(8), 25–31. DOI: 10.56397/rae.2024.08.04

Malysheva, O., Tokareva, E., Orchakova, L., & Smirnova, Y. (2022). The effect of online learning in modern history education. *Heliyon*, *8*(7). Advance online publication. DOI: 10.1016/j.heliyon.2022.e09965

Maria, J., Ahmad, A., & Awang, M. M. (2019, October). The applications of historical thinking skills in teaching and history learning: Between rhetoric and reality. In The 2nd International Conference on Sustainable Development and Multi-Ethnic Society (pp. 221-229). Redwhite Pres.

Martin, M., Chevalier, M., Burton, S., Bonvin, G., Besançon, M., & Deneux, T. (2023). Effects of introducing a learning robot on the metacognitive knowledge of students aged 8–11. In Balogh, R., Obdržálek, D., & Christoforou, E. (Eds.), *Robotics in education. RiE 2023. Lecture notes in networks and systems* (Vol. 747, pp. 169–183). Springer., DOI: 10.1007/978-3-031-38454-7_15

McCarthy, J., Minsky, M. L., Rochester, N., & Shannon, C. E. (2006). A Proposal for the Dartmouth Summer Research Project on Artificial Intelligence, August 31, 1955. *AI Magazine*, *27*(4), 12. DOI: 10.1609/aimag.v27i4.1904

Merriam, S. B., & Tisdell, E. J. (2016). *Qualitative research: A guide to design and implementation* (4th ed.). Jossey-Bass.

Miles, M. B., & Huberman, A. M. (1994). *Qualitative data analysis: An expanded sourcebook* (2nd ed.). Sage Publications, Inc.

Mojolou, D. N., Madli, F., Thomas, H., Sondoh, S. L.Jr, & Karunia, E. (2024). A trend in publishing Artificial Intelligence personalized education: Enhancing learning experiences for university students. *Journal of Information Systems and Technology Management*, *9*(37), 286–301. DOI: 10.35631/JISTM.937021

Mottl, J., & Musílek, M. (2024, May). Information technology as a tool for teaching history with a focus on Artificial Intelligence and audiovisual material. In *2024 47th MIPRO ICT and Electronics Convention (MIPRO)* (pp. 278–282). IEEE. doi: https://doi.org/DOI: 10.1109/MIPRO60963.2024.1056921

Muqorrobin, S., Arifin, S., Wutsqah, U., & Uulanian, H. (2024). Building character in the AI era (Combining technology and human values in education). Hikamatzu I. *Journal of Multidisciplinary*, *1*(1), 289–298. https://yasyahikamatzu.com/index.php/hjm/article/view/74

Nabiyev, V. (2021). *Yapay zekâ: makine öğrenmesi-stratejili oyunlar-örüntü tanıma-doğal dil işleme* [Artificial Intelligence: machine learning-strategic games-image recognition-natural language processing]. Seçkin.

Najib, M., Supadi, S., & Hamidah, N. (2024). Utilization of Artificial Intelligence to increase interactivity in history learning for high school students. *Jurnal Ilmiah Rumpun Ilmu Pendidikan, 1*(4), 01-20. doi: https://doi.org/DOI: 10.63760/jirip.v1i4.24

Nguyen, N. D. (2023). Exploring the role of AI in education. *London Journal of Social Sciences*, (6), 84–95. DOI: 10.31039/ljss.2023.6.108

Ni, L. B., & Hassan, N. B. (2024). The relevance of history learning in the age of Artificial Intelligence: Understanding its impact on critical thinking and ethical decision-making. *Journal of Language. Linguistics and Literature*, *2*, 1–10. DOI: 10.59232/LLL-V2I2P103

Nurhayati, T. N., & Halimah, L. (2024, August). The value and technology: Maintaining balance in social science education in the era of Artificial Intelligence. *Proceedings of the International Conference on Applied Social Sciences in Education, 1*(1), 28-36. doi: https://doi.org/DOI: 10.31316/icasse.v1i1.6840

Ofianto, Aman, Ningsih, T. Z., & Abidin, N. F. (2022). The development of a historical thinking assessment to examine students' skills in analyzing the causality of historical events. *European Journal of Educational Research, 11*(2), 609–619. DOI: 10.12973/eu-jer.11.2.609

Onesi-Ozigagun, O., Ololade, Y. J., Eyo-Udo, N. L., & Ogundipe, D. O. (2024). Revolutionizing education through AI: A comprehensive review of enhancing learning experiences. *International Journal of Applied Research in Social Sciences, 6*(4), 589–607. DOI: 10.51594/ijarss.v6i4.1011

Open, A. I. (2023). *ChatGPT* [Large language model]. https://chat.openai.com

Orhan Özen, S., & Çubukçu, Z. (2022). An investigation of the learners' personalized feedback paths based on e-Assessment. *Kastamonu Education Journal, 30*(2), 411–426. DOI: 10.24106/kefdergi.825787

Pedró, F., Subosa, M., Rivas, A., & Valverde, P. (2019). *Artificial Intelligence in education: Challenges and opportunities for sustainable development* (Working papers on education policy, No. 7). UNESCO. doi: https://unesdoc.unesco.org/ark:/48223/pf0000366994

Prasetyowati, D. I. & Sunarti. (2024, August). The role of Artificial Intelligence media in learning social studies education for elementary schools. In *International Conference on Applied Social Sciences in Education, 1*(1), 247-250. doi: https://doi.org/DOI: 10.31316/icasse.v1i1.6998

Qushwa, F. G., & Onia, S. I. (2024). AI innovation in education: Realizing personalized learning in the digital age. *Educative: Jurnal Ilmiah Pendidikan, 2*(3), 178–187. DOI: 10.70437/educative.v2i3.822

Radojčić, M. R., Perera, R. S., Chen, L., Spector, T. D., Hart, D. J., Ferreira, M. L., & Arden, N. K. (2022). Specific body mass index trajectories were related to musculoskeletal pain and mortality: 19-year follow-up cohort. *Journal of Clinical Epidemiology, 141*, 54–63. DOI: 10.1016/j.jclinepi.2021.09.020

Rajaram, K. (2023). *Learning Intelligence: Innovative and digital transformative learning strategies: Cultural and social engineering perspectives*. Springer.

Roméro, M., Heiser, L., Lepage, A., Gagnebien, A., Bonjour, A., Lagarrigue, A., Palaude, A., Boulord, C., Gagneur, C.-A., Mercier, C., Caucheteux, C., Guidoni-Stoltz, D., Tressols, F., Henry, J., Alexandre, F., Céci, J.-F., Camponovo, J., Fouché, L., Métral, J.-F., . . . Borgne, Y. L. (2023). Teaching and learning in the age of Artificial Intelligence. *In arXiv (Cornell University)*. Cornell University. doi: https://doi.org//arxiv.2303.06956DOI: 10.48550

Roy, K., & Swargiary, K. (2024). Exploring the impact of AI integration in education: A mixed-methods study. doi: https://doi.org/DOI: 10.2139/ssrn.4857648

Ružic, I. M., & Dumancic, M. (2015). Gamification in education. *Informatologia, 48*(3–4), 198–204. DOI: 10.3390/encyclopedia3040089

Saleem, S., Aziz, M. U., Iqbal, M. J., & Abbas, S. (2025). AI in education: Personalized learning systems and their impact on student performance and engagement. *The Critical Review of Social Sciences Studies, 3*(1), 2445–2459. DOI: 10.59075/c35qa453

Saputra, I., Astuti, M., Sayuti, M., & Kusumastuti, D. (2023). Integration of Artificial Intelligence in Education: Opportunities, challenges, threats and obstacles. A literature review. *Indonesian Journal of Computer Science, 12*(4). Advance online publication. DOI: 10.33022/ij /ij"cs.v12i4.3266

Sarpkaya, R., & Yılmaz, T. (2021). The place of the teacher in student-centred education and an evaluation of the pandemic process [Öğrenci merkezli eğitimde öğretmenin yeri ve pandemi sürecine ilişkin bir değerlendirme] [Eleştirel Pedagoji]. *Critical Pedagogy, 68*, 75–79.

Selanik-Ay, T. (2024). Social studies teaching with Artificial Intelligence. [Yapay zekâ ile sosyal bilgiler öğretimi] In Özdinç, F., Aydoğdu, B., & Kasapoğlu, E. (Eds.), *The future of the classroom: Teacher–Artificial Intelligence collaboration* [*Sınıfın geleceği: Öğretmen–yapay zekâ işbirliği*]. Nobel Akademik.

Seyhan, A. (2024). Social studies teachers' views on the use of Artificial Intelligence in education [Sosyal bilgiler öğretmenlerinin eğitimde yapay zeka kullanımına ilişkin görüşleri] [Uluslararası Eğitim Bilimleri Detgisi]. *The Journal of International Education Science*, *11*(41), 100–125. DOI: 10.29228/INESJOURNAL.78798

Sheng, X. (2023). The role of Artificial Intelligence in history education of Chinese high schools. *Journal of Education* [EPHHR]. *Humanities and Social Sciences*, *8*, 238. DOI: 10.54097/ehss.v8i.4255

Shu, X., & Ye, Y. (2023). Knowledge discovery: Methods from data mining and machine learning. *Social Science Research, 110*(April 2022), 102817. doi: https://doi.org/DOI: 10.1016/j.ssresearch.2022.102817

Singh, P., & Singh, N. (2020). Blockchain with IoT & AI: A review of agriculture and healthcare. *[IJAEC]. International Journal of Applied Evolutionary Computation*, *11*(4), 13–27. DOI: 10.4018/IJAEC.2020100102

Singh, P., Singh, R., Singh, N., & Singh, M. K. (2020). A distributed Artificial Intelligence: The future of AI. In Yadav, S. P., Mahato, D. P., & Thi Dieu Linh, N. (Eds.), *Distributed_artificial_intelligence: A_modern_approach* (pp. 263–276). Routledge Publishing.

Sivakumar, J., & Al Harthy, K. (2024). AI-Powered Teaching Plan: Present and Post Evaluation. In *Utilizing AI for Assessment, Grading, and Feedback in Higher Education* (pp. 162-188). IGI Global.

Sürme, M., & Atılgan, E. (2020). A research to determine the satisfaction levels of individual tours in the virtual museum. *Journal of Turkish Tourism Research*, *4*(3), 1794–1805. DOI: 10.26677/TR1010.2020.451

Susyanah, S., & Fajar, A. (2024, August). The Artificial Intelligence, *Social Sciences Learning Innovation Catalyst. In International Conference on Applied Social Sciences in Education*, *1*(1), pp. 114-120.

Swargiary, K., & Roy, K. (June 01, 2024). The impact of stress on academic performance and memory recall in K12 students: A controlled laboratory study. doi: http://dx.doi.org/DOI: 10.2139/ssrn.4877823

Szmyd, K., & Mitera, E. (2024). The impact of Artificial Intelligence on the development of critical thinking skills in students. *European Research Studies Journal, 27*(2), 1022–1039. DOI: 10.35808/ersj/3876

Tirado-Olivares, S., Navío-Inglés, M., O'Connor-Jiménez, P., & Cózar-Gutiérrez, R. (2023). From human to machine: Investigating the effectiveness of the conversational AI ChatGPT in historical thinking. *Education Sciences*, *13*(8), 803. DOI: 10.3390/educsci13080803

Trust, T., & Maloy, R. W. (2023). AI in the history classroom: Strategies for rethinking teaching and learning. *Teaching History*, *57*(3), 10–15.

UDL(Universal Design for Learning)-IRN. (2011). *Critical Elements of UDL in Instruction* (Version 1.2). Lawrence, KS: Author. The original MITS Critical Elements are located at http://mits.cenmi.org/

Uladi, A. İ., & Arı, E. S. (2023). Big data, big data analysis and aplication areas [Büyük veri, büyük veri analizi ve uygulama alanları] [Yönetin Bilişim Sistemleri Dergisi]. *Journal of Management Information Systems*, *9*(1), 1–14.

UNESCO. (The United Nations Educational, Scientific and Cultural Organization). (2021). *Recommendation on the Ethics of Artificial Intelligence*. Paris: United Nations Educational, Scientific and Cultural Organization. https://unesdoc.unesco.org/ark:/48223/pf0000380455

UNESCO. (2025, January 22). *UNESCO's International Education Day 2025: Embracing the future of Artificial Intelligence in education*. FundsforNGOs. https://news.fundsforngos.org/2025/01/22/unescos-international-education-day-2025-embracing-the-future-of-artificial-intelligence-in-education/

VanLehn, K. (2011). The relative effectiveness of human tutoring, intelligent tutoring systems, and other tutoring systems. *Educational Psychologist*, *46*(4), 197–221. DOI: 10.1080/00461520.2011.611369

Viator, M. G. (2012). Developing historical thinking through questions. *Social Studies*, *103*(5), 198–200. DOI: 10.1080/00377996.2011.606438

Waruwu, D. E. R. (2024). The future of IPS learning: The potential and challenges of implementing AI in the classroom. *International Conference on Applied Social Sciences in Education, 1*(1), 420–424. doi: https://doi.org/DOI: 10.31316/icasse.v1i1.6864

Wei, Y., Jiang, Y. H., Liu, J., Qi, C., Jia, L., & Jia, R. (2025, March). The advancement of personalized learning potentially accelerated by generative AI. In *Society for Information Technology & Teacher Education International Conference* (pp. 991–1000). Association for the Advancement of Computing in Education (AACE).

Williamson, B., & Eynon, R. (2020). Historical threads, missing links, and future directions in AI in education. *Learning, Media and Technology*, *45*(3), 223–235. DOI: 10.1080/17439884.2020.1798995

Xu, W., & Ouyang, F. (2022). The application of AI technologies in STEM education: A systematic review from 2011 to 2021. *IJ STEM Ed*, *9*, 59. DOI: 10.1186/s40594-022-00377-5

Yalçın, A. (2024). Evaluating the opinions of ChatGPT an Artificial Intelligence supported language processing model on social studies lesson [Yapay zekâ destekli dil işleme modeli olan ChatGPT'nin sosyal bilgiler dersi ile ilgili görüşlerinin değerlendirilmesi] [Uluslararası Karamanoğlu Mehmetbey Eğitim Araştırmaları Dergisi]. *International Journal of Karamanoğlu Mehmetbey Educational Research*, *6*(2), 136–152. DOI: 10.47770/ukmead.1485504

Yaşar, Ş., Köse, T. Ç., Göz, N., & Bayır, Ö. G. (2015). The effectiveness of student-centered teaching- learning processes in the social studies: A meta-analysis study [Sosyal bilgiler dersinde öğrenci merkezli öğretme-öğrenme süreçlerinin etkililiği: Bir meta analiz çalışması]. *Anadolu Journal of Educational Sciences International*, *5*(1), 38–56. DOI: 10.18039/ajesi.87691

Yawar, M. E., & Amany, S. (2025). The Use of Artificial Intelligence in Teaching History and its Effects on Community Leadership. [Akademik Tarih ve Düşünce Dergisi]. *Academic Journal of History and Idea*, *12*(1), 319–332. DOI: 10.5281/zenodo.15618802

Yetişensoy, O., & Rapoport, A. (2023). Artificial Intelligence literacy teaching in social studies education. *Journal of Pedagogical Research*, *7*(3), 100–110. DOI: 10.33902/JPR.202320866

Yıldırım, A., & Şimşek, H. (2021). *Sosyal bilimlerde nitel araştırma yöntemleri* [Qualitative research methods in social sciences]. Seçkin.

Yıldırım, I., & Servet, D. (2014). Gamification and education [Oyunlaştırma ve eğitim]. *International Journal of Human Sciences*, *11*(1), 655–670. DOI: 10.14687/ijhs.v11i1.2765

Yılmaz, Ö. (2024). Personalised learning and Artificial Intelligence in science education: Current state and future perspectives. *Educational Technology Quarterly*, *2024*(3), 255–274. DOI: 10.55056/etq.744

Zhou, J., Zhang, J., & Li, H. (2023). Exploring using Virtual Reality in teaching management and evaluation based on citation space analysis. *Journal of Education and Educational Research*, *3*(2), 42–45. DOI: 10.54097/jeer.v3i2.9014

Chapter 6
Digital Age of Educational Learning for Human–Centered Strategies

Ashima Saxena
https://orcid.org/0000-0002-7289-1848
Department of Management and Commerce, The Northcap University, Gurugram, India

Preeti Chawla
Department of Management and Commerce, The Northcap University, Gurgaon, India

K. Praveenkumar
https://orcid.org/0009-0007-1807-6643
KPR IT, Coimbatore, India

ABSTRACT

In the online world of education, genuine connections are essential for academic engagement and personal development. In this chapter, we examine approaches for fostering authentic relationships within online and hybrid learning contexts. It discusses how digital communication technologies, social-emotional learning (SEL), and collaborative platforms can be used to promote belongingness and engagement They discuss the importance of empathy, active listening, and personalized interactions in virtual spaces, and how it differs from physical interactions, and the challenges of digital fatigue, miscommunication and other complexities. Designing a learning community: the role of collaborative teams. Human Centered Design embraces diversity among learners and encourages collaboration among educators. It offers insights and practical strategies for forging connections in digital education and finding a sense of authenticity and emotional well-being.

DOI: 10.4018/979-8-3373-2948-2.ch006

INTRODUCTION

Digital technology has developed rapidly, changing the way people interact, communicate, and learn. In this era of blending traditional classroom learning with virtual platforms, how we interact and build relationships has changed drastically. As you are aware, digital learning provides flexibility and accessibility, along with creative approaches to pedagogy, but it raises some challenges about depth of connection, mental health and the extent to which social and collaborative learning relationships can exist to support development and would. The action of the Water is enough to develop and grow academically, personally and as a full human being. By extension, learning how to nurture nurturing, healthy, authentic relationships in online learning platforms has become the new practical challenge to modern education (Starkey, 2012).

These structures must be founded on authentic relationships that are the backbone of education and determine student engagement, motivation, and wellbeing. In traditional physical set up, based on shared space co-existence, has been giving opportunities for unplanned discussions, emotions support, and sense of belonging. But with the advent of the digital age, these relationship-building interactions have been utterly transformed, and the ways we connect have evolved into something that demands entirely new approaches to establishment and maintenance. These challenges include feelings of isolation, miscommunication and low emotional presence in online learning environments. Lack of in person communication contributes a downturn in social cues. Therefore, it requires that teachers and learning institutions engage in mindful practices to cultivate deep, supportive, and authentic connections in the online learning space between learners and teachers (Brown, 2001).

If used well, technology allows the creation of a form of learning community that engages and inspires. These efforts, combined with other digital tools — video conferencing, discussion forums, interactive platforms, AI-based learning and feedback assistants — have transformed students' interaction with teachers/peers beyond the traditional approach. Such techniques enable resourceful platforms that promote real-time engagement, personalized feedback, and collaborative learning experiences (Baym, 2015). It is worth noting that a mere integration of tech in education will not lead to the fostering of authentic relationships between the learners and the teachers. The real challenge is how to use these tools to foster meaningful engagement, real involvement, and affective bonding. By fostering relationship-building through interactive discussions, group projects, and mentorship opportunities in digital learning spaces, instructors can help students navigate through the distance of technology to find and experience humanity (Livingstone & Sefton-Green, 2016).

The role of social-emotional learning (SEL) is another key element for cultivating connections in digital learning. As such, SEL promotes emotional intelligence, self-awareness, empathy, and good communication skills, all of which are necessary to get along with others. Facilitating emotional intelligence is even more critical in a virtual learning environment where misunderstandings can frequently occur due to the lack of nonverbal cues. By incorporating SEL strategies in their own approaches, educators can build a welcoming environment for their students where they feel heard, valued, and understood. ASMR, mindfulness exercise, sharing sessions, and peer-support groups can enhance emotional connection and promote your sense of community among digital learners (Hartnett et al., 2014).

The personalization of digital education is a key component in nurturing real relationships. Teachers can also build close relationships when working with students face to face — getting to know them as individual, including what they do best, what makes them struggle and what their preferred learning style is. In an online environment, this process takes a more intentional approach. These platforms help educators understand their students' needs and provide tailored support such as personalized learning experiences, adaptive assessments, and one-on-one virtual meetings. Students who feel that their individual voices and learning styles are respected are more likely to participate actively and build meaningful relationships with their instructors and peers (Saykılı, 2019).

While digital avenues enhance learning, digital fatigue, disconnection, and technology overreliance must be remedied lest authentic relationships remain sustainable. Overindulgent screen time and a relative lack of fellow-feeling interaction can lead to lonelier times and disengagement. Educational institutions and educators should balance the desired technological efficiency of such systems with a human-centered approach to learning. Some of these issues, such as taking students out for real-world experiences, and encouraging interactions between classmates beyond digital devices, can help alleviate some of the challenges caused by digital tools to get the most out of your students. Sustaining relationships through digital education is a process of intentionally building a culture of care through which students can feel comfortable expressing themselves to each other and seeking out support(Agrawal et al., 2023a).

The Future of LearningThough the digital landscape is rapidly changing, the future of learning is an amalgamation of the physical and virtual worlds. Hybrid learning models that combine in-person and digital interaction could create an opportunity to bring the best of both worlds together. And with that technology comes the ability to address the key facts that connect students: a model for education that prioritizes relationships as much as it does knowledge. It is imperative that institutions, educators, and students work towards a successful learning environment where technology supports, rather than supplant genuine interactions(Vaithianathan et al., 2024; Yadav et al., 2024).

Only through a multidimensional combination of technology, emotional intelligence, personalisation and intentional engagement strategies can we nurture flourishing and authentic relationships in the digital age of learning. Although the shift to digital is not without its challenges central to education itself, it is also an opportunity to reshape the ways we build and maintain relationships in learning spaces. It is through more generative acts of learning that educators can foster spaces where their students learn, yes, but also learn to learn the social skills needed to succeed in a faster, more chaotically putting world (Rao et al., 2024; Yadav et al., 2024). A human-centered approach to digital learning is key to provide this balance, and ensuring that relationships remain the epicenter of learning.

Objectives

In this chapter, we seek to describe how to achieve authentic and flourishing relationships within digital learning environment. It aims to explore how technology can nurture authentic connections, as well as the challenges of isolation and miscommunication. The chapter also emphasizes social-emotional learning (SEL) as an essential practice in making digital connections stronger. It also has a goal of giving educators actionable strategies to differentiate learning experiences and promote student engagement. Manuals for human-centered digital learning can help close the gap between the digital world and emotion to create supportive human-to-human relationships for learners, teachers and educators alike.

Figure 1. Process of building and maintaining authentic relationships in digital education

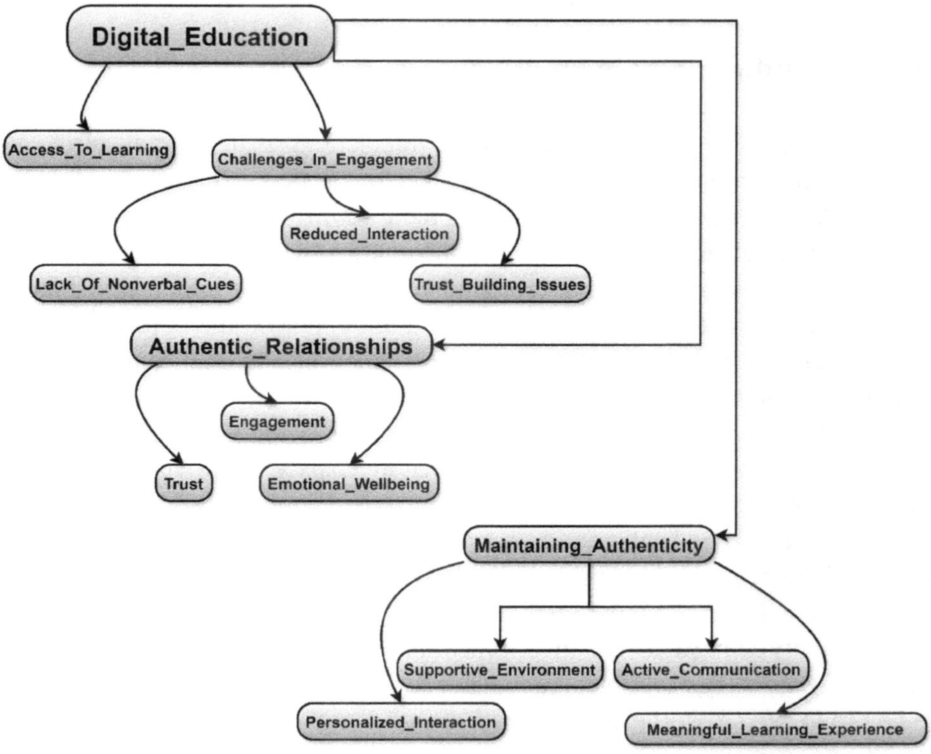

FUNDAMENTALS: AUTHENTIC RELATIONSHIPS IN DIGITAL EDUCATION

With the shift from face-to-face settings to virtual platforms for communication, the digital transformation of education has changed how students and educators engage. Technology has created a pathway for broader access to learning, but also challenges in authentic and meaningful relationships. In turn, authentic relationships in education help lay the foundation of trust, engagement and emotional well-being that ultimately help wash the experience of school to be productive and meaningful (Johnston, 2023; Pahomov, 2014). Maintaining authenticity in digital spaces — where nonverbal cues and face-to-face interactions are scarce — relies on deliberate steps. This includes grasping how authenticity, emotional connection, and the dynamics that underlie relationship-building in virtual spaces work in tandem to create a digital learning environment that is supportive and enriching. The process of building and maintaining authentic relationships in digital education is illustrated in Figure 1.

Defining Authenticity in Online Interactions

Digital Learning Environments: Online interactions that are real, clear and aim to communicate with other students, educators & peers in a meaningful way in face-to-face classrooms, authenticity is practiced through body language, intonation and dialogic interactions. While in the real world these cues are present, in digital realms, they are missing or profoundly modified and require updated forms of building and maintaining real interactions. I think, one of the important angles to authenticity in digital education is to consistency of communication. Trust is strengthened when educators and students engage in ways that resonate with their values, feelings, and worldviews. Clearly defined expectations, candid feedback, and active conversations are the bedrock of creating a space where students feel seen and heard." In addition, personalization is key to real connections. In response to virtual students' varied backgrounds, it is key to build connections: by recognizing where students are coming from, promoting self-expression, and being responsive to the individual needs of those attending class (Watson et al., 2011).

Authenticity demands active involvement and contribution from both the students and the educators. Passive interaction, save for one-way communication through pre-recorded lectures, often inhibits the forging of strong relationships. Rather than attempting to create a one-way lecture that simply mimics in-person learning, facilitating this two-way dialogue through interactive discussions, collaborative works, and real-time feedback can go a long way to engendering that sense of presence and authenticity that can be so hard to capture in a digital education space.

The Role of Emotional Connection in Learning

In a traditional classroom educators organically build relationships through personal interactions, classroom discussion and informal conversations. In digital learning, on the other hand, emotionally connecting is an intentional act harder to do due to the physical distance between students and instructors (Bell & Kornbluh, 2022). Studies have shown when students have emotional connections with their teachers and schoolmates, they show more engagement, perseverance, and achievement. Few strategies to develop emotional connection in digital education include empathy, personalized communication, and social-emotional learning (SEL) strategies. Educators who truly care about their students' well-being — who ask about their progress, listen to their challenges and cheer on their triumphs — strengthen that emotional bond (Venkatasubramanian et al., 2024; Yadav et al., 2024). Additionally, an inclusive and supportive online environment promotes emotional connection. Empowering cooperative learning experiences, peer-to-peer conversations, and group efforts will promoting student interaction and reduce sensations of isolation and disconnection The idea of social presence, which refers to the extent to which learners can perceive others as real and nonverbally interactive in online environments, also plays a vital role in enhancing emotional connections. Integrating video interactions, voice messages, personalized feedback, etc., can close the 'emotional gap' while studying online.

Factors Affecting Relationship-Building in Virtual Spaces

There are a number of factors that impact the building and sustaining of authentic relationships in digital education. These may include modes of communication, access to technology, the level of engagement, and the overall environment for learning (Pauleen & Yoong, 2001). Figure 2 depicts various factors that influence relationship-building in virtual spaces.

Figure 2. Factors affecting relationship-building in virtual spaces

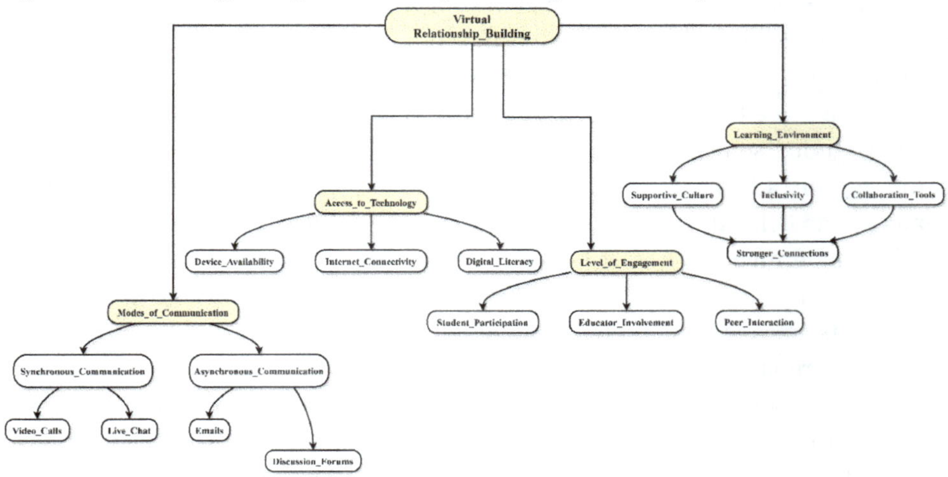

Limited Nonverbal Communication: The nature of digital learning does not involve face-to-face interaction so there is no opportunity to read body language, facial expressions and similar social cues. This can also lead to misunderstandings, misinterpretations and feelings of emotional detachment. Suggested approaches to defeat this are the use of emojis, video conferencing, and tone-aware text communication by educators and students.

Digital Fatigue and Engagement Challenges: Long hours of digital engagement can also lead to burnout, reducing student motivation and engagement. In order to combat this, we need to design digital learning with information for engagement — gamified learning, breakout room talking points, and asynchronous activities that allow flexibility.

Technological Barriers and Accessibility: These discrepancies affect the way relationships are formed, as students with less access may find themselves feeling left out of the loop. Keeling argues that the 2020 pandemic has emphasized the need for equitable learning opportunities and inclusive digital learning platforms; institutions simply cannot afford to blame learning part.

Trust and Psychological Safety: Personalizing the learning experience to cater to individual needs, interests, and challenges makes students feel valued and connected. Taking the time to get to know students and give individual feedback creates stronger connections with learners. Moreover, real-time interactions, discussion forums, and one-on-one mentorship would contribute to social presence, which can ultimately lead to feelings of connectedness within digital spaces.

Personalization and Social Presence: Learners recognized and valued as unique individuals who are connected to something larger can help them feel valued and connected. And these relationships are strengthened when educators take the time to get to know their students and offer constructive feedback designed for that student's needs. Furthermore, other methods of encouraging social presence - such as giving students the opportunity to interact with each other in real-time, facilitating threads of discussion on relevant topics, or simply pairing them with mentors - can help administrators and educators promote social presence in virtual learning environments.

Genuine relationships in digital education play an important role in maintaining students' engagement, motivation, and well-being. Building rapport Teaching through a computer screen poses specific challenges in establishing relationships with learners, but strategies such as the touch of a message, the warmth touch or presence of the instructor, and the personal touch can make learning continue to thrive in digital spaces. Conclusion By understanding the elements that drive virtual communication, as well as enforcing habits that promote authenticity, educators and students can forge the deep, lasting relationships important in contemporary learning environments.

THE ROLE OF TECHNOLOGY IN FOSTERING CONNECTIONS

Technology is changing the way education is delivered, and better access to learning experience, flexibility, and engagement. Digital education creates some of the most potential changing the way students, educators and peers interact with each other without local limitations being disruptive. Indeed, technology provides an array of technologies to improve communication and collaboration, but approaches to use tech for people relations please have to be considered when it is integrated into the contexts of learning. In this chapter, we deal with the role of interactive technologies in learning, the use of tools for virtual communication and the challenge of creating engaging and supportive digital experience by combining technology with human-centered interaction (Haleem et al., 2022). Figure 3 illustrates the significant role of technology in fostering connections in digital education.

Figure 3. Role of technology in fostering connections in digital education

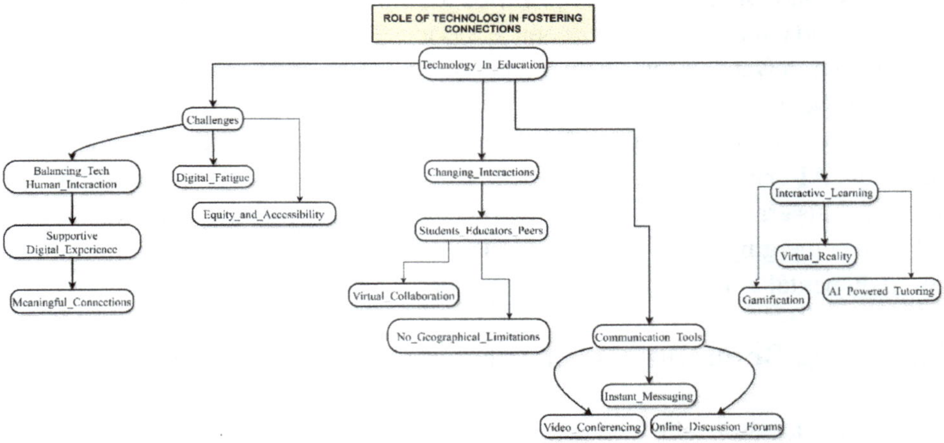

Digital Tools for Interactive Learning

What technology offers is a multitude of facets that promote interaction, collaboration and participation in a well-designed remote learning environment. One of the most game-changing educational technology changes has been the advent of learning management systems (LMS) like Google Classroom, Moodle, and Blackboard. Unless you have been living under a social media-resistant rock, you will have heard of these platforms, which enable educators to structure the coursework, present materials, keep a dialogue going and help personalize the process through creative feedback, becoming an interactive space for learning (Wassell & Crouch, 2008).

Video conferencing applications like Zoom, Microsoft Teams, and Google Meet have gained popularity during digital education. These digital platforms facilitate face-to-face engagement within virtual classrooms where teachers can have synchronous access to students via direct conversations, lectures, and activities in breakout rooms. Features such as sharing screens, virtual whiteboards and real-time polling that boost collaboration and active learning. Professional development focusing specifically on how educators can harness these tools as they teach has the potential to transform and energize classrooms. Collaborative platforms such as Padlet, Miro, and Trello are other types of interactive digital tools that facilitate group work, encourage idea sharing, and present information in visually appealing ways. Such platforms promote collaboration, creativity, and knowledge-sharing while making online learning more fun and community-oriented experience (Yadav et al., 2024).

Kahoot, and Duolingo are all gamification tools that use game-based learning to engage and enhance the educational experience. Features such as quizzes, competition, and reward systems help maintain motivation and engagement and create a bond between students and instructors. Artificial intelligence (AI) chatbots and virtual tutors are also being implicated into greater roles in personalized digital education. AI-driven tools can provide immediate feedback, answer questions, and help students grasp complex concepts. When combined with human interaction, AI and other emerging technologies can improve learning experiences while retaining the fundamental emotional and social elements of the education process.

Enhancing Communication Through Virtual Platforms

Digital education relies heavily on good communications to strengthen relationships. The pandemic has minimized the interaction via the use of virtual platforms, allowing their students and educators to socialize and communicate. But the success of virtual communication is contingent upon using these tools to create authoring conversations with each other. Discussion forums and online communities — whether integrated into an LMS space or existing in their cohesive environments, such as Discord, Reddit, or Slack — provide students with opportunities to communicate beyond the classroom. Aspects of these platforms foster peer interaction, sharing of knowledge and collaborative solving of problems, keeping students connected and feeling supported. But for these forums to work, educators must take the bull by the horns and facilitate discussion, ask relevant questions, and encourage students to participate (Haleem et al., 2022).

In digital education, messaging and email communication is a cornerstone in sustaining the student-instructor relationship. Prompt and responsive communication through emails, chat functions in LMS platforms or instant messaging tools like WhatsApp and Telegram allows students to feel like they are heard and supported. The establishment of communication norms, such as expected response times, availability hours, etc. assures that students are able to engage in the communication process in a timely way with regard to the feedback and assistance they receive.

Even social media integration helped to create more connectiveness in digital education. Students also use social media to participate in academic discussions, follow subject matter experts and help each other on projects via platforms such as LinkedIn, Twitter and Facebook. Social media can also be used to develop professional networks and share research ideas; however, it needs to be done with caution to not affect the compartmentalization of the personal and academic lives. The use of multimedia content is one of the main contributors to improving communication in digital education. Formats such as podcasts, video lectures, interactive infographics, or storytelling-based educational content draw learners in, allowing them to see themselves in what they are learning and thus creating immersive learning experiences. Online tools like YouTube, TED-Ed and Empuzzled allow educators to simplify complex ideas with engaging visuals and presentations No longer limited to static lessons and audios, online learning has become more immersive, allowing for interaction and participation.

Balancing Technology and Human Connection

Technology offers a plethora of tools to facilitate clinical communication and interaction, but in reality, the most important attribute of education at any level is the human relationship. A significant challenge of digital learning is to ensure that technology adds to, rather than takes away from, the relationships students, educators and peers have with one another (Pauleen & Yoong, 2001; Wassell & Crouch, 2008).

Another significant point about balancing technology and human connection is about having a sense of presence in digital learning environments. Social presence—that feeling of everyone being "real" and emotionally invested in an online environment—is essential to building authentic relationships. Video interactions, voice messages, and live Q&A sessions can foster this sense of presence and lack of isolation. Another key component is the personalization of digital education. When educators respond to individual learning styles, provide specific feedback and call students by name, they have concentrated on a process in which learners feel valued and formative. While AI-based analytics and adaptive learning platforms can adjust coursework to meet individual needs, there is no substitute for an involved human mentor and guide.

Preventing the issues of digital fatigue and excessive screen time is another challenge associated with digital learning. Extended screen time and a passive approach to online lectures may contribute to disengagement and fatigue. This can be prevented by ensuring teachers make the most of offline activities as well as hands-on learning opportunities, encouraging students to apply what they learn in their real life environment. With the potential to strike that balance, hybrid learning models can effectively integrate digital spaces within human-centered forms of education.

Fostering Authentic Relationships — Culture of Care and Empathy in Digital Education Teachers can do this by checking in on students' well-being, fostering open discussion and creating a supportive learning environment. A balance of technology and human interaction can be achieved by fostering trust and collaboration which will discourage hard content delivery, give priority to emotional intelligence over rigid delivery (Vijayakumar et al., 2024).

Through interactive learning and engagement, it has provided virtual communication, connectedness, collaboration, and continuity in learning. Yet the key to developing meaningful relationships in online education is how these tools are used. Educators create a thriving learning environment by answering yes to the use of active technology engagement, but a no to student screen engagement, while also having the ability to p produce asynchrony, creating sustainable and relevant learning experiences. Ultimately, the journey of digital education is new and exciting, and we must center our efforts on approaches that foster relationships and make students feel connected, supported, and invested in their learning.

SOCIAL-EMOTIONAL LEARNING (SEL) IN THE DIGITAL AGE

Social-Emotional Learning (SEL) is essential in education; it helps the learner develop emotional intelligence, self-awareness, empathy, and relationship skills. In traditional classes, SEL comes easily, thanks to personal interactions, group work and classroom talks. But in digital education, which places students and educators at physical distance, the intentional integration of SEL is that much more important. In the online learning environment, without the opportunity for face-to-face interaction, the risk of isolation, disengagement and lack of emotional connection is high; hence, there is need to devise the approach that allows to build significant casual communication, meaningful relationship and ideals of emotional wellbeing during online learning. This chapter discusses how important SEL is for digital education, tips for building emotional intelligence, and how to create a strong virtual learning environment(Sapra, 2019).

The Importance of SEL in Online Education

When interactions take place over the vast expanse of the digital world—through screens—it is even more important to understand, express, and manage emotions in order to keep students engaged and help promote productive learning relationships. SEL encourages students to improve self-regulation, resilience, and sense of belonging, which are linked to academic success as well as developing successful well-being. Lack of social presence — the feeling of being with other people in a virtual world — is one of the most serious problems of online education. In classrooms, students form relationships through shared experiences, casual conversation and nonverbal communication. Still, in the virtual context, those casual interactions are greatly limited, paving the way for emotional detachment. SEL goes a long way to fill this gap by teaching students how to be emotionally engaged and empathetic toward their digital interactions (Whitehead, 2017).

Both motivation and self-discipline, which are necessary ingredients for online learning, significantly improve with SEL. "It requires students to be really self-managing without the physical structure of a classroom to keep their heads down on their schoolwork so that their work is done," he said. SEL promotes goal-setting, time management and self-reflection, which are all critical components of a student's ability to succeed in a digital learning environment. The digital learning experience can also be stressful, and students have reported feelings of anxiety and isolation when they are not on track with their coursework or feel disconnected from their peers. SEL helps students learn to manage stress, cope with challenges, and seek help when necessary. It brings a sense of community and emotional resilience, assuring students that they have support and that they can thrive in their educational journey.

Strategies for Developing Emotional Intelligence

Emotional intelligence EQ is one element of social and emotional learning SEL that enables students to identify, understand, manage their emotions, and be aware of others' emotions. In the world of online education, EQ is something that must be cultivated with other delivery models that promote self-awareness, social awareness, and emotional regulation intentionally (Effrem & Robbins, 2019; Whitehead, 2017).

1. **Self-Awareness and Reflection:** Teachers can promote self-awareness by prompting students to reflect on how they feel and what they experience. You can do this through journaling, mindfulness-based activities such as guided

meditation or writing your goals. Through journaling, students can process their thoughts, manage stress, and maintain focus. Moreover, the self-motivation and resilience is promoted by a learning environment where students set academic and personal goals.

2. **Building Empathy and Social Awareness:** Empathy is a key element for any meaningful connection, it is all the more important in a digital world. Some of these strategies are: Virtual Group Discussion, Role Playing and Scenario-Based Learning, Diversity & Inclusion Activity. By engaging students to each share their perspective on different topics, these methods can build understanding and mutual respect. Such real-life scenarios and discussions around cultural differences nurture inclusivity and respect, allowing students to better empathize with people around them.
3. **Emotional Regulation and Conflict Resolution:** The role of emotions in a good online learning experience. Strategies might include encouraging open communication, teaching conflict resolution skills, and giving positive feedback. Other people open communication established trust and emotional well-being, where conflict resolution set fires prevention and strengthen relations. Acknowledging student efforts fosters confidence and emotional resilience.

Creating a Supportive Digital Learning Environment

A digital learning environment that supports students is one with emotional well-being at its core; that helps kids feel like part of the community (Johnston, 2023).

1. **Establishing a Sense of Community:** Online learning engagement increases by feeling connected. Online Icebreakers — A great way for educators to create a welcoming digital space is to host icebreaker activities, encourage peer collaboration (for example, through group projects) and establish an inclusive classroom culture. These skills ensure students feel welcome, authenticated, and promote collaboration and relationship-building. This positive learning environment is also shaped by establishing norms that respect diversity of thought and belief.
2. **Strengthening Student-Teacher Relationships:** A good student-teacher relationship increases engagement and emotional support. Educators can also create connections by giving personalized feedback, holding virtual office hours, and showing kindness and understanding. "Calling students by name, providing individual check-ins and acknowledging students' challenges can go a long way in providing motivation and the impetus to a positive state of mind," she adds.

3. **Promoting Mental Health and Well-Being:** As digital learning can lead to burn-out and stress, it is important to integrate well-being practices. Schools and educators can promote breaks and screen-free times, access to mental health resources, and normalization of mental health conversations. Finding a balance between real-life and online activities helps fight against unintentional digital fatigue, while also encouraging the sharing of info regarding counseling services, as well as mindfulness exercises to maintain emotional wellness.

Digital education relies heavily on social emotional learning (SEL) which aids students in developing emotional intelligence, resilience and building significant relationships. As students feel lonely and disconnected online, those intentional, albeit indirect, approaches can still help students feel supported, engaged and valued. Educators can help students navigate digital learning in a way that gives them confidence using self-awareness activities, empathy-building exercises, and emotional regulation strategies to integrate SEL. Furthermore, by focusing on aspects like building community so that students feel connected and supported, as well as building relationships with teachers and providing mental health activities, we have seen improvements in the health of learners overall. As we move forward into the digital education evolution, the importance of SEL will become even more important to our students in the areas of academic success and emotional and social well-being in our digital future.

Figure 4. Personalization and Student Engagement in digital education

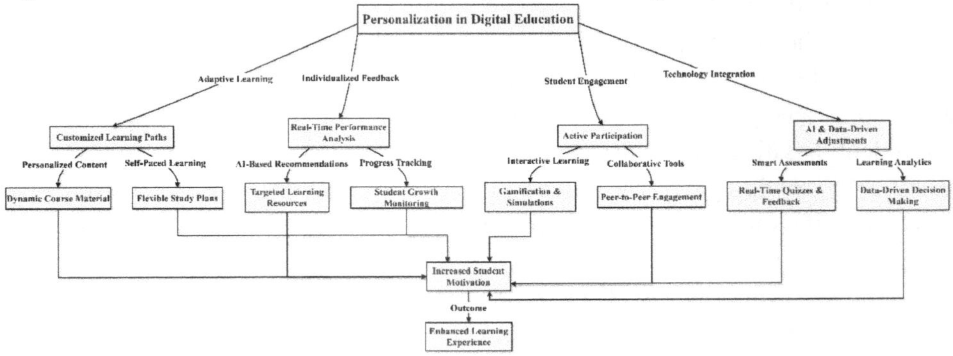

PERSONALIZATION AND STUDENT ENGAGEMENT

Personalized learning has gained prominence in the realm of digital education as a revolutionary concept that provides customized experiences based on the unique requirements, learning styles, and advancements of each learner. Personalized learning by contrast uses technology to dynamically adjust the materials, feedback, and engagement that students receive to their individual needs — away from one-size-fits-all approaches (Bhimavarapu, 2025). Personalization is essential for online courses as it helps mitigate students' feelings of disconnectedness from their peers, teachers, and the content itself caused by the absence of physical presence, thereby increasing motivation, trust, and participation in the course. This chapter examines the importance of adaptive learning, how individualized support aids in the development of trust, and how to build active engagement in digital spaces. Figure 4 depicts the impact of personalized learning on student engagement in digital education.

Adaptive Learning and Personalized Feedback

Adaptive learning technology is changing everything about the way we educate by providing tailored learning opportunities based on a student's strengths, weaknesses, and learning pace. Unlike static curricula, adaptive learning platforms utilize data-driven insights to modify instructional content, tailoring the experience to the appropriate level of challenge and support (Das et al., 2024; Gopi et al., 2024; Kalaiselvi et al., 2024).

A few of the high-impact implementations of adaptive learning is in the form of AI-powered learning websites such as Smart Sparrow. These platforms assess student engagement and performance and adapt course content to individual requirements. If a student has difficulty with a certain concept or problem, for example, the system responds by providing more resources, different explanations, or targeted exercises. Conversely, if a student is demonstrating mastery, they're invited to progress without force redundancy, leaving learning both efficient and engaging.

Adaptive learning is also furthered by personalized assessments, which move us away from traditional, standardized testing. Digital education can even allow for formative feedback in the way of quizzes with instant feedback, self-paced assignments, gamified learning experiences that adapt based on how students answer. The ability to adapt in real-time keeps learners motivated by avoiding the risk of being overwhelmed with information that either is too difficult or too simple. Personalized feedback is essential in adaptive learning and crucial for directing students towards improvement. In contrast to traditional grading that offers little in terms of insights, digital learning environments create room for feedback that is immediate, constructive, and actionable.

- Automated feedback systems provide instant responses to quizzes and assignments, enabling students to identify mistakes and rectify them immediately.
- Personalized instructor feedback allows students to receive targeted guidance based on their essays, projects, and discussions, providing a closer engagement and better understanding of the material.
- Peer feedback and collaborative reviews promote interaction and knowledge-sharing among students, enriching their learning journey.

They specifically provide a customized and granted access and help the students in resolving their issues related to projects and assignments.

Building Trust Through Individualized Support

Trust is particularly important when teaching remotely because students have far less access to their instructors and each other than in traditional classroom settings, so if they don't trust the materials, they will not feel obliged to stay motivated and engaged. Research in education suggests that trust and respect between students and teachers are key factors in creating a positive learning culture (Rafiq et al., 2025).

Building trust in digital education is best achieved through individualized support. When teachers invest effort into getting to know the nuances of every child's needs, learning styles, and life situations, students develop a sense of connection and purpose. There are several important strategies for establishing trust in the team:

a) Regular One-on-One Check-Ins: Virtual meetings encourage one-on-one mentorship, providing academic and emotional guidance, enhancing the human element of digital education.
b) Creating a Safe Environment for Open Communication: Open-door policies, like discussion boards, email access, or virtual office hours, can help students feel included and trusted.
c) Constant Recognition of Individual Successes: Class discussions and compliments on acknowledgments at home improve student confidence and motivation with praise. Badges, progress tracking and certificates are examples of digital platforms that recognize students for what they have completed, helping them see their progress.
d) Personalization according to student interest: If the learning material can connect to the parallel world or whatever a student might like, it will make

the content much more relatable and engaging. "When students choose their project topics, we give them responsibility.

Encouraging Active Participation in Online Spaces

The good participation rate is a dead giveaway that students are engaged in online learning. Yet, creating meaningful interaction in virtual classrooms will require conscious plans to facilitate collaboration, discussion, and a sense of presence in a community (Bhimavarapu, 2025; Rafiq et al., 2025).

1. **Creating Interactive and Engaging Learning Environments:** Using interactive tools can make the online landscape feel more familiar and easier to access. Kahoot, and Socrative, for example, promote live engagement in your session, while virtual breakout rooms within Zoom or Microsoft Teams open the floor for more directed discussions. Gamified learning experiences, such as game-based activities, make learning more enjoyable and help students to better retain concepts.
2. **Encouraging Student-Led Discussions and Contributions;** Promote active student engagement — enable student-led forums, multimedia-based inputs, and tasks that solve real-world problems. They allow for accountability, creativity, and interaction within the classroom, while also providing students with real-world applications of their knowledge through various teaching styles such as case studies, debates, and problem-based learning. It promotes ownership and investment of the students.
3. **Providing Consistent and Encouraging Feedback:** Feedback is critical for ensuring ongoing student motivation and engagement. Reward participation and call out contributions in both online discussions as well as in individual forums, and create incentives for participation; tackle passive engagement with targeted encouragement. The act of responding to students' posts, identifying insightful or particularly key points, and posing a follow-up or related question in the follow-up reply will help maintain interest. Identifying such factors can also help inspire less engaged students(Chandra et al., 2025; Sreedhar et al., 2024).

Through the use of interactive learning experiences, student-led discussions, and constructive feedback, instructors can establish an active digital learning community where students are engaged and empowered. But, that is only half the job done, the other half lies in personalization and student engagement in a digital education environment. Adaptive learning, personalized feedback, and individualized learning experiences allow educators to fine-tune the learning environment and meet students' diverse needs. Individualized support builds trust, making students feel that they belong and are in a safe, empathetic environment where they will be taken care of, which is motivating and inspiring. Moreover, using interactive tools, trusting students to lead discussions or exploring real-world applications amplify learning outcomes and create a strong digital learning community. Therefore, as online education matures, critical focus areas to offer deep and impactful digital learning are personalized learning along with continuous student engagement.

CHALLENGES IN NURTURING RELATIONSHIPS IN DIGITAL LEARNING

In a world of increasingly digital learning, educators and students both find themselves with unique challenges to establish and maintain meaningful relationships. As technology pictures options to accessibility and flexibility, it additionally poses challenges which may hamper engagement, social connection, and equitable participation. The lack of physical presence, dependence on virtual communication, and unequal access to technology serve as obstacles that need to be overcome in order to develop real connections in digital teaching (Gee et al., 2017). This chapter will review three critical distractions, digital exhaustion and social disconnection, communication issues in a virtual environment, and equity and access issues, and explore ways to mitigate these distractions. Figure 5 outlines the challenges in nurturing relationships in digital learning.

Figure 5. Challenges in Nurturing Relationships in Digital Learning

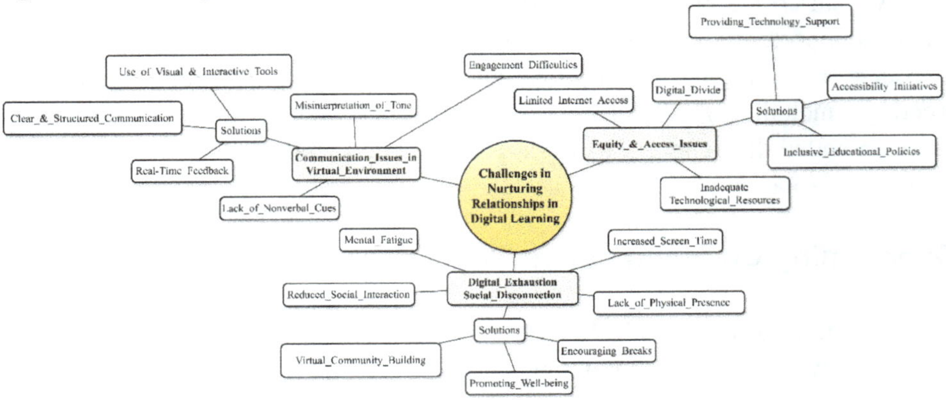

Digital Fatigue and Social Disconnection

One of the most pressing issues of digital learning is the rising phenomenon of digital fatigue leading to students as well as educators suffering from fatigue induced by an overload of screen exposure, a consistent diet of online content while being devoid of the physical interaction that has become a thing of the past. In contrast to traditional classrooms, where students move between activities, interact face to face and enjoy informal socialization opportunities, online learning may involve long stretches of focus on screens. But this can likewise result in a lack of motivation, poor engagement and separation from the learning process (Nussbaum-Beach & Hall, 2011).

Digital fatigue is interlinked with social disconnection, as digital online learning environments can be isolating environments with very few opportunities to engage in serendipitous interactions, informal exchanges and gestures that all help develop a richer connection. In brick and mortar schools, students bond through common experiences, teamwork and nonverbal cues. But these phenomena are often displaced with structured discussions, scheduled meetings, and more text-based communication, such as e-mails and messaging, in virtual settings. The above can lead to a sense of isolation, withdrawal, and disengagement from academic content and peers.

Finally, you can perpetuate these strategies as an educator by adding in screen-free assignments, incorporating asynchronous learning experiences, and prompting students to take breaks in between activities to avoid digital fatigue and social disconnection. The combination of synchronous and asynchronous education gives students the opportunity to cover and digest matter at their own pace, relieving pressure to be present 24/7 online. Similarly, encouraging informal social interaction (e.g., virtual coffee breaks, online study groups, and peer-mentoring programs) provides opportunities for students to engage in social dialogue beyond academic discourse. Encouraging use of video conferencing for small-group interpersonal meetings, including gamified learning experiences, and using discussion forums for open-ended dialogue are also ways to enhance social engagement and reduce feelings of isolation.

Overcoming Communication Barriers in Virtual Settings

Communication is a critical element of relationships in any learning environment; however, barriers in communication tend to inhibit collaboration, trust, and engagement in a digital education space. Face-to-face conversations help us use tone, expressions, and body language to understand what is being communicated, but communication in a remote workplace is mostly limited to text, emails, and scheduled calls. Leaving out a crucial aspect of human communication, tones, adds to misunderstandings, emotional distance, and intent. Moreover, students who are less confident in writing will likely feel reluctant to join discussions, resulting in a low engagement level and sense of belonging (Hutchison et al., 2020).

The lack of spontaneous interaction is one of the key communication barriers in virtual environments. In the physical class rooms, students can ask questions, clarify doubts, and talk to each other casually as well as with the instructors. In contrast, most online communication has to be scheduled or formalized (e.g., writing an email), which can slow the process and make responses seem less urgent. This obstacle is made even more problematic when students feel reluctant to reach out due to fear of being judged, lack of confidence or uncertainty about digital communication etiquette.

In online learning, language barriers, differences in digital literacy and technological challenges may also impact communication. It can be challenging for students from diverse linguistic backgrounds to articulate their ideas in a language they don't use in their daily lives, especially in text-based discussions where tone and intent can be more difficult to interpret. Moreover, for individuals less adept with digital tools, grappling with utilizing learning platforms, accessing course materials, or participating efficiently in virtual discussions can pose an additional challenge.

Educators can address these barriers by laying out clear communication norms and can encourage multimode interactions (e.g. discussions as video, voice messages, collaborative digital whiteboards, etc.) Offering multiple approaches to engagement (such as discussion forums, live chat features, and breakout rooms) provides students with more options for how and when they want to communicate. Clearly doing so is one way to help students feel more at home: setting expectations for response times, guidelines for respecting other people's speech in person and online and for creating a loving space, etc. In addition, providing language support, accessibility features, and digital literacy training is essential in ensuring that students of all backgrounds are equipped to communicate effectively in virtual settings.

Addressing Equity and Accessibility Issues

And equity and accessibility are crucial in a digital learning environment; the divide in equitable access in both technology and learning environments can affect how easily students are able to engage in a meaningful way. In addition to offering opportunities for remote and flexible learning, online education has also highlighted pre-existing inequalities; students from low-income backgrounds, rural areas and those who are disabled are particularly impacted (Bhimavarapu, 2025).

For all the apparent convenience and flexibility of digital learning, one of the most significant challenges is the digital divide, which divides students with high-speed internet access, updated devices and a conducive learning atmosphere, versus those without. Many students must use family computers, live with unstable internet access or lack a quiet study space, making it hard for them to log on when a live session is in progress, when to submit work and participate in collaborative activities that are possible in class. This leads to uneven learning outcomes and perpetuates socio-economic inequalities.

Beyond access to technology, access to learning is a major barrier for students with disabilities. Not all online platforms are designed with accessibility in mind, making it difficult for students with visual, auditory or motor impairments to navigate course content. Not providing closed captions for all videos, screen reader compatibility for content used, and alternative text for images can create barriers to access to information for students who require assistive technologies. Pre-defined and rigid course structures which do not cater to different learning needs can leave neurodiverse students behind, as they may need other instructional methods or more guidance or help than the standard, offered course.

In addition to being prepared for emergencies, institutions must focus on digital inclusion, offering things like loaner devices, subsidized internet access and community learning spaces for students who have limited access to technology. Developing learning platforms with accessibility in mind, providing diverse content formats (text, audio, video), and utilizing assistive technologies are ways to make digital education more accessible. Educators can utilize universal design for learning (UDL) principles that advocate for a more flexible learning path that suits diverse ways in which learners work. Examples of flexible / adaptable approaches: providing alternative means of assessment, granting extensions, providing materials in ways that all students can engage with regardless of their needs or context.

In digital learning, nurturing relationships can be more challenging, including digital fatigue, communication barriers and equity concerns. Although technology can support flexible and remote learning, it demands conscious work to build connection, engagement and perception of belonging. To combat digital fatigue, we can try to balance out screen time and encourage more spontaneous social interactions, aside from classes; combining various modes of formal learning can also address feelings of isolation. In overcoming communication barriers, it is important to develop inclusive and multimodal communication strategies that support different types of learners. Institutional commitment to bridging the digital divide and supporting students with diverse needs is critical to ensuring equity and accessibility in digital education. Educators and institutions can also do more to pre-emptively explore alternatives to mitigation in such spaces—especially where digital interactions are concerned—to promote authentic relationships and meaningful learning experiences.

BEST PRACTICES FOR EDUCATORS AND INSTITUTIONS

Digital education is always evolving, but forming meaningful relationships and creating engagement is still a focus for educators and institutions. Since studying in online environments can be lonely, it is important to have techniques for establishing community, encouraging collaboration, and building peer-to-peer communication. With the right balance of technology and human connection, virtual learning can be more engaging and supportive, and it is up to educators to make it happen. This part focuses on top practices when it comes to community, virtual collaboration, and mentorship in digital education (Davidson et al., 2010; Davidson & Goldberg, 2009).

Fostering a Sense of Community in Online Learning

Fostering a community is instrumental in students feeling engaged, motivated, and academically successful in online teaching and learning. A sense of connection with others — peers and instructors — will help students feel a sense of engagement and create positive learning experiences. Establishing a welcoming online atmosphere begins with clear lines of communication, expectations for interaction, and encouragement of frank conversation (Davidson et al., 2010).

Teachers can start off by customizing the learning, using video an introduction, message boards and virtual meet and greet to get acquainted with classmates and the relationship building from there. And encouraging students to share their background information, interests, and learning goals can make the classroom atmosphere more relatable and engaging. Regular check-ins and feedback loops—via surveys, and one-on-one meets can also augment the sense of connection, making sure that students feel heard and given the support they need amidst their learning journey.

Strategies for Effective Virtual Collaboration

Traditional teamwork can be tough when working remotely because time zone differences, the lack of face-to-face interactions, and varying levels of digital fluency can be a challenge. Still, when cooperation is well-designed, it can be enormously powerful. Educators can design structured group projects, providing students with defined roles and responsibilities with deadlines to uphold accountability and participation. Collaborative tools: Using collaborative tools (like Google Workspace, Microsoft Teams, and Miro) allows students to work together in real time which improves productivity and interaction(Butler et al., 2018).

Another key is synchronic and synchronic collaboration. While live sessions make it easy to ask questions and engage in discussions, asynchronous methods — including shared documents, recorded discussions and threaded message boards —

provide freedom to engage, giving students with differing schedules the opportunity to participate. Moving as much interaction to the digital space as possible in setting up virtual brainstorming sessions, peer review work, and collaborative web-based work areas fosters a sense of foamed collaboration and the team working within an enterprise to get things done.

Educators need to promote constructive feedback and reflection by advising what good feedback/language looks like in a virtual environment. Enhancing collaboration effectiveness: top tips Teaching etiquette of communicating digitally, upholding dialogues respectfully, including peer evaluation mechanisms. Institutional support for collaboration can also help with professional development workshops for educators on practices for good virtual teamwork and classroom management online.

Encouraging Peer-to-Peer Interaction and Mentorship

Peer-to-Peer and Mentor Interaction online learning presents new challenges in developing relationships and building rapport — vital aspects for successful learning, as peer-to-peer and mentor-pupil interaction and support is arguably more important online than in person. Offering structured peer mentorship programs enable students to help one another, as this can minimize feelings of isolation and improve learning outcomes. Creating friendships between new students and already experienced students strengthens an environment of collaborative learning and leads to academic and personal development(Clough, 2013).

Peer-led discussion groups and study circles allow students the opportunity to engage in meaningful discussions that may not happen in the traditional classroom setting. Platforms like Slack, Discord, or institutional learning management systems (LMS) act as informal discussion, collaborative problem-solving, and peer support forums. Educators could also facilitate peer feedback on assignments to promote creating communities of interaction and learning.

For long-term mentorship sustainability, institutions can establish alumni engagement programs in which alumni give advice to students. Guest speakers, online networking, community-building activities are all ways to build more connections in the online learning ecosystem. Through the implementation of mentorship opportunities, collaboration, and strong virtual communities, a more engaging, inclusive, and impactful digital learning experience can be developed for all via educators and institutions.

THE FUTURE OF RELATIONSHIP-BUILDING IN DIGITAL EDUCATION

Personalized learning, interaction and relationship: The emerging future of school education paradigm in the AI & global hi-technology artefacts era. The move towards blended instruction, the rise of artificial intelligence (AI) and greater use of virtual platforms, provide both opportunities and challenges in creating meaningful connections. So when new technologies offer us additional strategies for collaboration or engagement, the challenge is in how to humanize learning so that these remain emotional, trusting, and personal(Najjar et al., 2025). This chapter sees how change growing from hybrid learning models, AI and innovations affect relationships in education, whilst bringing human centered back in. Figure 6 depicts the future of relationship-building in digital education.

Figure 6. The Future of Relationship-Building in Digital Education

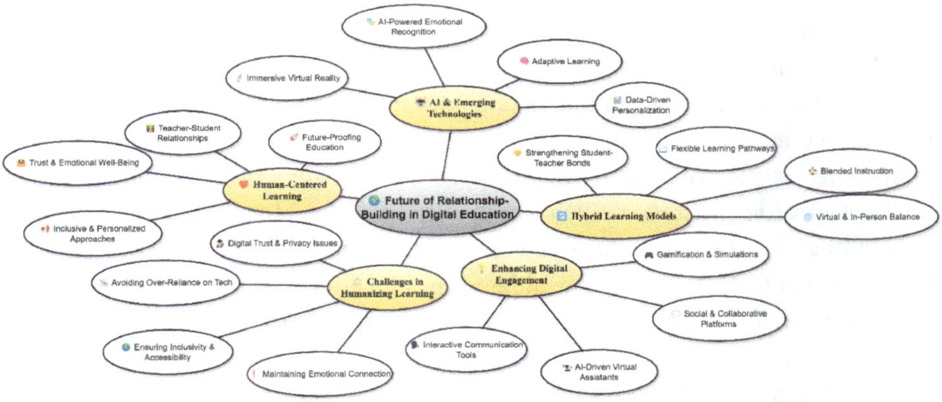

Hybrid Learning Models and Their Impact

One of the most under-discussed topics is the rise of hybrid learning. That said, a flexible solution like this—combined with traditional face-to-face opportunities as needed—would enable students to participate in the benefits of synchronous and asynchronous activities. Hybrid learning model implementation has far-reaching consequences in the area of building relationships as it connects physical and virtual classrooms and helps better connect students with educators. One major benefit of hybrid learning is that it offers a blend of digital engagement and face-to-face interactions. Although online modes of learning are useful in terms of accessibility and convenience, face-to-face interactions allow for group instructiveness, reading body language, and observation components. The combination lets students forge deeper connections with each other and their leaders while enjoying the flexibility of digital education(Straub, 2025).

However, hybrid learning also creates inequality in engagement to in-percentiles and online students. Without intentional strategies, virtual learners may feel disconnected from what is happening with their classroom, resulting in them participating less. To tackle this challenge, institutions need to utilize technology that enables seamless integration, including real-time collaboration tools, interactive discussion boards, and live-streamed sessions that promote active participation among remote and in-person learners alike. Educators may also institute turn-based arrangements, in which students switch between in-person and virtual attendance, engendering a feeling of inclusion and belonging.

The Role of AI and Emerging Technologies

AI and other emerging technologies are changing the way relationships are formed and maintained in education. The systems powered by AI can contribute in a number of ways and the input can be tailored to the individual student needs. AI can help improve Personalized Learning by analyzing student engagement with lessons, allowing instructors to identify which topics students need help with and give them specific assistance. Such a high level of personalization has the potential for strengthening the particular dynamics of the student-teacher relationship and allows learners to feel seen and validated in their journey (Chandra et al., 2025; Varalakshmi et al., 2025). 'Intelligent tutoring systems' are yet another major contribution of AI that are able to provide real-time guidance and adaptive feedback. Such systems allow for a persistent space of interaction prior to, during and after the course. AI-driven chatbots and virtual assistants can respond to common queries from students, provide learning suggestions, and promote peer collaboration through study groups guided by common interests and goals (Clough, 2013).

Moreover, the use of virtual reality (VR) and augmented reality (AR) are further improving relationships in digital education by immersing students in an experience-based learning environment. VR classrooms let students participate in realistic simulations, promoting teamwork and interaction like no other type of online course. Similarly, AR overlays can drive collaboration, making digital education more engaging.

While the applications of AI will continue to grow, it will be important to use those emerging technologies with ethics in mind, so that we do not find ourselves replacing human relationship with AI, but rather augmenting them. Automation can improve processes, certainly, but no matter how advanced, it still lacks the emotional intelligence, the mentorship and human connection that teachers bring, and AI will never take that away.

Maintaining Human-Centered Learning in a Digital World

While this technology is evolving to educate digitally, we must keep a human face so that we can engage meaningfully with each other. Technology can help in communication and engagement, but necessarily students need to be given time when they can learn emotionally, psychologically. Human-centered education places a premium on student well-being, empathy, and community-building, making sure that learning digitally is about granting people an experience that is personal and fulfilling. Active engagement strategies, such as live discussions, group projects, and personalized feedback around learning objectives, are among the most fail-safe approaches to maintaining human-centered learning. Recognize that video conferencing, voice notes, and interactive storytelling can help educators develop trust and rapport with students. Promoting reflective techniques, including journaling and peer mentoring, further connects students with what they are learning and with one another (Najjar et al., 2025).

Mental health and social-emotional learning (SEL) must also be prioritized within digital education in our institutions. Online learning can be isolating, and students may have trouble with motivation and stress in virtual environments. By incorporating Social Emotional Learning (SEL) elements, like emotional intelligence, resilience and self-awareness, teachers can cultivate spaces where students feel accepted as individuals, which enhances their academic performance. By offering access to counseling services, virtual wellness programs, and peer support groups, educators can foster a culture of well-being and support in digital education.

Finally, relationship building in digital education needs to be based on inclusive and equitable learning practices. Such that with changes in accessibility, diverse representation, and culturally responsive pedagogy all students feel a sense of belonging. These institutions would be well served to invest in training their educators to navigate effective digital relationship-building with the goals of engagement, empathy, and meaningful connection in their virtual and hybrid classrooms(Agrawal et al., 2023b).

The blending of hybrid learning models, AI-driven innovations, and a focus on human-centered learning will redefine relationship-building in this new era of digital education. Implementing hybrid models will allow for a balance between digital contact and face-to-face learning and will support new technology to deliver tailored, personalized, interactive learning experiences, stronger human bonds are a must, demanding intentional nurturing of emotional investment, inclusivity, and well-being. Through developing these types of relationships, we can ensure that digital education is not only technologically high-powered, it also remains deeply human and profoundly important.

CONCLUSION

One of the essential skills needed in the online teaching world is the ability to stimulate True Relationships which leads to engagement, trust and more. With the rise of virtual classrooms, educators and institutions should implement strategies that combine technology with human interaction in a sensitive and effective way. Educational relationships play a vital role in the success of digital learning environments, positively affecting students' motivation and emotional well-being while also contributing to academic success and thus cannot be excluded from educational interactions.

Hybrid learning models are a response and, when properly implemented, a solution to the problems involved in remote learning. If thoughtfully designed, hybrid environments have the potential to unite digital and face-to-face experiences, enabling students to form closer relationships with peers and educators. Just as AI and other emerging technologies are disrupting just about every industry on the planet, so too are they changing the landscape of education itself with personalized learning experiences, real-time feedback, and interactive engagement. Using these tools can have the potential to enhance our connections, but they also need to be used mindfully, with the focus on supplementing — not replacing — our human interactions. The human-centered approach continues to be critical in sustaining productive relationships in online education. Implementing strategies like social-emotional learning (SEL), active and hands-on participation, mentorship programs or partnerships, and using inclusive practices makes students feel welcome and as though they belong in the learning environment. Similarly, barriers to effective communication and a lack of access must be considered to avoid limiting equitable access for all learners.

As technology reinvents education, we must not lose sight of creating authentic, supportive, inclusive relationships. Using communication tools that work well with technology, supporting social and emotional health as well as academics, and fostering collaboration among students, educators can create a digital learning experience that is not only state-of-the-art but also personal. To create the future of education, innovation needs to be married with empathy so that digital learning environments can continue to be environments of connection, growth and lifelong experience.

REFERENCES

Agrawal, A. V., Pitchai, R., Senthamaraikannan, C., Balaji, N. A., Sajithra, S., & Boopathi, S. (2023a). Digital Education System During the COVID-19 Pandemic. In *Using Assistive Technology for Inclusive Learning in K-12 Classrooms* (pp. 104–126). IGI Global.

Agrawal, A. V., Pitchai, R., Senthamaraikannan, C., Balaji, N. A., Sajithra, S., & Boopathi, S. (2023b). Digital Education System During the COVID-19 Pandemic. In *Using Assistive Technology for Inclusive Learning in K-12 Classrooms* (pp. 104–126). IGI Global.

Baym, N. K. (2015). *Personal connections in the digital age*. John Wiley & Sons.

Bell, S., & Kornbluh, M. (2022). Networking in the digital age: Identifying factors that influence adolescents' online communication and relationship building. *Applied Developmental Science*, *26*(1), 109–126.

Bhimavarapu, U. (2025). Personalized Learning in the Digital Era: Unlocking Potential Through. *Optimizing Research Techniques and Learning Strategies With Digital Technologies*, 187.

Brown, J. S. (2001). Learning in the digital age. *The Internet and the University: Forum*, *71*(72), 65–71.

Butler, D., Leahy, M., Twining, P., Akoh, B., Chtouki, Y., Farshadnia, S., Moore, K., Nikolov, R., Pascual, C., & Sherman, B. (2018). Education systems in the digital age: The need for alignment. *Technology. Knowledge and Learning*, *23*, 473–494.

Chandra, S., Ghule, G., Bilfaqih, S. M., Thiyagarajan, A., Sharmila, J., & Boopathi, S. (2025). Adaptive Strategies in Online Marketing Using Machine Learning Techniques. In *Digital Transformation Initiatives for Agile Marketing* (pp. 67–100). IGI Global.

Clough, G. W. (2013). *Best of both worlds: Museums, libraries, and archives in the digital age*. Smithsonian Institution.

Das, S., Lekhya, G., Shreya, K., Shekinah, K. L., Babu, K. K., & Boopathi, S. (2024). Fostering Sustainability Education Through Cross-Disciplinary Collaborations and Research Partnerships: Interdisciplinary Synergy. In *Facilitating global collaboration and knowledge sharing in higher education with generative AI* (pp. 60–88). IGI Global Scientific Publishing.

Davidson, C. N., & Goldberg, D. T. (2009). *The future of learning institutions in a digital age*. The MIT press.

Davidson, C. N., Goldberg, D. T., & Jones, Z. M. (2010). *The future of thinking: Learning institutions in a digital age*. The MIT Press.

Effrem, K., & Robbins, J. (2019). Social-Emotional Learning: K-12 Education as New Age Nanny State. White Paper No. 192. *Pioneer Institute for Public Policy Research.*

Gee, E., Takeuchi, L., & Wartella, E. (2017). *Children and families in the digital age: Learning together in a media saturated culture*. Routledge.

Gopi, B., Kokila, M. S., Bibin, C. V., Sasikala, D., Howard, E., & Boopathi, S. (2024). Distributed technologies using AI/ML techniques for healthcare applications. In *Social Innovations in Education, Environment, and Healthcare* (pp. 375–396). IGI Global.

Haleem, A., Javaid, M., Qadri, M. A., & Suman, R. (2022). Understanding the role of digital technologies in education: A review. *Sustainable Operations and Computers*, *3*, 275–285.

Hartnett, M., Brown, M., & Anderson, B. (2014). Learning in the digital age: How are the ways in which we learn changing with the use of technologies. *Facing the Big Questions in Teaching: Purpose, Power and Learning,* 116–125.

Hutchison, K., Paatsch, L., & Cloonan, A. (2020). Reshaping home–school connections in the digital age: Challenges for teachers and parents. *E-Learning and Digital Media*, *17*(2), 167–182.

Johnston, J. B. (2023). What is an Authentic Relationship? *Jesuit Higher Education, 12*(2).

Kalaiselvi, D., Ramaratnam, M., Kokila, S., Sarkar, R., Anandakumar, S., & Boopathi, S. (2024). Future developments of higher education on social psychology: Innovation and changes. In *Social Innovations in Education, Environment, and Healthcare* (pp. 146–169). IGI Global.

Livingstone, S., & Sefton-Green, J. (2016). *The class: Living and learning in the digital age*. New York University Press.

Najjar, N., Rouphael, M., Bitar, T., & Hleihel, W. (2025). The rise and drop of online learning: Adaptability and future prospects. *Frontiers in Education*, *10*, 1522905.

Nussbaum-Beach, S., & Hall, L. R. (2011). *The connected educator: Learning and leading in a digital age*. Solution Tree Press.

Pahomov, L. (2014). *Authentic learning in the digital age: Engaging students through inquiry*. ASCD.

Pauleen, D. J., & Yoong, P. (2001). Relationship building and the use of ICT in boundary-crossing virtual teams: A facilitator's perspective. *Journal of Information Technology*, *16*(4), 205–220.

Rafiq, S., Zaki, K. A., & Nawaz, A. (2025). PERSONALIZED LEARNING IN THE DIGITAL AGE: HARNESSING TECHNOLOGY FOR STUDENT SUCCESS. *Contemporary Journal of Social Science Review*, *3*(1), 1515–1528.

Rao, S., Behera, G., Meenakshi, S., Rajini, J., Pravin, T., & Boopathi, S. (2024). Entrepreneurial insights from higher education. In *Advances in Business Strategy and Competitive Advantage* (pp. 101–132). IGI Global.

Sapra, R. (2019). Social and emotional learning in digital age: Future trajectories for children and adolescents. *International Journal of Education and Management Studies*, *9*(4), 237–239.

Saykılı, A. (2019). Higher education in the digital age: The impact of digital connective technologies. *Journal of Educational Technology and Online Learning*, *2*(1), 1–15.

Sreedhar, P. S. S., Sujay, V., Rani, M. R., Melita, L., Reshma, S., & Boopathi, S. (2024). Impacts of 5G Machine Learning Techniques on Telemedicine and Social Media Professional Connection in Healthcare. In *Analyzing Current Digital Healthcare Trends Using Social Networks* (pp. 209–234). IGI Global Scientific Publishing.

Starkey, L. (2012). *Teaching and learning in the digital age*. Routledge.

Straub, S. (2025). Inclusive Citizenship Education in Teacher Education through Interaction and Active Relationship Building. In *Inclusive Citizenship: Interdisziplinäre Perspektiven auf Bürgerschaft und politische Bildung* (pp. 413–422). Springer.

Vaithianathan, V., Shastri, D. S., Nandakumar, V., Misba, M., Kumar, P. S. V. V. S. R., & Boopathi, S. (2024). NEP Policy Implementation Strategies in Education in India. In *Educational Philosophy and Sociological Foundation of Education* (pp. 325–356). IGI Global., DOI: 10.4018/979-8-3693-3587-1.ch013

Varalakshmi, S., Thakur, D., Sharma, R. V., Al Habsi, L. S., Chandra, S., & Boopathi, S. (2025). Taxing Innovation for Leveraging Tax Policy to Foster Growth and Learning in the Digital Economy. In *Navigating Strategic Partnerships for Sustainable Startup Growth* (pp. 391–420). IGI Global Scientific Publishing.

Venkatasubramanian, V., Chitra, M., Sudha, R., Singh, V. P., Jefferson, K., & Boopathi, S. (2024). Examining the Impacts of Course Outcome Analysis in Indian Higher Education: Enhancing Educational Quality. In *Challenges of Globalization and Inclusivity in Academic Research* (pp. 124–145). IGI Global.

Vijayakumar, G. N. S., Domakonda, V. K., Farooq, S., Kumar, B. S., Pradeep, N., & Boopathi, S. (2024). Sustainable Developments in Nano-Fluid Synthesis for Various Industrial Applications. In *Adoption and Use of Technology Tools and Services by Economically Disadvantaged Communities: Implications for Growth and Sustainability* (pp. 48–81). IGI Global.

Wassell, B., & Crouch, C. (2008). Fostering connections between multicultural education and technology: Incorporating weblogs into preservice teacher education. *Journal of Technology and Teacher Education*, *16*(2), 211.

Watson, K., McIntyre, S., & McArthur, I. (2011). Trust and relationship building: Critical skills for the future of design education in online contexts. *Iridescent*, *1*(1), 22–29.

Whitehead, L. (2017). Social-emotional development in the digital age. *Exchange*, *19460406*(236), 16–20.

Yadav, U., Pitchai, R., Gopal, V., Kumar, K. R. S., Talukdar, M., & Boopathi, S. (2024). Powers of Higher Education Leadership: Navigating Policy and Management in Academic Institutions. In *Navigating Leadership and Policy Management in Education* (pp. 103–136). IGI Global., DOI: 10.4018/979-8-3693-9215-7.ch004

Chapter 7
From One-Size-Fits-All to Individualized Support: AI in the Inclusive Classroom

Mustafa Kayyali
https://orcid.org/0000-0003-3300-262X
Maaref University of Applied Sciences, Syria

ABSTRACT

As classrooms grow increasingly diverse, the limitations of one-size-fits-all instruction become harder to ignore. This chapter explores how artificial intelligence is reshaping inclusive education by offering dynamic, real-time support tailored to each learner's needs. Moving beyond theoretical ideals, we examine how AI-powered scaffolding tools can bridge learning gaps, foster autonomy, and create more equitable learning environments. Yet, personalization through AI is not without tension—it raises pressing questions about bias, agency, and the role of the human teacher. Through a critical and reflective lens, this chapter interrogates both the promise and complexity of using AI to transform inclusivity from aspiration into actionable reality.

INTRODUCTION

There was a time when classrooms were imagined as uniform spaces—rows of desks, identical books, a single teacher, and a singular way of delivering knowledge. For decades, education systems operated on the comforting illusion that students learn in similar ways and at a similar pace (Mifsud, 2023). This model, rooted in the industrial age, thrived on efficiency and standardization. Yet, real classrooms have always been messier, more complex, and far more human. Learners bring with

DOI: 10.4018/979-8-3373-2948-2.ch007

them a kaleidoscope of experiences, languages, abilities, emotional landscapes, and cognitive differences that simply do not fit neatly into standard molds.

In recent years, the call for inclusive education has grown louder. No longer just a moral imperative or a legal mandate, inclusion is increasingly recognized as essential to pedagogical excellence. But while the ideal is widely accepted, the path to achieving truly individualized support remains elusive. Teachers, often overburdened and under-resourced, struggle to tailor lessons to students with learning disabilities, language barriers, neurodiversity, or trauma histories—let alone to the quiet needs of gifted or disengaged learners. The sheer variety of learning profiles in any given classroom can make individualized support feel more like an aspiration than an achievable goal.

Enter artificial intelligence. AI is not a silver bullet—but it offers something education has long lacked: scalable personalization (Dembe, 2024). With the rise of AI-powered tools in education, we're beginning to witness a shift from static, linear instruction to adaptive learning environments that respond to each student's progress, preferences, and needs in real time. AI doesn't just help teachers *do* things differently—it invites them to *think* differently about what teaching and learning can be (Shah, 2023). The one-size-fits-all approach starts to fracture, making space for dynamic, student-centered models that adjust with remarkable granularity. But as we step into this new terrain, we must proceed thoughtfully. AI's integration into inclusive education is full of paradoxes. It promises support but may also reproduce bias. It empowers learners, but might diminish human connection. It can foster equity—and yet, in the wrong hands or poorly designed systems, it can deepen existing disparities. The technology's potential is immense, but so too are the ethical, pedagogical, and emotional complexities it introduces.

This chapter is an invitation to sit with that complexity. It explores the intersection of artificial intelligence and inclusive education—not as a seamless success story, but as an ongoing dialogue. We'll examine how AI can meet learners where they are, without replacing the teacher's empathy, intuition, or cultural knowledge. We'll ask hard questions about what it means to personalize learning in ways that are meaningful, just, and sustainable. And we'll consider how educators can remain not only relevant, but central, in an age of intelligent machines.

Inclusive education is not merely a destination—it is a commitment to listening, adapting, and evolving alongside our learners. In the chapters of education history, AI may become one of the most powerful tools we've ever had to realize that commitment. But only if we wield it wisely.

RETHINKING INCLUSIVITY IN THE AGE OF AI: A PARADIGM SHIFT IN EDUCATION

Inclusivity. It's a word we've heard so often in educational discourse that its meaning has, in some ways, become dulled—like a once-bright coin handled too frequently. Yet, peel back the layers of policy documents and reform talk, and what remains at the heart of inclusivity is simple: belonging. Not just physical presence in a classroom, but deep, dignified inclusion—being seen, heard, and valued for who one is, and how one learns. The kind of inclusion that demands we reorganize not just our seating charts, but our priorities. And now, in the age of artificial intelligence, that reorganization takes on a new urgency—and a new possibility.

Let's admit it: education has long flirted with the fantasy of uniformity. We built our systems to accommodate the mythical "average" student (Bennett, 2021). Standardized tests. Grade-level benchmarks. Mass-produced textbooks. Curricula that march in straight lines. But anyone who's ever taught knows the truth is messier. Learners defy symmetry. They stutter and soar at different moments. They carry invisible histories. Some arrive already on the margins. Some get pushed there. The so-called inclusive classroom has often felt more like an ambitious slogan than a lived reality. Until now. Or at least, that's the hope AI offers—the chance to disrupt the old mold, not just modify it.

Artificial intelligence didn't originate in education, of course. It came to us from tech giants, from neural networks, from the logic of pattern recognition and machine learning (Martin et al, 2021). It was built for optimization. Prediction. Efficiency. But now, it's in our schools, our lesson plans, even our students' hands. And with it comes the possibility to reshape the very contours of inclusion.

Still, we must ask: what does inclusivity *mean* when mediated by an algorithm? Can it remain a human value in a machine-driven age? At its most optimistic, AI in education holds the promise of precision. It doesn't tire. It doesn't overlook the quiet kid in the back who struggles to process auditory information (Kayyali, 2025 B). It doesn't forget that Jamal reads two grade levels behind or that Fatima shines in visual-spatial reasoning but falters in timed assessments. It can track. Adapt. Suggest. Respond. Not reactively, but preemptively. In theory, it meets each learner not where we think they are, but where they *actually* are—based on data, not guesswork. And that alone can be revolutionary. But let's not romanticize it.

There's something eerie, maybe even uncomfortable, about imagining a machine scanning through a child's learning habits, making real-time decisions about what they should see next. The intimacy of teaching—the eye contact, the intuitive hunch, the improvisation—is hard to replicate with lines of code (Jerve, 2023). And more than that, there's the risk of something quieter, subtler: outsourcing care.

You see, when we hand over personalization to algorithms, we risk forgetting what inclusion really asks of us. Not just differentiated instruction, but *human responsiveness.* The willingness to sit with discomfort. The ethical responsibility to hold space for contradiction and ambiguity. AI can mimic patterns. It can't make moral judgments. It can't discern when a student's poor performance isn't a learning gap, but a sign of grief (Sullivan & Fosso Wamba, 2022). Or hunger. Or fear. Inclusivity has always been emotional work. Political work. Social work. AI doesn't erase that. It only reconfigures the landscape on which we must now do it. But let's circle back. Why is this moment different? Why are so many educators—some cautiously, others enthusiastically—talking about AI as the next frontier of inclusive education?

Because scale has always been the barrier. We know how to support students individually—small class sizes, custom lesson plans, learning accommodations. But the system isn't built to do that *for everyone*. AI, in its ideal form, offers scalability. It can simultaneously adjust content for a student with dyslexia, scaffold language for an emergent bilingual learner, and challenge a gifted student with extension tasks (Mitra, 2024). It does not forget. It does not fall ill. It does not take offense. And in this way, AI becomes a kind of mirror. It reflects back to us what might be possible if we were truly able to give each child the attention they deserve. That mirror is both hopeful and haunting. Because it also shows us how far we've fallen short. But let's not be too quick to surrender the narrative. AI does not have to be the story's protagonist. We still hold the pen. And the way we design, deploy, and interpret AI tools will determine whether they serve the cause of inclusion—or undermine it.

Let's be real for a moment. Data is not neutral. The datasets we use to train educational AI systems are shaped by historic inequities, cultural blind spots, and unconscious biases (Lewis, 2025). If a system learns from flawed input, it will perpetuate flawed output. Imagine an AI tutor that unintentionally favors dominant language structures. Or a recommendation algorithm that flags certain behaviors as "off-task" when they're actually cultural expressions of engagement. The implications are sobering. So, the paradigm shift is not just technological. It must also be philosophical. Epistemological. What do we mean by learning? By success? By inclusion? These are not static concepts. They are culturally embedded, and AI forces us to interrogate them in ways we've long postponed. And then there's the matter of agency.

Who gets to decide how a student's path is personalized? The algorithm? The teacher? The student themselves? True inclusion does not just mean *being accommodated*. It means having voice, choice, and ownership over one's learning journey. It means we must design AI tools that do not *do* things to students, but *with* them. That allow for self-correction, refusal, questioning. That treat students not as data points, but as co-authors. I've spoken with teachers who both marvel at and recoil from AI-driven platforms. "It's helpful," one said, "but it also makes me feel… replaceable." That tension is real. And it deserves attention. If AI is going to be part of inclusive education, then it must also be inclusive of teachers—their judgment, their relationships, their professional identities. We cannot build systems that strip educators of their roles as moral and emotional anchors. We must design tools that complement, not supplant.

There's also something to be said about time. AI promises speed. Instant feedback. Rapid adaptation. But inclusion, as anyone who has practiced it knows, is often slow (Challoumis, 2024). It unfolds in moments of patience, repetition, trust-building. How do we reconcile these temporalities? Can a high-speed machine help us slow down in the right ways? Can it make room for the kind of learning that resists metrics?

We must be brave enough to ask. Let me offer a speculative scene: a student logs into an AI-powered learning platform. The system tracks her keystrokes, her pauses, her error patterns. It adjusts accordingly. She's presented with a new set of tasks—easier in one area, harder in another. She progresses. But what it doesn't see is the bruise hidden under her sleeve. The way she hesitated before logging in because her brother needed help with the baby. The fact that she speaks two languages at home, and neither one is English. The way her eyes light up when she's asked to tell a story orally, but go blank when she's handed a worksheet. AI can't know that. Not yet, anyway. Which is why, even as we lean into its possibilities, we must hold onto the messiness of the human. The contradictions. The stories. The moments that don't fit the model. To rethink inclusivity in the age of AI is to walk a tightrope between efficiency and empathy (Vallor, 2024). Between automation and attention. Between what machines can calculate, and what only humans can hold.

We need new literacy—technological, certainly, but also ethical, emotional, even spiritual. The kind that asks not just "What can we do?" but "What should we do?" and "Whom does this serve?" and "At what cost?" Because inclusion is not a checkbox. It is not achieved by plugging in a new platform. It is not measured solely by accessibility metrics or dashboard analytics. It is lived. Felt. Practiced in real time, in real classrooms, with real people. And that's the paradox, perhaps: AI may help us reach deeper levels of inclusion, but only if we remain *more* human in the process, not less (De Cremer & Kasparov, 2021). Let this be the shift we seek—not just a change in tools, but a change in values. Let us use AI not as a substitute for care, but as a scaffold for it. Let us build systems that respond to data, yes, but are also grounded in dignity. Let us remember that at the heart of every inclusive classroom is not an algorithm, but a relationship. That's where the future of education begins. Not in the wires. But in the willingness to listen.

UNDERSTANDING LEARNER DIVERSITY: NEEDS, GAPS, AND THE LIMITS OF UNIFORM INSTRUCTION

Walk into any classroom on any given day, and you'll find more than just bodies in chairs. You'll find micro-worlds. A constellation of minds, each orbiting around its own experiences, abilities, memories, fears, and dreams. Some of them are wide-eyed and eager, others guarded and half-asleep. A few may be fluent in the dominant language; others may be silently translating every word in their heads. One might be wrestling with algebra, while another is mourning a grandparent, or nursing invisible wounds that no test can measure. And yet, most systems expect them to be taught as though they're essentially the same.

This is the central contradiction of modern schooling: we talk about learner diversity as if it's self-evident—something every teacher knows, accepts, even celebrates. But the machinery of education still hums along on the premise of sameness. It thrives on uniform benchmarks. Standardized pacing. One textbook per subject. A collective, forward motion dictated not by readiness, but by calendars. And in the space between our recognition of diversity and our methods of instruction, a painful gap yawns open. Let's linger in that gap for a while. Because it's where most of our students actually live.

The Myth of the Average Learner

Somewhere along the way, education became obsessed with the notion of "average." We built entire curricula, school calendars, and assessment rubrics around this spectral, statistical middle—the "typical" child, the "expected" reader, the "standard" performer. But here's the thing: the average learner does not exist. At least not in any meaningful, flesh-and-blood way. You will never find a student who is precisely average in reading, writing, numeracy, attention, emotional regulation, processing speed, and creativity all at once (Baron, 2023). It's a chimera. A myth stitched together from aggregate data. Yet this mythical learner shapes everything. Lessons are planned around them. Exams are written for them. Interventions are triggered by how far a real student deviates from this imaginary norm. And so, students who don't fit the mold—who are slower, faster, quieter, louder, more chaotic, less compliant—are flagged as problems to be fixed, not as voices to be heard. We call it remediation. We call it extension. We call it differentiation. But all too often, these are afterthoughts—patches sewn onto a garment never meant to fit everyone in the first place.

Diversity Isn't Just a Label—It's a Landscape

When we talk about diversity in classrooms, we tend to fall into tidy categories: special education, English language learners, gifted and talented, neurodivergent, at-risk (Harry & Klingner, 2022). But human variation resists tidy lines. It spills over, mixes, contradicts itself. Consider Maria. She's an English learner, but also profoundly gifted in mathematics. She draws intricate diagrams when she's bored. She zones out in group work but thrives in one-on-one discussion. Her speech is slow, but her thinking fast. Where does she "fit" in our categories? How do we serve her? Does she get pulled for ESL support or accelerated math? Or think about Amir. Diagnosed with ADHD, he's been called disruptive more times than he can count. He speaks out of turn, forgets homework, taps his pencil incessantly. But he's also the first to notice when a classmate is hurting. He asks questions that others are too afraid to pose. What kind of data captures that? Diversity, in truth, isn't about labels. It's about complexity. It's about honoring the full tapestry of how humans learn—not just in terms of ability or language, but in emotion, motivation, history, and culture. It's messy. And profoundly beautiful. But here's the hard part: teaching to this complexity—*really* teaching to it—is almost impossible within the logic of one-size-fits-all instruction.

The Tyranny of Uniformity

Uniform instruction, despite its noble intentions, often becomes a form of quiet violence. That sounds dramatic, maybe. But think about what it feels like to be constantly behind. To see everyone else grasp something that confuses you. Or to be perpetually ahead, waiting while the rest of the class catches up. To be misunderstood, mislabeled, mismeasured. Over time, these experiences leave marks. Not just academic gaps, but internalized beliefs: *I'm not smart. I don't belong here. School isn't for people like me.* And let's not forget the teachers, caught in the crossfire. Most teachers don't *want* to teach uniformly. They know their students are different. They feel it every day. But they're also asked to cover a syllabus, meet pacing guides, prepare students for high-stakes tests. There's pressure to move, to complete, to report. In that space, personalization becomes a luxury—a thing to do *after* the "real" teaching is done (Simons & Masschelein, 2021). And so the system grinds on. Some students fall through the cracks. Others float just above them, barely holding on. A few thrive, but not because the system is designed for them—more often, they succeed in spite of it. We can't pretend that tweaking around the edges will fix this. We need a new model.

Learning Gaps: Symptoms, Not Deficiencies

Let's talk about gaps. "Learning gaps" has become a buzzword—especially post-pandemic. Policymakers invoke it like a rallying cry. Schools issue reports. Curricula are rewritten to "catch students up." But gaps are not just academic absences. They are *symptoms*—of mismatch, of disconnection, of systems that failed to recognize a student's way of learning before it was labeled as "behind." Take the case of Meera, who struggled with reading for years. Everyone assumed she had a decoding issue. It wasn't until someone realized she had undiagnosed vision problems—coupled with anxiety—that the picture made sense. Her "gap" wasn't a lack of effort or intelligence. It was a compound effect of unmet needs, misunderstood signals, and late intervention. Or look at Jacob, who rarely participates in class discussions. Teachers assume he's disengaged. But he's autistic, and open-ended verbal participation overwhelms him. When given a digital forum to respond in writing, he thrives—offering rich insights his peers hadn't considered. The "gap" disappears when the method shifts. What we call a gap is often just the visible surface of a deeper disconnect—between what a learner needs and what the system offers. So, what would it look like to flip the script? To design for difference, rather than retrofit it?

From Accommodation to Anticipation

Historically, educational responses to learner diversity have been reactive. A student struggles (Rowan et al, 2021). A referral is made. An Individualized Education Plan is created. Supports are layered on. But this approach—while well-intentioned—reinforces a deficit mindset. It treats the student as the deviation, the outlier. The one who needs to be *brought back* into alignment. What if, instead, we designed systems that *expect* diversity? Not as an exception, but as the starting point. This is where the concept of universal design for learning (UDL) begins to reshape the landscape (Fovet, 2023). At its heart, UDL asks: How can we make learning accessible, flexible, and meaningful *from the outset*? How do we provide multiple means of representation, engagement, and expression—not because some students "need" it, but because *all* students benefit from it? The shift here is philosophical as much as practical. It requires us to stop viewing accommodations as add-ons and start seeing them as foundational. It asks us to let go of rigid sequencing and embrace branching paths. It demands a pedagogy of *presence*—one that doesn't rush past the learner in pursuit of curriculum coverage, but lingers, listens, adapts (Kayyali, 2025 D). AI, as we'll explore further in this book, has the potential to support this shift. It can provide real-time feedback. Offer personalized scaffolds. Identify patterns of engagement that might otherwise go unnoticed. But only if it's rooted in a framework that values human complexity, not just performance optimization.

Emotional and Cultural Layers of Diversity

So far, we've spoken largely about cognitive and behavioral differences. But diversity runs deeper still. A student's cultural background shapes not only how they learn, but how they interpret the learning environment. Eye contact. Silence. Questioning authority. What counts as participation or respect. These aren't universal. They're cultural scripts. And when teachers unknowingly default to their own norms, students from different backgrounds may be misread—graded unfairly, disciplined disproportionately, or excluded from full participation. There's also the emotional weight students carry into the classroom. Trauma. Poverty. Racialized experiences. Bullying. These don't sit quietly in the corner during math lessons. They walk in with the learner, shadow every interaction, shape every risk taken—or not taken. To truly understand learner diversity, we must attend to these invisible currents. We must learn to see what's not on the worksheet. We must develop what some call "educational empathy"—the capacity to recognize that every behavior is communication, every silence a kind of speech. And here again, we must tread carefully with data-driven tools. Because emotional and cultural nuances are hard to quantify. They resist tidy classification. They require presence, not just processing.

Reimagining the Role of the Teacher

All of this raises a pressing question: if learner diversity is this vast, this multidimensional, how can one teacher possibly meet all these needs? The answer is: alone, they can't. But in a reimagined system—one that blends human insight with technological support—they might not have to (Zhang & Tian, 2024). Let's not reduce the teacher's role to content delivery. That's not what learners crave. They crave connection. Encouragement. Curiosity. Someone who sees them not as a profile or a datapoint, but as a whole, becoming person. Technology can handle some of the heavy lifting—tracking progress, suggesting resources, flagging concerns. But only the teacher can interpret that data in context. Only the teacher can notice the look in a student's eyes that says *something's wrong today*. Only the teacher can build the trust that makes learning safe. In this light, the teacher becomes less of a transmitter and more of a translator (Chen, 2025). A curator. A guide who knows when to step in and when to step back. And in doing so, they honor diversity not by managing it, but by embracing it. We've spent too long contorting learners to fit the system. It's time the system learns to bend. To flex. To stretch itself around the glorious, unpredictable, and profoundly human messiness of the classroom. And it begins with understanding—truly, deeply understanding—that learner diversity is not a hurdle. It's the heartbeat of education. And unless we listen to it, we'll always be out of rhythm with those we seek to serve.

AI AS A RESPONSIVE ALLY: PERSONALIZING LEARNING PATHWAYS IN REAL TIME

Picture this: a student, let's call her Noor, sits quietly at the back of the classroom. She's not disruptive. She's not particularly behind. But she's invisible. Not in the ghostly sense, but in the way that happens when you're somewhere between thriving and struggling—just enough to go unnoticed. Her questions never quite make it to the surface. Her misunderstandings stay tucked beneath polite nods. And each day, she slips a little further into the fog of "fine."

Now imagine something else. Imagine that the system watching over Noor—the digital scaffolding behind her learning—doesn't just track correct or incorrect answers. It notices her hesitation before answering a question. It picks up on her repeated rereading of a particular sentence. It recognizes that she performs better when visual aids accompany instructions, or that her comprehension drops when her emotional tone signals stress. And then it does something radical. It adjusts. In that moment, and many more like it, artificial intelligence becomes more than a tool. It becomes a kind of *responsive presence*—an ally working in tandem with the teacher to personalize learning in real time, to restore visibility to the learners who've been quietly drifting through the margins. That's the promise, isn't it? But before we lose ourselves in the poetry of possibility, let's unpack the mechanics—and the meaning—of this shift.

Personalization Without Permission: The Double-Edged Sword of Adaptivity

There's something magical—almost eerie—about systems that seem to "know" what a learner needs before the learner does. Algorithms trained on vast swaths of behavioral data can now predict, with stunning accuracy, when a student might fail a test, disengage from a lesson, or require extra support (Firat, 2023). It's like having a digital intuition. And yet, it's not magic. It's math. It's probability. It's pattern. The danger, of course, lies in the illusion of certainty. When a machine determines that a student should be rerouted to remedial material based on a subtle lag in response time, we must ask: is that a helpful nudge, or a premature judgment? Personalization, when driven entirely by metrics, can begin to feel like preemption. The student may never have a chance to struggle productively—to surprise even themselves. We walk a fine line between empowerment and overreach. Real-time personalization must be rooted in *context*. A student's slowness on a Tuesday morning may be caused by cognitive fatigue, yes—but it might also stem from hunger, a broken night's sleep, or the aftermath of a family argument. Algorithms don't always see that. Teachers sometimes don't either. But together—machine and human—there's potential for something more layered. What if AI didn't just "decide" what to show the student next? What if it *suggested*—and then invited the teacher or student to respond, override, engage? In this way, personalization becomes a dialogue, not a directive.

Responsiveness as a Pedagogical Principle

Let's pause here, because the word "responsive" deserves some space. It implies more than reaction. It suggests awareness. Attunement. The ability to not only register a signal, but to *feel* its rhythm and respond in kind. That's what good teachers do—they scan the room, they notice the slump of a shoulder, the flicker of frustration. They pivot. They adapt their tone, slow their pace, find another metaphor. Can a machine ever truly do that? Not in the full, human sense. But in its own way, AI is learning to approximate this pedagogical responsiveness (Huang, 2022). And in doing so, it expands the range of what's possible—especially in crowded classrooms, especially for learners who are often overlooked. Let's consider an example. In a blended learning environment, a student named Ray is working through a math module. His scores are middling—not alarmingly low, not high enough to attract attention. But the system registers a curious pattern: Ray consistently excels at spatial reasoning problems, but struggles with multi-step word problems. It doesn't just flag this to the teacher—it tailors Ray's path accordingly, offering scaffolded prompts, visual breakdowns, and mini-refresher lessons on reading comprehension. Meanwhile, the teacher receives an alert—not a red exclamation mark of failure, but a nuanced snapshot: *Ray demonstrates strength in visual logic. Reading load may be impeding problem-solving accuracy. Consider integrating multimodal representations in your next group activity.* This kind of insight, delivered gently and in real time, enables *relational* personalization. Not just "here's the next task," but "here's how you might understand your student better." And this is where AI begins to shift from being a cold calculator to a responsive co-educator.

The Temporal Fluidity of Real-Time Support

Let's talk about time. Because traditional instruction is painfully linear. You teach a unit. Assess. Move on. Students who get it move forward. Students who don't... well, sometimes they catch up. Sometimes they don't. The system keeps marching. AI disrupts this. It breaks the tyranny of the timeline. In a responsive learning environment, time becomes elastic. Students can loop back to review prior concepts without fear of holding up the class (Tolman & Kremling, 2023). They can move ahead when ready. Pacing is no longer dictated by the group average, but by the learner's readiness, fatigue, curiosity, even mood. And this flexibility is not just logistical—it's emotional. It tells students: *Your process matters. Your timing is valid.* That's no small thing. Because for so many learners—especially those who've been marginalized by rigid systems—the ability to move at one's own pace is a form of liberation. It's an antidote to shame. A restoration of agency.

From Mass Instruction to Micro-Moments of Insight

Real-time AI feedback doesn't just benefit learners. It transforms teaching. In the traditional classroom, formative assessment is a challenge. Teachers can't be everywhere at once. They rely on raised hands, facial expressions, incomplete homework, hunches. By the time a misunderstanding becomes visible, it may have already calcified. But with AI, every click, pause, and keystroke becomes a data point. The system can detect confusion before the student verbalizes it. It can surface trends that would otherwise remain buried. This isn't about surveillance—it's about surfacing signals that help teachers intervene earlier, more precisely. It's about *micro-moments* of insight. A student struggling with multiplication isn't just sent back to practice drills—they're guided through targeted conceptual breakdowns, with support tailored to the exact point of friction (Newton et al, 2024). The system knows whether the issue lies in number sense, procedural memory, or simple fatigue. And the teacher? They receive a distilled narrative, not a spreadsheet. They see patterns across the class—who's stuck, who's slipping, who's soaring. They don't have to guess where to intervene. They can spend less time firefighting and more time connecting.

Agency in the Algorithmic Age

Still, there's something we must hold onto with white-knuckled care: student agency. Personalization, if not handled thoughtfully, can become a form of algorithmic paternalism—students being guided by systems they don't understand, down paths they didn't choose (Carreira, 2024). It's a subtle kind of disempowerment, dressed up as support. That's not what inclusion looks like. So how do we build systems that personalize *with* students, not *for* them? We give them visibility into the process. We let them see how and why the system makes recommendations. We allow them to opt out, to push back, to steer. We design interfaces that invite reflection: *Why do you think this task was suggested? How did that lesson feel? Want to try something different next time?* We restore human voice in the loop. We also design for variability in self-direction. Not every learner wants full control. Some crave structure, others autonomy. AI systems can—and should—adapt their *level* of adaptivity. And they should always leave room for dialogue. Because in the end, true personalization is not about perfect fit. It's about meaningful participation. It's about co-creating a path.

Quiet Revolutions: What We Don't Always See

Here's what we don't often talk about. AI, used well, has the power to humanize education—not dehumanize it. Yes, it's built on abstraction (Aberšek et al, 2023). Yes, it runs on invisible rules. But when designed with care, it can re-center the learner's experience. It can lift burdens from teachers' shoulders. It can reveal invisible brilliance in students who've long been seen only through the lens of deficiency. And sometimes, it can do something even softer. It can make a student feel *known*. Imagine a student who's always been behind. Who's used to red marks and sighs of disappointment. Who suddenly receives feedback that says: *You're improving at identifying patterns. Nice work today.* Imagine how that lands. Not as a generic badge, but as a whisper of recognition. That matters. These quiet revolutions—moments of affirmation, glimpses of growth—are where AI's true power lies. Not in dashboards or heat maps, but in the micro-shifts that change a learner's story.

Let's be clear: AI is not a pedagogue. It doesn't understand joy. It doesn't recognize sarcasm. It can't hear the subtle tremble in a student's voice when they say, "I'm fine." But it can assist. It can scaffold. It can whisper insights to teachers who are too tired to notice patterns. It can help students explore pathways they didn't know existed. And it can, in its own quiet way, make room for more human teaching. When we treat AI not as a replacement, but as a responsive ally—an extension of our ethical, emotional, pedagogical selves—we begin to unlock new forms of care. New ways of listening. New architectures of inclusion. This is the future worth building. Not one in which machines teach and humans monitor, but one in which intelligence—human and artificial—collaborate to shape learning that is truly personal, truly responsive, and truly alive.

EQUITY, ETHICS, AND AGENCY: NAVIGATING CHALLENGES IN AI-DRIVEN SUPPORT

It's tempting—seductive, even—to imagine artificial intelligence in education as a neutral actor. A silent orchestrator of personalization. A tireless assistant. A fixer of old problems. It sifts through mountains of data, identifies gaps, makes predictions, adapts resources, streamlines feedback. It seems almost elegant, how efficiently it tailors learning to individual needs. But let's pause that image for a moment. Look again. Beneath the surface—beneath the dashboard colors and the auto-generated progress reports—lie questions that can't be answered with code. Questions about fairness. About power. About who gets to decide what "support" really means. Because for all its potential, AI doesn't arrive in schools as a blank slate. It drags behind it a heavy suitcase of assumptions—assumptions we may not notice until they've shaped the learning landscape in ways we didn't anticipate, and can't easily undo. This is the terrain where ethics and equity collide. And agency—human agency—gets negotiated, often quietly, beneath layers of algorithms and interface design. Let's unpack this terrain carefully.

The False Promise of Neutrality

We've been told, often, that data doesn't lie. That AI, being machine-driven, sidesteps human error, bias, and subjectivity. That it is fairer because it is *not* human. But this is a dangerous myth (Almada & Dymitruk, 2022). Every dataset used to train an AI system was created by humans. Designed by humans. Filtered through human values, priorities, oversights. The algorithm reflects not some objective truth, but the worldview of its creators—and, often, the socio-political contexts in which it was trained. When an AI system recommends a reading level, flags a behavioral pattern, or suggests a "just-right" activity, it's not drawing from a universal standard of learning. It's drawing from data. And that data may be incomplete, unbalanced, or skewed by decades of structural inequality. Here's the quiet danger: bias in educational AI isn't always loud or malicious. It's subtle. It's embedded in what's measured and what's ignored. It's present in the way engagement is defined—often through Western behavioral norms—or in how success is tracked, usually through test scores rather than creative expression or cultural relevance. A student who fidgets, for example, may be flagged as off-task. But what if that student is autistic and focusing deeply in their own way? Or what if they come from a cultural background where movement is part of learning? The system doesn't know that. It sees deviation from pattern and labels it. And just like that, the so-called "support" becomes surveillance.

The Unequal Landscape of Access

Then there's the matter of who gets the AI in the first place. Not all schools are created equal. Not all students come to the table with the same tools. In wealthier districts, AI platforms may be embedded within robust tech infrastructures—supported by trained staff, strong broadband, updated devices. In under-resourced schools, those same platforms may glitch, lag, or go underused due to lack of training or unreliable internet. Even within classrooms, there's a digital stratification. Students with stronger literacy skills may navigate the interface more easily. Those with prior exposure to technology may adapt quicker. Learners with disabilities may struggle with inaccessible design, unless universal access was built into the system from the start. And let's not forget language. A student who speaks Arabic at home may find the AI's feedback tone confusing. A child from a rural background may be disoriented by culturally unfamiliar examples. AI doesn't just need to *work*—it needs to *resonate*. If we're not vigilant, AI may deepen the very inequities it's meant to solve—offering the most adaptive learning to those who already have the most advantage, while reinforcing barriers for those with fewer resources (Mitchell, 2021). So, equity in AI isn't just about distributing devices. It's about designing systems that are aware of difference. Systems that don't assume English fluency, neurotypical behavior, or Western cultural norms as defaults. Otherwise, we're just digitizing discrimination.

The Erosion of Agency

Let's talk now about something harder to measure: choice. As AI systems grow more sophisticated, more predictive, more "helpful," there's a creeping risk that they begin to *choose* for learners (Bailey, 2023). And that, at first, feels benign. After all, isn't it nice when the system serves you the perfect lesson? Isn't it efficient when it routes you away from content you're "not ready for"? But efficiency can be a double-edged sword. Personalization can morph into paternalism. Imagine a student repeatedly struggling with advanced texts. The system, recognizing this, begins offering simpler material. The student improves—but only within a limited range. The system, in trying to support, has quietly capped their ceiling. And the student? They may never know they were diverted. That's the danger. When AI starts shaping learning pathways invisibly, students may stop being active participants in their own growth. They stop choosing. They stop wondering. They follow the path laid out, trusting its authority, even when it subtly narrows their horizons. True personalization isn't just about tailored content. It's about *inviting* the learner into the process. Asking: What are you curious about today? Where do you want to stretch? How do you want to learn this? Agency requires transparency. Students—and teachers—should understand *how* the AI makes decisions, and have the power to intervene, redirect, challenge. Otherwise, we risk turning learners into passive consumers of machine logic, rather than co-constructors of meaning.

Consent, Privacy, and the Ethics of Data

And now, the thorniest root in the garden: data ethics. In order for AI systems to function well in education, they need data. Lots of it. Clicks. Scores. Time spent. Facial expressions (in some cases). Eye movement. Audio. Emotion detection. But how much is too much? When we collect that data, who owns it? Where is it stored? Who has access? And perhaps most importantly—was the student ever *asked*? Most educational systems operate under the assumption of implied consent. Students log in. The system tracks. That's it. But that's not real consent. That's institutional compliance. Children—and their families—deserve more. They deserve to know what's being tracked. Why. For how long. They deserve the right to delete their data, to opt out, to say no. And yet, in most classrooms, these questions are never asked. The tech is rolled out. The data is harvested. And the ethics get filed under "policy later." This isn't just a legal issue. It's a moral one. Because when we reduce learners to datapoints, we start to see them that way. Their complexity gets flattened. Their stories disappear. And the classroom—once a space of possibility—becomes a site of extraction. We must resist that. AI in education must be built not just on performance metrics, but on consent. On care. On deep respect for the dignity of every learner.

Teachers at the Crossroads: Mediators of Meaning

And what about teachers? Where do they stand in this web of automation, ethics, and equity? They are the human firewall. The moral compass. The last line of defense. Teachers are not just implementers of technology. They are interpreters. They're the ones who must ask: *Does this suggestion make sense for Jamal? Does this path feel right for Anya? Is the AI supporting my intuition—or contradicting it?* But this role is heavy. And often unsupported. Teachers are being asked to navigate unfamiliar platforms, interpret analytics, manage dashboards, and address equity—all while still teaching, mentoring, caring, and surviving. Many weren't trained in data ethics (Howard et al, 2022). Few have time to scrutinize every AI recommendation. Some don't even realize they can override the system. If we want ethical AI in education, we must invest in teachers (Kayyali, 2025 E). Train them. Trust them. Give them not just access to tools, but the authority to reshape them. Make them co-designers, not just end users. AI should amplify teacher insight, not override it. And it should never replace the warmth of human presence.

Building for Justice: Designing Ethically from the Ground Up

The question isn't whether AI belongs in education. It's already here. The question is: what kind of AI do we want? What values do we want embedded in it? Whose voices do we want shaping it? We must build systems that are culturally responsive, linguistically inclusive, emotionally intelligent, and ethically transparent. That means involving marginalized communities in the design process. Listening to students. Paying attention to those most likely to be harmed. It means slowing down. We live in a culture that fetishizes innovation. Faster platforms. Smarter systems. More features. But ethics isn't fast. Equity takes time. Listening is slow. Let's not rush past the hard questions just because the technology is shiny. Let's ask: Who is this system for? Who benefits? Who might be harmed? Let's embed values into code—yes—but also into practice, into policy, into pedagogy.

There's something sacred about learning. It's not just the acquisition of skills or the mastery of standards. It's a human act—a dance between uncertainty and discovery (Kim et al, 2023). Between not knowing and wanting to know. Between fear and flight. When we introduce AI into this delicate space, we must tread with reverence. Not because AI is dangerous, but because learning is precious. Equity, ethics, and agency are not afterthoughts. They are the very foundations on which AI must stand if it is to support inclusive education. Let's not build systems that only serve the most measurable learners. Let's build ones that can hear the quiet child. Respect the rebellious one. Support the struggling one. And challenge the soaring one. And let's never forget that inclusion is not just a feature. It's a commitment. A way of seeing. A way of being. If AI can help us live that commitment more fully, more deeply—then it truly becomes an ally. But we must choose that path. Every line of code. Every policy. Every click. We must choose it, again and again.

TOWARD A MORE HUMAN-CENTERED FUTURE: LESSONS FROM THE INCLUSIVE AI CLASSROOM

There's something quietly humbling about watching a child learn. Not the polished version—the test scores, the tidy portfolios—but the raw, uncertain, beautiful process of a mind reaching outward. The way eyes flicker when a concept begins to make sense. The long pause before a brave question. The sudden laughter when something clicks. These are human moments. Irregular. Often fragile. And yet, they're the heart of education. So, as we talk about AI in classrooms, as we weigh its power to scaffold, personalize, analyze, and optimize, we must return to this question, over and over: **What kind of future are we building, and who is it for?** Because technology doesn't just shape outcomes. It reshapes the way we *see* each other (Bailey et al, 2022). And if we're not careful, even well-intentioned innovations can lead us into colder, more mechanical forms of learning—ones that serve efficiency at the expense of meaning (Kayyali, 2025 C). But it doesn't have to be that way. If we listen carefully—if we treat classrooms not as testbeds for tools but as living ecosystems—we can begin to extract something more essential: not just what works, but what matters. Not just speed or scale, but soul. This is about more than design principles. It's about memory, presence, emotion, and the art of holding space for difference. So, let's gather what we've learned from the AI-inclusive classroom—not just data points or best practices, but the slower, softer truths that emerge when we pause, notice, and ask harder questions.

Lesson One: Connection Is the Metric That Matters Most

The AI-driven classroom hums with a peculiar kind of intelligence (Bu u, 2024). Dashboards flicker with insights (Kayyali, 2026). Engagement graphs rise and fall. Learning pathways branch and shift in real time. And yet, amidst all this technical choreography, the most vital indicator of success isn't always on the screen. It's in the relationship. Between teacher and student. Between student and student. Between a child and their own sense of capability. You can personalize all you want—feed the algorithm endless data, adjust the difficulty, tailor the pace. But if a learner doesn't *feel* safe, doesn't feel *seen*, the learning won't stick. Not in a way that transforms. Not in a way that endures. We've watched students light up when the AI finally gets it right—when it offers a challenge that excites rather than overwhelms, when it praises effort in a way that feels authentic (Kayyalli, 2024). But we've also seen the reverse. When too much automation makes a learner feel monitored, managed, boxed in. Inclusion is not just about access. It's about emotional belonging. AI must be designed in ways that honor that—through voice, tone, timing, and transparency. Through interfaces that feel like invitations, not interrogations. Through systems that support, rather than replace, the delicate bonds of trust that make real learning possible. And teachers? Their connection to students is not a variable. It's the anchor. AI should orbit around that, not the other way around.

Lesson Two: Flexibility Is Not Optional—It's Foundational

One of the quiet revelations of AI-infused classrooms is how much rigidity still exists in our educational thinking. We speak of differentiation, but we still crave uniform outputs. We say we value creativity, but we measure comprehension with multiple-choice tests. We love the idea of personalized learning, but we distrust anything that can't be cleanly assessed. But when AI is used with care—with *sensitivity*—it begins to loosen those old habits. A student can respond to a prompt with a voice recording, rather than a typed essay (Sharples, 2022). A math problem can be solved through drawing, through logic, through real-life application. A history lesson can branch into storytelling, debate, or virtual exploration. Suddenly, flexibility isn't a side feature. It's the design. And when learners sense that flexibility—not just in format, but in the timing, the pacing, the framing—they begin to show up more fully. They take risks. They self-direct. They move from compliance to curiosity. This is especially true for students who've struggled under traditional models—neurodivergent learners, multilingual students, children with trauma histories. For them, the ability to access knowledge *on their terms* isn't a luxury. It's a lifeline. The lesson here is not just that flexibility works. It's that inflexibility was always a barrier—and we can no longer pretend it wasn't.

Lesson Three: Technology Without Human Judgment Is Incomplete

Let's be honest: the allure of AI lies in its promise of precision (Evans et al, 2021). It sees patterns we miss. It delivers feedback faster than we can. It scales personalization in ways that feel miraculous. But it doesn't understand nuance. It doesn't account for silence. It doesn't know when a learner is disengaged because they're bored, or because their family is in crisis. That's the teacher's domain. In classrooms where AI is implemented most effectively, you'll often find a teacher who uses it not as a crutch, but as a companion (Kayyali, 2025 A). They scan the data, yes—but they also trust their gut. They know when to override a suggestion. When to pause a lesson. When to just sit with a student and *ask*. The AI might say, "This student needs more scaffolding." The teacher might say, "No, this student needs sleep. Or safety. Or a moment of joy." That's not anti-tech. That's deeply human-centered tech. That's pedagogy with teeth and tenderness. The machines are smart. But they're not wise. We must keep the human in the loop—not just to correct errors, but to restore context. To ask questions the system can't, and likely never will.

Lesson Four: Bias Hides in the Architecture

Bias doesn't announce itself. It doesn't say, "I'm excluding your culture from this word problem," or "I'm mislabeling your dialect as a reading deficit." It just sits quietly in the background, shaping the parameters, weighting the probabilities, reinforcing old narratives. In AI systems, bias hides in the training data. In the assumptions baked into models (Gichoya et al, 2023). In what counts as "success." In who designs the platform and whose stories it tells. This matters. Deeply. Because when AI is used to personalize learning, any bias in its foundations gets scaled. Multiplied. Cemented. And learners on the margins—Black, brown, disabled, neurodivergent, multilingual—get subtly misread, misdiagnosed, misdirected. The inclusive AI classroom, then, must be constantly interrogated. Not just used. Who built this tool? Who tested it? What values are embedded in its design? Is it adaptable across languages? Across cultures? Does it amplify deficit thinking, or does it recognize diverse strengths? Educators must be trained not only to use AI but to *question* it. Students, too. Ethical literacy is no longer optional. It's essential. We don't just need tech-savvy learners. We need critically aware learners. Ones who ask, "Why is the system sending me this?" and "What story is the data telling about me, and do I agree?" The future classroom isn't just a space for learning—it's a site of resistance and reclamation.

Lesson Five: Metrics Don't Tell the Whole Story

There's a peculiar tyranny to data, especially when it comes in colorful dashboards and real-time reports (Mikhaylova & Pettersson, 2025). It feels authoritative. Final. "This student is behind." "That one is excelling." But what gets measured is not always what matters. A student may appear disengaged because they're not clicking as often—but maybe they're thinking deeply. Maybe they're processing differently. Maybe they're resisting in ways that are, paradoxically, signs of strength. Another student may be completing tasks rapidly. But are they growing? Are they challenged? Or just playing the game? AI thrives on measurable input. But humans are not neat input-output systems. We carry histories. We perform. We adapt. We hide. The most human-centered AI systems are the ones that leave space for the unmeasurable. That allow for narrative. For reflection. For slowness. For not knowing. This means schools must resist the pressure to reduce learning to numbers—even beautiful ones. They must stay messy. Stay open. The story of a learner is not a curve. It's a landscape.

Lesson Six: Inclusion Is Not an Endpoint—It's a Posture

Too often, we treat inclusion as a goal to be reached. A checklist to complete. A thing to "achieve." But in the AI-powered classroom, inclusion becomes something else entirely: a posture. A way of being. It's not just about adding accessibility features (Lata, 2024). It's about designing *from* difference. Starting with the assumption that variability is the norm. That struggle is not a failure. That learners come to us whole, not broken. And it means committing to constant adaptation—not just by the system, but by the people within it. Teachers who revise. Systems that listen. Students who shape their own paths. Administrators who ask deeper questions, not just for compliance, but for care. This isn't a one-time fix. It's a living practice. It's the willingness to sit in discomfort. To say, "We don't know yet," and to mean it with humility. AI, when used wisely, supports that practice. It doesn't finish the work. It opens it.

The future isn't built all at once. It's shaped moment by moment—by the choices we make, the tools we choose, the silences we break. In classrooms across the globe, small revolutions are already underway. A student discovers joy in a task they once feared. A teacher reclaims time to connect. A learner with a disability receives support before they ask for it. A bilingual child sees their home language reflected in an assessment. These are not headlines. They're human lines. Subtle. Quiet. Transformative. And they remind us of something essential: AI doesn't make a classroom more human. People do. So, if we want a human-centered future, we have to build it that way—deliberately, vulnerably, together. Let the algorithms run, yes. Let the data flow. But let our deepest metrics be kindness. Creativity. Curiosity. Belonging. Let us measure the future not just in outcomes, but in how many students feel like they matter. Like they are not problems to be solved, but possibilities to be honored. That is the promise of inclusive education. And if AI can help us reach for it—then let it (Neisser, 2024). But let it follow, not lead. Let it serve, not steer. Let it amplify our humanity, not automate it. Always. Unapologetically. First.

CONCLUSION

As we reflect on the promises and pitfalls of integrating AI into inclusive classrooms, a complicated but compelling picture begins to take shape. We are standing at a pedagogical crossroads—on one hand, the weight of centuries-old educational models that prized conformity and efficiency; on the other, a vision of learning that is fluid, personal, and deeply responsive. AI is not just a new tool in the teacher's kit—it is a disruptor, a catalyst, and potentially, a mirror reflecting the values embedded within our systems.

The notion of inclusion is, at its core, radical. It challenges educators not just to bring marginalized students into the classroom, but to reconstruct the classroom itself in a way that acknowledges difference as a strength rather than a problem to be managed. In this reimagining, AI offers an infrastructure of possibility. With its capacity to analyze data patterns, identify learning gaps, and adapt instruction in real time, AI brings us closer than ever to the elusive goal of personalized learning. No longer does the teacher have to choose between reaching the average learner and supporting the outliers—AI can help hold space for both.

But let us not mistake capacity for commitment. Technology does not, in itself, guarantee transformation. The tools we build reflect the priorities we set. If our data is biased, our models will be biased. If our goals are reductionist—focused only on test scores or behavioral compliance—we risk automating exclusion in subtler, more insidious ways. The algorithms may hum along, but the human cost can be immense. Inclusion cannot be automated; it must be cultivated, continually, with vigilance and heart.

Moreover, AI must never replace the nuanced role of the teacher. No matter how sophisticated the system, it cannot replicate the intuitive judgments, ethical discernment, or emotional attunement of a skilled educator. The teacher's presence—compassionate, adaptive, and deeply human—is what gives learning its soul. The role of AI, then, is not to replace, but to reinforce. To lift some burdens, reveal unseen patterns, and offer new ways of seeing learners who might otherwise remain unseen.

Perhaps the most profound promise of AI in the inclusive classroom is not efficiency or novelty, but *possibility*. The possibility of reshaping what equity looks like in practice. The possibility of hearing every student's voice—not just the loudest or most fluent. The possibility of turning differentiation from a daily struggle into a natural part of classroom life. If we are intentional, ethical, and human-centered in our approach, AI can be more than a technical solution. It can be a pedagogical partner in the long, unfinished work of justice in education.

This journey will require humility, imagination, and courage. We must listen closely—not just to what the technology tells us, but to what our students, especially the most vulnerable, are trying to say. We must be willing to shift, to unlearn, to redesign. And in doing so, we affirm a truth that predates technology and will outlive it: that every child matters, and every learner deserves to be seen, heard, and supported—uniquely and fully. Let that be the legacy we build—not just with AI, but with intention, care, and the unwavering belief in each learner's right to thrive.

REFERENCES

Aberšek, B., Flogie, A., & Aberšek, M. K. (2023, June). Transformation of Education: From Dehumanization to Re-Humanization of Society. In International Baltic Symposium on Science and Technology Education. Scientia Socialis Ltd. 29 K. Donelaicio Street, LT-78115 Siauliai, Republic of Lithuania.

Almada, M., & Dymitruk, M. (2022). Data protection and judicial automation. In *Research Handbook on EU Data Protection Law* (pp. 270–289). Edward Elgar Publishing.

Bailey, D. E., Faraj, S., Hinds, P. J., Leonardi, P. M., & von Krogh, G. (2022). We are all theorists of technology now: A relational perspective on emerging technology and organizing. *Organization Science*, *33*(1), 1–18.

Bailey, J. (2023). AI in Education: The leap into a new era of machine intelligence carries risks and challenges, but also plenty of promise. *Education Next*, *23*(4), 29–36.

Baron, N. S. (2023). *Who wrote this?: how AI and the lure of efficiency threaten human writing*. Stanford University Press.

Bennett, P. (2021). Teaching itself: a mythology of learning in theory and practice.

Bu u, A. F. (2024). Unleashing the Potential of AI in Classrooms. *Revista de Stiinte Politice*, (81), 34–42.

Carreira, M. B. F. D. C. (2024). AI-powered personalization: A behavioural economics perspective in marketing (Master's thesis).

Challoumis, C. (2024). The Imperative of Skill Development in an AI Revolution. In *XIX International Scientific Conference*. London. Great Britain (pp. 132-168).

Chen, E. (2025). "We Are Bridges": Bilingual Latina Teachers as Cultural Mediators in Family–School Partnerships. *Education Sciences*, *15*(6), 717.

De Cremer, D., & Kasparov, G. (2021). AI should augment human intelligence, not replace it. *Harvard Business Review*, *18*(1), 1–8.

Dembe, A. (2024). Advancing personalized learning through educational artificial intelligence: Challenges, opportunities, and future directions. *Res Invent J Eng Phys Sci*, *3*(1), 89–101.

Evans, O., Cotton-Barratt, O., Finnveden, L., Bales, A., Balwit, A., Wills, P., . . . Saunders, W. (2021). Truthful AI: Developing and governing AI that does not lie. arXiv preprint arXiv:2110.06674.

Firat, M. (2023). Predicting student disengagement: Harnessing visual cues for intelligent tutoring systems. London journal of social sciences, (6), 75-83.

Fovet, F. (2023). The Changing Landscape of Inclusive Education: A Shift towards Universal Design for Learning. In The Routledge International Handbook of Children's Rights and Disability (pp. 483-499). Routledge.

Gichoya, J. W., Thomas, K., Celi, L. A., Safdar, N., Banerjee, I., Banja, J. D., & Purkayastha, S. (2023). AI pitfalls and what not to do: Mitigating bias in AI. *The British Journal of Radiology*, *96*(1150), 20230023. PMID: 37698583

Harry, B., & Klingner, J. (2022). *Why are so many students of color in special education?: Understanding race and disability in schools*. Teachers College Press.

Howard, N. R., Schaffer, R., & Thomas, S. (2022). *Closing the gap: Digital equity strategies for teacher prep programs*. International Society for Technology in Education.

Huang, J. S. (2022). Pedagogical Responsiveness to Every Student in Singapore–Can Artificial Intelligence for Education Be a Solution to Embrace the Complexity in Teaching and Learning? In *Pedagogical Responsiveness in Complex Contexts: Issues of Transformation, Inclusion and Equity* (pp. 75–94). Springer International Publishing.

Jerve, K. R. (2023). Learning to Un-sing: A study of free improvisation vocalists' ideas, strategies, and techniques (Master's thesis).

Kayyali, M. (2025a). Ethical Implications of Generative AI in Education: Privacy, Bias, and Integrity. In Transformative AI Practices for Personalized Learning Strategies (pp. 185-218). IGI Global Scientific Publishing.

Kayyali, M. (2025b). Generative AI and Education: Transforming Teaching and Learning Through Collaborative Intelligence. In Humans and Generative AI Tools for Collaborative Intelligence (pp. 25-52). IGI Global Scientific Publishing.

Kayyali, M. (2025c). The Future of AI in Education: Predictions and Emerging Trends. Next-Generation AI Methodologies in Education, 367-406.

Kayyali, M. (2025d). AI in Higher Education: Revolutionizing Curriculum and Administration. In AI Adoption and Diffusion in Education (pp. 31-62). IGI Global Scientific Publishing.

Kayyali, M. (2025e). Ethical Implications of Generative AI in Education: Privacy, Bias, and Integrity. In Transformative AI Practices for Personalized Learning Strategies (pp. 185-218). IGI Global Scientific Publishing.

Kayyali, M. (2026). The Impact of AI on Classroom Dynamics in Higher Education: Shifting Roles for Professors and Students. In Responsible AI Integration in Education (pp. 151-180). IGI Global Scientific Publishing.

Kim, H., Lee, B. K., Lee, H., Hwang, D., Park, S., Min, K., & Choo, J. (2023). Learning to discover skills through guidance. *Advances in Neural Information Processing Systems*, *36*, 28226–28254.

Lata, P. (2024). Towards Equitable Learning: Exploring Artificial Intelligence in Inclusive Education.

Lewis, A. A. (2025). Unpacking Cultural Bias in AI Language Learning Tools: An Analysis of Impacts and Strategies for Inclusion in Diverse Educational Settings. *International Journal of Research and Innovation in Social Science*, *9*(1), 1878–1892.

Martin, S. M., Casey, J. R., & Kane, S. (2021). History of artificial intelligence and personalized learning. In *Serious games in personalized learning* (pp. 27–47). Routledge.

Mifsud, D. (2023). Rethinking the concept of teacher education: a problematization and critique of current policies and practices. In *Teacher education as an ongoing professional trajectory: implications for policy and practice* (pp. 1–23). Springer International Publishing.

Mikhaylova, T., & Pettersson, D. (2025). The timeless beauty of data: Inventing educational pasts, presents and futures through data visualisation. *Critical Studies in Education*, *66*(2), 142–158.

Mitchell, M. (2021). Why AI is harder than we think. arXiv preprint arXiv:2104.12871.

Mitra, D. S. (2024). AI-Powered Adaptive Education for Disabled Learners. Available at *SSRN* 5042713.

Neisser, U. (2024). General, academic, and artificial intelligence. In *The nature of intelligence* (pp. 135–144). Routledge.

Newton, N., Record, A. E., & Mello, A. J. (2024). *Fluency Doesn't Just Happen in Multiplication and Division: Strategies and Models for Teaching the Basic Facts*. Taylor & Francis.

Rowan, L., Bourke, T., L'Estrange, L., Lunn Brownlee, J., Ryan, M., Walker, S., & Churchward, P. (2021). How does initial teacher education research frame the challenge of preparing future teachers for student diversity in schools? A systematic review of literature. *Review of Educational Research*, *91*(1), 112–158.

Shah, P. (2023). *AI and the Future of Education: Teaching in the Age of Artificial Intelligence*. John Wiley & Sons.

Sharples, M. (2022). Automated essay writing: An AIED opinion. *International Journal of Artificial Intelligence in Education, 32*(4), 1119–1126.

Simons, M., & Masschelein, J. (2021). Looking after school: A critical analysis of personalization in education.

Sullivan, Y. W., & Fosso Wamba, S. (2022). Moral judgments in the age of artificial intelligence. *Journal of Business Ethics, 178*(4), 917–943.

Tolman, A. O., & Kremling, J. (Eds.). (2023). *Why students resist learning: A practical model for understanding and helping students*. Taylor & Francis.

Vallor, S. (2024). *The AI mirror: How to reclaim our humanity in an age of machine thinking*. Oxford University Press.

Zhang, H., & Tian, M. (2024). Unpacking the multi-dimensional nature of teacher competencies: A systematic review. *Scandinavian Journal of Educational Research*, , 1–22.

Chapter 8
AI and Differentiated Instruction:
Supporting Every Learner's Journey

Mustafa Kayyali
https://orcid.org/0000-0003-3300-262X
Maaref University of Applied Sciences, Syria

ABSTRACT

In today's classrooms, where learner diversity is more visible and complex than ever, artificial intelligence is quietly reshaping how we support every student's unique path. This chapter explores how AI can act as both a mirror and a guide—reflecting learner needs and scaffolding instruction in real time. Drawing on the principles of differentiated instruction, it unpacks how AI-powered platforms can tailor pace, content, and assessment to individual profiles. Yet, this journey is not without tension. Ethical considerations around equity, bias, and teacher autonomy emerge as essential parts of the conversation. Rather than presenting AI as a panacea, the chapter invites a thoughtful look at how we can use it to amplify—not replace—the deeply human art of teaching, ensuring no learner is left behind.

INTRODUCTION

In every classroom, visible or hidden, lies a spectrum of learning differences—variations in pace, background knowledge, cognitive styles, emotional readiness, and more. Educators have long wrestled with the challenge of reaching every student, of making instruction not only accessible but meaningful. Differentiated instruction emerged as a response to this complexity: an acknowledgment that equity does not

DOI: 10.4018/979-8-3373-2948-2.ch008

mean sameness, and that effective teaching must stretch beyond a one-size-fits-all approach. But as any teacher can attest, differentiation is not easy. It demands a level of planning, adaptability, and real-time insight that is often aspirational in under-resourced or overburdened educational systems.

Enter artificial intelligence—not as a magic wand, but as a quietly disruptive force (Maeda, 2025). The term “AI in education” may conjure up images of cold algorithms replacing warm human interaction, or of surveillance systems reducing students to data points. But in truth, AI is neither savior nor villain. It is a tool—and like any tool, its value depends on how, why, and by whom it is used (Chanan, 2023). What makes AI particularly compelling in the context of differentiated instruction is its potential to lift the heavy cognitive and logistical load that teachers have carried for too long.

At its best, AI enables educators to see what might otherwise go unnoticed: patterns of struggle, bursts of progress, gaps in comprehension, hidden strengths (Shah, 2023). It can adapt content delivery, scaffold tasks, and assess understanding with a degree of precision and responsiveness that few human-led systems can achieve alone. This is not to say that AI should replace human judgment, but rather that it can serve as a co-pilot—offering timely insights that inform instructional choices and empower teachers to be more responsive.

Yet, this promise must be met with caution. With AI’s increasing presence in education comes a set of ethical questions that we cannot ignore (Kayyali, 2025 A). Who designs these systems, and whose cultural assumptions shape their logic? What data is being collected, and how is it used? Can personalization inadvertently lead to labeling or tracking that limits students’ potential? These are not just technical concerns; they are deeply human ones. If we are to use AI to differentiate instruction meaningfully, we must do so in a way that honors student dignity, protects teacher agency, and resists the reduction of learning to metrics alone.

This chapter is an invitation to rethink differentiated instruction in light of emerging technologies—not with blind enthusiasm or cynical dismissal, but with measured curiosity and a commitment to inclusive pedagogy. It draws from research, classroom examples, and theoretical reflections to explore how AI can support the diverse journeys of learners, especially those who are often marginalized by traditional systems. It examines the practical applications of AI-driven tools, their affordances and limitations, and the philosophical tensions they surface in our understanding of what it means to teach and to learn. Ultimately, this is not a chapter about technology; it is a chapter about people—about how we can create environments where every learner feels seen, supported, and capable of growth, with AI as a partner in that process.

REIMAGINING LEARNER DIVERSITY IN THE AGE OF AI

I still remember the late-afternoon hush of my first classroom, fluorescent tubes hissing overhead while thirty stories unfolded in parallel—some bold, some brittle, all hoping to be heard. Amir read aloud in cautious spurts, each vowel cradled by his mother tongue. Lena, code-savvy and impatient, sprinted through the worksheet, then doodled fractals in the margins. Rayyan's eyes danced between the page and the window where clouds looked like dragons; Mariam copied every line twice, terrified of mistakes. *That* tangle of tempos, accents, hopes, and hidden wounds is what we call "diversity."

For decades, teachers have tried to honor that tangle with differentiated instruction: small-group rotations, tiered tasks, color-coded folders, heroic but exhausting (Schroeder-Schock, 2024). The truth? Even the most devoted educator can't monitor thirty cognitive landscapes simultaneously, let alone sculpt bespoke pathways in real time. Enter artificial intelligence—glamorous headline, slippery promise. Algorithms can crunch click-streams faster than we can sip coffee; sensors can register hesitation in milliseconds. Yet the prospect of a machine parsing human complexity feels equal parts thrilling and unsettling, like handing a Stradivarius to a robot and asking for Mozart. How, then, do we reimagine learner diversity when data flows like water and predictive models hum behind every screen?

Shattering the Old Labels

First, we loosen our grip on the tidy boxes we once relied upon. "Visual." "Auditory." "Gifted." Labels made lesson planning easier, but they flattened students into caricatures. AI systems, trained on oceans of granular data, reveal patterns that upend those boxes: the shy poet who masters geometry through augmented-reality sandboxes; the extrovert who prefers quiet asynchronous discussion boards (Zhu et al, 2021). Diversity, in other words, is fractal—zoom in and new details bloom (Kayyali, 2025 B). Yet data points can masquerade as truths if we're not vigilant. An adaptive platform may note that Mei stumbles on fraction questions and instantly tag her "below benchmark," nudging her toward remedial drills. It may never see the quiet rapture on her face when she studies fractal art, where fractions birth spirals. If we allow AI to calcify difference into deficit, we haven't reimagined diversity; we've shrunk it. The challenge isn't only to collect finer-grained data; it's to interpret it with humility, always remembering that numbers are shadows of lived experience, not the experiences themselves.

Turning Algorithms into Empathic Listeners

Imagine a platform that listens to pauses the way a jazz musician treasures silence between notes—attuned not just to wrong answers but to pregnant hesitations that signal budding insight or simmering confusion. Picture an interface that lets students nudge the tempo of instruction like adjusting podcast playback speed: slow motion for conceptual knots, double-time when the concept clicks (Wolf & Putnam, 2023). Here, diversity becomes choreography. Learners sometimes leap ahead of the beat, sometimes linger on a downstroke; the tool keeps tempo without shaming anyone for dancing off-meter. I want to linger on stories, though, because stories complicate data. Consider Noor, a refugee who arrives mid-semester with a hesitant smile and memories in languages I don't speak. Traditional differentiation suggests simplified texts, a buddy system, perhaps some extra scaffolding. An AI-powered translator can render her favorite Syrian folktales into English, map vocabulary to astronomy articles (her passion), and generate pronunciation drills tuned to her accent. Suddenly, differentiation feels less like triage and more like hospitality—*Welcome, Noor; bring your cosmos with you.*

Trust, Transparency, and the Ghost in the Machine

Trust is the oxygen of any learning ecosystem, and algorithms can suffocate it if left opaque (Galés, 2024). If Rashid fears that the grammar checker will flag his vibrant code-switching as error, he'll shrink himself to fit the machine's brittle rules. Demystifying the black box becomes critical: show learners how recommendations arise, where their data travels, how they can contest an automated judgment. In practical terms, that might look like dashboards with "Why am I seeing this?" links, toggle-switches to refuse certain data uses, and student-owned portfolios in which algorithmic nudges are annotated—*The system thinks I struggle with inferential questions, but here's my counter-evidence.* We must also confront cultural nuance. AI, like any artifact, inherits the fingerprints of its makers. An adaptive reader trained mostly on Western narratives may misread indigenous storytelling, flattening metaphor or misclassifying genre (Kodó, 2024). Reimagining diversity means feeding the machine a diet as heterogeneous as the learners it hopes to serve, then continually auditing its digestion. That's not tech-maintenance; that's justice work.

The Resource Question: From Flashy Pilot to Everyday Infrastructure

Skeptics will ask—rightly—whether under-resourced schools can implement such nuanced systems. Reimagining diversity with AI is not a shiny plug-in arriving

Tuesday; it's a slow cultural shift (Malek, 2021). It begins with micro-moments: a speech-to-text feature that liberates a dysgraphic student; real-time captions that invite a hard-of-hearing learner into the din of discussion; a predictive dashboard that flags a disengaged teen before she drifts beyond rescue. If these tools prove their worth in classrooms squeezed for time and bandwidth, momentum builds. Think solar panels: once fringe, now roofing staple. Yet the more we lean on adaptive systems, the more urgently we must revisit the teacher's role. Educators risk becoming flight attendants on autopilot flights—clicking buttons, rarely steering. The antidote is repositioning teachers as sense-makers who filter algorithmic whispers through human wisdom. Picture a conductor guiding an orchestra where AI instruments hum continuously; the conductor decides which crescendos to amplify, which discordant notes to mute, when silence is the music students need.

Assessment without Reduction

Traditional exams capture slivers of competence and reward those who test well. AI can open the door to multimodal evidence: eye-tracking to surface engagement patterns, keystroke analyses to spotlight problem-solving strategies, sentiment analysis in reflection journals (Subasi et al, 2024). But metrics can muffle mystery. Some of the most transformative learning moments hide in productive struggle—zones the algorithm may deem inefficient. Our task is to protect that fertile muddle, to design analytics that recognize *productive uncertainty* as a sign of depth, not delay.

Equity at the Crossroads

Globally, classrooms swell with linguistic, neurological, cultural, and socioeconomic variety—COVID-19 only amplified the gaps (Ehsan, 2024). If only affluent districts can afford sleek dashboards, personalization becomes a gated luxury. We need policy frameworks that treat adaptive learning as basic infrastructure, akin to electricity or clean water. Otherwise we risk a bifurcated future: algorithmic tailwinds for the wealthy, algorithmic headwinds for everyone else. Equity, in this sense, is not a courtesy upgrade; it's the runway (Kayyali, 2022). At the same time, the more we individualize pathways, the more we must nurture collective empathy. When an AI tutor guides each learner down a bespoke tunnel, peer learning can atrophy. Designers should embed collaborative affordances: algorithms that notice complementary strengths and propose peer mentors, or group tasks where heterogeneity is an asset, not a hurdle. Imagine a math platform that pairs a spatial-reasoning whiz with a verbal analogist, their distinct cognitive blueprints converging on the same puzzle. Diversity then becomes not an obstacle to manage but a source of generative friction.

Affect, Privacy, and Consent

Emotions saturate cognition. Some AI tools now infer mood from facial cues or voice timbre. The ethics are thorny—privacy, cultural misreads, surveillance creep (Puplampu, 2024). Still, brushing off affective computing ignores learners who silently disengage. The middle path is consent-based, student-controlled affective support: dashboards where learners self-report stress, triggering adaptive pacing; optional pulse checks that invite mindfulness breaks. In this paradigm, learners are co-authors of their data stories, not passive characters in someone else's plot.

Guarding Space for Serendipity

Part of me worries that by bottling diversity into data we may domesticate its wildness. Some of the richest lessons erupt when Jamal derails the agenda with a question sparked by last night's sci-fi series. Algorithms adore pattern; creativity loves disruption. Reimagining diversity must leave elbow-room for chaos—features that let students train micro-models on emergent interests, or "wild-card days" when the dashboard goes silent and curiosity leads. Language, too, deserves fresh lenses. Real-time translation already whispers captions, but what if the algorithm *championed* translanguaging, recognizing the rhetorical power of code-meshing? Instead of punishing bilingual students for "mixed register," the system could highlight their linguistic agility, inviting cross-disciplinary riffs in heritage tongues (Macháček et al, 2023). Diversity becomes linguistic jazz—scales bending, sliding, recombining. AI's role shifts from grammar sentinel to improvisational accompanist.

Neurodiversity and Co-Design

Learners with ADHD may thrive on gamified micro-bursts; autistic students might crave predictable visual schedules. Yet neurotypical norms still lurk in default settings. Genuine inclusion means co-designing with neurodiverse stakeholders, asking them which fonts calm or agitate, which notification sounds jangle or soothe (Kelly, 2023). When the default color scheme triggers sensory overload, a customization slider isn't a nice-to-have; it's dignity. Data sovereignty also matters. Indigenous communities craft protocols to guard cultural knowledge from exploitative scraping. Reimagining diversity requires honoring those protocols inside educational platforms—embedding consent layers, tagging sacred stories as "share-restricted," and giving communities veto power over algorithmic use.

Quantum processors may one day predict not just academic progress but well-being trajectories; holographic mentors might float beside Sofia at her kitchen table, lessons synced to her circadian rhythm (SWARGIARY, 2024). Those futures can dazzle—and distract. Reimagining diversity starts now, in the messy present, where the Wi-Fi hiccups mid-quiz and students laugh it off in the chat (Kayyali, 2025 C). It starts where teachers tinker during lunch break, configuring a free open-source recommender to help Abdul master phonics without shame. It starts with district leaders who insist on interoperable data standards so kids don't lose their personalized settings when they change schools. AI is a lens. Point it only at deficits and you design interventions steeped in remediation. Point it at possibility and you craft ecosystems where differences shimmer as assets. Reimagining learner diversity in the age of AI is less about silicon circuits than moral circuitry—a collective act of imagination that calls technologists to write code that breathes, policymakers to legislate with empathy, educators to stay endlessly curious, and learners to claim authorship of their journeys (Vallor, 2024). If we get it right, classrooms will no longer be places where diversity is accommodated grudgingly, like an afterthought. They'll be gardens where variety is the point—where every outlier, every overlap, every quirky cognitive signature has room to unfurl. And the algorithms? They'll be the silent gardeners, tilling data into insight, watering roots of potential we once overlooked, always answerable to the human hands that planted the seeds.

UNDERSTANDING DIFFERENTIATED INSTRUCTION: NEEDS, GAPS, AND POSSIBILITIES

Walk into any classroom—anywhere, any grade level, any country—and you'll quickly notice it: the quiet chaos of difference (Winek, 2025). One child hums the right answer before the teacher finishes the question. Other stares blankly, still grappling with the vocabulary in the question itself. A third draws patterns in the margins of their notebook, lost in thoughts that have nothing to do with the lesson at hand. These are not anomalies. They are the norm. The myth of the homogenous classroom—of rows of students learning the same content at the same pace in the same way—has long been dead. If it ever truly lived, it did so only in policy documents and outdated instructional models. And yet, despite this deeply human reality, education systems have struggled to design for such complexity. They standardize, streamline, and sort. They craft curriculum as if learners are factory inputs, not fluid, evolving beings with wildly varying needs. Differentiated instruction emerged as an attempt to break that mold. Not a fix-all, not a revolution, but a philosophy—and a practice—that acknowledges a simple truth: children learn differently. And that difference, if embraced, can become a catalyst rather than a constraint. But let's not romanticize. Differentiated instruction is hard. Really hard. It asks teachers to become part diagnostician, part designer, part juggler. It requires flexible planning, intuitive responses, relentless patience. When it works, it can be transformative.

When it doesn't, it can feel like chaos in disguise. So, how do we make sense of this idea, this aspiration, in a way that's honest about its difficulties but open to its possibilities? That's what this section seeks to explore—not as an abstract ideal, but as a living, breathing tension point within real classrooms.

What It Is—and What It Isn't

Let's begin with what differentiated instruction is not. It is not simply "giving some students more work" or "watering down the content for those who struggle." It's not about making ten separate lesson plans or labeling kids so tightly that the labels become cages. It's not just flexible seating or letting kids choose between drawing a poster or writing a paragraph. Those things might be *tools*, sure. But they're not the essence. At its heart, differentiated instruction is an orientation—a mindset—that treats learner variance not as a problem to fix, but as a reality to design for (Herner-Patnode & Lee, 2021). It involves adapting the *content* (what is being taught), the *process* (how it is being taught), the *product* (how students demonstrate learning), and the *environment* (where and with whom they learn). These adaptations are based on students' readiness levels, interests, and learning profiles. Not just ability. Not just performance. But the whole ecology of how a student comes to know and understand. Carol Ann Tomlinson, perhaps the most cited voice in this field, once described differentiation as "doing what's fair for students." Fair, not equal. That distinction matters. Equal means everyone gets the same; fair means everyone gets what they need. It's a subtle shift, but once internalized, it changes everything. The classroom is no longer a monolithic structure but a responsive, breathing system.

Why the Need is So Urgent Now

The world has changed. Dramatically. We live in a hyperconnected age where information floods our devices, where students arrive with experiences shaped by migration, trauma, neurodiversity, multilingualism, and a host of other factors that defy easy categorization. Add to that the lingering disruptions of the pandemic, and what you get is a classroom landscape that is messier, more uneven, and more urgent than ever before. Some students return to school having thrived in remote learning environments—self-paced, free from classroom anxiety (Rodrigues, 2024). Others return having slipped through the cracks—two years behind, confidence shattered. Some flourish when they can express themselves through video or voice; others crave the tactile comfort of pen and paper. The gap between the fastest and slowest learners in a single classroom can now span *years*. What's at stake isn't just academic success. It's belonging. When students consistently experience work that is either too easy or too difficult, they disengage. They feel unseen. Repeated often enough, this becomes identity-shaping: *I'm not smart. I don't get math. School isn't for me.* Differentiated instruction, at its best, intervenes before that narrative takes root.

The Gaps Between Theory and Practice

Let's be honest: while the theory of differentiation is elegant, its application can feel maddening. Teachers are expected to meet every learner where they are, in real time, often without the training, time, or tools to do so (Sjølie et al, 2021). It's no wonder some educators throw up their hands. *You want me to scaffold every lesson for three different levels, create interest-based pathways, and modify assessments—all while managing behavior, meeting IEPs, and covering the curriculum? Are you kidding?* The gap between expectation and support is vast. Many schools speak the language of differentiation but operate on schedules and structures that make it nearly impossible. Rigid timetables. Overcrowded classrooms. One-size-fits-all testing regimes. There's also a professional development gap. Most teacher training touches on differentiation, but often in vague terms—more inspirational than instructional (Tyrina, 2021). Teachers are told *why* it matters but rarely shown *how* to do it at scale. And then there's the equity gap. Differentiation done poorly can reinforce inequities rather than dismantle them. If "low group" students get busywork while "high group" students get enrichment, we've not differentiated—we've tracked. If we lower expectations rather than offer appropriate scaffolds, we're not empowering—we're limiting. Differentiation must walk a tightrope: it must meet students where they are *without* locking them there.

Possibilities Emerging from the Margins

Despite these challenges, the possibilities are real—and they often emerge in the margins. In classrooms where teachers are given room to innovate, differentiation becomes an art form (VanTassel-Baska et al, 2021). I've seen it. A history teacher who uses learning stations not just to manage behavior, but to let students explore revolutions through different lenses: art, economics, biography. A math teacher who offers three versions of a problem set—core, challenge, and extension—and invites students to self-select based on how they're feeling that day. A language teacher who uses podcasting as an alternative assessment, allowing students to code-switch between languages and speak from their lived experience (Green, 2022). What binds these examples isn't a specific method? It's an ethos. A willingness to be responsive. A belief that all students can learn, just not in the same way or on the same day. These teachers don't always follow the textbook. They build flexible scaffolds, knowing that some students need a ramp and others a ladder. And the students? They notice. They lean in. They try harder—not because the work is easy, but because it feels like it was made *for* them. That's the magic of well-done differentiation. It doesn't pander; it invites.

The Emotional Labor of Differentiation

Let's not gloss over this part. Differentiated instruction is emotionally demanding. It requires educators to care deeply and constantly—to pay attention, to adapt, to listen, to rework plans that "should've worked." It can feel like pouring yourself into a sieve (Tomlinson, 2022). When it clicks, it's exhilarating. When it doesn't, it's demoralizing. There's also the quiet grief that comes from watching a student struggle, despite your best efforts. The lesson you tailored to their interests that still didn't land. The student who refuses every differentiated offering because they've learned not to trust school. Differentiation, in this sense, is as much about resilience as it is about strategy. This is where systemic support matters. Differentiation can't rest on the shoulders of individual teachers alone. It needs to be a schoolwide commitment, embedded in schedules, team planning, curriculum design. It requires time—sacred, protected time—for teachers to plan, collaborate, reflect. Without that, even the best intentions wither.

A Glimpse Ahead

Now, with AI entering the classroom not as a concept but a tool—sometimes clumsy, sometimes astonishing—we have the chance to rethink differentiation altogether (Dlask, 2024). AI won't solve the problem. It can't care. It can't notice that a student is unusually quiet or that their humor masks deep insecurity. But it *can* extend the teacher's reach. It can analyze patterns across weeks that the eye might miss. It can recommend content that adjusts in real time. It can offer multilingual supports, voice-to-text tools, reading levels that scale. In short, it can help make differentiation *doable*—if, and only if, it's used ethically, thoughtfully, and in partnership with human judgment. But we must be vigilant. Differentiation driven by data, not empathy, risks becoming clinical. The moment a student's learning profile becomes a static label in an algorithm, we've failed. The goal must remain what it has always been: to see each learner as fully human, to craft experiences that challenge and support, to keep the flame of curiosity alive.

In the End, It's About Relationships

What makes differentiation work is not the template or the strategy. It's the relationship. The teacher who notices when Aisha's eyes drift because the content doesn't connect. The one who sees potential in a rough draft and offers just the right nudge. The one who listens—not just to what students say, but to how they say it. That relational awareness, that attunement, is the soil in which all differentiation grows. Differentiated instruction is not a checklist. It's a posture. It's what happens when we teach not to the middle, but to the edges. When we stop asking, *How do I cover the content?* and start asking, *How do I uncover the learner?* It's messy. It's unpredictable. But it's also the only kind of teaching that meets students where they are, while gently nudging them toward where they could be. And that—that refusal to settle for sameness, that insistence on designing for difference—is not just pedagogical. It's moral. It's a commitment to equity, to humanity, to hope. Let the lesson plans be flexible. Let the outcomes be open-ended. Let the learners surprise us. Let's teach not just to the test, but to the child. Differentiation, for all its demands, reminds us why we got into this work in the first place—not to replicate knowledge, but to cultivate growth. Not to manufacture outcomes, but to nurture lives. And in that vision, the possibilities are endless.

HOW AI TOOLS PERSONALIZE LEARNING PATHWAYS

There's something hauntingly beautiful—and daunting—about standing in front of a classroom, eyes scanning a sea of students who are, in some strange way, all walking different roads while sitting in the same room. Same chairs, same fluorescent glow, same content objective scribbled on the whiteboard. But what's happening inside each student? Different velocities, different maps, different weight in their backpacks—emotional, cognitive, cultural. And here we are, as teachers, expected to guide them all to the same destination by the same time, with the same resources. It's a rigged game. Or at least it has been. But something has shifted. Artificial intelligence—once the domain of science fiction, now humming quietly in the background of more and more classrooms—is changing the rules. Not replacing teachers (let's kill that fear right here), but offering something else: *precision*. Not the cold, mechanical kind. But something warmer, more intuitive. The ability to actually *see* where each student is on their journey and offer pathways that respond—not reactively, but responsively—to their unique rhythm (Tomlinson & Jarvis, 2023). The promise of AI in personalized learning isn't that it knows best. It's that it *notices* faster. It listens more than it speaks (Laak & Aru, 2024). And when designed well, it lets students be seen more fully, more faithfully, more frequently than a single human—however brilliant and attentive—can manage on their own.

Listening to the Silences: What AI Detects That We Can't Always Catch

Let's begin here: AI doesn't teach. It watches. It listens. It gathers. It maps. Not in some Big Brother, dystopian, every-keystroke-is-being-surveilled sort of way—but more like a meticulous, tireless observer who tracks every stumble, every pause, every click, and turns that behavioral breadcrumb trail into a constellation. Take, for instance, a student who hesitates for 18 seconds on a multiple-choice question, changes their answer twice, then submits the correct option. A human teacher might see the end result—"correct"—and move on (Lan & Chen, 2024). But the AI flags the hesitation. Maybe it recognizes a pattern: similar hesitations around abstract language in science passages (Kayyali, 2025 D). It nudges the system—perhaps the reading level was a little too high, or the vocabulary too domain-specific. Based on that, the next assignment might adapt: same concept, simpler language. Or maybe a pre-lesson vocabulary primer. No red ink. No callout. Just a subtle redirection. And for the student? It feels seamless. There's no stigma, no public correction. The path simply shifts. Quietly. Intelligently.

Micro-Adaptive Feedback: A Real-Time Mirror

In traditional classrooms, feedback often comes after the fact—days later, sometimes weeks (Tragant et al, 2022). A graded essay. A returned quiz. A comment scrawled in red ink. But what if the feedback could come *mid-thought*? What if it could intervene during the process, not after the product? AI tools now offer micro-adaptive feedback—miniature, real-time reflections that guide without interrupting (Akibu, 2024). Think of a math platform that gently prompts a student mid-step: "Are you sure you want to subtract here?" Or a writing assistant that flags tone before submission, asking, "This sentence sounds more informal than your introduction. Would you like to revise for consistency?" These nudges are not corrections. They're conversation starters. Mirrors, not magnifying glasses. And here's the subtle brilliance: students begin to internalize this feedback loop. They start to anticipate it. Eventually, they develop metacognition. They begin to ask those questions themselves, even when the AI is silent.

Multiple Pathways, Not Just Multiple Levels

There's a danger in conflating personalization with leveling. Not every student needs to move "up" or "down" a ladder. Some need a different *angle*, a different *mode*, a different *motivation.* AI tools that personalize learning effectively don't just adjust difficulty—they diversify the experience itself (Davis et al, 2024). Let's imagine three students learning about photosynthesis. One receives a simulation-based activity, manipulating variables to test how light affects plant growth. Another watches a narrative animation, rich in visuals and storytelling, walking through the process step-by-step. The third engages with an interactive reading, laced with pop-up vocabulary supports and embedded comprehension checks. All three cover the same standard. But the road they take? Completely different. This is where AI shines—not in sorting students by perceived ability, but in offering *choice without chaos*. The teacher doesn't have to manually assign 30 pathways. The system, informed by student profiles, previous interactions, and stated preferences, makes intelligent recommendations. And the student? They feel like the work was crafted *for them*. Because, in a very real sense, it was.

The Dance Between Autonomy and Guidance

Too much choice, and students flounder. Too little, and they disengage. AI-powered personalization strikes a balance, offering what I like to think of as *bounded autonomy*—choice within structure. Consider a language learning platform. A student completes a short diagnostic on grammar, comprehension, and speaking fluency (NETI FERLINA, 2023). Based on this, the system recommends a learning path—but it also offers alternatives: "You can focus on past tense mastery *or* conversational fluency this week. Your scores suggest both would be helpful." The student picks. That pick matters. It signals ownership. And when a learner feels they have agency, they show up differently. They lean in. But here's the kicker: the AI still watches. If the chosen path isn't fruitful, it quietly reroutes. A bit like a GPS. Not in a punitive way—no "recalculating" scolding. Just a recalibration. A new suggestion. A fresh prompt. Because the goal isn't the *route*. It's the *destination*. And every detour is data.

Personalization Without Isolation: Designing for Community

There's a quiet risk in personalized learning that nobody talks about enough—the risk of isolation (Gunawardena et al, 2024). When every learner is on a different path, the classroom can start to feel like a silent study hall. Everyone with their headphones. Everyone in their algorithmic lane. But learning isn't just cognitive—it's social. AI systems that truly *understand* personalization don't just optimize for individual growth; they create opportunities for collaborative convergence. Imagine a scenario: four students, each with different strengths, are grouped by an AI tool for a collaborative project. One excels in visual design. One in research. One in verbal presentation. One in organization. The system doesn't just throw them together randomly. It pairs them intentionally, based on complementary profiles, prior engagement, even interest data from past lessons. Now the learning pathway becomes a shared space. Not uniform, but united. Each student contributes from their zone of strength, and in the process, learns from others. Personalization doesn't mean isolation. It means precision in *how* we bring students together, not just *why*.

Beyond Academics: Affect-Aware Personalization

Not all data is cognitive. In fact, some of the richest personalization comes from recognizing the emotional contours of learning. A student's pace may slow not because they don't understand—but because they're anxious. Another may click "next" repeatedly, not out of boredom, but from overwhelm. Newer AI tools are beginning to integrate affect-aware models (Triantafyllopoulos et al, 2024). They pick up on hesitation patterns, keystroke rhythms, even eye movement (in proctored environments), to detect cognitive load, stress, or disengagement. Based on these signals, the system can pause, adjust, or even offer a mental wellness check-in: "Would you like to take a short break? Here's a mindfulness activity, or a quick drawing task before we continue." This isn't about infantilizing students. It's about honoring the emotional reality of learning. The best personalization tools know when to push—and when to pause.

The Ethical Edge: When Personalization Goes Too Far

Let's not get dreamy-eyed. With great data comes great responsibility. Personalization, if misused, can veer into manipulation. If an AI system continually steers struggling students toward "easier" content without challenge, it risks capping their potential (Shah, 2023). If it feeds high-achievers only more and more acceleration, it may miss the soft skills—collaboration, empathy, patience—that don't show up in keystroke data. Then there's the issue of bias. AI models trained on skewed datasets can make personalization feel alienating. If cultural references, language idioms, or assessment norms are biased toward one dominant group, the system may misread student ability altogether. The solution? Transparent algorithms. Educators in the loop. Students with access to their own data and the ability to contest or recalibrate how they're being guided. Personalization must never become a form of invisible tracking.

AI as a Co-Teacher, Not a Commander

In every personalized system, there's a heartbeat missing if the teacher is not central. The AI may surface insights, suggest strategies, even scaffold pathways—but it cannot understand the nuance of a raised eyebrow, a slumped posture, a half-whispered "I don't get it." The teacher sees those things. The teacher *knows*. The most powerful AI learning platforms are designed not to supplant educators, but to serve them (Srinivasa et al, 2022). Dashboards that surface struggling students in real-time. Reports that show which concepts are sticking and which need reteaching. Suggestions—not prescriptions—for small-group configuration. In this sense, AI becomes a kind of mirror for the teacher. It reflects what might otherwise go unnoticed. It offers just enough light to illuminate the next step. But the teacher decides which path to take.

Personalized learning isn't about making everyone brilliant (Dhananjaya et al, 2024). It's about making everyone *seen.* It's about creating a system that says, "We know you're different. We planned for it." That kind of design is radical. It shifts the burden from the learner to the system. No longer does the student have to bend to fit the lesson. The lesson bends to meet the student. And AI, when wielded wisely, helps us do that. Not with mechanical coldness, but with the subtlety of attentive presence. Not to control learning, but to *free* it. The real promise of personalized AI learning pathways isn't efficiency (Zhang, 2024). It's humanity. It's the quiet dignity of a child realizing that the work they've been given? It fits. It makes sense. It's neither too much nor too little. It was meant for *them.* And that feeling—that rare, vital, golden feeling of being met where you are—is where real learning begins. Would you like me to develop this into a visual framework, include case studies, or cross-reference current tools like Century Tech, Squirrel AI, or DreamBox?

NAVIGATING ETHICAL AND PRACTICAL COMPLEXITIES IN AI-DRIVEN DIFFERENTIATION

Somewhere in the not-so-distant past, the teacher's red pen gave way to the algorithm's invisible hand (Kayyali, 2025 E). The shift was subtle—first, a recommendation engine for reading levels; then, real-time flags on student performance; now, adaptive systems that nudge learners down personalized pathways based on a swirl of micro-decisions they may not even remember making. At a glance, it seems like progress. A smoother ride for the learner, a dashboard of insight for the educator. But beneath the gloss, something stirs—a quiet unease, a murmur of questions no chart can answer. What exactly are we building? And who gets to decide what *learning* looks like in a world where decisions are increasingly mediated by lines of code? The ethics of AI-driven differentiation are not a footnote (Xu et al, 2024). They're the plot. Because what we call "personalized" can just as easily become *predictive.* And when we let systems predict too much, they begin to prescribe. Before long, the story a student could write for themselves is quietly overwritten by what the machine *thinks* they are capable of. Not because of malice. But because the data said so. This is where the practical collides with the philosophical. And the stakes couldn't be higher.

The Illusion of Neutrality: Bias in the Bones

Let's start with the most uncomfortable truth: there is no such thing as neutral AI. Every dataset, every model, every output reflects the decisions—conscious or not—of the people who built it. If a predictive engine was trained primarily on middle-class, monolingual students from Western urban centers, then it carries those assumptions into every classroom it enters, whether in rural Uganda or inner-city Detroit. Here's a scenario: a student from a linguistically rich household—say, they speak Arabic at home, French in their community, and English at school—writes an essay full of translanguaging. Code-switching, metaphor, rhythmic phrasing inherited from oral traditions. The AI grammar checker flags it as "confusing." The writing assistant suggests "clarity" revisions that flatten the voice, sand away the texture (Wallwork, 2024). The score drops. Feedback loops begin. What's lost here isn't just a grade. It's cultural expression. Linguistic identity. The student learns not just *what* to say, but *how* to say it "correctly"—according to the logic of a machine that never spoke their tongue. Bias isn't just offensive; it's formative. Left unchecked, it doesn't just reproduce inequality—it *automates* it.

Consent, Transparency, and the Ghost Curriculum

Have you ever been in a room where you were being observed, even if silently? A classroom with a camera, a meeting with someone taking notes? It changes how you behave (Kayyali, 2026). Now imagine a student who knows that every click, every scroll, every pause is being captured. Not necessarily judged—but captured. Stored. Analyzed. Used. Do they still take risks? Do they still make glorious, clumsy mistakes? Or do they start performing for the algorithm? This is the ghost curriculum—what students learn *about themselves* from the systems meant to support them. If personalization is built on data, then we need to talk about *data literacy*. Not just for educators, but for students (Gebre, 2022). They deserve to know what's being tracked, how it's being interpreted, and—most critically—how to push back. If a student is labeled "below benchmark" based on two weeks of post-pandemic struggle, that label can haunt them for years unless there's a way to contest it, to explain, to *recontextualize*. AI needs an appeals process. A way to raise your hand and say, "Actually, that's not who I am." Otherwise, personalization becomes predestination.

The Myth of Scalability: Efficiency vs. Meaning

One of the biggest selling points for AI in education is scalability (Gebre, 2022). The idea that we can finally offer individualized learning to *everyone*, not just those in private schools or with dedicated tutors. Sounds wonderful. But here's the catch: scaling differentiation through automation often trims away the very nuance that makes it *meaningful*. Think of it like mass-produced art. Technically accurate. Visually pleasing. But it lacks the little imperfections—the unexpected brushstroke, the smudge, the hesitation—that make a piece *alive*. When we design AI tools for efficiency, we risk building systems that *optimize for average*. They personalize, yes—but within pre-coded boundaries. Students can choose their pace, maybe their modality. But can they choose their *purpose*? Their *voice*? Real differentiation isn't just about adjusting levels. It's about honoring complexity. And complexity doesn't scale easily. It needs time. Dialogue. Space for the unscripted. This is why human teachers can never be replaced. Because what they offer isn't just instruction. It's *interpretation*. A way of reading the learner beyond the data.

The Role of the Educator: From Sage to Sensemaker

If we're honest, some educators are wary of AI not because they fear job loss, but because they fear relevance loss. Will the AI know more about my students than I do? Will I become a glorified babysitter, watching while the system does the real work? These fears are valid. But they're also misplaced. In AI-driven differentiation, the role of the teacher *changes*, but it becomes even more essential. No longer the sole source of knowledge, the teacher becomes the *sensemaker*—the one who filters the machine's suggestions through human intuition (Pedwell, 2024). The one who says, "Yes, the system thinks Jamal needs simpler texts, but I know he rises to the challenge when it's about civil rights history. Let's try this article instead." The teacher becomes the ethical gatekeeper. The cultural translator. The advocate. But only if we design the system that way. Only if teachers are *in the loop*, not out of it. That means interfaces built *with* educators, not just for them. That means professional development that's not an afterthought. That means respecting the teacher's judgment *more* once data enters the room, not less.

Practical Realities: Infrastructure, Access, and Implementation Chaos

Let's shift from the theoretical to the painfully practical. Some schools can barely keep the lights on. Cracked projectors, ancient laptops, spotty internet, no IT staff to speak of. In these places, the dream of AI-powered differentiation sounds like a cruel joke. Personalized dashboards? Real-time analytics? Let's start with working Wi-Fi. Even when the tech is there, implementation is messy. Teachers get new tools with little training. Systems don't talk to each other. Students log into five different platforms, each with its own quirks and logic. Fatigue sets in. Data fatigue. Tech fatigue. Pedagogical fatigue. And let's not forget the pressure from above. Districts want results—measurable, printable, fundable. So the personalization becomes performance-focused. Speed. Completion. Benchmark mastery. The human gets lost in the metrics. This isn't a reason to abandon AI. But it is a reason to slow down. To pilot, not impose. To ask questions before demanding answers.

When Differentiation Becomes Differentiationism

Here's a provocative thought: can differentiation become a form of discrimination? If we're not careful, yes. Imagine this: a student is consistently recommended "lower" level tasks. Over time, they internalize that. Teachers stop expecting depth. Peers see them as "low group." The student stops raising their hand (Hulings, 2022). What began as a well-meaning attempt to meet them where they are becomes a trap. A subtle, invisible ceiling. This is what I call *differentiationism*—the moment when personalization hardens into limitation. It's a failure not of the tool, but of imagination. Of courage. The best AI systems not only recommend content—they offer *exit ramps*. "You've mastered this level—want to try the next?" "You've shown creative thinking—ready for a more open-ended task?" The system nudges upward, outward. Always with respect, but never with finality. Because no learner should be defined by a snapshot.

Whose Future Are We Building? Student Agency and Participatory Design

If AI is shaping learning, students must shape AI. Too often, educational technology is designed by adults, for adults, and imposed on children. But students are not passive recipients of learning. They are co-authors. They deserve to be part of the design conversation. What would that look like?

- Student councils that test and review edtech tools before adoption.
- Feedback systems that let learners flag when personalization *doesn't* feel personal.
- Portfolios where students can annotate their own data, offering context behind the numbers.
- Systems that don't just recommend, but ask: *How do you like to learn? What helps you grow? What would you like to try next?*

When students feel ownership, they lean in. When they feel surveilled, they withdraw (Leekeenan & White, 2021). The line is thin. And it's our job to walk it with care. AI-driven differentiation is not a villain. It's a mirror. It reflects back what we put into it—our values, our biases, our hopes. It can be a force for equity or a vehicle for control. A tool of liberation or a mechanism of standardization. We get to choose. But only if we stay awake. Only if we keep asking messy, human questions. Questions without tidy answers. Like—

- What does *growth* really look like?
- Who defines *success* in this system?
- Are we creating conditions for learners to surprise us—or just conform to predictions?

Because that's what real education is about. Surprise. Discovery. Change. Not just in the student, but in us. AI can help us teach more responsively. More insightfully. But only if we remain *responsible*. Only if we keep the human at the center—not just as the subject of learning, but as its purpose. So, let's build systems that don't just track what students *do*, but ask who they're *becoming*. Let's use the data not just to differentiate instruction—but to deepen connection. And let's never forget: the most important thing we personalize is not the content. It's the *care*. The attention. The belief that behind every data point is a person—messy, luminous, growing. Just like us.

TOWARDS AN INCLUSIVE, HUMAN-CENTERED FUTURE OF AI IN EDUCATION

The future always arrives a little crooked. Not in straight lines, not in polished timelines, not in the tidy shapes of white papers or marketing decks. It stumbles in, half-baked, trailing both promise and peril. Artificial Intelligence in education is no exception. It didn't burst in like a revolution (Bulathwela et al, 2024). It crept in—quietly, incrementally—through adaptive quizzes, chatbots, automated grading tools, reading recommendation engines. Now it's everywhere and nowhere at once. It's in the background, whispering to us through dashboards and nudging decisions behind screens. But if we're going to let machines into our learning spaces—if we're going to let them influence what students learn, how they learn it, and how that learning is judged—then we need to step back and ask the question that almost no algorithm is equipped to answer:

Who is this for?

Not just in the general sense of "learners." Not just in the marketing sense of "stakeholders." But *who*, specifically. Which students? Which needs? Which stories? Which futures? Because a future built on AI, if not designed with brutal honesty and soft compassion, risks becoming efficient but blind. And that's the danger we face now: not the rise of evil machines, but the slow, unthinking drift into systems that reflect and reinforce existing inequities while wearing the mask of innovation. What we need, urgently, is a different vision—one grounded not in optimization but in *inclusion*. Not in automation but in *attention*. Not in the cold metrics of performance, but in the warm, flickering complexity of human potential. This is an attempt to imagine that kind of future. Not as a utopia. Not as a blueprint. But as a call to build—with care, with courage, and with others.

The Limits of "Personalization" Without Humanity

Let's start with something that might seem heretical in the age of personalized learning: personalization, as it is often currently implemented, is not inherently human-centered. Just because a student's path is tailored does not mean it is humane. Just because the system adapts does not mean it *understands*. You can build an AI that adjusts content to match reading levels, vocabulary preferences, even learning styles (Kanchon et al, 2024). You can offer a choice of formats—video, text, interactive modules—and feel proud of the range. But if that AI can't pause for grief, can't register cultural dissonance, can't see that a student is silent not because they're disengaged but because they're processing a trauma that doesn't fit into a rubric—then what we've created isn't personalization. It's mimicry. Real personalization requires *presence*. It requires that someone—not something—is listening. That someone is willing to say, "Forget the lesson plan. Tell me what's really going on." AI can't do that. Not yet. Probably not ever. So, the future we should aim for isn't one where AI becomes the teacher (Shah, 2023). It's one where AI supports teachers in being more *human*—more available, more responsive, more attuned. A future where the machine says, "This student has taken the same quiz five times. Their accuracy keeps dropping." And the teacher, hearing that whisper, walks over and kneels beside the desk—not with a new worksheet, but with a simple, *Are you okay?* That's the kind of personalization that matters. The kind rooted in relationship.

Who Gets to Design the System?

There's an uncomfortable reality beneath most of our conversations about educational AI: the people designing the systems are not the ones using them. They're not the teachers. They're not the students. They're often not even educators. They're engineers, data scientists, venture capitalists, startup founders—many of them brilliant, no doubt—but working from a vantage point far removed from the rhythm of classrooms. And that matters. Because every decision in AI design—what data gets collected, how it's interpreted, what the "correct" outcome looks like—is a value judgment. It encodes assumptions. About intelligence. About success. About what's normal and what's not. If those assumptions go unchallenged, we end up with tools that may work well for students who already fit the system, but fail (or worse, harm) those who don't. Neurodivergent learners. Multilingual students. Those living in poverty. Those with cultural reference points the algorithm was never trained to recognize (Leung, 2024). The fix isn't just to tweak the training data. It's to open the design process. To make it participatory. To bring in students, teachers, parents—not as "user testers" at the end of development, but as *co-creators* from the beginning. Ask them what they need. What they fear. What they've learned from systems that failed them. Because unless we democratize the design, the tools we build will always serve the powerful first.

Slowing Down the Speed of EdTech

We're conditioned to think of innovation as speed. Launch faster. Iterate. Disrupt. But education doesn't move like a startup. Learning is slow. Messy. Deep. And it resists metrics in all the best ways. The danger is that AI, with its promise of rapid insight and real-time feedback, encourages us to treat learning like a series of transactions (Paramesha et al, 2024). Input. Output. Score. Adjust. Move on. But real growth? Real meaning? That often happens in silence. In the gap between struggle and insight. In the wandering. If we're not careful, AI will start rushing the process—pushing students to mastery before they've had a chance to dwell. Nudging them forward when what they need is to *pause*. So, we need to bake slowness into our systems. Not inefficiency, but spaciousness. Time to reflect. Time to fail. Time to *not know*. And that means resisting the pressure to optimize everything. It means sometimes choosing the longer path because it's more *human*.

Designing for the Margins, Not the Middle

There's a phrase in universal design: *If you design for the margins, you serve everyone better.* That should be the mantra for AI in education. Instead of optimizing for the average learner—the mythical middle—we should start with those furthest from the center. Students who have been historically excluded. Who learn differently. Who speak other languages (Anya, 2021). Who need extra support not because they're deficient, but because the system wasn't built with them in mind.

When we start there, our tools get better. They become more flexible, more empathetic, more robust. Accessibility isn't an afterthought. It's the foundation. This also means rethinking how we define success. Not every student wants to be a coder or an engineer. Not every student thrives in competitive environments. The AI of the future should be able to ask, "What kind of learner do you want to be?" and adapt accordingly. Let students set their own metrics. Let them define growth on their terms. That's not chaos. That's dignity.

Embedding Ethics in the Everyday

Ethics isn't a policy you paste on top of your product. It's not a checklist. It's a *habit.* A way of seeing. And in education, it has to start with the question: *What kind of human being are we helping to shape?* That's not hyperbole. It's reality. Because when an AI decides what a student sees, how quickly they move through content, what feedback they get—that *shapes* their self-concept. Their motivation. Their willingness to try again. So, we need ethics not just in the code, but in the classroom. Students should know how the system works. What data it collects. What it assumes (Khoa et al, 2023). They should be able to challenge it. Annotate it. Say, "That score doesn't reflect what I learned." We also need to think about data sovereignty. Who owns the learning record? How long is it stored? Who gets to see it? Right now, most students have no idea where their educational data goes. That's not just a technical issue. It's a trust issue. And if students don't trust the system, they won't engage with it honestly. They'll game it. Perform for it. Or disengage entirely. Transparency isn't optional. It's foundational.

What Would a Human-Centered AI Actually Look Like?

Let's imagine, for a moment, a classroom five years from now—not a fantasy, but a possible near-future grounded in care. Each student logs into their learning platform. But it doesn't start with a quiz or a progress bar (Srbecky et al, 2023). It starts with a question: *How are you feeling today?* And based on the answer, it adjusts—not just the content, but the pace, the tone, the challenge level. It doesn't just flag errors. It asks, *Would you like help with this? Would you prefer a video or a conversation?* It doesn't track just performance. It tracks patterns of curiosity. It remembers that Fatima asked three questions about ecosystems last week and nudges her toward a biodiversity module—*not* because of a test score, but because she showed wonder. It gives teachers a dashboard—not filled with grades, but with stories. Snapshots of student growth. Moments of resilience. Places where the teacher's intuition might matter more than the algorithm's advice. And when something goes wrong—because it will—the system doesn't hide. It explains. It says, *Here's what I saw. Here's why I made this choice. Do you agree?* That's not just tech. That's trust.

We talk a lot about rigor. About outcomes. About equity. All important. But what about joy? What about designing systems that make students *feel alive*? That spark laughter? That offer wonder? Because education, at its best, isn't just preparation. It's liberation. It's a kind of becoming. What if AI could help us get *closer* to that? Not by replacing teachers. Not by reducing learning to a series of clicks. But by freeing up space—for relationships, for creativity, for slow, deep, messy thinking. That's the future I want (Kayyali, 2024). And if we build it together—honestly, inclusively, humanely—it won't just be smart. It'll be *wise*. It'll be ours.

CONCLUSION

Differentiated instruction has always asked educators to see the full humanity of their students—to recognize the mosaic of abilities, experiences, and needs that define every classroom. With the arrival of AI-powered tools, this vision no longer has to be merely aspirational. We now have the capacity to personalize instruction with a level of nuance and immediacy that was once unthinkable. But with that capacity comes a responsibility—one that demands intentionality, reflection, and a critical awareness of what is at stake.

As we stand at the crossroads of pedagogy and technology, one truth must anchor us: **education is a profoundly human endeavor**. AI can process patterns, but it cannot perceive the tremble in a student's voice when they're too anxious to ask a question. It can recommend the next lesson, but it cannot celebrate a hard-won breakthrough or understand the silence of a student who has just experienced loss. What this means is that AI, no matter how advanced, must remain in service to human judgment, human relationships, and human values.

This does not diminish the transformative potential of AI—it clarifies it. When designed ethically and implemented thoughtfully, AI can extend the teacher's reach. It can provide a flexible scaffolding that bends to student needs, identifies learning gaps in real time, and adapts instruction to meet diverse learners where they are. It can surface hidden patterns that guide more equitable teaching decisions. And for students with disabilities, language barriers, or other obstacles, AI can offer support that is timely, personalized, and empowering. But we must guard against two risks. The first is **automation without meaning**—the seduction of dashboards, analytics, and performance metrics that forget the student behind the data. The second is **equity without context**—deploying "personalized" tools that, in practice, replicate biases or entrench inequalities under the guise of objectivity. If we do not confront these risks head-on, we may find ourselves with more efficient systems, but less just classrooms.

So, what does responsible innovation look like? It begins with involving educators in the design of AI tools, ensuring they align with pedagogical values and classroom realities. It means equipping teachers with the training and time they need to interpret data critically and use it wisely. It calls for transparency around how algorithms work, and accountability when they fail. Most importantly, it demands that we center students—not just as users, but as full participants in their own learning journeys.

The future of differentiated instruction will not be decided by technology alone. It will be shaped by the choices we make as educators, designers, and communities. Will we use AI to sort and separate, or to support and uplift? Will we build systems that scale efficiency, or ones that deepen empathy? These are not technical questions. They are moral ones.

In the end, the goal is not to teach with AI—it is to teach better *because* of it. To notice more, not less. To respond more fully, not more rigidly. To make space for every learner's journey, in all its complexity and potential. And perhaps, if we get it right, to ensure that no student feels invisible again—not to their teacher, not to the system, and not to the future.

REFERENCES

Akibu, A. (2024). Tomorrow's Classrooms: An Exploration of AI's Role in Adaptive Learning (Doctoral dissertation, University of Pennsylvania).

Anya, U. (2021). Critical race pedagogy for more effective and inclusive world language teaching. *Applied Linguistics*, *42*(6), 1055–1069.

Bulathwela, S., Pérez-Ortiz, M., Holloway, C., Cukurova, M., & Shawe-Taylor, J. (2024). Artificial intelligence alone will not democratise education: On educational inequality, techno-solutionism and inclusive tools. *Sustainability*, *16*(2), 781.

Chanan, M. (2023). Artificial stupidity: on the alienation of intelligence. Free Associations, 36(88).

Davis, C., Bush, T., & Wood, S. (2024). Artificial intelligence in education: Enhancing learning experiences through personalized adaptation. *International Journal of Cyber and IT Service Management*, *4*(1), 26–32.

Dhananjaya, G. M., Goudar, R. H., Kulkarni, A., Rathod, V. N., & Hukkeri, G. S. (2024). A digital recommendation system for personalized learning to enhance online education: A review. *IEEE Access : Practical Innovations, Open Solutions*.

Dlask, J. (2024). Promoting Differentiation in the English Classroom with the Help of Generative AI.

Ehsan, M. M. (2024). Impact of COVID-19 Lockdowns on Learning Losses: Structural and Individual Factors (Master's thesis, Hamad Bin Khalifa University (Qatar)).

Galés, N. L. (2024). Trust and connection in the artificial intelligence educational ecosystem: From algorithmism to algoritharism. *Revista Catalana de Pedagogia*, *26*, 4–37.

Gebre, E. (2022). Conceptions and perspectives of data literacy in secondary education. *British Journal of Educational Technology*, *53*(5), 1080–1095.

Green, V. (2022). "Use Your Teacher Voice": How a Podcast Could Support ESOL Teachers' Voices in Advocacy.

Gunawardena, M., Bishop, P., & Aviruppola, K. (2024). Personalized learning: The simple, the complicated, the complex and the chaotic. *Teaching and Teacher Education*, *139*, 104429.

Herner-Patnode, L., & Lee, H. J. (2021). Differentiated Instruction to Teach Mathematics: Through the Lens of Responsive Teaching. *Mathematics Teacher Education and Development*, *23*(3), 6–25.

Hulings, M. (2022). What are they bringing with them? Understanding past science experiences of preservice elementary teachers and what they mean for the science methods course. *Journal of Research in Science Teaching*, *59*(8), 1465–1488.

Kanchon, M. K. H., Sadman, M., Nabila, K. F., Tarannum, R., & Khan, R. (2024). Enhancing personalized learning: AI-driven identification of learning styles and content modification strategies. *International Journal of Cognitive Computing in Engineering*, *5*, 269–278.

Kayyali, M. (2022). Equity, Equality, Diversity, and Inclusion as Key Performance Indicators in Higher Education. *Online Submission*, *3*(5), 1–3.

Kayyali, M. (2024). Future possibilities and challenges of AI in education. In *Transforming education with generative AI: Prompt engineering and synthetic content creation* (pp. 118–137). IGI Global Scientific Publishing.

Kayyali, M. (2025a). Ethical Implications of Generative AI in Education: Privacy, Bias, and Integrity. In Transformative AI Practices for Personalized Learning Strategies (pp. 185-218). IGI Global Scientific Publishing.

Kayyali, M. (2025b). Generative AI and Education: Transforming Teaching and Learning Through Collaborative Intelligence. In Humans and Generative AI Tools for Collaborative Intelligence (pp. 25-52). IGI Global Scientific Publishing.

Kayyali, M. (2025c). The Future of AI in Education: Predictions and Emerging Trends. Next-Generation AI Methodologies in Education, 367-406.

Kayyali, M. (2025d). AI in Higher Education: Revolutionizing Curriculum and Administration. In AI Adoption and Diffusion in Education (pp. 31-62). IGI Global Scientific Publishing.

Kayyali, M. (2025e). Ethical Implications of Generative AI in Education: Privacy, Bias, and Integrity. In Transformative AI Practices for Personalized Learning Strategies (pp. 185-218). IGI Global Scientific Publishing.

Kayyali, M. (2026). The Impact of AI on Classroom Dynamics in Higher Education: Shifting Roles for Professors and Students. In Responsible AI Integration in Education (pp. 151-180). IGI Global Scientific Publishing.

Kelly, S. (2023). Let me play, too! Co-designing inclusive sensory play spaces in collaboration with neurodiverse and neurotypical children (Doctoral dissertation, Queensland University of Technology).

Khoa, B. T., Hung, B. P., & Hejsalem-Brahmi, M. (2023). Qualitative research in social sciences: Data collection, data analysis and report writing. *International Journal of Public Sector Performance Management*, *12*(1-2), 187–209.

Kodó, K. (2024). Storytelling: Adaptability and Expansion of American Indian and Indigenous Culture.

Laak, K. J., & Aru, J. (2024). AI and personalized learning: bridging the gap with modern educational goals. arXiv preprint arXiv:2404.02798.

Lan, Y. J., & Chen, N. S. (2024). Teachers' agency in the era of LLM and generative AI. *Journal of Educational Technology & Society*, *27*(1), I–XVIII.

Leekeenan, K., & White, H. (2021). Recognition and respect: Centering students' voices through writing groups. *English Journal*, *110*(4), 92–99.

Leung, H. (2024). Artificial Intelligence as Agents to Support Neurodivergent Creative and Critical Thinking Modules.

Macháček, D., Dabre, R., & Bojar, O. (2023). Turning whisper into real-time transcription system. arXiv preprint arXiv:2307.14743.

Maeda, J. (2025). *How to Speak Machine, with a new preface by the author: A Gentle Introduction to Artificial Intelligence*. MIT Press.

Malek, A. (2021). *Intersection: Reimagining the future of mobility across traditional boundaries*. SAE International.

NETI FERLINA, N. F. (2023). THE CORRELATION BETWEEN STUDENTS'GRAMMAR ABILITY AND STUDENTS'SPEAKING ABILITY (Doctoral dissertation, UNIVERSITAS SULAWESI BARAT).

Paramesha, M., Rane, N. L., & Rane, J. (2024). Big data analytics, artificial intelligence, machine learning, internet of things, and blockchain for enhanced business intelligence. *Partners Universal Multidisciplinary Research Journal*, *1*(2), 110–133.

Pedwell, C. (2024). The Intuitive and the Counter-Intuitive: AI and the A ffective Ideologies of Common Sense. *New Formations*, *112*(112), 70–93.

Puplampu, R. (2024). *What Everyone Should Know About the Rise of AI: AI Transparency, Privacy, and Ethics Best Practices*. Puplampu Books.

Rodrigues, M. (2024). Returning to School After a Pandemic: Secondary Teacher Perspectives on Students Returning to School in Regard to Academic Achievement, Behavior, Mindset, and Social Connections (Doctoral dissertation, University of Massachusetts Global).

Schroeder-Schock, A. (2024). *Coaching First-Grade Teachers On Differentiated Instructional Practices For Learners With Mathematical Promise: An Action Research Study*. The College of William and Mary.

Shah, P. (2023). *AI and the Future of Education: Teaching in the Age of Artificial Intelligence*. John Wiley & Sons.

Sjølie, E., Strømme, A., & Boks-Vlemmix, J. (2021). Team-skills training and real-time facilitation as a means for developing student teachers' learning of collaboration. *Teaching and Teacher Education*, *107*, 103477.

Srbecky, R., Colutto, S., Wetzel, S. A., Winterhagen, M., Fraas, W., Dettmers, J., & Hemmje, M. (2023). Realization of adaptive progress bars in moodle for attested competencies and qualifications for learners in higher education institutions psychology courses considering qualifications-based learning. In EDULEARN23 Proceedings (pp. 1736-1742). IATED.

Srinivasa, K. G., Kurni, M., & Saritha, K. (2022). Harnessing the Power of AI to Education. In *Learning, teaching, and assessment methods for contemporary learners: pedagogy for the digital generation* (pp. 311–342). Springer Nature Singapore.

Subasi, A., Qaisar, S. M., & Nisar, H. (Eds.). (2024). *Artificial Intelligence and Multimodal Signal Processing in Human-Machine Interaction*. Elsevier.

SWARGIARY. K. (2024). The Quantum Leap: Exploring the Power and Potential of Q-Star AI in Academia and Beyond. EdTech Research Association, Scottsdale, Arizona, US.

Tomlinson, C. A. (2022). *Everybody's classroom: differentiating for the shared and unique needs of diverse students*. Teachers College Press.

Tomlinson, C. A., & Jarvis, J. M. (2023). Differentiation: Making curriculum work for all students through responsive planning & instruction. In Systems and models for developing programs for the gifted and talented (pp. 599-628). Routledge.

Tragant, E., Pinyana, À., Mackay, J., & Andria, M. (2022). Extending language learning beyond the EFL classroom through WhatsApp. *Computer Assisted Language Learning*, *35*(8), 1946–1974.

Triantafyllopoulos, A., Christ, L., Gebhard, A., Jing, X., Kathan, A., Milling, M., ... & Schuller, B. W. (2024). Beyond Deep Learning: Charting the Next Frontiers of Affective Computing. Intelligent Computing, 3, 0089.

Tyrina, A. (2021). *Investigating the Attitudes, Beliefs and Practices of High School Chemistry Teachers Regarding the Differentiation of Instruction*. The University of Maine.

Vallor, S. (2024). *The AI mirror: How to reclaim our humanity in an age of machine thinking*. Oxford University Press.

VanTassel-Baska, J., Hubbard, G. F., & Robbins, J. I. (2021). Differentiation of instruction for gifted learners: Collated evaluative studies of teacher classroom practices. Handbook of giftedness and talent development in the Asia-Pacific, 945-979.

Wallwork, A. (2024). *AI-assisted Writing and Presenting in English*. Springer Nature.

Winek, A. (2025). Making Space for Quiet Joy in the Classroom. Joy-Centered Pedagogy in Higher Education: Uplifting Teaching and Learning for All.

Wolf, A. T., & Putnam, K. (2023). *Beyond the Static Page: An Interactive Learning Approach for Students*. AT Wolf & Company.

Xu, C., Sun, Y., & Zhou, H. (2024). Artificial aesthetics and ethical ambiguity: Exploring business ethics in the context of AI-driven creativity. *Journal of Business Ethics*, , 1–22.

Zhang, Q. (2024). Harnessing Artificial Intelligence for Personalized Learning Pathways: A Framework for Adaptive Education Management Systems. *Applied and Computational Engineering*, *82*, 167–172.

Zhu, X., Wang, D., Pedrycz, W., & Li, Z. (2021). A design of granular classifier based on granular data descriptors. *IEEE Transactions on Cybernetics*, *53*(3), 1790–1801. PMID: 34936563

Compilation of References

Aberšek, B., Flogie, A., & Aberšek, M. K. (2023, June). Transformation of Education: From Dehumanization to Re-Humanization of Society. In International Baltic Symposium on Science and Technology Education. Scientia Socialis Ltd. 29 K. Donelaicio Street, LT-78115 Siauliai, Republic of Lithuania.

Adams, C., Pente, P., Lemermeyer, G., & Rockwell, G. (2023). Ethical principles for Artificial Intelligence in K-12 education. *Computers and Education: Artificial Intelligence*, *4*, 100131. DOI: 10.1016/j.caeai.2023.100131

Admane, R., Sawale, P. S., Jayasree, R., Kurup, S. J., & Thomas, S. A. (2024). Artificial intelligence in education: Tailoring curriculum to individual student needs through AI-based systems. *Library of Progress-Library Science. Information Technology & Computer*, *44*(3), 8847–8856. DOI: 10.48165/bapas.2024.44.2.1

Agrawal, A. V., Pitchai, R., Senthamaraikannan, C., Balaji, N. A., Sajithra, S., & Boopathi, S. (2023a). Digital Education System During the COVID-19 Pandemic. In *Using Assistive Technology for Inclusive Learning in K-12 Classrooms* (pp. 104–126). IGI Global.

Agrawal, A. V., Pitchai, R., Senthamaraikannan, C., Balaji, N. A., Sajithra, S., & Boopathi, S. (2023b). Digital Education System During the COVID-19 Pandemic. In *Using Assistive Technology for Inclusive Learning in K-12 Classrooms* (pp. 104–126). IGI Global.

Akibu, A. (2024). Tomorrow's Classrooms: An Exploration of AI's Role in Adaptive Learning (Doctoral dissertation, University of Pennsylvania).

Akinwalere, S. N., & Ivanov, V. (2022). Artificial Intelligence in Higher Education: Challenges and Opportunities. *BORDER CROSSING*, *12*(1), 1. DOI: 10.33182/bc.v12i1.2015

Akyel, Y., & Tur, E. (2024). Prospects, challenges, and future directions in the research and investigation of Artificial Intelligence's potential and applications in educational sciences [Yapay zekanın potansiyelinin ve eğitim bilimlerindeki uygulamalarının araştırılması ve araştırmalarda beklentiler, zorluklar ve gelecek Yönelimleri] [Ahi Evran Üniversitesi Kırşehir Eğitim Fakültesi Dergisi]. *Ahi Evran University Journal of Kırşehir Education Faculty*, *25*(1), 645–711. DOI: 10.29299/kefad.1322341

AlAfnan, M. A., Dishari, S., Jovic, M., & Lomidze, K. (2023). Chatgpt as an educational tool: Opportunities, challenges, and recommendations for communication, business writing, and composition courses. *Journal of Artificial Intelligence and Technology*, *3*(2), 60–68.

Aldemir, U., Caner, S., Akın, P., & Kaplan, A. (2024) Student-centered learning models in education [Eğitimde öğrenci merkezli öğrenme modelleri]. *International QMX Journal, 3*(3), 1280-1285. ISSN: 3023-6037. doi: https://doi.org/DOI: 10.5281/zenodo.10899512

Ali, A., Al-rimy, B. A. S., Tin, T. T., Altamimi, S., Qasem, S. N., & Saeed, F. (2023). Empowering Precision Medicine: Unlocking Revolutionary Insights through Blockchain-Enabled Federated Learning and Electronic Medical Records. *Sensors (Basel)*, *23*(17), 7476. DOI: 10.3390/s23177476 PMID: 37687931

Ali, M. (2024). AI and intelligent tutoring systems: A new paradigm for student-centered learning. *Journal of AI Integration in Education*, *1*(2), 1–11.

Alkattan, H., Subhi, A. A., Adelaja, O. A., Abotaleb, M., Mijwil, M. M., Mishra, P., Sekiwu, D., Bamwerinde, W., & Turyasingura, B. (2023). Employing data mining techniques and machine learning models in classification of students' academic performance. *Babylonian Journal of Artificial Intelligence*, *2023*, 43–54.

Allen, T. J., & Mizumoto, A. (2024). ChatGPT over my friends: Japanese English-as-a- Foreign-Language learners' preferences for editing and proofreading strategies. *RELC Journal. Article, 00336882241262533*. Advance online publication. DOI: 10.1177/ 00336882241262533

Almada, M., & Dymitruk, M. (2022). Data protection and judicial automation. In *Research Handbook on EU Data Protection Law* (pp. 270–289). Edward Elgar Publishing.

Almazrou, S., Alanezi, F., & Almutairi, S. A.. (2024). Enhancing medical students' critical thinking skills through ChatGPT: An empirical study with medical students. *Nutrition and Health (Berkhamsted, Hertfordshire)*. Advance online publication. DOI: 10.1177/02601060241273627 PMID: 39150341

Alpar, D., Batdal, G., & Avcı, Y. (2012). Educational technology applications in student-centred education [Öğrenci merkezli eğitimde eğitim teknolojileri uygulamaları] [Hasan Ali Yücel Eğitim Fakültesi Dergisi]. *HAYEF Journal of Education*, *4*(1), 19–31.

Alraddadi, M. M., & Zebehazy, K. T. (2023). Exploring inclusive teaching practices to enhance effective learning of students with visual impairments in a secondary school in Saudi Arabia using a self-regulated learning framework. *British Journal of Visual Impairment*, •••, 02646196231201770.

Altun, A. (2022). How can digital history affect history education? [Dijital Tarih, Tarih Eğitimini Nasıl Etkileyebilir?]. *8th International Symposium on History Education [8. Uluslararası Tarih Eğitimi Sempozyumu]* (ISHE 2022), (pp. 17-28). Adana, Türkiye.

Alvi, E., & Gillies, R. M. (2024). Investigating the individual nature of teacher beliefs and practices about self-regulated learning and how this shapes their practices for supporting student learning. *Educational Studies*, *50*(4), 516–538.

Amiraullt, R. J. (2019). The Next Great Educational Technology Debate: Personal Data, Its Ownership, and Privacy. *Quarterly Review of Distance Education*, *20*(2), 55. https://eric.ed.gov/?id=EJ1237016

Anya, U. (2021). Critical race pedagogy for more effective and inclusive world language teaching. *Applied Linguistics*, *42*(6), 1055–1069.

Anyichie, A. C., Butler, D. L., & Nashon, S. M. (2023). Exploring Teacher Practices for Enhancing Student Engagement in Culturally Diverse Classrooms. *Journal of Pedagogical Research*, *7*(5), 183–207.

Arslan, K. (2020). Artificial intelligence and applications in education [Eğitimde yapay zeka ve uygulamaları] [Batı Anadolu Eğitim Bilimleri Dergisi]. *Western Anatolia Journal of Educational Sciences*, *11*(1), 71–88.

Asad, M., Ali, S., & Wahid, I. (2022). The Role of Artificial Intelligence in Enhancing Learning Outcomes in Higher Education. *Journal of Educational Computing Research*, *58*(4), 666. DOI: 10.1177/07356331221122732

Ayala-Pazmiño, M. (2023). *Artificial intelligence in education: Exploring the potential benefits and risks. In 593 Digital Publisher CEIT, 8(3).*, DOI: 10.33386/593dp.2023.3.1827

Aydan, S. (2023). *From Little Acorns to Mighty Oaks: Self-Regulation Strategies of the Top Ranking Science High School Students in Türki ye and Factors Promoting These Strategies* [Doctoral dissertation, Middle East Technical University]. METU Library Database https://open.metu.edu.tr/handle/11511/104828

Azevedo, R., Rosário, P., Magalhães, P., Núñez, J. C., Pereira, B., & Pereira, A. (2023). A tool-kit to help students from low socioeconomic status background: A school-based self-regulated learning intervention. *European Journal of Psychology of Education, 38*(2), 495–518.

Bailey, D. E., Faraj, S., Hinds, P. J., Leonardi, P. M., & von Krogh, G. (2022). We are all theorists of technology now: A relational perspective on emerging technology and organizing. *Organization Science*, *33*(1), 1–18.

Bailey, J. (2023). AI in Education: The leap into a new era of machine intelligence carries risks and challenges, but also plenty of promise. *Education Next*, *23*(4), 29–36.

Baker, M., & Andriessen, J. (2022). *Arguing to learn* (3rd ed.). The Cambridge Handbook of the Learning Sciences.

Baker, R. S., Ocumpaugh, J., & Andres, J. M. (2024). BROMP quantitative field observations: A review. In *Handbook of artificial intelligence in education* (pp. 132–156). Edward Elgar Publishing.

Bandura, A. (1986). *Social Foundations of Thought and Action: A Social Cognitive Theory*. Prentice Hall.

Banks, S. (2011). *A Historical Analysis of Attitudes Toward the use of Calculators in Junior High and High School Math Classrooms in the United States since 1975* [Master's Thesis, Cedarville University]. Digital Commons. https://digitalcommons.cedarville.edu/education_theses/31/

Bano, M., Zowghi, D., Kearney, M., Schuck, S., & Aubusson, P. (2018). Mobile learning for science and mathematics school education: A systematic review of empirical evidence. *Computers & Education*, *121*, 30–58. DOI: 10.1016/j.compedu.2018.02.006

Bardach, L., Yanagida, T., Goetz, T., Jach, H., & Pekrun, R. (2023). Self-regulated and externally regulated learning in adolescence: Developmental trajectories and relations with teacher behavior, parent behavior, and academic achievement. *Developmental Psychology*, *59*(7), 1327. PMID: 37155294

Baron, N. S. (2023). *Who wrote this?: how AI and the lure of efficiency threaten human writing*. Stanford University Press.

Baym, N. K. (2015). *Personal connections in the digital age*. John Wiley & Sons.

Bell, S., & Kornbluh, M. (2022). Networking in the digital age: Identifying factors that influence adolescents' online communication and relationship building. *Applied Developmental Science*, *26*(1), 109–126.

Bennett, P. (2021). Teaching itself: a mythology of learning in theory and practice.

Benzer, S., & Benzer, R. (2024). Yapay zekâ ve eğitimin geleceği. [Artificial intelligence and the future of education] In Gökcearslan, S., & Yıldız Durak, H. (Eds.), *Yapay zekâ okuryazarlığı* [Artificial intelligence literacy]. (pp. 191–220). Nobel Akademik.

Berson, I. R., & Berson, M. J. (2023). The democratization of AI and its transformative potential in social studies education. *Social Education*, *87*(2), 114–118.

Bertram, C., Weiss, Z., Zachrich, L., & Ziai, R. (2021). Artificial intelligence in history education. Linguistic content and complexity analyses of student writings in the CAHisT project (Computational assessment of historical thinking). *Computers and Education: Artificial Intelligence*. doi: https://doi.org/DOI: 10.1016/j.caeai.2021.100038

Bhimavarapu, U. (2025). Personalized Learning in the Digital Era: Unlocking Potential Through. *Optimizing Research Techniques and Learning Strategies With Digital Technologies*, 187.

Bierstaker, J. L., Brink, W. D., Khatoon, S., & Thorne, L. (2024). Academic Fraud and Remote Evaluation of Accounting Students: An Application of the Fraud Triangle. *Journal of Business Ethics*, *195*(2), 425. DOI: 10.1007/s10551-024-05628-9

Bozkurt, A. (2023). Generative artificial intelligence (AI) powered conversational educational agents: The inevitable paradigm shift. *Asian Journal of Distance Education*, *18*(1), 198–204. DOI: 10.5281/zenodo.7716416

Briskin, J., & Land, S. M. (2020). Student-centered virtual design studio environments. In *The Routledge International Handbook of Student-Centered Learning and Teaching in Higher Education* (pp. 345–360). Routledge.

Brom, C., Šisler, V., & Slavik, R. (2010). Implementing digital game-based learning in schools: Augmented learning environment of "Europe 2045.". *Multimedia Systems*, *16*(1), 23–41. DOI: 10.1007/s00530-009-0174-0

Brown, J. S. (2001). Learning in the digital age. *The Internet and the University: Forum*, *71*(72), 65–71.

Buber, M. (1958/2000). *I and thou*. Scribner Classics.

Bukharin, N. (2021). *Historical Materialism*. Critical Editions. (Original work published 1925)

Bulathwela, S., Pérez-Ortiz, M., Holloway, C., Cukurova, M., & Shawe-Taylor, J. (2024). Artificial intelligence alone will not democratise education: On educational inequality, techno-solutionism and inclusive tools. *Sustainability*, *16*(2), 781.

Bulut, O., Beiting-Parrish, M., Casabianca, J. M., Slater, S. C., Jiao, H., Song, D., & Morilova, P. (2024). The rise of Artificial Intelligence in educational measurement: Opportunities and ethical challenges. *Journal of Educational Measurement and Evaluation*, *5*(3), 1–32. DOI: 10.59863/MIQL7785

Bussell, D. (2024). Historical thinking in the classroom: A multiple-case study. *Social Studies*, *115*(3), 129–145. DOI: 10.1080/00377996.2023.2274051

Bu u, A. F. (2024). Unleashing the Potential of AI in Classrooms. *Revista de Stiinte Politice*, (81), 34–42.

Butler, D., Leahy, M., Twining, P., Akoh, B., Chtouki, Y., Farshadnia, S., Moore, K., Nikolov, R., Pascual, C., & Sherman, B. (2018). Education systems in the digital age: The need for alignment. *Technology. Knowledge and Learning*, *23*, 473–494.

Callan, G., Longhurst, D., Shim, S., & Ariotti, A. (2022). Identifying and predicting teachers' use of practices that support SRL. *Psychology in the Schools*, *59*(11), 2327–2344.

Caro, M. F., Quitian, L., Giraldo, J. C., & Lengua-Cantero, C. (2023, November). A formal model for personalized learning path using Artificial Intelligence for instructional planning with a focus on 21st-century skills and environmental awareness. In *2023 IEEE Colombian Caribbean Conference (C3)* (pp. 1-6). IEEE.

Carreira, M. B. F. D. C. (2024). AI-powered personalization: A behavioural economics perspective in marketing (Master's thesis).

Carretero, M., & Gartner, E. (2024). Artificial Intelligence and historical thinking: A dialogic exploration of ChatGPT/Inteligencia Artificial y pensamiento histórico: una exploración dialógica del ChatGPT. *Studies in Psychology*, *45*(1), 80–102. DOI: 10.1177/021093952412413

Chalkiadakis, A., Seremetaki, A., Kanellou, A., Kallishi, M., Morfopoulou, A., Moraitaki, M., & Mastrokoukou, S. (2024). Impact of Artificial Intelligence and Virtual Reality on Educational Inclusion: A Systematic Review of Technologies Supporting Students with Disabilities. *Education Sciences*, *14*(11), 1223. DOI: 10.3390/educsci14111223

Challoumis, C. (2024). The Imperative of Skill Development in an AI Revolution. In *XIX International Scientific Conference*. London. Great Britain (pp. 132-168).

Chanan, M. (2023). Artificial stupidity: on the alienation of intelligence. Free Associations, 36(88).

Chandra, S., Ghule, G., Bilfaqih, S. M., Thiyagarajan, A., Sharmila, J., & Boopathi, S. (2025). Adaptive Strategies in Online Marketing Using Machine Learning Techniques. In *Digital Transformation Initiatives for Agile Marketing* (pp. 67–100). IGI Global.

Chang, D. H., Lin, M. P. C., Hajian, S., & Wang, Q. Q. (2023). Educational design principles of using AI chatbot that supports self-regulated learning in education: Goal setting, feedback, and personalization. *Sustainability*, *15*(17), 12921. DOI: 10.3390/su151712921

Chaudhry, M. A., & Kazim, E. (2022). Artificial Intelligence in Education (AIEd): A high-level academic and industry note 2021. *AI and Ethics*, *2*(1), 157–165. PMID: 34790953

Chen, E. (2025). "We Are Bridges": Bilingual Latina Teachers as Cultural Mediators in Family–School Partnerships. *Education Sciences*, *15*(6), 717.

Chetry, K. K. (2024). Transforming education: How AI is revolutionizing the learning experience. *International Journal of Research Publication and Reviews*, *5*(5), 6352–6356. DOI: 10.55248/gengpi.5.0524.1277

Chisega-Negrılă, A. M. (2024). Teaching and learning in an AI-powered world. *Bulletın of" Carol I. Natıonal Defence Unıversıty*, *13*(3), 105–116. DOI: 10.53477/2284-9378-24-33

Chiu, T. K. (2024). A classification tool to foster self-regulated learning with generative artificial intelligence by applying self-determination theory: A case of ChatGPT. *Educational Technology Research and Development*, *72*(4), 2401–2416. DOI: 10.1007/s11423-024-10366-w

Chiu, T. K. (2024). Future research recommendations for transforming higher education with generative AI. *Computers and Education: Artificial Intelligence*, *6*, 100197. DOI: 10.1016/j.caeai.2023.100197

Christodoulou, A., & Angeli, C. (2022). Adaptive Learning Techniques for a Personalized Educational Software in Developing Teachers' Technological Pedagogical Content Knowledge. *Frontiers in Education*, *7*. Advance online publication. DOI: 10.3389/feduc.2022.789397

Çığır Dikyol, D., & Şar İşbilen, E. (2020). The use of virtual reality technology in history teaching: The case of Çatalhöyük [Tarih öğretiminde sanal gerçeklik teknolojisi kullanımı: Çatalhöyük örneği] [Tarih Okulu Dergisi]. *Journal of History School*, *45*, 677–712. DOI: 10.29228/Joh40295

Clough, G. W. (2013). *Best of both worlds: Museums, libraries, and archives in the digital age*. Smithsonian Institution.

Çöpgeven, N. S., Özkaya, H., & Aydın, S. (2023). Artificial Intelligence-based gamification in open and distance learning [Açık ve uzaktan öğrenmede yapay zeka destekli oyunlaştırma] [Journal of Open Education Applications and Research]. *Açıköğretim Uygulamaları ve Araştırmaları Dergisi*, *9*(1), 386–407. DOI: 10.51948/auad.1203700

Corrales Serrano, M. (2023). Gamification and the history of art in secondary education: A didactic intervention. *Education Sciences*, *13*(4), 389. DOI: 10.3390/educsci13040389

Craig, S. D., & Schroeder, N. L. (2017). Reconsidering the voice effect when learning from a virtual human. *Computers & Education*, *114*, 193–205.

Creswell, J. W., & Creswell, J. D. (2018). *Research design: Qualitative, quantitative, and mixed methods approaches*. Sage.

Cuevas, H. F. (2024). Personalized feedback in formative assessment: A case study in Mexican higher education in the era of AI. *Eastern Journal of Languages. Linguistics and Literatures*, *5*(2), 12–21. DOI: 10.53906/ejlll.v5i2.340

Cunha, J., Guimarães, A., Martins, J., & Rosário, P. (2023). A self-regulation intervention conducted by teachers in a disadvantaged school neighborhood: Implementers' and observers' perceptions of its impact on elementary students. *Children (Basel, Switzerland)*, *10*(11), 1795. PMID: 38002886

D'Mello, S. K., & Graesser, A. (2023). Intelligent tutoring systems: How computers achieve learning gains that rival human tutors. In *Handbook of educational psychology* (pp. 603–629). Routledge.

Dao, X. Q., & Le, N. B. (2023). Investigating the effectiveness of ChatGPT in mathematical reasoning and problem solving: Evidence from the Vietnamese National High School Graduation Examination. *arXiv preprint arXiv:2306.06331*.

Das, S., Lekhya, G., Shreya, K., Shekinah, K. L., Babu, K. K., & Boopathi, S. (2024). Fostering Sustainability Education Through Cross-Disciplinary Collaborations and Research Partnerships: Interdisciplinary Synergy. In *Facilitating global collaboration and knowledge sharing in higher education with generative AI* (pp. 60–88). IGI Global Scientific Publishing.

Dasam, S., Goriparthi, P., Manchanda, M., Nowbattula, P. K., & Subhashini, R. (2024, December). *Enhancing writing skills with AI: Personalized feedback mechanisms for English learners*. In *2024 International Conference on Artificial Intelligence and Quantum Computation-Based Sensor Application (ICAIQSA)* (pp. 1–6). IEEE. doi: https://search.informit.org/doi/10.3316/informit.322842139237015

Davidson, C. N., & Goldberg, D. T. (2009). *The future of learning institutions in a digital age*. The MIT press.

Davidson, C. N., Goldberg, D. T., & Jones, Z. M. (2010). *The future of thinking: Learning institutions in a digital age*. The MIT Press.

Davis, C., Bush, T., & Wood, S. (2024). Artificial intelligence in education: Enhancing learning experiences through personalized adaptation. *International Journal of Cyber and IT Service Management*, *4*(1), 26–32.

De Cremer, D., & Kasparov, G. (2021). AI should augment human intelligence, not replace it. *Harvard Business Review*, *18*(1), 1–8.

Demartini, C. G., Sciascia, L., Bosso, A., & Manuri, F. (2024). Artificial Intelligence Bringing Improvements to Adaptive Learning in Education: A Case Study. *Sustainability*, *16*(3), 1347. DOI: 10.3390/su16031347

Dembe, A. (2024). Advancing personalized learning through educational artificial intelligence: Challenges, opportunities, and future directions. *Res Invent J Eng Phys Sci*, *3*(1), 89–101.

Dewar, J. A. (1998). *The information age and the printing press: Looking backward to see ahead*. RAND Corporation. https://www.rand.org/content/dam/rand/pubs/papers/2005/P8014.pdf

Dhananjaya, G. M., Goudar, R. H., Kulkarni, A., Rathod, V. N., & Hukkeri, G. S. (2024). A digital recommendation system for personalized learning to enhance online education: A review. *IEEE Access : Practical Innovations, Open Solutions*.

Dlask, J. (2024). Promoting Differentiation in the English Classroom with the Help of Generative AI.

Doyle, T. J., & Doyle, B. M. (2020). Learning and teaching in harmony with the brain: Insights from neuroscience, biology, cognitive science, and psychology. In *The Routledge International Handbook of student-centered learning and teaching in higher education* (pp. 75–91). Routledge.

Drakopoulos, V., & Sioulas, P.-V. (2021). Enhancing Primary School Teaching through Virtual Reality. *Journal of Computer Science Research, 3*(2), 11. DOI: 10.30564/jcsr.v3i2.2777

Durall, E., & Kapros, E. (2020). Co-design for a competency self-assessment chatbot and survey in science education. In *Learning and Collaboration Technologies. Human and Technology Ecosystems: 7th International Conference, LCT 2020, Held as Part of the 22nd HCI International Conference, HCII 2020, Copenhagen, Denmark, July 19–24, 2020* [Springer International Publishing.]. *Proceedings, 22*(Part II), 13–24.

Edelstein, D., Findlen, P., Ceserani, G., Winterer, C., & Coleman, N. (2017). Historical research in a digital age: Reflections from the mapping the republic of letters project. *The American Historical Review, 122*(2), 400–424. DOI: 10.1093/ahr/122.2.400

EDUCAUSE. (2024). *2024 EDUCAUSE Horizon Report: Teaching and Learning Edition*. Boulder, CO: EDUCAUSE. Retrieved from https://www.educause.edu/horizon-report-teaching-and-learning-2024

Effrem, K., & Robbins, J. (2019). Social-Emotional Learning: K-12 Education as New Age Nanny State. White Paper No. 192. *Pioneer Institute for Public Policy Research*.

Egunjobi, D., & Adeyeye, O. (2024). Revolutionizing Learning: The Impact of Augmented Reality (AR) And Artificial Intelligence (AI) on Education. *International Journal of Research Publication and Reviews, 5*(10), 1157. DOI: 10.55248/gengpi.5.1024.2734

Ehsan, M. M. (2024). Impact of COVID-19 Lockdowns on Learning Losses: Structural and Individual Factors (Master's thesis, Hamad Bin Khalifa University (Qatar)).

Erol Şahin, A. N. (2024). Generative Artificial Intelligence in history teaching: Prospective teachers' perceptions and ethical concerns [Tarih Öğretiminde Üretken Yapay Zekâ: Öğretmen Adaylarının Algıları ve Endişeleri]. *Xth International Symposium on History Education [10. Uluslararası Tarih Eğitimi Sempozyumu]* (ISHE 2024), 1–15, Kars, Türkiye.

Essel, H. B., Osei-Poku, P., Acheampong, A., & Anning, A. (2022). Exploring the effectiveness of AI chatbots in higher education: A student-centered study. *Education and Information Technologies, 27*(6), 8801–8822. DOI: 10.1007/s10639-022-11048-3

Essel, H. B., Vlachopoulos, D., Essuman, A. B., & Amankwa, J. O. (2024). ChatGPT effects on cognitive skills of undergraduate students: Receiving instant responses from AI- based conversational large language models (LLMs). *Computers and Education: Artificial Intelligence*, *6*, 100198. Advance online publication. DOI: 10.1016/j.caeai.2023.100198

Evans, O., Cotton-Barratt, O., Finnveden, L., Bales, A., Balwit, A., Wills, P., . . . Saunders, W. (2021). Truthful AI: Developing and governing AI that does not lie. arXiv preprint arXiv:2110.06674.

Ferreira, P. C., & Simão, A. M. V. (2012). Teaching practices that foster self-regulated learning: A case study. *Educational Research E-journal, 1*(1), 1–16.

Firat, M. (2023). Predicting student disengagement: Harnessing visual cues for intelligent tutoring systems. London journal of social sciences, (6), 75-83.

Fisher, M., & Jacobs, H. H. (2023). Prompt literacy: A key for AI-Based Learning. *Educational Leadership*, *80*(9), 18–19. https://www.ascd.org/el/articles/prompt-literacy-a-key-for-ai-based-learning

Fisk, R. (2023). The rise of ChatGPT and Generative A.I. and what it means for Schools. *AASA Journal of Scholarship & Practice, 20*(1), 37-46. https://www.aasa.org/docs/default-source/publications/journal-of-scholarship-and-practice/2023-spring-issue/rise-chatgpt-generativeai.pdf

Flayyih, M. F., & Hassan, T. O. U. T. (2024). Predictive analytics model for students' grade prediction using machine learning. *Babylonian Journal of Artificial Intelligence*, *2024*, 83–101.

Foucault, M. (1972/2010). *The archaeology of knowledge and the discourse on language*. Vintage Books.

Fovet, F. (2023). The Changing Landscape of Inclusive Education: A Shift towards Universal Design for Learning. In The Routledge International Handbook of Children's Rights and Disability (pp. 483-499). Routledge.

Frasson, C. (2023). The future of learning assessment. In du Boulay, B., Mitrovic, A., & Yacef, K. (Eds.), *Handbook of Artificial Intelligence in education* (pp. 637–639). Edward Elgar Publishing.

Friesen, N. (2017). *The textbook and the lecture: Education in the age of new media*. Johns Hopkins University Press.

Fuchs, K. (2023). Exploring the opportunities and challenges of NLP models in higher education: Is ChatGPT a blessing or a curse? *Frontiers in Education*, •••, 8.

Galés, N. L. (2024). Trust and connection in the artificial intelligence educational ecosystem: From algorithmism to algoritharism. *Revista Catalana de Pedagogia*, *26*, 4–37.

Gebre, E. (2022). Conceptions and perspectives of data literacy in secondary education. *British Journal of Educational Technology*, *53*(5), 1080–1095.

Gee, E., Takeuchi, L., & Wartella, E. (2017). *Children and families in the digital age: Learning together in a media saturated culture*. Routledge.

Gichoya, J. W., Thomas, K., Celi, L. A., Safdar, N., Banerjee, I., Banja, J. D., & Purkayastha, S. (2023). AI pitfalls and what not to do: Mitigating bias in AI. *The British Journal of Radiology*, *96*(1150), 20230023. PMID: 37698583

Gidiotis, I., & Hrastinski, S. (2024). Imagining the future of Artificial Intelligence in education: A review of social science fiction. *Learning, Media and Technology*, •••, 1–13. DOI: 10.1080/17439884.2024.2365829

Gitomer, D. H., Curtis, M. E., Glaser, R., & Lensky, D. B. (1987). Processing differences as a function of item difficulty in verbal analogy performance. *Journal of Educational Psychology*, *79*(3), 212.

Gligorea, I., Cioca, M., Oancea, R., Gorski, A.-T., Gorski, H., & Tudorache, P. (2023). Adaptive Learning Using Artificial Intelligence in e-Learning: A Literature Review. *Education Sciences*, *13*(12), 1216. DOI: 10.3390/educsci13121216

Glowa, L., & Goodell, J. (2016). Student-centered learning: Functional requirements for integrated systems to optimize learning. *International Association for K-12 Online Learning*. doi: https://files.eric.ed.gov/fulltext/ED567875.pdf

Gluz, J. C., Flores, C. D., & Vicari, R. M. (2007). Formal Aspects of Pedagogical Negotiation in AMPLIA System. In Nedjah, N., Mourelle, L. M., Borges, M. N., & Almeida, N. N. d. (Eds.), *Intelligent Educational Machines. Studies in Computational Intelligence* (Vol. 44). Springer., DOI: 10.1007/978-3-540-44921-8_6

Goel, A. K., & Polepeddi, L. (2016). *Jill Watson: A virtual teaching assistant for online education*. Georgia Institute of Technology.

Gopi, B., Kokila, M. S., Bibin, C. V., Sasikala, D., Howard, E., & Boopathi, S. (2024). Distributed technologies using AI/ML techniques for healthcare applications. In *Social Innovations in Education, Environment, and Healthcare* (pp. 375–396). IGI Global.

Grájeda, A., Burgos, J., Olivera, P. C., & Sanjinés, A. (2023). Assessing student-perceived impact of using Artificial Intelligence tools: Construction of a synthetic index of application in higher education. In *Cogent Education, 11* (Vol. 1). Taylor & Francis., DOI: 10.1080/2331186x.2023.2287917

Green, V. (2022). "Use Your Teacher Voice": How a Podcast Could Support ESOL Teachers' Voices in Advocacy.

Gregory, S. (2023). Empowering Teaching With Prompt Engineering: How to Integrate Curriculum, Standards, and Assessment for a New Age. In Sharma, R. C., & Bozkurt, A. (Eds.), *Transforming Education with Generative AI: Prompt Engineering and Synthetic Content Creation*. IGI Global.

Grubaugh, S., & Levitt, G. (2024). The Future of Elementary Social Studies: Harnessing AI's Potential Through Evidence-Based Practices. *Technium Soc. Sci. J.*, *58*, 87–93. DOI: 10.47577/tssj.v58i1.10991

Guan, H. (2023). Advantages and challenges of using Artificial Intelligence in primary and secondary school education. *Journal of Education. Humanities and Social Sciences*, *22*, 377–383. DOI: 10.54097/ehss.v22i.12469

Guasti, L., Ferrini, A., & Pieraccini, G. (2023). Teaching Blockchain at School. In: Kubincová, Z., Caruso, F., Kim, Te, Ivanova, M., Lancia, L., Pellegrino, M.A. (Eds.) Methodologies and Intelligent Systems for Technology Enhanced Learning, Workshops - 13th International Conference. MIS4TEL 2023. Lecture Notes in Networks and Systems, vol 769, pp. 378-387. Springer, Cham. doi: https://doi.org/ DOI: 10.1007/978-3-031-42134-1_38

Gunawardena, M., Bishop, P., & Aviruppola, K. (2024). Personalized learning: The simple, the complicated, the complex and the chaotic. *Teaching and Teacher Education*, *139*, 104429.

Haleem, A., Javaid, M., Qadri, M. A., & Suman, R. (2022). Understanding the role of digital technologies in education: A review. *Sustainable Operations and Computers*, *3*, 275–285.

Hallarte, D. K., Camaongay, Q. M., Congson, J., Cuamag, S., Datosme, J., Laude, V. K. B., Milano, M. L., Gonzales, R., & Gonzales, G. (2024). Modeling self-regulation in learning mathematics through teacher-promoting interaction and parental support among STEM learners: The mediating role of intrinsic motivation. *Social Sciences & Humanities Open*, *10*, 101135. DOI: 10.1016/j.ssaho.2024.101135

Halverson, R., Grigg, J., Prichett, R., & Thomas, C. (2007). The New Instructional Leadership: Creating Data-Driven Instructional Systems in School. *Journal of School Leadership, 17*(2), 159. DOI: 10.1177/105268460701700202

Hanna, A., & Bender, E. M. (August 12, 2023). AI Causes Real harm. Let's Focus on that over the End-of-Humanity Hype. *Scientific American*. https://www.scientificamerican.com/article/we-need-to-focus-on-ais-real-harms-not-imaginary-existential-risks/

Harry, A., & Sayudin, S. (2023). Role of AI in Education. [INJURITY]. *Interdiciplinary Journal and Hummanity*, *2*(3), 260–268. DOI: 10.58631/injurity.v2i3.52

Harry, B., & Klingner, J. (2022). *Why are so many students of color in special education?: Understanding race and disability in schools*. Teachers College Press.

Hartnett, M., Brown, M., & Anderson, B. (2014). Learning in the digital age: How are the ways in which we learn changing with the use of technologies. *Facing the Big Questions in Teaching: Purpose, Power and Learning,* 116–125.

Hassani, H., & Silva, E. S. (2023). The role of ChatGPT in data science: How ai-assisted conversational interfaces are revolutionizing the field. *Big Data and Cognitive Computing*, *7*(2), 62. DOI: 10.3390/bdcc7020062

Heirweg, S., De Smul, M., Merchie, E., Devos, G., & Van Keer, H. (2022). The long road from teacher professional development to student improvement: A school-wide professionalization on self-regulated learning in primary education. *Research Papers in Education*, *37*(6), 929–953.

Herft, A. (2023). A Teacher's Prompt Guide to ChatGPT aligned with 'What Works Best' Guide. Retrieved on January 23 2023 from https://drive.google.com/file/d/15qAxnUzOwAPwHzoaKBJd8FAgiOZYcIxq/view

Herner-Patnode, L., & Lee, H. J. (2021). Differentiated Instruction to Teach Mathematics: Through the Lens of Responsive Teaching. *Mathematics Teacher Education and Development*, *23*(3), 6–25.

Hew, K. F., Huang, W., Du, J., & Jia, C. (2021, August). Using chatbots in flipped learning online sessions: Perceived usefulness and ease of use. In *International Conference on Blended Learning* (pp. 164-175). Cham: Springer International Publishing.

Hogan, E., & Payne, B. (2024). A mixed-methods study of teachers' use of feedback within middle school social studies classrooms to promote reading comprehension. *Learning and Instruction*, *92*, 101938. DOI: 10.1016/j.learninstruc.2024.101938

Holmes, W., Persson, J., Chounta, I.-A., Wasson, B., & Dimitrova, V. (2022). Artificial intelligence and education: A critical view through the lens of human rights, democracy, and the rule of law. *Council of Europe*. https://rm.coe.int/1680a956e3

Holmes, W., Bialik, M., & Fadel, C. (2019). *Artificial Intelligence in education. Promises and implications for teaching and learning* (1st ed.). Center for Curriculum Redesign., https://static.googleusercontent.com/media/edu.google.com/en// pdfs/Intelligence-Unleashed-Publication.pdf

Holmes, W., Porayska-Pomsta, K., Holstein, K., Sutherland, E., Baker, T., Shum, S. B., & Koedinger, K. R. (2022). Ethics of AI in education: Towards a community-wide framework. *International Journal of Artificial Intelligence in Education, 32*(3), 504–526.

Howard, N. R., Schaffer, R., & Thomas, S. (2022). *Closing the gap: Digital equity strategies for teacher prep programs*. International Society for Technology in Education.

Hsu, T. C., Chang, C., & Jen, T. H. (2023). Artificial intelligence image recognition using self-regulation learning strategies: Effects on vocabulary acquisition, learning anxiety, and learning behaviors of English language learners. *Interactive Learning Environments*, •••, 1–19.

Huang, C. W., Coleman, M., Gachago, D., & Van Belle, J. P. (2023). Using ChatGPT to encourage critical AI literacy skills and for assessment in higher education. In *Annual conference of the southern african computer lecturers' association* (pp. 105–118). Nature Switzerland. Cham: Springer.

Huang, A. Y. Q., Lu, O. H. T., & Yang, S. J. H. (2022). Effects of Artificial Intelligence–Enabled personalized recommendations on learners' learning engagement, motivation, and outcomes in a flipped classroom. []). Elsevier BV.]. *Computers & Education, 194*, 104684.

Huang, J. S. (2022). Pedagogical Responsiveness to Every Student in Singapore–Can Artificial Intelligence for Education Be a Solution to Embrace the Complexity in Teaching and Learning? In *Pedagogical Responsiveness in Complex Contexts: Issues of Transformation, Inclusion and Equity* (pp. 75–94). Springer International Publishing.

Hulings, M. (2022). What are they bringing with them? Understanding past science experiences of preservice elementary teachers and what they mean for the science methods course. *Journal of Research in Science Teaching, 59*(8), 1465–1488.

Hussein, H., Elmogy, M., & Guirguis, S. (2014). Automatic English question generation system based on template driven scheme. [IJCSI]. *International Journal of Computer Science Issues, 11*(6), 45.

Hutchison, K., Paatsch, L., & Cloonan, A. (2020). Reshaping home–school connections in the digital age: Challenges for teachers and parents. *E-Learning and Digital Media, 17*(2), 167–182.

International Telecommunication Union (ITU). (2021). *Measuring digital development: Facts and figures 2021*. ITU.

James, W. (1896/2011). *The collected works of William James*.

Jamieson, S. (2022). The AI "Crisis" and (Re)turn to Pedagogy. *Composition Studies, 50*(3), 153–158.

Jamilah, W. S. N., & Halimah, L. H. (2024, August). Innovative learning strategies for social studies in the era of Artificial Intellıgence. In *International Conference on Applied Social Sciences in Education, 1*(1), 181-187. doi: https://doi.org/DOI: 10.31316/icasse.v1i1.6842

Jaramillo, J. J., & Chiappe, A. (2024). The AI-driven classroom: A review of 21st-century curriculum trends. *Prospects, 54*, 645–660. DOI: 10.1007/s11125-024-09704-w

Jerve, K. R. (2023). Learning to Un-sing: A study of free improvisation vocalists' ideas, strategies, and techniques (Master's thesis).

Jian, M. J. K. O. (2023). Personalized learning through AI. *Advances in Engineering Innovation, 5*(1), 16–19. DOI: 10.54254/2977-3903/5/2023039

Jin, F., Lin, C. H., & Lai, C. (2025). Modeling AI-assisted writing: How self-regulated learning influences writing outcomes. *Computers in Human Behavior, 165*, 108538.

Jin, S. H., Im, K., Yoo, M., Roll, I., & Seo, K. (2023). Supporting students' self-regulated learning in online learning using artificial intelligence applications. *International Journal of Educational Technology in Higher Education, 20*(1), 37.

Jobin, A., Ienca, M., & Vayena, E. (2019). The global landscape of AI ethics guidelines. *Nature Machine Intelligence, 1*, 389–399. DOI: 10.1038/s42256-019-0088-2

Johnston, J. B. (2023). What is an Authentic Relationship? *Jesuit Higher Education, 12*(2).

Jones, M. (1985, May). Applications of Artificial Intelligence within education. *Computers & Mathematics with Applications (Oxford, England)*, *11*(5), 517–526. DOI: 10.1016/0898-1221(85)90054-9

Jung, H., & Park, J. H. (2023). Design and issues of writing literatures using ChatGPT. *Journal of Knowledge Information Technology and Systems*, *18*(1), 31–40. DOI: 10.3 4163/jkits.2023.18.1.004

Kalaiselvi, D., Ramaratnam, M., Kokila, S., Sarkar, R., Anandakumar, S., & Boopathi, S. (2024). Future developments of higher education on social psychology: Innovation and changes. In *Social Innovations in Education, Environment, and Healthcare* (pp. 146–169). IGI Global.

Kaledio, P., Robert, A., & Frank, L. (2024). The impact of Artificial intelligence on students' learning experience. SSRN *Electronic Journal*, February (1). doi: http://dx.doi.org/DOI: 10.2139/ssrn.4716747

Kamalov, F., & Gurrib, I. (2023). New Era of Artificial Intelligence in Education: Towards a Sustainable Multifaceted Revolution. *arXiv* (Cornell University). https://doi.org//arxiv.2305.18303DOI: 10.48550

Kanchon, M. K. H., Sadman, M., Nabila, K. F., Tarannum, R., & Khan, R. (2024). Enhancing personalized learning: AI-driven identification of learning styles and content modification strategies. *International Journal of Cognitive Computing in Engineering*, *5*, 269–278.

Kaswan, K. S., Dhatterwal, J. S., & Ojha, R. P. (2024). AI in personalized learning. In *Advances in technological innovations in higher education* (pp. 103–117). CRC Press.

Kayyali, M. (2025a). Ethical Implications of Generative AI in Education: Privacy, Bias, and Integrity. In Transformative AI Practices for Personalized Learning Strategies (pp. 185-218). IGI Global Scientific Publishing.

Kayyali, M. (2025b). Generative AI and Education: Transforming Teaching and Learning Through Collaborative Intelligence. In Humans and Generative AI Tools for Collaborative Intelligence (pp. 25-52). IGI Global Scientific Publishing.

Kayyali, M. (2025c). The Future of AI in Education: Predictions and Emerging Trends. Next-Generation AI Methodologies in Education, 367-406.

Kayyali, M. (2025d). AI in Higher Education: Revolutionizing Curriculum and Administration. In AI Adoption and Diffusion in Education (pp. 31-62). IGI Global Scientific Publishing.

Kayyali, M. (2025e). Ethical Implications of Generative AI in Education: Privacy, Bias, and Integrity. In Transformative AI Practices for Personalized Learning Strategies (pp. 185-218). IGI Global Scientific Publishing.

Kayyali, M. (2026). The Impact of AI on Classroom Dynamics in Higher Education: Shifting Roles for Professors and Students. In Responsible AI Integration in Education (pp. 151-180). IGI Global Scientific Publishing.

Kayyali, M. (2022). Equity, Equality, Diversity, and Inclusion as Key Performance Indicators in Higher Education. *Online Submission*, *3*(5), 1–3.

Kayyali, M. (2024). Future possibilities and challenges of AI in education. In *Transforming education with generative AI: Prompt engineering and synthetic content creation* (pp. 118–137). IGI Global Scientific Publishing.

Keegin, J. M. (2023, May 23). *ChatGPT is a plagiarism machine: So why do administrators have their heads in the sand?* The Chronicle of Higher Education. https://www.chronicle.com/article/chatgpt-is-a-plagiarism-machine

Kelly, S. (2023). Let me play, too! Co-designing inclusive sensory play spaces in collaboration with neurodiverse and neurotypical children (Doctoral dissertation, Queensland University of Technology).

Khoa, B. T., Hung, B. P., & Hejsalem-Brahmi, M. (2023). Qualitative research in social sciences: Data collection, data analysis and report writing. *International Journal of Public Sector Performance Management*, *12*(1-2), 187–209.

Kim, H., Lee, B. K., Lee, H., Hwang, D., Park, S., Min, K., & Choo, J. (2023). Learning to discover skills through guidance. *Advances in Neural Information Processing Systems*, *36*, 28226–28254.

Kodó, K. (2024). Storytelling: Adaptability and Expansion of American Indian and Indigenous Culture.

Kolovelonis, A., Goudas, M., & Dermitzaki, I. (2010). Self-regulated learning of a motor skill through emulation and self-control levels in a physical education setting. *Journal of Applied Sport Psychology*, *22*(2), 198–212.

Krstić, L., Aleksić, V., & Krstić, M. (2022). Artificial intelligence in education. *RE:view*.

Kuhail, M. A., Abdellatif, A., Shamsi, H., Alqudah, A. M., & Ali, R. (2023). Personalized chatbots to improve knowledge retention and learner engagement in higher education. *Education and Information Technologies*, *28*, 5781–5800. DOI: 10.1007/s10639-023-11797-3

Laak, K. J., & Aru, J. (2024). AI and personalized learning: bridging the gap with modern educational goals. arXiv preprint arXiv:2404.02798.

Labadze, L., Grigolia, M., & Machaidze, L. (2023). Role of AI chatbots in education: Systematic literature review. *International Journal of Educational Technology in Higher Education*, *20*(1). Advance online publication. DOI: 10.1186/s41239-023-00426-1

Lai, T., Xie, C., Ruan, M., Wang, Z., Lu, H., & Fu, S. (2023). Influence of Artificial Intelligence in education on adolescents' social adaptability: The mediatory role of social support. *PLoS One*, *18*(3), e0283170. DOI: 10.1371/journal.pone.0283170

Lampou, R. (2023). The integration of Artificial Intelligence in education: Opportunities and challenges. Review of Artificial Intelligence in Education. *Review of Artificial Intelligence in Education*, *4*(0), 1–12. DOI: 10.37497/rev.artif.intell.educ.v4i00.15

Lampropoulos, G., & Kinshuk. (2024). Virtual reality and gamification in education: A systematic review. *Educational Technology Research and Development*, *72*(3), 1691–1785. DOI: 10.1007/s11423-024-10351-3

Lan, Y. J., & Chen, N. S. (2024). Teachers' agency in the era of LLM and generative AI. *Journal of Educational Technology & Society*, *27*(1), I–XVIII.

Lata, P. (2024). Towards Equitable Learning: Exploring Artificial Intelligence in Inclusive Education.

Lee, B. N. (2023). Exploring the relationship between history learning and thinking skills: A synthesis of research. *Muallim Journal of Social Sciences and Humanities*, *7*(2), 18–30. DOI: 10.33306/mjssh/233

Leekeenan, K., & White, H. (2021). Recognition and respect: Centering students' voices through writing groups. *English Journal*, *110*(4), 92–99.

Lee, S.-M. (2019). A Systematic review of context-aware technology use in foreign language learning. *Computer Assisted Language Learning*, *25*(3), 294–318. DOI: 10.1080/09588221.2019.1688836

Leidinger, M., & Perels, F. (2012). Training self-regulated learning in the classroom: Development and evaluation of learning materials to train self-regulated learning during regular mathematics lessons at primary school. *Education Research International*, *2012*(1), 735790.

Leung, H. (2024). Artificial Intelligence as Agents to Support Neurodivergent Creative and Critical Thinking Modules.

Levitt, G., & Grubaugh, S. (2024). Why do I have to learn this stuff? Using AI to assist secondary teachers in teaching future-ready practical life skills with any social studies lesson. *Technium Social Sciences Journal, 59*, 327–341. DOI: 10.47577/tssj.v59i1.11241

Levstik, L. S., & Barton, K. C. (2015). *Doing history: Investigating with children in elementary and middle schools* (5th ed.). Routledge., DOI: 10.4324/9781315818108

Lewis, A. A. (2025). Unpacking Cultural Bias in AI Language Learning Tools: An Analysis of Impacts and Strategies for Inclusion in Diverse Educational Settings. *International Journal of Research and Innovation in Social Science, 9*(1), 1878–1892.

Liao, X., Zhang, X., Wang, Z., & Luo, H. (2024). Design and implementation of an AI- enabled visual report tool as formative assessment to promote learning achievement and self- regulated learning: An experimental study. *British Journal of Educational Technology, 55*, 1253–1276. DOI: 10.1111/bjet.1342

Lin, C. C., Huang, A. Y. Q., & Lu, O. H. T. (2023). Artificial intelligence in intelligent tutoring systems toward sustainable education: A systematic review. *Smart Learn. Environ., 10*, 41. DOI: 10.1186/s40561-023-00260-y

Lingard, L. (2023). Writing with ChatGPT: An illustration of its capacity, limitations & implications for academic writers. *Perspectives on Medical Education, 12*(1), 261. DOI: 10.5334/pme.1072 PMID: 37397181

Lin, H., & Mubarok, H. (2021). The impact of educational chatbots on students' writing performance and perception in EFL context. *Journal of Educational Computing Research, 59*(6), 1110–1131. DOI: 10.1177/0735633121992221

Lin, J.-J., & Lin, H. (2019). Mobile-assisted ESL/EFL vocabulary learning: A Systematic review and meta-analysis. *Computer Assisted Language Learning, 32*(8), 878–919. DOI: 10.1080/09588221.2018.1541359

Liu, Y., Le-Cong, T., Widyasari, R., Tantithamthavorn, C., Li, L., Le, X. B. D., & Lo, D. (2024). Refining chatgpt-generated code: Characterizing and mitigating code quality issues. *ACM Transactions on Software Engineering and Methodology, 33*(5), 1–26. DOI: 10.1145/3643674

Liu, Z., & Yushchik, E. (2024). Exploring the prospects of using Artificial Intelligence in education. *Cogent Education, 11*(1). Advance online publication. DOI: 10.1080/2331186X.2024.2353464

Livingstone, S., & Sefton-Green, J. (2016). *The class: Living and learning in the digital age*. New York University Press.

Li, X., & Jiang, Y. (2024). Artificial intelligence in education: Opportunities, current status, and prospects. *Geographical Research Bulletin, 3*, 146–174. DOI: 10.50908/grb.3.0_146

Luan, H., Géczy, P., Lai, H., Gobert, J. D., Yang, S. J. H., Ogata, H., Baltes, J., Guerra, R. da S., Li, P., & Tsai, C. (2020). Challenges and Future Directions of Big Data and Artificial Intelligence in Education. *Frontiers in Psychology, 11*. Advance online publication. DOI: 10.3389/fpsyg.2020.580820 PMID: 33192896

Lubis, F. (2019). Education in the disruption era. *Britain International of Linguistics, Arts, and Education Journal, 1*(2), 183–188. DOI: 10.33258/biolae.v1i2.85

Luckin, R. (2017). Towards artificial intelligence-based assessment systems. *Nature Human Behaviour, 1*(3), 1–3.

Luckin, R., Holmes, W., Griffiths, M., & Forcier, L. B. (2016). *Intelligence Unleashed. An argument for AI in education*. Pearson.

Luprichová, J. (2025). Enhancing historical understanding, gender perspectives, and critical thinking: Integrating AI-powered tools in university-level British history education. (2025). *Resources, 1*, 188–197. DOI: 10.53349/re-source.2025.is1.a1391

Lyell, I. (2024). Artificial Intelligence and the future of education. *Agora*, 59(2), 7–8. doi: https://search.informit.org/doi/10.3316/informit.T202407050001250 0610823061

Macháček, D., Dabre, R., & Bojar, O. (2023). Turning whisper into real-time transcription system. arXiv preprint arXiv:2307.14743.

Maeda, J. (2025). *How to Speak Machine, with a new preface by the author: A Gentle Introduction to Artificial Intelligence*. MIT Press.

Maghsudi, S., Lan, A., Xu, J., & van der Schaar, M. (2021). Personalized Education in the Artificial Intelligence Era: What to Expect Next. *IEEE Signal Processing Magazine, 38*(3), 37. DOI: 10.1109/msp.2021.3055032

Magomadov, V. S. (2020). The application of artificial intelligence and Big Data analytics in personalized learning. *Journal of Physics: Conference Series, 1691*(1), 12169. DOI: 10.1088/1742-6596/1691/1/012169

Mahmoud, C. F., & Sørensen, J. T. (2024). Artificial Intelligence in personalized learning with a focus on current developments and future prospects. *Research and Advances in Education, 3*(8), 25–31. DOI: 10.56397/rae.2024.08.04

Main, P. (2024). *Webb's Depth of Knowledge*. Structural Learning. https://www.structural-learning.com/post/webbs-depth-of-knowledge

Malek, A. (2021). *Intersection: Reimagining the future of mobility across traditional boundaries*. SAE International.

Malik, A., Prihatini, S., & Agustina, R. D. (2023). Study on collaborative creativity learning models and gender on students' creative thinking skills. *Jurnal Penelitian & Pengembangan Pendidikan Fisika*, *9*(1). Advance online publication. DOI: 10.21009/1.09109

Malysheva, O., Tokareva, E., Orchakova, L., & Smirnova, Y. (2022). The effect of online learning in modern history education. *Heliyon*, *8*(7). Advance online publication. DOI: 10.1016/j.heliyon.2022.e09965

Maria, J., Ahmad, A., & Awang, M. M. (2019, October). The applications of historical thinking skills in teaching and history learning: Between rhetoric and reality. In The 2nd International Conference on Sustainable Development and Multi-Ethnic Society (pp. 221-229). Redwhite Pres.

Marougkas, A., Troussas, C., Krouska, A., & Sgouropoulou, C. (2023). Virtual reality in education: A review of learning theories, approaches and methodologies for the last decade. *Electronics (Basel)*, *12*(13), 2832.

Martin, M., Chevalier, M., Burton, S., Bonvin, G., Besançon, M., & Deneux, T. (2023). Effects of introducing a learning robot on the metacognitive knowledge of students aged 8–11. In Balogh, R., Obdržálek, D., & Christoforou, E. (Eds.), *Robotics in education. RiE 2023. Lecture notes in networks and systems* (Vol. 747, pp. 169–183). Springer., DOI: 10.1007/978-3-031-38454-7_15

Martin, S. M., Casey, J. R., & Kane, S. (2021). History of artificial intelligence and personalized learning. In *Serious games in personalized learning* (pp. 27–47). Routledge.

McArthur, T. (1987). The English languages? *English Today*, *3*(3), 9–13. DOI: 10.1017/S0266078400013511

McCarthy, J., Minsky, M. L., Rochester, N., & Shannon, C. E. (2006). A Proposal for the Dartmouth Summer Research Project on Artificial Intelligence, August 31, 1955. *AI Magazine*, *27*(4), 12. DOI: 10.1609/aimag.v27i4.1904

Merriam, S. B., & Tisdell, E. J. (2016). *Qualitative research: A guide to design and implementation* (4th ed.). Jossey-Bass.

Metz, C. (June 10, 2023). *How could A.I. Destroy Humanity?* The New York Times. https://www.nytimes.com/2023/06/10/technology/ai-humanity.html

Mifsud, D. (2023). Rethinking the concept of teacher education: a problematization and critique of current policies and practices. In *Teacher education as an ongoing professional trajectory: implications for policy and practice* (pp. 1–23). Springer International Publishing.

Mikhaylova, T., & Pettersson, D. (2025). The timeless beauty of data: Inventing educational pasts, presents and futures through data visualisation. *Critical Studies in Education*, *66*(2), 142–158.

Miles, M. B., & Huberman, A. M. (1994). *Qualitative data analysis: An expanded sourcebook* (2nd ed.). Sage Publications, Inc.

Mitchell, M. (2021). Why AI is harder than we think. arXiv preprint arXiv:2104.12871.

Mitra, D. S. (2024). AI-Powered Adaptive Education for Disabled Learners. Available at *SSRN* 5042713.

Mojolou, D. N., Madli, F., Thomas, H., Sondoh, S. L.Jr, & Karunia, E. (2024). A trend in publishing Artificial Intelligence personalized education: Enhancing learning experiences for university students. *Journal of Information Systems and Technology Management*, *9*(37), 286–301. DOI: 10.35631/JISTM.937021

Molenaar, I. (2022). The concept of hybrid human-AI regulation: Exemplifying how to support young learners' self-regulated learning. *Computers and Education: Artificial Intelligence*, *3*, 100070.

Mottl, J., & Musílek, M. (2024, May). Information technology as a tool for teaching history with a focus on Artificial Intelligence and audiovisual material. In *2024 47th MIPRO ICT and Electronics Convention (MIPRO)* (pp. 278–282). IEEE. doi: https://doi.org/DOI: 10.1109/MIPRO60963.2024.1056921

Muqorrobin, S., Arifin, S., Wutsqah, U., & Uulanian, H. (2024). Building character in the AI era (Combining technology and human values in education). Hikamatzu I. *Journal of Multidisciplinary*, *1*(1), 289–298. https://yasyahikamatzu.com/index.php/hjm/article/view/74

Nabiyev, V. (2021). *Yapay zekâ: makine öğrenmesi-stratejili oyunlar-örüntü tanıma-doğal dil işleme* [Artificial Intelligence: machine learning-strategic games-image recognition-natural language processing]. Seçkin.

Najib, M., Supadi, S., & Hamidah, N. (2024). Utilization of Artificial Intelligence to increase interactivity in history learning for high school students. *Jurnal Ilmiah Rumpun Ilmu Pendidikan, 1*(4), 01-20. doi: https://doi.org/DOI: 10.63760/jirip.v1i4.24

Najjar, N., Rouphael, M., Bitar, T., & Hleihel, W. (2025). The rise and drop of online learning: Adaptability and future prospects. *Frontiers in Education, 10,* 1522905.

Neisser, U. (2024). General, academic, and artificial intelligence. In *The nature of intelligence* (pp. 135–144). Routledge.

Neji, W., Boughattas, N., & Ziadi, F. (2023). Exploring New AI-Based Technologies to Enhance Students' Motivation. *Issues in Informing Science and Information Technology*, *20*, 95. DOI: 10.28945/5149

NETI FERLINA, N. F. (2023). THE CORRELATION BETWEEN STUDENTS'GRAMMAR ABILITY AND STUDENTS'SPEAKING ABILITY (Doctoral dissertation, UNIVERSITAS SULAWESI BARAT).

Newman, R. S. (2023). Adaptive help seeking: A strategy of self-regulated learning. In *Self-regulation of learning and performance* (pp. 283–301). Routledge.

Newton, N., Record, A. E., & Mello, A. J. (2024). *Fluency Doesn't Just Happen in Multiplication and Division: Strategies and Models for Teaching the Basic Facts.* Taylor & Francis.

Ng, D. T. K., Tan, C. W., & Leung, J. K. L. (2024). Empowering student self-regulated learning and science education through ChatGPT: A pioneering pilot study. *British Journal of Educational Technology*, *55*(4), 1328–1353.

Nguyen, N. D. (2023). Exploring the role of AI in education. *London Journal of Social Sciences*, (6), 84–95. DOI: 10.31039/ljss.2023.6.108

Nguyen, V. (2025). The Use of Generative AI Tools in Higher Education: Ethical and Pedagogical Principles. *Journal of Academic Ethics*. Advance online publication. DOI: 10.1007/s10805-025-09607-1

Ni, L. B., & Hassan, N. B. (2024). The relevance of history learning in the age of Artificial Intelligence: Understanding its impact on critical thinking and ethical decision-making. *Journal of Language. Linguistics and Literature*, *2*, 1–10. DOI: 10.59232/LLL-V2I2P103

Nurhayati, T. N., & Halimah, L. (2024, August). The value and technology: Maintaining balance in social science education in the era of Artificial Intelligence. *Proceedings of the International Conference on Applied Social Sciences in Education, 1*(1), 28-36. doi: https://doi.org/DOI: 10.31316/icasse.v1i1.6840

Nussbaum-Beach, S., & Hall, L. R. (2011). *The connected educator: Learning and leading in a digital age*. Solution Tree Press.

Ofianto, Aman, Ningsih, T. Z., & Abidin, N. F. (2022). The development of a historical thinking assessment to examine students' skills in analyzing the causality of historical events. *European Journal of Educational Research, 11*(2), 609–619. DOI: 10.12973/eu-jer.11.2.609

Okonkwo, C. W., & Ade-Ibijola, A. (2021). Chatbots applications in education: A systematic review. *Computers and Education: Artificial Intelligence, 2*, 100033. DOI: 10.1016/j.caeai.2021.100033

Open, A. I. (2023). *ChatGPT* [Large language model]. https://chat.openai.com

Orhan Özen, S., & Çubukçu, Z. (2022). An investigation of the learners' personalized feedback paths based on e-Assessment. *Kastamonu Education Journal, 30*(2), 411–426. DOI: 10.24106/kefdergi.825787

Orji, F. A., & Vassileva, J. (2022). Automatic modeling of student characteristics with interaction and physiological data using machine learning: A review. *Frontiers in Artificial Intelligence, 5*. Advance online publication. DOI: 10.3389/frai.2022.1015660 PMID: 36406472

Pahomov, L. (2014). *Authentic learning in the digital age: Engaging students through inquiry*. ASCD.

Pajares, F. (2012). Motivational role of self-efficacy beliefs in self-regulated learning. In *Motivation and self-regulated learning* (pp. 111–139). Routledge.

Paramesha, M., Rane, N. L., & Rane, J. (2024). Big data analytics, artificial intelligence, machine learning, internet of things, and blockchain for enhanced business intelligence. *Partners Universal Multidisciplinary Research Journal, 1*(2), 110–133.

Pauleen, D. J., & Yoong, P. (2001). Relationship building and the use of ICT in boundary-crossing virtual teams: A facilitator's perspective. *Journal of Information Technology, 16*(4), 205–220.

Pedró, F., Subosa, M., Rivas, A., & Valverde, P. (2019). *Artificial Intelligence in education: Challenges and opportunities for sustainable development* (Working papers on education policy, No. 7). UNESCO. doi: https://unesdoc.unesco.org/ark:/48223/pf0000366994

Pedwell, C. (2024). The Intuitive and the Counter-Intuitive: AI and the A ffective Ideologies of Common Sense. *New Formations, 112*(112), 70–93.

Peng, H., Ma, S., & Spector, J. M. (2019). Personalized adaptive learning: An emerging pedagogical approach enabled by a smart learning environment. *Smart Learning Environments, 6*(1). Advance online publication. DOI: 10.1186/s40561-019-0089-y

Perkins, M. (2023). Academic integrity considerations of AI Large Language Models in the post-pandemic era: ChatGPT and beyond. *Journal of University Teaching & Learning Practice*, *20*(2), 7–24. DOI: 10.53761/1.20.02.07

Perry, N. E., Lisaingo, S., Yee, N., Parent, N., Wan, X., & Muis, K. (2020). Collaborating with teachers to design and implement assessments for self-regulated learning in the context of authentic classroom writing tasks. *Assessment in Education: Principles, Policy & Practice*, *27*(4), 416–443.

Pintrich, P. R. (2000). Multiple goals, multiple pathways: The role of goal orientation in learning and achievement. *Journal of Educational Psychology*, *92*(3), 544.

Prasetyowati, D. I. & Sunarti. (2024, August). The role of Artificial Intelligence media in learning social studies education for elementary schools. In *International Conference on Applied Social Sciences in Education, 1*(1), 247-250. doi: https://doi.org/DOI: 10.31316/icasse.v1i1.6998

Puplampu, R. (2024). *What Everyone Should Know About the Rise of AI: AI Transparency, Privacy, and Ethics Best Practices*. Puplampu Books.

Qushwa, F. G., & Onia, S. I. (2024). AI innovation in education: Realizing personalized learning in the digital age. *Educative: Jurnal Ilmiah Pendidikan*, *2*(3), 178–187. DOI: 10.70437/educative.v2i3.822

Radojčić, M. R., Perera, R. S., Chen, L., Spector, T. D., Hart, D. J., Ferreira, M. L., & Arden, N. K. (2022). Specific body mass index trajectories were related to musculoskeletal pain and mortality: 19-year follow-up cohort. *Journal of Clinical Epidemiology*, *141*, 54–63. DOI: 10.1016/j.jclinepi.2021.09.020

Rafiq, S., Zaki, K. A., & Nawaz, A. (2025). PERSONALIZED LEARNING IN THE DIGITAL AGE: HARNESSING TECHNOLOGY FOR STUDENT SUCCESS. *Contemporary Journal of Social Science Review*, *3*(1), 1515–1528.

Rajaram, K. (2023). *Learning Intelligence: Innovative and digital transformative learning strategies: Cultural and social engineering perspectives*. Springer.

Rao, S., Behera, G., Meenakshi, S., Rajini, J., Pravin, T., & Boopathi, S. (2024). Entrepreneurial insights from higher education. In *Advances in Business Strategy and Competitive Advantage* (pp. 101–132). IGI Global.

Reidenberg, J. R., & Schaub, F. (2018). Achieving big data privacy in education. *Theory and Research in Education*, *16*(3), 263–279.

Rizvi, M. (2023). Investigating AI-Powered Tutoring Systems that Adapt to Individual Student Needs, Providing Personalized Guidance and Assessments. *The Eurasia Proceedings of Educational and Social Sciences*, *31*, 67. DOI: 10.55549/epess.1381518

Robin, C. (2023, August 24). *How ChatGPT changed my plans for the fall.* The Chronicle of Higher Education. https://www.chronicle.com/article/the-end-of-the-take-home-essay

Rodrigues, M. (2024). Returning to School After a Pandemic: Secondary Teacher Perspectives on Students Returning to School in Regard to Academic Achievement, Behavior, Mindset, and Social Connections (Doctoral dissertation, University of Massachusetts Global).

Rodríguez-García, J. M., Gutiérrez-Rangel, H. F., & Cisneros-Reyes, Y. D. (2023). LA INTELIGENCIA ARTIFICIAL: RETOS Y ACTUALIDADES RESPECTO A LA EDUCACIÓN SUPERIOR. *Aura M. Torres Reyes Reina Castellanos Vega Cristhian Bonilla Rodríguez Alberto Villa Valencia*, 19.

Ross, B., Chase, A. M., Robbie, D., Oates, G., & Absalom, Y. (2018). Adaptive quizzes to increase motivation, engagement, and learning outcomes in a first-year accounting unit. *International Journal of Educational Technology in Higher Education*, *15*(1), 30.

Rowan, L., Bourke, T., L'Estrange, L., Lunn Brownlee, J., Ryan, M., Walker, S., & Churchward, P. (2021). How does initial teacher education research frame the challenge of preparing future teachers for student diversity in schools? A systematic review of literature. *Review of Educational Research*, *91*(1), 112–158.

Roy, K., & Swargiary, K. (2024). Exploring the impact of AI integration in education: A mixed-methods study. doi: https://doi.org/DOI: 10.2139/ssrn.4857648

Ružic, I. M., & Dumancic, M. (2015). Gamification in education. *Informatologia*, *48*(3–4), 198–204. DOI: 10.3390/encyclopedia3040089

Saleem, S., Aziz, M. U., Iqbal, M. J., & Abbas, S. (2025). AI in education: Personalized learning systems and their impact on student performance and engagement. *The Critical Review of Social Sciences Studies*, *3*(1), 2445–2459. DOI: 10.59075/c35qa453

Sapra, R. (2019). Social and emotional learning in digital age: Future trajectories for children and adolescents. *International Journal of Education and Management Studies*, *9*(4), 237–239.

Saputra, I., Astuti, M., Sayuti, M., & Kusumastuti, D. (2023). Integration of Artificial Intelligence in Education: Opportunities, challenges, threats and obstacles. A literature review. *Indonesian Journal of Computer Science, 12*(4). Advance online publication. DOI: 10.33022/ij /ij"cs.v12i4.3266

Sarpkaya, R., & Yılmaz, T. (2021). The place of the teacher in student-centred education and an evaluation of the pandemic process [Öğrenci merkezli eğitimde öğretmenin yeri ve pandemi sürecine ilişkin bir değerlendirme] [Eleştirel Pedagoji]. *Critical Pedagogy, 68*, 75–79.

Sasikala, P., & Ravichandran, R. (2024). Study on the impact of artificial intelligence on student learning outcomes. *Journal of Digital Learning and Education, 4*(2), 145–155.

Saykılı, A. (2019). Higher education in the digital age: The impact of digital connective technologies. *Journal of Educational Technology and Online Learning, 2*(1), 1–15.

Schei, O. M., Møgelvang, A., & Ludvigsen, K. (2024). Perceptions and use of AI chatbots among students in higher education: A scoping review of empirical studies. *Education Sciences, 14*(8), 922. DOI: 10.3390/educsci14080922

Schroeder-Schock, A. (2024). *Coaching First-Grade Teachers On Differentiated Instructional Practices For Learners With Mathematical Promise: An Action Research Study*. The College of William and Mary.

Schunk, D. H., & Greene, J. A. (2018). Historical, contemporary, and future perspectives on self-regulated learning and performance. In *Handbook of self-regulation of learning and performance* (2nd ed., pp. 1–15). Routledge/Taylor & Francis Group. Educational psychology handbook series.

Schunk, D. H., & Zimmerman, B. (Eds.). (2011). *Handbook of Self-Regulation of Learning and Performance*. Taylor & Francis.

Selanik-Ay, T. (2024). Social studies teaching with Artificial Intelligence. [Yapay zekâ ile sosyal bilgiler öğretimi] In Özdinç, F., Aydoğdu, B., & Kasapoğlu, E. (Eds.), *The future of the classroom: Teacher–Artificial Intelligence collaboration* [*Sınıfın geleceği: Öğretmen–yapay zekâ işbirliği*]. Nobel Akademik.

Selk, A. (2018, May 5). *One space or two spaces after a full stop? Scientists have finally found the answer.* The Independent. https://www.independent.co.uk/tech/one-space-or-two-spaces-after-a-full-stop-scientists-have-finally-found-the-answer-a8337646.html

Seo, K., Tang, J., Roll, I., Fels, S., & Yoon, D. (2021). The impact of artificial intelligence on learner-instructors in online learning. *International Journal of Educational Technology in Higher Education, 18*(1), 1–23. PMID: 34778540

Seyhan, A. (2024). Social studies teachers' views on the use of Artificial Intelligence in education [Sosyal bilgiler öğretmenlerinin eğitimde yapay zeka kullanımına ilişkin görüşleri] [Uluslararası Eğitim Bilimleri Detgisi]. *The Journal of International Education Science, 11*(41), 100–125. DOI: 10.29228/INESJOURNAL.78798

Shah, P. (2023). *AI and the Future of Education: Teaching in the Age of Artificial Intelligence*. John Wiley & Sons.

Sharples, M. (2022). Automated essay writing: An AIED opinion. *International Journal of Artificial Intelligence in Education, 32*(4), 1119–1126.

Sheng, X. (2023). The role of Artificial Intelligence in history education of Chinese high schools. *Journal of Education* [EPHHR]. *Humanities and Social Sciences, 8*, 238. DOI: 10.54097/ehss.v8i.4255

Shu, X., & Ye, Y. (2023). Knowledge discovery: Methods from data mining and machine learning. *Social Science Research, 110*(April 2022), 102817. doi: https://doi.org/DOI: 10.1016/j.ssresearch.2022.102817

Shuvo, S. A., & Islam, M. A. (2023). Blockchain Technology: A tool to solve the challenges of education sector in developing countries. *International Journal of Computational Systems Engineering, 7*(3), 1. DOI: 10.1504/ijcsyse.2023.10055995

Simons, M., & Masschelein, J. (2021). Looking after school: A critical analysis of personalization in education.

Singh, P., & Singh, N. (2020). Blockchain with IoT & AI: A review of agriculture and healthcare. [*IJAEC*]. *International Journal of Applied Evolutionary Computation, 11*(4), 13–27. DOI: 10.4018/IJAEC.2020100102

Singh, P., Singh, R., Singh, N., & Singh, M. K. (2020). A distributed Artificial Intelligence: The future of AI. In Yadav, S. P., Mahato, D. P., & Thi Dieu Linh, N. (Eds.), *Distributed_artificial_intelligence: A_modern_approach* (pp. 263–276). Routledge Publishing.

Sins, P., de Leeuw, R., de Brouwer, J., & Vrieling-Teunter, E. (2024). Promoting explicit instruction of strategies for self-regulated learning: Evaluating a teacher professional development program in primary education. *Metacognition and Learning, 19*(1), 215–247.

Sivakumar, J., & Al Harthy, K. (2024). AI-Powered Teaching Plan: Present and Post Evaluation. In *Utilizing AI for Assessment, Grading, and Feedback in Higher Education* (pp. 162-188). IGI Global.

Sjølie, E., Strømme, A., & Boks-Vlemmix, J. (2021). Team-skills training and real-time facilitation as a means for developing student teachers' learning of collaboration. *Teaching and Teacher Education, 107*, 103477.

Skinner, B. F. (1953). Some Contributions of an Experimental Analysis of Behavior to Psychology as A Whole. *The American Psychologist, 8*, 69–78.

Somasundaram, M., Junaid, K. M., & Mangadu, S. (2020). Artificial intelligence (AI) enabled intelligent quality management systems (IQMS) for the personalized learning path. *Procedia Computer Science, 172*, 438–442.

Spruce, R., & Bol, L. (2015). Teacher beliefs, knowledge, and practice of self-regulated learning. *Metacognition and Learning, 10*, 245–277.

Srbecky, R., Colutto, S., Wetzel, S. A., Winterhagen, M., Fraas, W., Dettmers, J., & Hemmje, M. (2023). Realization of adaptive progress bars in moodle for attested competencies and qualifications for learners in higher education institutions psychology courses considering qualifications-based learning. In EDULEARN23 Proceedings (pp. 1736-1742). IATED.

Sreedhar, P. S. S., Sujay, V., Rani, M. R., Melita, L., Reshma, S., & Boopathi, S. (2024). Impacts of 5G Machine Learning Techniques on Telemedicine and Social Media Professional Connection in Healthcare. In *Analyzing Current Digital Healthcare Trends Using Social Networks* (pp. 209–234). IGI Global Scientific Publishing.

Srinivasa, K. G., Kurni, M., & Saritha, K. (2022). Harnessing the Power of AI to Education. In *Learning, teaching, and assessment methods for contemporary learners: pedagogy for the digital generation* (pp. 311–342). Springer Nature Singapore.

Srinivasa, R. J., Dodson, S., Seo, K., Yoon, D., & Fels, S. (2021). NoteLink: A Point-and-Shoot Linking Interface between Students' Handwritten Notebooks and Instructional Videos. In *2021 ACM/IEEE Joint Conference on Digital Libraries (JCDL)* (pp. 140–149). IEEE.

Starkey, L. (2012). *Teaching and learning in the digital age*. Routledge.

Straub, S. (2025). Inclusive Citizenship Education in Teacher Education through Interaction and Active Relationship Building. In *Inclusive Citizenship: Interdisziplinäre Perspektiven auf Bürgerschaft und politische Bildung* (pp. 413–422). Springer.

Subasi, A., Qaisar, S. M., & Nisar, H. (Eds.). (2024). *Artificial Intelligence and Multimodal Signal Processing in Human-Machine Interaction*. Elsevier.

Sullivan, M., Kelly, A., & Mclaughlan, P. (2023). ChatGPT in higher education: Considerations for academic integrity and student learning. *Journal of Applied Learning & Teaching*, *6*(1), 1–10. DOI: 10.37074/jalt.2023.6.1.17

Sullivan, Y. W., & Fosso Wamba, S. (2022). Moral judgments in the age of artificial intelligence. *Journal of Business Ethics*, *178*(4), 917–943.

Suriano, R., Plebe, A., Acciai, A., & Fabio, R. A. (2025). Student interaction with ChatGPT can promote complex critical thinking skills. *Learning and Instruction*, *95*, 102011. Advance online publication. DOI: 10.1016/j.learninstruc.2024.102011

Sürme, M., & Atılgan, E. (2020). A research to determine the satisfaction levels of individual tours in the virtual museum. *Journal of Turkish Tourism Research*, *4*(3), 1794–1805. DOI: 10.26677/TR1010.2020.451

Susyanah, S., & Fajar, A. (2024, August). The Artificial Intelligence, *Social Sciences Learning Innovation Catalyst. In International Conference on Applied Social Sciences in Education*, *1*(1), pp. 114-120.

uteu, L. (2021). Teachers' beliefs about classroom practices that develop students' metacognition and self-regulated learning skills. *Acta Didactica Napocensia*, *14*(1), 165–173.

SWARGIARY. K. (2024). The Quantum Leap: Exploring the Power and Potential of Q-Star AI in Academia and Beyond. EdTech Research Association, Scottsdale, Arizona, US.

Swargiary, K., & Roy, K. (June 01, 2024). The impact of stress on academic performance and memory recall in K12 students: A controlled laboratory study. doi: http://dx.doi.org/DOI: 10.2139/ssrn.4877823

Szmyd, K., & Mitera, E. (2024). The impact of Artificial Intelligence on the development of critical thinking skills in students. *European Research Studies Journal*, *27*(2), 1022–1039. DOI: 10.35808/ersj/3876

Tahiru, F. (2021). AI in education: A systematic literature review. [JCIT]. *Journal of Cases on Information Technology*, *23*(1), 1–20.

Tirado-Olivares, S., Navío-Inglés, M., O'Connor-Jiménez, P., & Cózar-Gutiérrez, R. (2023). From human to machine: Investigating the effectiveness of the conversational AI ChatGPT in historical thinking. *Education Sciences*, *13*(8), 803. DOI: 10.3390/educsci13080803

Toh, L., & Yap, F. (2023). Leveraging AI for Personalized Learning in Higher Education: Challenges and Opportunities. *Educational Technology Review, 20*(1), 1–10. DOI: 10.1080/14261235.2023.2104921

Tolman, A. O., & Kremling, J. (Eds.). (2023). *Why students resist learning: A practical model for understanding and helping students.* Taylor & Francis.

Tomlinson, C. A., & Jarvis, J. M. (2023). Differentiation: Making curriculum work for all students through responsive planning & instruction. In Systems and models for developing programs for the gifted and talented (pp. 599-628). Routledge.

Tomlinson, C. A. (2022). *Everybody's classroom: differentiating for the shared and unique needs of diverse students.* Teachers College Press.

Tragant, E., Pinyana, À., Mackay, J., & Andria, M. (2022). Extending language learning beyond the EFL classroom through WhatsApp. *Computer Assisted Language Learning, 35*(8), 1946–1974.

Triantafyllopoulos, A., Christ, L., Gebhard, A., Jing, X., Kathan, A., Milling, M., ... & Schuller, B. W. (2024). Beyond Deep Learning: Charting the Next Frontiers of Affective Computing. Intelligent Computing, 3, 0089.

Trouche, L. (2005). Calculators in mathematics education: A rapid evolution of tools, with different effects. In Guin, D., Ruthven, K., & Trouche, L. (Eds.), *The didactical challenge of symbolic calculators: Turning a computational device into a mathematical instrument* (pp. 9–39). Springer.

Trust, T., & Maloy, R. W. (2023). AI in the history classroom: Strategies for rethinking teaching and learning. *Teaching History*, *57*(3), 10–15.

Tyrina, A. (2021). *Investigating the Attitudes, Beliefs and Practices of High School Chemistry Teachers Regarding the Differentiation of Instruction.* The University of Maine.

UDL(Universal Design for Learning)-IRN. (2011). *Critical Elements of UDL in Instruction* (Version 1.2). Lawrence, KS: Author. The original MITS Critical Elements are located at http://mits.cenmi.org/

Uladi, A. İ., & Arı, E. S. (2023). Big data, big data analysis and aplication areas [Büyük veri, büyük veri analizi ve uygulama alanları] [Yönetin Bilişim Sistemleri Dergisi]. *Journal of Management Information Systems, 9*(1), 1–14.

UNESCO. (2025, January 22). *UNESCO's International Education Day 2025: Embracing the future of Artificial Intelligence in education.* FundsforNGOs. https://news.fundsforngos.org/2025/01/22/unescos-international-education-day-2025-embracing-the-future-of-artificial-intelligence-in-education/

UNESCO. (The United Nations Educational, Scientific and Cultural Organization). (2021). *Recommendation on the Ethics of Artificial Intelligence.* Paris: United Nations Educational, Scientific and Cultural Organization. https://unesdoc.unesco.org/ark:/48223/pf0000380455

Urban, R., Kireš, M., & Hladká, A. (2023). Enhancing students' problem-solving and critical thinking skills through intelligent tutoring systems: A case study in secondary education. *Computers in Human Behavior Reports*, *9*, 100213. DOI: 10.1016/j.chbr.2022.100213

Usher, M., & Barak, M. (2024). Unpacking the role of AI ethics online education for science and engineering students. *International Journal of STEM Education*, *11*(1). Advance online publication. DOI: 10.1186/s40594-024-00493-4

Vaithianathan, V., Shastri, D. S., Nandakumar, V., Misba, M., Kumar, P. S. V. V. S. R., & Boopathi, S. (2024). NEP Policy Implementation Strategies in Education in India. In *Educational Philosophy and Sociological Foundation of Education* (pp. 325–356). IGI Global., DOI: 10.4018/979-8-3693-3587-1.ch013

Vallor, S. (2024). *The AI mirror: How to reclaim our humanity in an age of machine thinking*. Oxford University Press.

VanLehn, K. (2011). The relative effectiveness of human tutoring, intelligent tutoring systems, and other tutoring systems. *Educational Psychologist*, *46*(4), 197–221. DOI: 10.1080/00461520.2011.611369

VanTassel-Baska, J., Hubbard, G. F., & Robbins, J. I. (2021). Differentiation of instruction for gifted learners: Collated evaluative studies of teacher classroom practices. Handbook of giftedness and talent development in the Asia-Pacific, 945-979.

Varalakshmi, S., Thakur, D., Sharma, R. V., Al Habsi, L. S., Chandra, S., & Boopathi, S. (2025). Taxing Innovation for Leveraging Tax Policy to Foster Growth and Learning in the Digital Economy. In *Navigating Strategic Partnerships for Sustainable Startup Growth* (pp. 391–420). IGI Global Scientific Publishing.

Venkatasubramanian, V., Chitra, M., Sudha, R., Singh, V. P., Jefferson, K., & Boopathi, S. (2024). Examining the Impacts of Course Outcome Analysis in Indian Higher Education: Enhancing Educational Quality. In *Challenges of Globalization and Inclusivity in Academic Research* (pp. 124–145). IGI Global.

Viator, M. G. (2012). Developing historical thinking through questions. *Social Studies, 103*(5), 198–200. DOI: 10.1080/00377996.2011.606438

Vijayakumar, G. N. S., Domakonda, V. K., Farooq, S., Kumar, B. S., Pradeep, N., & Boopathi, S. (2024). Sustainable Developments in Nano-Fluid Synthesis for Various Industrial Applications. In *Adoption and Use of Technology Tools and Services by Economically Disadvantaged Communities: Implications for Growth and Sustainability* (pp. 48–81). IGI Global.

Voskamp, A., Kuiper, E., & Volman, M. (2022). Teaching practices for self-directed and self-regulated learning: Case studies in Dutch innovative secondary schools. *Educational Studies*, *48*(6), 772–789.

Vygotsky, L. S. (1978). *Mind in society: The development of Higher Psychological Processes*. Harvard University Press.

Wach, K., Duong, C. D., Ejdys, J., Kazlauskaitė, R., Korzynksi, P., Mazurek, G., Paliszkiewicz, J., & Ziemba, E. (2023). The dark side of generative artificial intelligence: A critical analysis of controversies and risks of ChatGPT. *Entrepreneurial Business and Economics Review*, *11*(2), 7–30.

Wachowski, Li., & Wachowski, La (1999). *The Matrix [Film]*. Warner Brothers. https://www.warnerbrothers.com/movies/matrix

Wallwork, A. (2024). *AI-assisted Writing and Presenting in English*. Springer Nature.

Wang, C. Y., & Lin, J. J. (2023). Utilizing artificial intelligence to support analyzing self-regulated learning: A preliminary mixed-methods evaluation from a human-centered perspective. *Computers in Human Behavior*, *144*, 107721.

Waruwu, D. E. R. (2024). The future of IPS learning: The potential and challenges of implementing AI in the classroom. *International Conference on Applied Social Sciences in Education, 1*(1), 420–424. doi: https://doi.org/DOI: 10.31316/icasse.v1i1.6864

Wassell, B., & Crouch, C. (2008). Fostering connections between multicultural education and technology: Incorporating weblogs into preservice teacher education. *Journal of Technology and Teacher Education*, *16*(2), 211.

Watson, K., McIntyre, S., & McArthur, I. (2011). Trust and relationship building: Critical skills for the future of design education in online contexts. *Iridescent*, *1*(1), 22–29.

Wei, Y., Jiang, Y. H., Liu, J., Qi, C., Jia, L., & Jia, R. (2025, March). The advancement of personalized learning potentially accelerated by generative AI. In *Society for Information Technology & Teacher Education International Conference* (pp. 991–1000). Association for the Advancement of Computing in Education (AACE).

Whitehead, L. (2017). Social-emotional development in the digital age. *Exchange, 19460406*(236), 16–20.

Williamson, B., & Eynon, R. (2020). Historical threads, missing links, and future directions in AI in education. *Learning, Media and Technology, 45*(3), 223–235. DOI: 10.1080/17439884.2020.1798995

Winek, A. (2025). Making Space for Quiet Joy in the Classroom. Joy-Centered Pedagogy in Higher Education: Uplifting Teaching and Learning for All.

Wolf, A. T., & Putnam, K. (2023). *Beyond the Static Page: An Interactive Learning Approach for Students*. AT Wolf & Company.

Wollny, S., Schneider, J., Di Mitri, D., Weidlich, J., Rittberger, M., & Drachsler, H. (2021). Are we there yet?-a systematic literature review on chatbots in education. *Frontiers in Artificial Intelligence, 4*, 654924. PMID: 34337392

Woolf, B. P., Arroyo, I., Muldner, K., Burleson, W., Cooper, D. G., Dolan, R., & Christopherson, R. M. (2010). The effect of motivational learning companions on low achieving students and students with disabilities. In: *International conference on intelligent tutoring systems* (pp. 327–337). Springer, Berlin, Heidelberg.

Xie, T., & Pentina, I. (2022). Attachment theory as a framework to understand relationships with social chatbots: a case study of Replika.

Xu, C., Sun, Y., & Zhou, H. (2024). Artificial aesthetics and ethical ambiguity: Exploring business ethics in the context of AI-driven creativity. *Journal of Business Ethics*, , 1–22.

Xu, W., & Ouyang, F. (2022). The application of AI technologies in STEM education: A systematic review from 2011 to 2021. *IJ STEM Ed, 9*, 59. DOI: 10.1186/s40594-022-00377-5

Yadav, U., Pitchai, R., Gopal, V., Kumar, K. R. S., Talukdar, M., & Boopathi, S. (2024). Powers of Higher Education Leadership: Navigating Policy and Management in Academic Institutions. In *Navigating Leadership and Policy Management in Education* (pp. 103–136). IGI Global., DOI: 10.4018/979-8-3693-9215-7.ch004

Yalçın, A. (2024). Evaluating the opinions of ChatGPT an Artificial Intelligence supported language processing model on social studies lesson [Yapay zekâ destekli dil işleme modeli olan ChatGPT'nin sosyal bilgiler dersi ile ilgili görüşlerinin değerlendirilmesi] [Uluslararası Karamanoğlu Mehmetbey Eğitim Araştırmaları Dergisi]. *International Journal of Karamanoğlu Mehmetbey Educational Research, 6*(2), 136–152. DOI: 10.47770/ukmead.1485504

Yang, Y., & Xia, N. (2023). Enhancing Students' Metacognition via AI-Driven Educational Support Systems. *International Journal of Emerging Technologies in Learning, 18*(24), 133–148. DOI: 10.3991/ijet.v18i24.45647

Yaşar, Ş., Köse, T. Ç., Göz, N., & Bayır, Ö. G. (2015). The effectiveness of student-centered teaching- learning processes in the social studies: A meta-analysis study [Sosyal bilgiler dersinde öğrenci merkezli öğretme-öğrenme süreçlerinin etkililiği: Bir meta analiz çalışması]. *Anadolu Journal of Educational Sciences International, 5*(1), 38–56. DOI: 10.18039/ajesi.87691

Yaseen, H., Mohammad, A. S., Ashal, N., Abusaimeh, H., Ali, A. A. A., & Sharabati, A. A. (2025). The Impact of Adaptive Learning Technologies, Personalized Feedback, and Interactive AI Tools on Student Engagement: The Moderating Role of Digital Literacy. *Sustainability, 17*(3), 1133. DOI: 10.3390/su17031133

Yawar, M. E., & Amany, S. (2025). The Use of Artificial Intelligence in Teaching History and its Effects on Community Leadership. [Akademik Tarih ve Düşünce Dergisi]. *Academic Journal of History and Idea, 12*(1), 319–332. DOI: 10.5281/zenodo.15618802

Yetişensoy, O., & Rapoport, A. (2023). Artificial Intelligence literacy teaching in social studies education. *Journal of Pedagogical Research, 7*(3), 100–110. DOI: 10.33902/JPR.202320866

Yıldırım, A., & Şimşek, H. (2021). *Sosyal bilimlerde nitel araştırma yöntemleri* [Qualitative research methods in social sciences]. Seçkin.

Yıldırım, I., & Servet, D. (2014). Gamification and education [Oyunlaştırma ve eğitim]. *International Journal of Human Sciences, 11*(1), 655–670. DOI: 10.14687/ijhs.v11i1.2765

Yılmaz, Ö. (2024). Personalised learning and Artificial Intelligence in science education: Current state and future perspectives. *Educational Technology Quarterly, 2024*(3), 255–274. DOI: 10.55056/etq.744

Zawacki-Richter, O., Marín, V. I., Bond, M., & Gouverneur, F. (2019). Systematic review of research on artificial intelligence applications in higher education: Are the machines taking over? *International Journal of Educational Technology in Higher Education*, *16*(1), 1–38. DOI: 10.1186/s41239-019-0171-0

Zeide, E. (2017). The Structural Consequences of Big Data-Driven Education. *Big Data*, *5*(2), 164. DOI: 10.1089/big.2016.0061 PMID: 28632444

Žerak, U., Juriševič, M., & Pečjak, S. (2024). Parenting and teaching styles in relation to student characteristics and self-regulated learning. *European Journal of Psychology of Education*, *39*(2), 1327–1351.

Zhang, H., & Tian, M. (2024). Unpacking the multi-dimensional nature of teacher competencies: A systematic review. *Scandinavian Journal of Educational Research*, , 1–22.

Zhang, Q. (2024). Harnessing Artificial Intelligence for Personalized Learning Pathways: A Framework for Adaptive Education Management Systems. *Applied and Computational Engineering*, *82*, 167–172.

Zhou, J., Zhang, J., & Li, H. (2023). Exploring the Use of Artificial Intelligence in Teaching Management and Evaluation Based on Citation Space Analysis. *Journal of Education and Educational Research*, *3*(2), 42. DOI: 10.54097/jeer.v3i2.9014

Zhu, X., Wang, D., Pedrycz, W., & Li, Z. (2021). A design of granular classifier based on granular data descriptors. *IEEE Transactions on Cybernetics*, *53*(3), 1790–1801. PMID: 34936563

Zimmerman, B. J., & Cleary, T. J. (2009). Motives to self-regulate learning: A social cognitive account. In Handbook of motivation at school (pp. 247–264). Routledge/ Taylor & Francis Group.

Zimmerman, B. J. (2000). Attaining self-regulation: A social-cognitive perspective. In Boekaerts, M., Pintrich, P., & Zeidner, M. (Eds.), *Handbook of self-regulation* (pp. 13–39). Academic Press., DOI: 10.1016/B978-0-12-109890-2.X5027-6

Zimmerman, B. J. (2002). Becoming a Self-Regulated Learner: An Overview. *Theory into Practice*, *41*(2), 64–70. DOI: 10.1207/s15430421tip4102_2

Zimmerman, B. J., & Schunk, D. H. (2011). In Zimmerman, B. J., & Schunk, D. H. (Eds.), *"Self-regulated learning and performance: an introduction and overview," in Handbook of Self-Regulation of Learning and Performance* (pp. 1–14). Routledge.

Zohery, M. (2023). ChatGPT in academic writing and publishing: A comprehensive guide. In *Artificial intelligence in academia, research, and science: ChatGPT as a case study* (1st ed., pp. 10–61). Achtago.

Zovko, V., & Gudlin, M. (2019, June). *Artificial intelligence as a disruptive technology in education*. [Conference Proceedings]. The Future of Education 2019.

About the Contributors

Scott Gregory is assistant professor of teacher education at Fort Hays State University.

***

Seda Aydan is a researcher and educator with a Ph.D. in Curriculum and Instruction from Middle East Technical University (2018–2023). She has completed her postdoctoral studies in the Department of Education Studies at the University of California, San Diego, USA (2024-2025). She has over 12 years of experience as an instructor at TED University in Ankara, Türkiye. Her areas of interest include teacher education, curriculum development and evaluation for K-12 education, self-regulated learning at the K-12 level, mixed-method research, and testing and assessment.

Bhavana S. Karmore working as Assistant Professor and Dean at BCA and MCA Department of G. H. Raisoni University, Amravati for U.G. and P. G. Department . Total Years of Experience 15+ . She publish more than 20+ Papers in International Journals . She work as International Expert at International Conferences. She worked as a Editorial Board Members in 5+ International Journals and Reviewer in 10+ International Journals and International Conferences . Project Guided 10+ PG students and 10+ UG Students . She publish more than 10+ books of Electronics and Computer Engg. subjects. 3 Design patent, 2 copyright .

Mustafa Kayyali is an ardent advocate for excellence in higher education, driven by a relentless pursuit of quality, recognition, and innovation. Their journey in academia started with a Master's in Quality Management and Evaluation in Higher Education from Universitat Oberta de Catalunya, followed by a Ph.D. in Quality Management from Azteca University. These academic pursuits have laid a strong foundation for their expertise in Accreditation, Quality Assurance, and Higher

Education Rankings. As an entrepreneur, researcher, translator, and publisher, they are deeply involved in various facets of the academic world. Their diverse interests encompass Management, Translation, Interpretation, and Academic consulting, contributing to a well-rounded understanding of the industry. Throughout their career, they have made significant contributions to academic literature, with more than 40 published papers and 30 book chapters to my name. Additionally, they take pride in having translated 6 books, bridging language gaps, and promoting knowledge exchange on a global scale. They are committed to fostering positive change in higher education and contributing to its continuous improvement.

Shraddha N. Zanjat currently serves as an Assistant Professor in the EEE Department at the School of Engineering and Technology (SOET), Sandip University, Nashik. With 10 years of teaching experience and 2 years of industry exposure, she brings a wealth of knowledge to her role. She holds a post-graduation degree, a Master of Technology in Electronics and Communication, from RTMN University. Additionally, she is pursuing her PhD at Sandip University, Nashik. Prof. Shraddha N. Zanjat has presented ten conference papers at both national and international levels and has published five papers in esteemed international journals such as IEEE, UGC, and others. Furthermore, she has obtained five Indian design patents. She is also a member of two technical association bodies. Prof. Shraddha N. Zanjat has registered four copyrights under her name and has published two book chapters in Scopus-indexed publications. Additionally, she has authored more than 50 books with international publications and has received royalties of about 20k.

Index

H

I

L

O

P

R

S

T

V

www.ingramcontent.com/pod-product-compliance
Lightning Source LLC
LaVergne TN
LVHW080857300926
849162LV00003B/448